Troubleshooting and Repairing PCs

Troubleshooting and Repairing PCs

Beyond the Basics
Third Edition

Michael F. Hordeski

McGraw-Hill

New York   San Francisco   Washington, D.C.   Auckland   Bogotá
Caracas   Lisbon   London   Madrid   Mexico City   Milan
Montreal   New Delhi   San Juan   Singapore
Sydney   Tokyo   Toronto

Library of Congress Cataloging-in-Publication Data

Hordeski, Michael F.
    Troubleshooting and repairing PCs : beyond the basics / Michael F.
Hordeski.—3rd ed.
        p. cm.
    Third ed. of: Repairing PCs.
    Includes index.
    ISBN 0-07-030555-2 (hc). — ISBN 0-07-030556-0 (pc)
    1. IBM Personal Computer—Maintenance and repair. 2. IBM
microcomputer—Maintenance and repair. 3. IBM–compatible
computers—Maintenance and repair. I. Hordeski, Michael F.
Repairing PCs. II. Title.
TK7889.I26H673   1997
621.39'16—dc21   96-48864
                                                                CIP

McGraw-Hill

A Division of The **McGraw·Hill** *Companies*

1 2 3 4 5 6 7 8 9 0   DOC/DOC   9 0 2 1 0 9 8 7

ISBN 0-07-030555-2 (HC)

ISBN 0-07-030556-0 (PC)

*The sponsoring editor for this book was Scott Grillo, the editing supervisor was
Christina Palaia, and the production supervisor was Pamela Pelton. It was set in
ITC Century Light by North Market Street Graphics.*

Printed and bound by R. R. Donnelley & Sons Company.

McGraw-Hill books are available at special quantity discounts to use as premiums and
sales promotions, or for use in corporate training programs. For more information,
please write to the Director of Special Sales, McGraw-Hill, 11 West 19th Street,
New York, NY 10011. Or contact your local bookstore.

 This book is printed on recycled, acid-free paper containing a minimum of 50% recycled
de-inked fiber.

Contents

3 The System Unit   *101*

4 Diagnostic Hardware and Software   *151*

Introduction

This book illustrates how to clean, maintain, adjust, and repair the parts in your IBM PC computer. It covers the early models, which you are likely to find little information on, as well as newer models such as the Pentium, and newer products such as CD-ROMs and sound cards. The more information you have on PCs and their components, the easier it is to get your system up and running when you have a breakdown.

You will also find this book helpful if you need to compare the characteristics of the different IBM PC families and compatibles. The operation of the different components is clarified and common buzzwords and acronyms are defined. Effective troubleshooting techniques are demonstrated and illustrated with easily understood flow diagrams.

Each chapter starts with a basic introduction of the topic—no previous knowledge is assumed. This allows nontechnical and novice users to become knowledgeable and lose their fear of PCs. Building upon the basic introduction, each chapter goes into details of the hardware differences and their related problems, so even more experienced users can expand upon their knowledge.

This book should help you to identify and solve problems more quickly and easily. It will also make you more informed on your PC's performance and functionality.

You will learn about the most cost-effective approaches to maintenance, troubleshooting, and repair. Since there are many ways a PC can fail, you should know how to detect these failures and make the appropriate repairs when they are needed.

It is important to understand the problem of data disasters as well as inner workings of hard disk drives. Failures in a PC's data storage are often critical since these failures often mean loss of data. Many of these failures are not hardware faults. They are often correctable data defects. This book presents techniques for diagnosing and treating both kinds of failure.

This book should make you more technically proficient. It will provide a good working knowledge of how PCs are built and how they function. You will gain in-depth information about how critical hardware and software elements can malfunction and practical tips for dealing with those problems.

You will learn how to use diagnostic programs for troubleshooting. You can find memory faults using only DOS, but there are ways to make this task much easier with commercial diagnostic software. There are also ways to fix hard disks before problems occur and techniques to recover data that DOS cannot read. These diagnostic skills are available using state-of-the-art programs that are available today.

You will find how to test processors, memory, hard disks, mouse units, networks, and power supplies without using special equipment. If you learn how to maintain your system, you can reduce downtime and the cost of being down. Since most computer malfunctions are not caused by defective components, it is easy to make these repairs. These simple repairs can often be lifesavers, since they can save you from costly downtime.

You can learn how to diagnose computer problems, and then decide when you can repair it yourself or when you should use an outside service. In many cases, all that is required are your fingers and no tools. You should know how to aid technicians, when they are needed, with diagnoses that will save time, money, and quickly get you operating again.

Anyone who works with an IBM PC or compatible should find the book helpful. If you are an end user, you can save hours of time by taking care of simple problems on your own. If you are a computer support staff member who supports end users, you can learn valuable tips that will help you with your job. If you are responsible for repairs, you will be able to make intelligent decisions.

This revised edition includes Windows troubleshooting tips, green PCs, and more material on 486 and Pentium-based computers. There is also a section on portable computers including pen types, laptops, and notebooks.

Chapter 1 has been expanded to include non-Intel 486 and Pentium-based processors. Chapter 2 has added details of the 386, 486, and Pentium caches, bus systems, and power supplies.

Chapter 3 has expanded coverage of 386, 486, and Pentium internal memory, problems, solutions, and audio circuits. There are additional details on 486 and Pentium circuit boards including some of the newer chip sets being used for these boards.

Chapter 5 has additional tips and problems that can occur with SCSI controllers. Chapter 6 has details on some of the newer chip sets used in the video systems of 486 and Pentium computers. There are also additional tips on monitor adjustment and construction, and a section on sound card construction and troubleshooting in Chap. 6.

Chapter 8 has been expanded with additional details on small networks including thick and thin cables and their restrictions. Chapter 9 has additional material on touch panel input devices. Chapter 10 includes more troubleshooting equipment.

This book has many useful tips for beginners and intermediate users, including those with advanced 486 machines as well as Pentium-based machines. As newer machines replace the older units, many older models find new homes. Many repairs on older machines can be accomplished, but the technology is changing rapidly as newer machines replace the older models.

All of us involved in this book, including the staff at McGraw-Hill, have tried to make it as complete and useful as possible. This latest edition has detailed troubleshooting charts that provide a quick look for visualizing what could possibly be wrong. This will allow you to estimate the extent of most computer problems and tell you if you should tackle the job yourself or go to an outside service. There are also many additional drawings and photographs that should help you with construction details, disassembly, and maintenance.

Many thanks to Dee who did much to organize the entire project and to Bill Skotnica for all of his help.

The IBM PC Architecture

You will be better able to understand and repair PCs if you have a good background knowledge of the many types and brands of PCs that you might encounter. Also, a brief history of some of the developments in PCs is interesting as well as helpful.

The IBM PC computer

The IBM PC computer shown in Fig. 1-1 has a modular design. It uses an 8088 16-bit processor. The PC-DOS (personal computer disk operating system) allows you to use software packages available from a wide range of independent suppliers.

Refer to Fig. 1-2 for a block diagram showing the PC system functions. The 8088 processor controls the disk drive reading and writing of data. The 8088 processor controls the monitor, the keyboard, the communications connectors, and all options added to the system.

The first IBM PC came with 16 to 64K (kilobytes) of main memory. A *byte* represents one character position. You could expand the memory to 256K with the addition of a memory extension option. The computer also came with a disk drive that holds 180 or 360K of auxiliary memory on single- or double-sided 5¼-inch diskettes. With a second disk drive, you could bring the total auxiliary memory to 720K.

The PC design made it easy to install, comfortable to operate, and easy to repair. Human engineering considered the total relationship between you and the computer. The system design minimized conditions that might have led to strain and fatigue. It was also flexible so that you had the freedom to adapt it to your needs.

The modular construction of this type of computer allows you to place the three components in different locations. You can use a floor stand to hold the system unit and keep your work surface free. The components are relatively light, compact, and portable. The keyboard comes with a 6-foot cord that lets you place it anywhere that is comfortable, even on your lap.

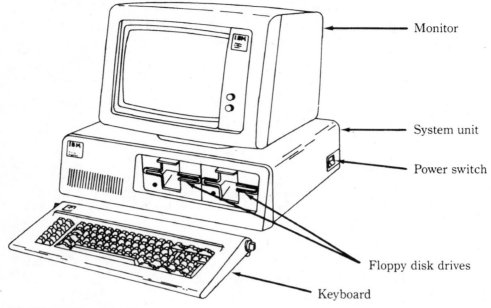

Monitor

System unit

Power switch

Floppy disk drives

Keyboard

1-1 IBM personal computer.

The monitor

The PC computer monitor contains a video screen whose diagonal dimension is 30.5 centimeters (12 inches) (Fig. 1-3). Do not touch the screen because fingerprints show easily. A monitor supplies video information, and the video control system is in the video adapter board inside the system unit. Adjustments on the monitor back or side let you adjust the screen brightness and contrast levels as on a television set.

The keyboard

The PC computer has a low-profile keyboard which has 84 keys, as shown in Fig. 1-4. The standard keys at the center and left provide you the uppercase and lowercase alphabets, numbers, and punctuation. To the right of these keys are the basic editor keys: Insert, Delete, End, Home, Print Screen, Page Down, Page Up, Number Lock, and the cursor arrow keys. The numeric keypad is on the same side.

Special function keys for different applications are on the left side of the keyboard: word processing, electronic mail, accounting, and spreadsheets.

Keyboard features

Keyboard features are as follows:

- A low profile that allows you access to the disk drives in the system unit, in case you want to place the two components on the same table or desk.
- Key-click sounds as the keys are pressed. You can often adjust the key-click volume or turn it off.

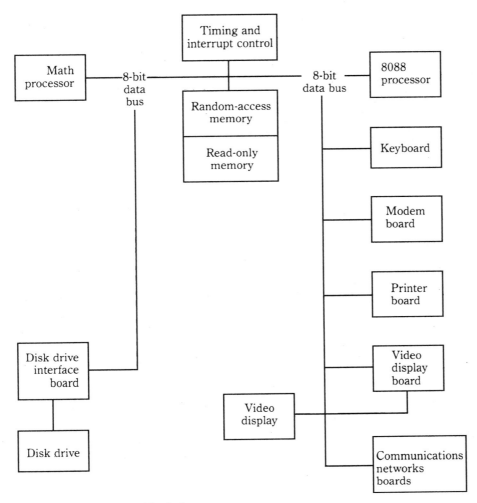

1-2 IBM PC computer block diagram.

- A keyboard tone generator that produces a margin bell. The tone volume might also be adjustable.
- Auto-repeat of all keys on the main keypad array, the numeric keypad, and the function keys (including Space, Del Char, and Tab).

The keys are arranged in an electrical matrix, and the system continually scans the keyboard for keys that are pressed. A single-chip, 8-bit processor detects whenever a key is pressed and transmits the event to the system module. A click sounds when a key is pressed. You might be able to turn the key-click feature on or off or adjust its volume through a setup feature. Many keyboards have lights that the system turns on and off. These lights have specific functions during normal system operation; an example of a keyboard light is one that lights when you have pressed the Caps Lock key.

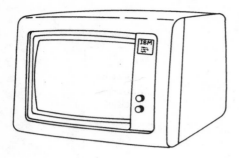

1-3 IBM PC computer monitor.

The floppy disk drive

The PC computer family uses a compact disk subsystem that consists of a *disk controller board* (Fig. 1-5) and a *floppy disk drive* (Fig. 1-6), which controls the diskettes on a single spindle. These disks or diskettes provide mass storage, data exchange, and file backup capabilities. The early diskettes stored 180 to 360K of information. Later, this capacity was expanded to 1.2MB (megabytes).

Disk storage capacity is usually expressed in terms of megabytes and kilobytes (a 30MB hard disk drive, for example, or a 360K floppy disk). The CPU (central processing unit) cannot directly access items stored on disk. A disk controller connects the disk to the CPU. The controller can be a separate expansion board, or it can be part of the main system board.

The disk drive has a single spindle turned by the drive motor. The drive accesses the diskettes with a single-head carriage assembly (if it is single-sided) or with a dual-head assembly (if it is double-sided). In either case, a stepper motor/lead screw combination moves the assembly.

The disk drive has two sensors that detect when you have inserted a diskette into the drive. These sensors also look for the notch on the side of the diskette protective cover to see if the diskette is write protected. If the write-protect notch is covered, the disk drive cannot *write* (store data) on the diskette.

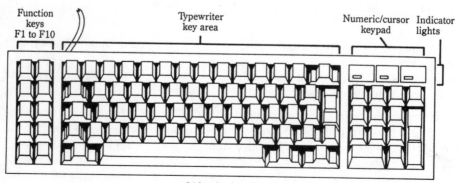

1-4 84-key board.

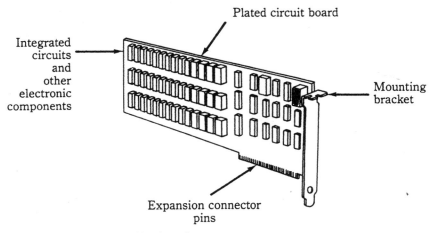

1-5 Typical disk controller board.

The IBM PC family

The original PC-DOS IBM Personal Computer used an Intel 8088 microprocessor that ran at a speed of 4.77 MHz (megahertz). The memory of the first units was only 16 to 64K; later, this was upgraded to 256 to 640K of RAM (random-access memory) and 40K of ROM (read-only memory). Two 5¼-inch floppy disk drives provided data storage.

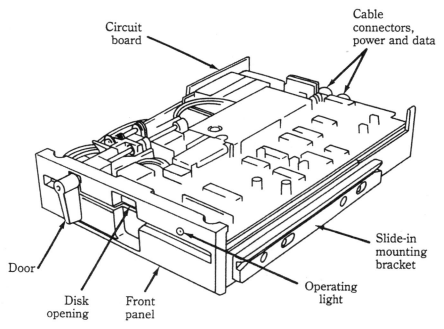

1-6(A) Floppy disk drive.

1-6(B) Top view showing spindle.

The IBM PC offered five expansion slots and an optional expansion unit to accommodate eight additional boards. For additional storage capacity, up to two 10MB hard disk drives were offered.

IBM PC/XT

The IBM PC/XT uses an Intel 8088 CPU running at 4.77 MHz. The memory is also 128 to 640K of RAM with 40K of ROM. Storage is one or two 5¼-inch 360K floppy disk drives, or one 5¼-inch 360K floppy disk drive and one 10MB hard disk drive. The IBM PC/XT includes eight expansion slots with one floppy drive and one hard disk drive. An optional expansion unit gives you the availability of eight additional slots. For increased storage capacity, you can install a 10MB hard disk and one 180 or 360K floppy drive.

1-6(C) Bottom view showing stepper motor and lead screw.

IBM PC/AT

The IBM PC/AT offers more raw processing power by using an Intel 80286 CPU running at 6 MHz. Internal memory was expanded and could range from 256K to 3MB of RAM. Storage was increased with a 1.2MB floppy disk drive and a 20MB hard disk drive. Seven I/O (input-output) expansion slots are available for adding peripherals. You can expand the standard AT memory to 3MB of RAM, and you can improve the capacity with an available 40MB hard disk drive.

XT/AT compatibles

Many of the better-known compatibles are described in this section.

AT&T

The AT&T Personal Computer 6300 uses an Intel 8086 CPU running at 8 MHz. The internal memory ranges from 128 to 640K of RAM for the floppy version, 256 to 640K of RAM for the 10MB hard disk version, and 512 to 640K RAM for the 20MB hard disk version. Storage is two 5¼-inch 360K floppy disk drives or one 5¼-inch 360K floppy and one 10 or 20MB hard disk drive. A socket is provided for an optional 8087 math coprocessor. The floppy disk system has seven available expansion slots, and there are six available slots on the hard disk system. A 16/8-bit data-bus converter is provided for communications interfacing.

Compaq

The Compaq Deskpro (Model 4) also uses the 8086 CPU, which runs at 4.77 or 8 MHz. The internal memory is 128 to 640K of RAM with 8K of ROM. Standard storage is one 5¼-inch 360K floppy disk drive and one 10MB hard disk drive. The Model 4 includes a 10MB tape backup system, and you can expand storage capacity to accommodate a 30MB hard disk drive. The system has a socket for an 8087 math coprocessor and includes one parallel and one serial port. It also has four available expansion slots. A switchable clock speed gives you software compatibility with older programs.

The Compaq Deskpro 286 (Model 2) uses an 80286 CPU running at 6 or 8 MHz. The memory is 512K to 8.2MB of RAM with 8K of ROM. Standard storage is one 3½-inch 1.4MB micro floppy disk drive and one 30MB hard disk. Storage capacity can be expanded with a 70MB hard disk drive, and a 10MB tape backup system is also available. You can improve system performance with an optional 80287 math processor, and there are four available expansion slots. The Model 2 has one parallel and one serial port and a switchable clock speed for improved software compatibility.

Corona

The Corona ATP-6-QD from Corona Data Systems uses an 80286 CPU running at 6 MHz. The internal memory range is 512K to 16MB RAM. Standard storage is one 5¼-inch 360K floppy disk drive and one 3½-inch 1.4MB floppy. You can upgrade the Corona ATP-6-QD system with an Intel 80287 math processor. The unit has five expansion slots.

The system also includes one serial and one parallel port. The Corona ATP-6-Q20 is standard with one 1.2MB floppy and a 20MB hard disk drive.

Ericsson

The Ericsson Personal Computer Model S02 from Ericsson Information Systems uses an 8088 CPU running at 4.77 MHz. Internal memory is 256 to 640K of RAM with 8K of ROM. Standard storage is two 5¼-inch 360K floppy disk drives. A socket allows upgrading the Ericsson Personal Computer with an optional Intel 8087 math coprocessor. The PC has five IBM bus-compatible expansion slots, one serial port, and one parallel port.

Hewlett-Packard

The Touchscreen II from Hewlett-Packard uses an 8088 CPU that runs at 8 MHz. Internal memory is 256 to 640K RAM. Standard storage is two 3½-inch 720K floppy disk drives or one 3½-inch 720K floppy and one 10, 20, or 40MB hard disk drive. This computer is upgraded from the HP-150, with touch-screen features. The standard system has four available expansion slots and four serial ports. For additional storage capacity, you can add a 10, 20, or 40MB hard disk drive.

ITT

The ITT Xtra XP from ITT Information Systems uses an 80286 CPU running at 4.77 or 6 MHz. Internal memory is 512K to 1.6MB of RAM and 64K of ROM.

Standard storage is one 5¼-inch 360K floppy disk drive and a 10 or 20MB hard disk. You can upgrade the ITT Xtra XP with an optional Intel 80287 math coprocessor, and you can expand the memory to 1.6MB. The XP has four available expansion slots after the monitor is added. Three are on the hard disk version after the controller board is installed. There is one parallel and one serial port. A switchable clock speed improves compatibility with applications software.

Kaypro

The Kaypro 286i (Model A) uses an 80286 microprocessor that runs at 6 MHz. The internal memory is 512K to 15MB of RAM and 32K of ROM. Standard storage is one 5¼-inch 1.2MB floppy disk drive. The 286i is a typical clone of IBM's AT. The Kaypro 286i has a socket for an 80287 math coprocessor. You can expand system memory up to 15MB of RAM with additional boards. The system has seven expansion slots.

The Model B has one floppy and one 10MB hard disk drive, five expansion slots, one serial and two parallel ports, and an RGB (red, green, blue) interface for a PC/AT-compatible monitor.

Leading Edge

The Leading Edge Personal Computer Model D uses an 8088 CPU that runs at 4.77 MHz. Internal memory ranges from 256 to 640K of RAM. Storage is two 5¼-inch 360K floppy disk drives or one floppy and one 10MB hard disk. The Leading Edge Model D has four available IBM-compatible expansion slots. The system can accommodate an optional 8087 math coprocessor. Also included are one parallel and one serial port.

NCR

The NCR PC6 uses an 8088-2 CPU that runs at 4.77 or 8 MHz. The standard internal memory is 256 or 512 to 640K of RAM and 40K of ROM. Storage is two 5¼-inch 360K floppy disk drives or one 360K floppy and one 20MB hard disk. An alternative option is one 360K floppy drive, one 20MB hard disk, and one 10MB streaming-tape backup. The unit has six expansion slots available for additional cards. Five slots are available on the hard disk versions. One RS232 port and one parallel port are standard. The NCR PC8 uses an 80286 microprocessor running at 6 MHz. Internal memory is 256K to 4MB of RAM and 40K of ROM. Standard storage is one 5¼-inch 1.2MB floppy disk drive. The unit has six expansion slots, and the system storage capacity can include a 40MB hard disk drive.

The PC8 enhanced version has 512K RAM, five expansion slots, a 1.2MB floppy drive, a 20MB hard disk drive, one serial port, and one parallel port.

Tandy

The Tandy 1200 HD uses an 8088 CPU running at 4.77 MHz. Internal memory is 256 to 640K of RAM. Storage is one internal 5¼-inch 360K floppy disk drive and a 10MB hard disk drive. You can use the motherboard to add an Intel 8087 math coprocessor. Five IBM-compatible expansion slots are available. Four are available after the monitor board is installed. You can get this unit with an external 35MB hard disk drive. One parallel port is standard.

TeleVideo

The TeleVideo AT (Model I) from TeleVideo Systems uses the 80286 CPU and runs at 6 or 8 MHz. The internal memory is 256K to 15MB of RAM and 32K of ROM. Standard storage is one 5¼-inch 1.2MB floppy disk drive.

The TeleVideo AT has eight expansion slots for adding peripheral cards along with a socket for an 80287 math coprocessor. You can expand memory to 15MB with additional memory boards and storage to 40MB. One serial and one parallel port are standard. The TeleVideo Telecat 286 is a desktop PC with a 20MB disk drive. A version with a 30MB disk drive is also available. The disk drives operate more slowly than those on IBM's PC AT, and the power supply is smaller. The 80286 microprocessor runs at either 6 or 8 MHz.

Wang

The Wang PC-PK6 from Wang Laboratories uses the 8086 microprocessor running at 8 MHz. Internal memory can range from 128 to 640K of RAM. Standard storage is one 5¼-inch 360K floppy disk drive and one 10MB hard disk. There are four available expansion slots; an RS232C port and a parallel port are standard.

Zenith

The Z-200 Advanced PC from Zenith Data Systems uses the 80286 CPU running at 6 MHz. Internal memory is 512K to 16MB. Storage is one 5¼-inch 1.2MB floppy disk drive with or without a 20MB hard disk. The computer has seven expansion slots and a socket for adding an 80287 math coprocessor.

Some history of PCs, XTs, and ATs

In the mid-1980s, many computer makers marketed PC and XT versions following IBM's lead in the personal-computer market. While these manufacturers were still following the IBM by developing PC- and XT-compatible systems, IBM developed and released the Personal Computer AT, leading the way into a second generation of microcomputers.

A number of manufacturers then released AT clones in an attempt to gain a part of this new market. Typical of these AT-compatible computers were Compaq Computer's Deskpro 286, Corona Data Systems' Corona ATP, Texas Instruments' Business Pro, TeleVideo Systems' TeleVideo AT, and Kaypro Corporation's Kaypro 286i.

IBM first released the AT as a higher-end system in August, 1984. By March of 1985, about 10 percent of IBM's microcomputer unit shipments were ATs. By July of 1985, there were about 110,000 ATs in use.

The manufacturers of compatible systems included upgrades from the AT with improved clock speeds and greater disk storage. With the more powerful features, the AT and its clones were more useful in business applications. Enhanced versions allowed users to expand hard disk storage capacity to 60MB or more.

Early in 1985, the combined sales of the AT and compatibles averaged around 15,000 and 20,000 units per month. For the first seven months of the year, IBM sold about 80 percent of these units, but competition slowly began to grow. The total number of units for 1985 was 700,000 units, and IBM had about 70 percent of these.

Most of the compatibles are clones of the IBM desktop machines. But some manufacturers, such as Corona Data Systems and Compaq, began offering portable XT- and AT-compatible machines. Most of the portables use the same circuitry, but the size of the circuit boards has been reduced to provide units that can easily be transported. These portable PCs are generally not hardware-compatible, although some can use standard expansion boards.

Tables 1-1, 1-2, and 1-3 list the various early PC types (IBM, XT, and AT compatibles) that are covered in this book, along with their basic characteristics. Table 1-4 summarizes other essential characteristics of the PC family.

Table 1-1. IBM Personal computers PC and AT

Processor	MHz	Memory	Storage
IBM personal 8088 computer	4.77	256 to 640K RAM; 40K ROM	One or two 5¼-in floppy disks
IBM personal 8088 computer XT	4.77	256 to 640K RAM; 40K ROM	One 5¼-in floppy disk; One 10MB disk
IBM personal 80286 computer AT	6	256K to 3MB	1.25MB floppy disk; One 20MB hard disk

Table 1-2. Typical XT-compatible computers

Company	Processor	MHz	Memory	Storage
Athena Canon	8086	4.77	256 to 512K RAM; 16K ROM	Two 360K 5¼-in floppy disks
AT&T Personal computer	8086	8	128 to 640K	One 360K 5¼-in floppy and one 10MB hard disk; two 360K floppy disks and a 10MB hard disk
BIOS (basic input-output system)	8088	10	640K	360K floppy disk; one 40MB hard disk
Commodore PC	8088	4.77	PC XT 640K	Two 360K 5¼-in floppy disks
DTK Data	8088	4.77/10	640K	360K and 20MB
Epson Equity	8088	8	640K	360K
Ericsson personal computer	8088	4.77	256 to 640K RAM; 8K ROM	Two 360K 5¼-in floppy disks
Model S02 Headstart II	8088	10	640K	5¼- and 3½-in floppy disks, 360 and 720K
ITT Xtra	8088	4.8	128 to 640K RAM; 320K ROM	One 360K disk
Leading Edge personal color computer	8088-2	7.16/ 4.77	256 to 640K RAM; 20K ROM	Two 360K 5¼-in floppy disks or one floppy and one 10MB hard disk
NCR PC4	8088	4.77	128 to 640K RAM; 8K ROM	Two 360K 5¼-in floppies or one 360K floppy and one 10MB hard disk
Tandy 1000	8088	4.77	128 to 640K disk	One 360K 5¼-in floppy
Z-150 Zenith Data	8088	4.77	320 to 720K RAM; 32K ROM	Two 5¼-in 320/360K floppy disks or one floppy and one 10MB hard disk

Table 1-3. Typical AT-compatible computers

Company	Processor	MHz	Memory (RAM)	Storage
AGI/Everex 1700C	80286	12	1Mb	1.2MB, 40MB
AST Premium drive	80286	6/12	512K	1.2MB floppy disk 1.2MB, 40MB
Compaq E Model 1	80286	12	1Mb	1.2MB
DTK Tech 1260	80286	8/12	640K	1.2MB, 20MB
Epson Equity II Plus	80286	12	640K	1.2MB, 40MB
Leading Edge D2	80286	8/12	640K	1.2MB, 50MB
Packard Bell PB-286	80286	8/12	640K	1.2MB, 40MB

486 and 386 PCs

The typical 486 or 386 computer brings the advantages of a powerful microprocessor to a small, high-performance personal computer. With many 386 and 486 computers, you have the ability to switch operating speeds with keystrokes, so the computers can provide you full IBM PC AT compatibility in addition to the microprocessor native speed. One or two megabytes of SIMM (single inline memory module) system-board memory are minimum, and most boards are expandable to 16MB. A full-size 101-key keyboard is standard, and the computers have one or two built-in serial ports, a built-in parallel port, and a built-in mouse port.

The expansion slots will accept 8-, 16-, or 32-bit or PC-compatible expansion boards. These slots can hold boards for auxiliary disk or tape-drive controllers, network interfaces, modems, and special video display adapters.

The computer includes at least one 3½-inch 1.44MB floppy drive with the floppy controller on the system board as well as a built-in connector for IDE (integrated drive electronics) hard drives. The integrated VGA (video graphics array) hardware provides enhanced video and graphics capabilities without using an expansion slot (Fig. 1-7).

Shadow RAM (random-access memory) provides faster execution of the BIOS (basic input-output system). The computer copies the BIOS from ROM (read-only memory) into high-speed, write-protected RAM, and executes it from RAM.

IBM PS/2

Since the introduction of the IBM PC in 1981, the use of the personal computer has grown and the size of applications has also increased. Disk storage requirements have grown significantly. The size of the components has decreased and the proliferation of personal computers in all areas has been significant. Substantial advancements resulted in higher-capacity, faster, smaller, and less-expensive systems.

The IBM PS/2 (Personal System/2) family borrowed technology from IBM's large systems and customized IBM circuit integration. Some of IBM's goals in developing the PS/2 family were to enhance reliability, improve overall quality, and increase component meantime between failures. A repackaged physical component design, with reduced

Table 1-4. PC family characteristics

DOS versions	Compatibles generally use the latest release of MS-DOS. IBM machines use some version of PC-DOS.
BIOS manufacturer and release date	This characteristic refers to the brand name and revision date of the BIOS (basic input-output system) firmware chip. Early chips might not be completely software-compatible.
Processor type	The type of main processor used in the PC determines the relative performance of the machine.
Intel 8088	Used in the IBM PC, XT, and most turbo compatibles.
Intel 8086	This chip is usually found in higher performance XT-type machines such as the AT&T PC 6300.
NEC V20/V30	These chips are clones of the Intel 8088 and 8086 chips. They operate faster than the Intel versions. These chips are found in some compatibles or they are installed to improve performance.
Intel 80188/80186	These processors are later versions of the 8088 and 8086 chips. They are similar functionally to the earlier processors but they can process instructions faster and run at a faster clock rate. These processors are often found on early accelerator boards.
Intel 80286	Machines using this processor are generally AT-class PCs. The IBM PC/AT uses the 80286 chip, and most PC compatibles of the 286 class use the 80286 processor.
Intel 80386 SX	Machines using this processor use a 16-bit bus like the AT but are faster and operate at higher speeds.
Intel 80386 DX	Machines using this processor use a 32-bit bus for faster information processing and operate at higher speeds than the AT computer.
Intel 80486	This processor is a more powerful version of the 386, and it can be run at higher speeds. It has a built-in math coprocessor.
Pentium Bus Type	Pentium is a 64-bit processor with some features of the 486. In addition to the processor type, there are several possible bus types that affect the relative performance of the machine.
XT bus	This refers to an 8-bit bus such as that found in an IBM PC or XT. This bus is used in machines with an 8088, 8086, V20, or V30 processor.
AT bus	This refers to the 16-bit bus that is used in the IBM AT or compatibles. Also called the ISA bus.
Micro Channel	The IBM Micro Channel bus is used in the PS/2 Model 50 and other more powerful models.
EISA	Extended ISA bus that adds another 16 bits.
VESA-VL	A local or mezzanine bus used in 486 and Pentium systems.
PCI	PCI stands for *peripheral component interconnect,* a local, or mezzanine, bus used in Pentium systems.

size, weight, heat, and noise, was the result. One of the major changes was a new bus/channel architecture. System throughput and overall capacity was increased, and new graphics capabilities were introduced.

The PS/2 family includes desktop models as well as floor-standing models along with the IBM PC Convertible. All models have front controls and indicator lights. The power

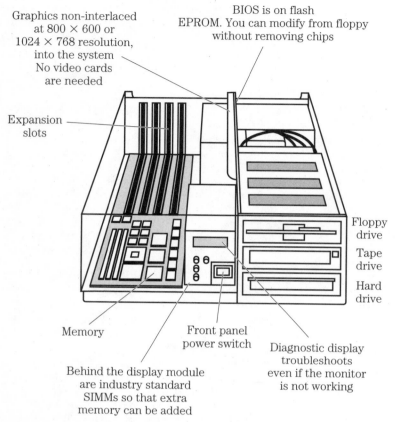

Graphics non-interlaced
at 800 × 600 or
1024 × 768 resolution,
into the system
No video cards
are needed

BIOS is on flash
EPROM. You can modify from floppy
without removing chips

Expansion
slots

Floppy
drive

Tape
drive

Hard
drive

Memory

Front panel
power switch

Diagnostic display
troubleshoots
even if the monitor
is not working

Behind the display module
are industry standard
SIMMs so that extra
memory can be added

1-7 A 486 desktop system chassis.

switch is in the front of the system. Low-profile 3½-inch diskette drives have a single push-button diskette release. The noise levels on the PS/2 models are up to 75 percent lower than for the IBM PC. The noise reduction is possible because of the design of the fan and airflow.

Models 30, 50, 60, and 80 use the Enhanced Keyboard with replaceable keytops and a detachable keyboard cord. Model 25 uses the IBM Space Saving Keyboard or the Enhanced PC Keyboard. IBM based the Models 25 and 30 on the traditional IBM PC architecture. Models 50, 60, and 80 use the Micro Channel architecture.

Micro Channel architecture

IBM designed the initial PC architecture in 1981 for entry-level personal-computing requirements. These stand-alone systems handled one application at a time using a small or moderate amount of memory. The PS/2 line was designed for more advanced applications.

The Micro Channel architecture was first used in PS/2 Models 50, 60, and 80; it has 32-bit data paths and analog channel for voice and analog signals. It also has redesigned interrupt servicing, automatic attachment detection, and automatic configuration optimizing.

System-board integration

The PS/2 system-board design integrates the functions that occupy four to five adapter cards on an IBM Personal Computer AT system using VLSI (very large-scale integration) and SMT (surface-mount technology). The system board includes memory expansion, display, parallel, serial port, and mouse ports. On the system board, there is also a video subsystem as well as the diskette controller.

IBM custom-designed gate arrays replace lower-level components. The internal data paths have been designed to reduce cables with direct connections between components.

Memory

IBM uses SIP (single inline package) technology in the PS/2 Models 25, 30, 50, and 60. The memory modules snap onto a custom-designed connector on the system board. They use SMT that requires less space and power and produces less heat. The Model 80 uses high-speed (80 ns, or 80 nanoseconds) 1MB technology, which is the same memory used in IBM's 3090, 9370, and other IBM systems.

Storage media

Models 30 and 50 use a 20MB 3½-inch fixed disk; Models 60 and 80 use 40, 70, 115, or 314MB disks (5¼-inch). Model 30 uses an integrated controller. IBM also introduced an optical disk drive with removable cartridge disks. Each removable disk can contain up to 200MB of data. The optical disk uses light beam access with WORM (write-once-read-many) technology. You can use the optical disk drive for archiving data.

Graphics

The PS/2 Models 25 and 30 integrate the graphics function on the system board by using a gate array chip called the MCGA (MultiColor Graphics Array). The MCGA is fully compatible with the IBM Color Graphics adapter. An improved 8 × 16 character box is used. The MCGA also determines which type of display is attached and appropriately converts the image to 64 shades of gray for a monochrome display. This process is *color summing*. The MCGA can display 256 colors from a palette of more than 256,000 colors. In the entry-addressability color graphics mode (320 × 200), the MCGA can display 256 colors simultaneously for a television type of image. In the high-addressability mode (640 × 480), high-quality graphics can be displayed in greater clarity with two colors simultaneously.

Models 50, 60, and 80 use a higher-addressability character box (9 × 16) in the VGA (video graphics array). Performance and color variety are improved by VGA compared to EGA (extended graphics array). The IBM 8514/A provides functions beyond VGA including 1024 × 768 screen modes and increased color capability for PS/2 Models 50, 60, and 80.

Model 25

The Model 25 uses an Intel 8086, which runs at 8 MHz. You can add an 8087 math coprocessor. Internal memory is 512K on the system board for the standard unit and 640K on the system board for the collegiate unit.

The standard unit has one 720K 3½-inch diskette drive, and the collegiate unit has two 720K 3½-inch diskette drives. Options include a second 720K 3½-inch diskette drive, a 4869 5¼-inch external diskette drive, or an external 3363 optical disk drive. A 12-inch analog monochrome or color display is used. The MultiColor Graphics Array (MCGA) has an 8×16 character box with either 640×480 or 320×200 resolution.

The Model 25 uses a 64K video RAM along with an analog display interface. Integrated functions include serial I/O up to 9600 bps (bits per second), parallel I/O, an audio earphone connector, and diskette controller. Expansion is one full-size expansion slot and one 8-inch expansion slot. The monochrome unit has a 90-W (watt) power supply, and the color unit has a 115-W supply.

Model 30

The Model 30 has an Intel 8086 running at 8 MHz. You can add an 8087 math coprocessor. The Model 30 has 640K of RAM on the system board. Storage is either two 720K 3½-inch diskette drives or one 720K 3½-inch diskette drive and a 20MB hard disk. Options include an external 3363 optical disk drive, a 6157 streaming-tape drive, or a 4869 5¼-inch external diskette drive.

Video and integrated functions are the same as the Model 25 except that a hard disk controller is also available. Three expansion slots are available to accept IBM PC cards. It has a 70-W switching power supply.

Model 50

The Model 50 uses an Intel 80286 running at 10 MHz. You can add an 80287 math coprocessor. The system board has 1MB RAM on the system board. The RAM is expandable to 7MB on adapter cards. Model 50 has one 1.44MB 3½-inch diskette drive and one 20MB fixed disk. Options include an external 3363 optical disk drive, a 6157 streaming-tape drive, and a 4869 5¼-inch external diskette drive. The video graphics array (VGA) uses a 9×16 character box with a 720×400 text mode. Graphics modes are 640×480 pels with 16 colors from a 256K palette and 320×200 pels with 256 colors from a 256K palette. A 256K video RAM is used with an analog display interface.

Serial and parallel interfaces are included along with a diskette controller and a hard disk controller adapter. There are three available expansion slots. The power supply is a 94-W switching unit.

Model 60

The processor in a Model 60 is an 80286 running at 10 MHz. You can add an 80287 math coprocessor. There is 1MB RAM on the system board that is expandable to 15Mb with adapter cards. Storage is one 1.44MB 3½-inch diskette drive with a 44 or 70MB hard disk. A second 1.44MB 3½-inch diskette drive can be used along with a second hard disk of 44MB. A 115MB hard disk is available along with an internal or external 3363 optical disk drive, a 6157 streaming-tape drive, and a 4869 5¼-inch external diskette drive.

The video graphics array (VGA) uses a 9×16 character box with a 720×400 text mode. Graphics modes include 640×480 pels with 16 colors from a 256K palette and 320×200 pels with 256 colors. Video RAM is 256K. An analog display interface is used.

The unit includes serial and parallel interfaces along with the diskette controller and hard disk controller adapter. An ST-506 interface is used with the smaller hard disks. An ESDI (enhanced small device interface) is used with the large hard disks. Seven expansion slots are available. The tower case has a 207- or 225-W switching power supply.

Model 80

The Model 80 uses an 80386 running at 16 or 20 MHz. An 80387 math coprocessor is an option. The 16-MHz system board has 1MB of RAM on the system board, which can be expandable to 2MB. The internal memory is expandable to 16MB with adapter cards. The 20-MHz system board has 2MB of RAM on the system board that is expandable to 4MB. The system is expandable to 16MB of RAM using adapter cards.

Storage ranges from one 1.44MB 3½-inch diskette drive and one 44MB fixed disk to one 1.44MB 3½-inch diskette drive and one 314MB hard disk. Options include a second 1.44MB 3½-inch diskette drive and a second hard disk of 44 to 314MB. There is also an internal or external 3363 optical disk drive, a 6157 streaming-tape drive, and a 4869 5¼-inch external diskette drive.

The video graphics array (VGA) uses a 9 · 16 character box with a 720 · 400 text mode. Graphics modes use 640 · 480 pels with 16 colors from a 256K palette or 320 · 200 pels with 256 colors from a 256K palette. A 256K video RAM is used along with an analog display interface.

The computer includes serial and parallel interfaces with a diskette controller and disk controller adapter. An ST-506 interface is included with the smaller hard disks and an ESDI with the larger disks. Model 80 has four 16-bit expansion slots and three 16/32-bit expansion slots available. The tower case has a 207- or 225-W switching power supply. Table 1-5 shows the basic characteristics of the PS/2 models.

The 386 architecture

The 386 microprocessor was introduced in 1986 and is based on a 32-bit family of chips. The 386 DX microprocessor has 32 address lines and can directly access 4GB (gigabytes) of main memory and 64 terabytes (64 trillion bytes) of virtual memory. The virtual memory addressing capabilities allow systems to operate with less physical memory, which reduces the system cost. Many of the techniques used in the 386 microprocessor came from mainframe computers. The 386 DX CPU performance has increased at least 25 percent per year with the introduction of new speeds since 1986, including 33-MHz chips such as the 386 DX CPU, the 387 math coprocessor, and the 82385 cache controller.

The 486 microprocessor

The introduction of the 486 microprocessor in 1989 extended the 386 architecture to even greater performance. The 486 CPU integrates a 386 DX CPU enhanced with RISC (reduced instruction set computer) technology, a 387 math coprocessor, and a cache memory. The result provides at least double the performance of the 386 DX CPU at the same clock speed. At a clock speed of 25 MHz, the 486 CPU performance is equivalent to most 32-bit RISC processors.

386–486 compatibility

The 486 processor shares the 32-bit software architecture of the 386 family. The 486 improves the 386 architecture performance within the bounds of compatibility with earlier processors. Like the 386 processor, the 486 CPU runs all 8086 and 80286 software.

Table 1-5. Personal Systems/2 model characteristics

Model	25	30	50	60	80
Microprocessor type	8086	8086	80286	80286	80386
speed (MHz)	8	8	10	10	16 or 20
Permanent memory (ROM) (K)	64	64	128	128	128
User memory (RAM) base	512/640K	640K	1MB	1MB	1/2MB
maximum	640K	640K	7MB	15MB	16MB
Disk storage					
standard (Mb)		20	20	44/70	44/70
maximum (Mb)		20	20	185	628
Diskette drives 3½-in capacity	720K	720K	1.44MB	1.44MB	1.44MB
number as standard	1-1	2	1	1	1
Integrated					
functions					
parallel/serial/					
pointing	X	X	X	X	X
device port					
MCGA graphics	X	X			
VGA graphics		X	X	X	
port					
diskette	X	X	X	X	X
controller					
disk adapter		X	X	X	X
clock/calendar		X	X	X	X
Optical disk					
drive					
internal				X	X
external	X	X	X	X	X
max storage (GB)	4	4	12	16	16
6157 tape	X	X	X	X	
drive					
Expansion					
slots	2–3	3	3	7	7

Software that runs on the 386 will run with no changes on the 486 CPU. Software written for the 486 processor also will run on any 386 processor. Table 1-6 shows the differences between the 386 and 486 processors.

SX machine

The 386 SX processor was designed to deliver 386 functions at a 16-bit price. The 386 architecture, including the 486 processor, runs software written for DOS, OS/2, 32-bit OS/2, UNIX, and XENIX 386. The 286 systems only run a subset of 386 family software. Typical SX computers include the following.

Table 1-6. Processor comparison

Processor	386 SL	386 SX	386 DX	486 SX	486 DX
Internal bus width	32 bits	32 bits	32 bits	32 bits	32 bits
External bus width	16 bits	16 bits	32 bits	32 bits	32 bits
Virtual address space	4GB	4GB	4GB	4GB	4GB
Physical address space	32MB	16MB	4GB	4GB	4GB
Clock frequencies	20, 25 MHz	16, 20 MHz	20, 25, 33 MHz	16, 20, 25 MHz	25, 33, 50 MHz
Coprocessor	387 SX	387 SX	387 DX	487 SX	Built-in
Cache controller	Built-in	80385 SX, 80395 SX	80385 DX 80395 DX	Built-in	Built-in

ALR PowerFlex

ALR's PowerFlex 20C SX is a 20-MHz machine with a 5MB limit on CPU-speed RAM. The CPU board plugs into a special slot, which makes it easy to change to a 486 by swapping boards. Because a 32-bit 486 has to access motherboard memory through the 16-bit memory bus, you do not get the full benefits of the 486. In addition to the SX CPU, the motherboard has a 286. If the CPU or processor board fails, you can use the Power-Flex as a 286. VGA is not built into the motherboard, so you have to use a separate board. ALR's VGA video board also contains the system mouse port. This VGA board runs in 800 × 600 super-VGA mode.

Although the PowerFlex has room for four drives, the chassis is not designed for moving drives around. If you need to change a drive in one of the center drive bays, you will need to remove the CPU board, any full-length expansion boards, and the drives in the right-hand bays. Changing expansion boards and the right-hand drives is not a problem.

AST Premium II

The AST Premium II is a small-footprint PC with the CPU, system memory, and math coprocessor on a removable CPU board, so it is easy to change it to a 25- or 33-MHz 386 DX or a 25-MHz 486. The system has good expansion capacity with five drive bays and five available expansion slots. Thumbscrews make it easy to open and close the case, and the internal design lets you change drives without having to remove expansion boards or other drives. The power switch and monitor controls are on the front panel, and it has a reset switch along with a second serial port and a mouse port.

Compaq Deskpro

Compaq's Deskpro 386/s20 is a 20-MHz 386 SX. It includes a 4K RAM cache and uses 60 and 120MB hard disk drives. The Deskpro 386/s20 has 2MB of RAM with room for 16MB on the motherboard. It uses a 3½-inch floppy disk drive and either a 60 or

120MB hard disk. The case is removed by loosening a few thumbscrews. Changing RAM or the math coprocessor is easy, and changing a drive requires removing a few screws. The memory uses standard SIMMs instead of the special memory modules used in some Compaq units.

All power and monitor controls are on the front panel. It has an integrated VGA adapter and 2MB of RAM. You can increase the RAM to 13MB using a special high-speed RAM expansion slot. There are four 8/16-bit expansion slots, one of which is used for ordinary operation. Deskpro has a 1.44MB floppy disk drive, with a 40 or 80MB hard disk installed in its internal drive bay.

Compaq 33L

The Deskpro 386/33L has a modular processor board, seven available EISA slots, drive array technology, and a 100MB capacity for RAM. Compaq worked with Western Digital to develop IDE (integrated drive electronics) hard drives, which run from a controller located on the motherboard. The drive array technology uses multiple hard drives that act as one.

Two 110MB drives can perform as a fast 220MB drive or as a single 110MB drive that backs itself up as it is used. The drive array technology must be used with Compaq drives.

You must use proprietary memory modules, which cost several times as much as standard SIMMs. You can change to a 486 CPU by changing processor cards. The system case uses thumbscrews.

Compaq's small-footprint case appeared in 1988 with the Deskpro 386s. Compaq uses a longitudinal 140-W power supply that runs along the full depth of the machine. Three front-panel bays can be used for storage, which can include 3½ and 5¼ inch.

Deskpro 386N and 286N

The 386N is a 16-MHz 386 SX computer. It has built-in serial, parallel, and mouse ports along with built-in floppy and hard disk controllers, and a 16-bit VGA controller. The 386N has three expansion slots. Two of them are ISA standard 8/16-bit slots (full length), and the third is a high-speed memory slot. With 1MB of RAM as standard, this can be increased with 7MB of additional memory on the motherboard and 8MB more in the memory slot.

The Deskpro 286N has the same features as the 386N, but it uses a 12-MHz 286 instead of a 386.

NEC PowerMate

The NEC PowerMate uses custom boards and each must fit into its own dedicated slot on the motherboard. The CPU and math coprocessor are on one of those boards. Other proprietary boards provide an 800×600 super-VGA adapter and RAM expansion. The IDE (integrated drive electronics) controller is built-in along with four expansion slots and three drive bays. The keyboard and mouse ports, on/off switch, and the monitor controls are on the front panel. The system has a 12MB limit for fast RAM. Many systems offer the EISA (Extended Industry Standard Architecture) bus. This bus allows higher throughput as well as backward compatibility with standard AT-style boards.

Besides speed, RAM capacity is the other advantage that the standard 80386 chip has over the less-expensive SX. The maximum for the SX chip is 16MB of CPU-speed RAM. Typical 386 DX machines include the following.

PowerMate.   The PowerMate has plenty of room for working in. It can take 16Mb of RAM. A proprietary ASIC (application-specific integrated circuit) chip is used for memory management. Five slots are present for EISA, and the PowerMate uses motherboard switches to set up the system. There is also a floor stand so the unit can stand up like a tower.

Arche Legacy.   The Legacy uses an AT box with five half-height drive slots and it can accommodate a full-height drive. Five expansion slots are available, but for more than 8MB of RAM, it uses one of the two RAM slots, which can also take standard 8/16-bit cards. To bring the memory up to its full 32MB capacity it takes two of these slots.

   The Legacy has no front-panel on/off switch, and installing a coprocessor requires removing the motherboard. There is a front-panel reset button and an LED display to indicate the processor speed. The motherboard uses several proprietary chips. These chips reduce the component count and increase machine reliability.

AST Premium.   The Premium has a tower case with good room to work and 80Mb of RAM capacity. The tower case provides eight available EISA slots and six drive bays. You can easily change the CPU.

AT&T.   AT&T's machine uses a floor-standing case and has eight drive bays. The front panel has a reset button, and the on/off switch is down near the floor. Configuring RAM, printer, and serial port settings can be time-consuming because a number of jumper pins must be changed on the system board. They have room for one or two internal hard drives with four full-length 8/16-bit ISA expansion slots.

   Compaq has integrated VGA graphics and built-in floppy and VGA graphics and built-in floppy and hard disk controllers. The serial, parallel, and mouse ports are on the motherboard. These ports would normally take several expansion cards. Four full-length 8/16 slots are available for expansion. In addition to saving a slot, the IDE disk controller provides faster data transfer than the earlier ST-506 controllers. IDE hard disks also tend to cost less than others. The Compaq Flex Architecture separates the system memory bus from the peripheral bus for high-speed access to memory.

Dell.   The Dell DX system provides six available AT-style slots. There are four half-height drive bays and the system can take 16Mb of RAM. Also included are super-VGA graphics. The unit has a small-footprint chassis and opens with thumbscrews. It also has front-panel on/off and reset switches.

Tandy.   The Tandy machine has four drive bays with 16Mb of RAM and a RAM cache. The 80386 is mounted on a modular board, but you can replace it with a 486 board. Five AT-style expansion slots and four drive slots are available, but two of these are for third-height drives. The compact chassis has on/off and reset controls on the front panel.

Zenith.   The Zenith unit has a caching disk controller, which can operate four ESDI, seven SCSI, and two floppy drives at the same time. This board uses one EISA slot; VGA and I/O take up two more slots, leaving four available slots. The standard AT-style chassis allows five half-height drives. Table 1-7 lists several 386 DX computers with their major characteristics.

The IBM 486

The IBM PS/2 XP 486 machines include two Model 90 desktops and two Model 95 towers. The XPs use the XGA (extended graphics array) that is built into all Model 90 motherboards and comes as an expansion board with the Model 95 towers. Like IBM's 8514/AZ, XGA offers 1024 × 768 resolution with 256 colors. A special mode allows XGA to display up to 65,536 colors at standard VGA resolution.

The tower case offers more drive bays and slots (Fig. 1-8), but the tower and desktop configurations are similar internally. The CPU board is removable; it fits into a Micro Channel slot. This board holds the 486, memory controller, and related circuitry, making it easier to change CPUs.

The XP models have 4MB of CPU-speed memory and can take 32MB. The standard memory uses 70-ns (nanosecond) chips and uses 1, 2, or 4MB single inline memory modules (SIMMs).

The memory architecture gives the 486 interleaved access to two 32-bit memory banks. It also allows you to add a 256K secondary memory cache. Many other systems either have a hard-wired secondary cache or cannot be modified. XPs store part of the BIOS on disk and copy it into RAM, which aids both performance and future upgrades. The throughput for serial ports has been increased from 19,200 bits per second to a potential 345,000 bits per second for high-speed modems. Parallel and mouse ports are standard. All the systems use IBM's 32-bit SCSI bus-master controller, which is built-in and handles up to seven SCSI drives for gigabytes of storage.

Table 1-7. Typical 386 DX computers

Company	Processor	MHz	Memory	Storage
AST Model 45	80386 DX	16	1MB RAM	1.2 or 1.4, 40MB
Compaq Model 40	80386 DX	20	1MB RAM	1.2, 40MB
DTK	80386 DX	20	0K RAM	Optional
Epson Equity	80386 DX	20	1MB RAM	1.2, 40/90MB
Hewlett-Packard HP Vectra QS/20	80386 DX	20	1MB RAM	108MB
Leading Edge D-3	80386 DX	16	1MB RAM	1.2, 65MB
Televideo Teloas III, Model NH	80386 DX	16	1MB RAM	1.2, 40MB
Zenith Z-386	80386 DX	16	1MB RAM	1.2, 80MB

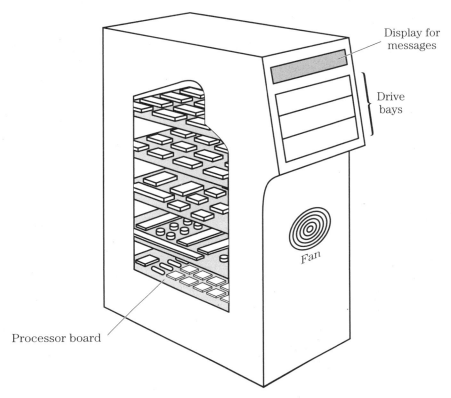

1-8 A 486 tower system.

The Model 90 desktop

The Model 90 is a little larger than the 386-based Model 70. With XGA on the system board, there are three 32-bit Micro Channel slots. One of the slots has a special pass-through extension that hooks into XGA, for boards such as IBM's M-Motion multimedia unit. This unit holds up to five storage devices. Two 5¼-inch bays can hold CD ROM drives, tape backup units, or a half-height 5¼-inch floppy drive. On the motherboard, two vertical racks of sockets hold up to four SIMMs each. The power supply is 194 W, and there are two serial ports and one parallel port.

Model 95

The Model 95 uses a tower slightly smaller than the Model 80 and has eight 32-bit slots. Two of the slots have XGA pass-through extensions. The SIMMs plug into the system board. The machine uses a 329-W power supply and seven storage bays. Model 95 has two bays for floppy disks, CD ROM drives, or tape backup and five for hard disks. This capacity allows up to 1.6GB with IBM drives. The tower case has an 8-character LED diagnostic display in front.

Other 486 computers

Some 486 computers of other manufacturers are described in the following text.

Compaq Systempro

The Systempro floor-standing tower system has room for 11 mass-storage devices and 11 full-size expansion slots. The Flex/MP architecture uses four expansion slots. The slots are dedicated for up to 256MB of RAM and for CPU expansion. In one of the Flex/MP slots is a processor card that can use either an 80386 or 80486. The 80386 processor card has a 64K RAM cache and supports the Weitek 3167-33 and Intel 80387-33 math coprocessors. The 80486 processor card has an integrated coprocessor, 8K of on-chip cache, and a Server Cache that uses 512K of 25-ns static RAM in a second-level cache. You can make the Systempro run faster with an additional 386 or 486 processor card.

Instead of a single, large hard disk drive, the Systempro uses *drive-array technology* that uses teams of smaller disk drives that act like one drive to the operating system and the user. The incoming data is split up and written to several drives simultaneously.

The *data-guarding feature* stores an image of the data. Each time a byte is written to any drive in the array, the IDE controller reads the byte occupying the same position on all the other drives. It performs a mathematical calculation on the byte values and writes the result on the data guard drive. Then, if a drive fails, its contents are reconstructed by reading the guard drive and interpreting the stored values.

The technique is used with four or eight drives and would fail if two drives in the same array crashed at the same time. For critical data, you can set the controller so it automatically and continuously performs *drive mirroring,* using half the system storage to duplicate information written to the other half. You can also use *controller duplexing* with two IDA controllers and two sets of drive arrays, providing redundancy for the two disk subsystems and the data is always accessible.

The base configuration has 240MB of storage, 8MB of RAM, and one 386 processor. The Intelligent Array Expansion System has 2.6GB of mass storage.

Deskpro 486/33L

The Compaq Deskpro 486/33L has an EISA expansion bus and an integrated VGA adapter. The Deskpro comes in a wide-body chassis with seven 8/16/32-bit EISA expansion slots. The following controllers and interfaces are built in: floppy disk controller, IDE hard disk controller, parallel port, tape drive controller, mouse port, two serial ports, and an Integrated Video Graphics System with a Graphics Accelerator.

In addition to the seven EISA slots, there are two additional 32-bit slots. One holds the processor card with the 33-MHz 80486 CPU and a socket for a Weitek 4167 numeric coprocessor. The second slot can hold up to 100MB of RAM. The processor has 8K of on-chip cache memory and takes another 128K of cache.

The Deskpro 486/33L Model 120 comes with a 120MB IDE hard disk that provides 19-ms (millisecond) access times. The 320 or 650MB systems provide access times of 18 ms and an even faster data transfer, because of the enhanced ESDI controller used with these drives. Seven bays for mass storage devices allow the Deskpro to store up to 1.3GB internally. The Deskpro 486/33L also can use the same Intelligent Drive Array controller used on the Systempro.

Acer 486 SX

The AcerPower 486 SX was one of the first 486 SX systems, which are compact ISA (Industry Standard Architecture) desktop systems. The 16-bit ISA I/O bus is a lower-cost product than the 32-bit EISA (Extended Industry Standard Architecture) bus.

The Acer 486 SX includes an Intel 486 SX processor, 2MB of system memory, an integrated Ultra-VGA graphics chip set, a 101-key enhanced PS/2 keyboard, a PS/2 mouse, four expansion slots for 16- or 8-bit ISA board, two serial ports (9-pin and 25-pin), and a parallel port. The system also comes with a 3½-inch 1.44MB floppy diskette drive. It has four 3½-inch half-height storage bays. You can convert two of the 3½-inch bays to a 5¼-inch half-height bay.

The AcerPower 486 SX uses its own ChipUp technology. ChipUp technology allows the system to detect automatically the type of CPU installed, so you do not have to worry about setting switches or configuring software when the 486 DX chip is installed. The second coprocessor is designed for the Weitek 4167 coprocessor for more floating-point capability. Memory is accessed through a separate 128-bit memory bus. The system memory uses a technique called *page-mode interleave.* Page-mode interleave speeds up the processing. The internal memory is *DRAM,* or *dynamic RAM,* which has to refresh itself constantly to keep from losing data. The time DRAM spends refreshing itself is time lost from processing tasks, which slows the system down.

Page-mode interleaving splits the DRAM (dynamic RAM) into two banks. Even addresses are accessed from one bank, and odd addresses are accessed from the other bank, which reduces the time the CPU spends waiting for DRAM to refresh itself and fetch the data. These times are called *wait states.*

Along with page-mode interleaving, the unit uses an 8K internal RAM cache. The RAM cache uses static RAM to hold frequently used instructions and data. Static RAM is faster than dynamic RAM because it does not have to continually refresh itself.

A cachable BIOS (basic input-output system) lets you put BIOS code into the 8K RAM cache. BIOS code in the cache can improve the performance by 25 percent. Cachable BIOS is sometimes confused with shadow RAM.

Shadow RAM designates a section of conventional RAM for the BIOS. So, when you boot up the machine, the contents of system and video BIOS are copied into shadow RAM, which is faster than the EPROM (erasable programmable read-only memory), which normally stores the BIOS.

The base memory is 2MB, with three available SIMM sockets. Different combinations of SIMM chips can be used. The AcerPower 486 SX supports six types of commercial SIMMs: 1, 2, 4, 8, 16, and 32MB. Table 1-8 summarizes the characteristics of IBM PCs up to the basic 486.

Pentium systems

The Pentium chip followed the Intel 386 and 486 microprocessors. The Pentium processor has all of the features of the 486 with the following enhancements and additions: superscalar architecture; dynamic branch prediction; pipelined, floating-point unit; improved instruction execution; separate code and data caches; write-back data cache; 64-bit data bus; bus-cycle pipelining; address parity; and internal parity checking.

Table 1-8. Intel processor evolution

8086/8088	IBM PC XT	1978	Basic computing power in a PC platform; clock speeds 4.77–10 MHz
80286	IBM PC AT	1982	10 times faster than original 8086 chip; runs in either real or protected mode, but does not run well in both modes at the same time, thus, not a good chip for running multi-tasking Windows; clock speeds 6–12 MHz
80386		1985	At least 50 percent faster than the 286; allowed for real multitasking, switching between real and protected mode; 32-bit data bus and processes 32 bits of data internally as opposed to 16 bits of earlier chips; clock speeds 16–33 MHz; DX: full 32-bits; SX: 16-bits
80486		1989	At least 50 percent faster than 386 chip; includes math coprocessor; DX versions 8K on-chip cache, FISC-like core, SL technology; clock speeds 25 to 100 MHz

The Pentium has two instruction pipelines and floating-point units that are capable of independent operation. Each pipeline issues frequently used instructions in a single clock, and the two pipelines can issue two integer instructions in one clock or one to two floating-point instructions in one clock. The floating-point unit has faster algorithms to speed some math operations up to 10 times. Separate code and data caches are on the chip. The data bus is 64 bits, which improves the data transfer rate. Burst read and write-back cycles are supported as well as bus-cycle pipelining that allows two bus cycles to take place simultaneously.

VL and PCI buses

Some Pentium systems use a local or mezzanine bus. A *local bus* is a direct extension of the processor lines and operates on the same clock. The VESA (Video Electronics Standards Association) is a local bus used in many 486 systems (Fig. 1-9).

A *mezzanine bus* is a cross between a local bus and an I/O bus. Its signals are buffered from the processor signals, and its clock is usually one-half or one-third the CPU speed. Another example is the Intel PCI (peripheral component interconnect) specification and chip set, which is also used as a mezzanine bus in Pentium systems (Fig. 1-10).

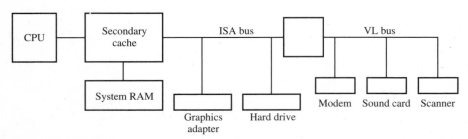

1-9 The (VL) VESA local bus.

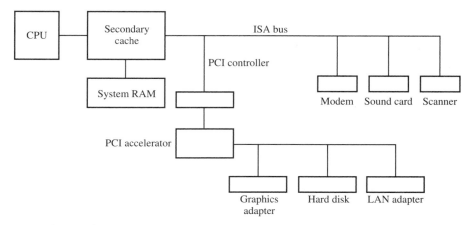

1-10 The PCI bus.

PCI started with 32 bits and operated at half the speed of the Pentium's external clock. Next, it supported 64-bit addressing and 3.3-V (volt) operation. It also defines a PCI connector slot for add-in cards. An alternative to PCI is VESA's VL-Bus, which is used in many 486 systems. There are chip sets that support the Pentium and VL-Bus as well as inexpensive VL-Bus controllers.

Like the PCI, the VL-Bus started at 32 bits, then it provided support for 64 bits. The VL-Bus for Pentium has more controllers available compared to an early lack of controllers and add-ins for PCI.

The VL-Bus is not as powerful as PCI and might suffer from performance problems above 50 MHz because its timing was designed to work at 40 MHz or less. PCI is a better design for a high-speed local bus. Because the VL-Bus was really designed for the 486 chip, a fair amount of logic is needed to use it as a mezzanine bus for the Pentium and this drives up the cost.

A few Pentium systems use the VL-Bus. Some use a proprietary local bus for video. Others use Compaq and NCR implement PCI. Low-speed functions, such as serial I/O for mice and modems, still use the low-cost ISA bus.

Some Pentium systems designed as network servers include EISA slots. Most servers need eight or more slots, and you cannot put that many on VL or PCI.

Pentium systems require more cooling so there are bigger or more fans, special cooling hardware, and tanklike cases that must be kept closed to prevent damage to the electronics inside.

Most Pentium systems are based on existing 486 designs. The vendors tried to build flexibility into their 486 designs to accommodate the Pentium. To hold the Pentium, most vendors use either a daughtercard or a processor card. The designs of the cards vary. Some can contain the processor, cache, DMA (direct memory access), and memory with a 64-bit interface, but others hold the processor and support circuitry with a 32-bit interface.

The ALR Evolution V-Q is one machine that has Pentium on the motherboard. It and the NCR System 3360 use completely new system designs for the Pentium.

Cooling problems

All these machines create a lot of heat. A 66-MHz Pentium uses about 15 W itself, and the high-speed support chips add to this. Many Pentium chips have their own fan mounted directly to them. Others use at least a heat sink. Some, such as the Compaq and Zenith units, have both a heat sink and a fan mounted directly to the IC. Some of the systems designed for the Pentium, such as the multiprocessor NCR System 3360, have separate air channels and pathways for processor cooling. If the channels or pathways are damaged or changed, major heating problems could occur.

Other systems, such as the Acer AcerFrame 3000MP, use a large conductive cooling plate. The IBM Model 95 66-MHz Pentium server has a row of squirrel-cage fans mounted near the processor.

High processor speed and circuit complexity mean more electrical power. Pentium systems tend to have larger power supplies, and a power supply of 400 W or more is common. The larger power supply also adds more heat. The faster 486 systems handle this by separating the power supply and its cooling fan from the rest of the system. Most Pentium systems isolate the power supply cooling airflow (Fig. 1-11). If you suspect

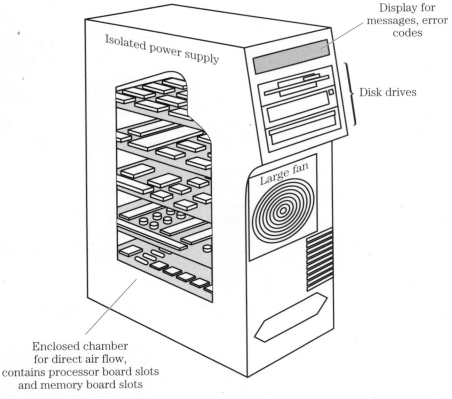

1-11 Pentium floor-standing tower system.

heating problems in your Pentium, try to trace or measure the temperature of the air-flow; you might have to add another fan in some cases. These small cooling fans are available from many electronics supply houses.

Typical Pentium systems

Some typical Pentium systems are listed in the following text.

IBM PC server series

The PC server 300 is available with a 486DX2 66- or 60-MHz Pentium processor. It has EISA and PCI buses with 8MB of memory that is expandable to 128MB. There is a 728Mb hard drive with 8 open slots and 9 bays.

The 320 uses a 90-MHz Pentium that is multiprocessor-enabled. It has 16MB of memory and is expandable to 256MB. There are 6 open slots with 9 bays. A CD-ROM drive is standard. The 500 is similar, except it has double the memory and 18 bays. It also uses the MCA bus. The 720 uses a 100-MHz Pentium and doubles the memory again.

AcerFrame 3000MP

The AcerFrame processor speed is 60 MHz, and the processor-to-memory band-width is 32 bits. The memory uses ECC (error checking and correction) checking. The cache is 256K and the expansion bus has EISA and ISA slots. The RAM is 16MB. Acer uses a metal plate to heat-sink the processor board that sits next to the expansion slots. It supports four processors that share the memory and the EISA bus peripherals.

ALR

The ProVeisa machine has a processor speed of 60 MHz with a processor-to-memory bandwidth of 32 bits. The memory uses parity checking and the cache is 512K. The expansion bus slots are EISA and ISA. RAM is 32MB, and there is a four-drive 540MB SCSI array. The ProVeisa uses a 1024 × 768, 14-inch monitor. The ALR Evolution has a processor speed of 60 MHz with a processor-to-memory bandwidth of 128 bits. The memory also uses parity checking and the cache is 512K. The expansion bus is EISA and VL. RAM is 32MB, and there is a four-unit 540MB SCSI drive array and a 1024 × 768, 14-inch monitor. The processor is mounted on the system board.

Compaq Deskpro 5/66M

The processor speed of the 5/66M is 66 MHz, and the processor-to-memory band-width is 128 bits. The memory uses parity checking, and the cache is 256K. The expansion slots are EISA, and the RAM is 16MB. A 510MB IDE is included with a 20-inch, 1280 × 1024 monitor. Compaq uses its TriFlex architecture, in which the processor has its own board with the other timing critical parts like the cache and DMA circuits.

DECpc 560ST

The DECpc processor runs at 60 MHz, and the processor-to-memory bandwidth is 32 bits. The DECpc uses parity memory checking, and the cache is 256K. The expansion bus is EISA, and there is 16MB of RAM. The computer also has a 1GB SCSI drive and a 1024 × 768 monitor.

Hewlett-Packard NetServer 5/60 LM

The NetServer has a processor speed of 60 MHz, and the processor-to-memory bandwidth is 32 bits. The memory uses parity checking and the cache is 256K. The expansion slots are EISA and there is an integrated SCSI-2 controller. It has 16MB of RAM and a 4GB SCSI drive.

IBM Model 95

The IBM Model 95 is a 66-MHz Pentium server with a processor-to-memory bandwidth of 64 bits. The memory uses ECC checking and the cache is 256K. The expansion bus is Micro Channel MC, and there is 16MB of RAM. The Model 95 has two 540MB SCSI drives and a 1024 × 768 monitor.

NCR System 3360

NCR System 3360 processor speed is 60 MHz, and there is a processor-to-memory bandwidth of 128 bits. The memory can use parity checking or EDAC. A 256K cache is used along with a Micro Channel expansion bus. There is 64MB of RAM and a 1GB SCSI drive. A 1280 × 1024, 19-inch monitor is used. This system has an isolated power supply located on the top end of the tower case. It will accept several processors in an enclosed chamber, that has a large fan for good airflow. The system uses custom memory management chips and a proprietary local bus for video. This feature allows whichever bus is free to update the display.

Siemens Nixdorf PCE-5S

The processor speed of the Nixdorf is 60 MHz, and the processor-to-memory bandwidth is 64 bits. The memory uses EDAC, and the cache is 256K. The expansion bus slots use EISA, ISA, and VL. The PCE-5S has an integrated SCSI-2 controller and 16MB of RAM. A 510MB SCSI drive is used along with 1024 × 768 video.

Unisys PW Advantage Plus 5606

The Advantage Plus has a processor speed of 60 MHz and a processor-to-memory bandwidth of 32 bits. Parity-checking memory is used along with a 256K cache. The expansion bus is EISA, and there is an integrated SCSI-2 controller. The RAM is 16MB; the system includes a 1.2GB SCSI drive and 1024 × 768 video.

Z-Server LT 466XE Model 500

The Z-Server processor runs at 66 MHz, and the processor-to-memory bandwidth is 64 bits. The memory uses parity checking, and the cache is 256K. The expansion bus is EISA, and there is an integrated SCSI-2 controller. The RAM is 16MB, and there is a 3.5GB SCSI drive and 1024 × 768 video. Table 1-9 lists some other Pentium 66-MHz systems as well as a representative DX4-100 system.

Pentium versus 486

In 1993, when Intel introduced the Pentium chip, the following technological advances set the Pentium apart from previous chips. The Pentium's enhanced floating-point-processor (FPU) design is especially useful in high-end graphics applications.

Table 1-9. Pentium-66, DX4-100 systems

	Axik Evolution V ST/66	Dell Ace Cache 586-66PCI/ MPC	Gateway OptiPlex 4100/L	ALR P5-66
CPU	Pentium-66	Pentium-66	DX4-100	Pentium-66
CPU/upgrade socket	273-pin	273-pin	238-pin ZIF	273-pin ZIF
BIOS	Phoenix 1.02.04M	Award 12/27/93	Phoenix 80486 RBP	Phoenix 1/24/94
Installed/maximum RAM (MB)	16/128	16/192	8/64	16/128
SIMMs	72-pin	72-pin	72-pin	72-pin
SIMM sockets/free	8/4	6/4	4/2	4/0
Secondary RAM cache installed/maximum (K)	256/256	256/512	128/128	256/256
Case style	Tower	Tower	Compact	Tower
Free drive bays				
Accessible	0/3	0/2	0/1	0/3
Internal 3½/5¼-in	1/0	3/2	0/0	3/0
Free slots				
32-bit	0/5/0	0/3/0	0/3/0	0/4/0
32-bit EISA/16-bit ISA/ 8-bit ISA slots				
PCI or VL slots/free	3 VLB/1	3 PCI/1	0/0	0/4/0
Hard disk	WD Caviar 2540 540MB	Quantum LPS 525S 525MB	WD Caviar 1170 170MB	WD Caviar 2540 540MB
Adapter	Alpha S475I VLB	OEM/PCI-SC200 SCSI	Integrated	Integrated
Floppy drives	1.44MB	1.44MB	1.44MB	1.44MB
Parallel/serial/mouse ports	1/2/1	1/2/0	1/2/1	1/2/1

Multiple data pipelining allows the processor to move more information more quickly, but to take advantage of this and other new features of the Pentium, manufacturers have to recompile existing software applications. Not a lot of software has been recompiled for the Pentium, but most new software is optimized to work on Pentium systems. Windows 95 is optimized for the Pentium processor.

Superscalar technology enables the chip to move more information at one time through the use of multiple data paths. *Branch prediction* is a technique that predicts the routing of data, so that the microprocessor does not have to slow down to determine what to do next. The 16K on-chip cache is twice the size of the 486.

While the 486 processor was the first Intel processor to include RISC-like technology, the Pentium incorporates more RISC technology by processing the most frequently used instructions much more quickly.

Floating-point bug

The early Pentiums had a *floating-point bug,* which produced errors in advanced mathematical calculations. Intel, at first, denied the scope of the problem and then started to replace only chips that could be proven to be defective. It later agreed to replace any Pentium chip that the customer desired. It was the FPU that was found to cause math errors, but Intel reported that only one in 9 billion floating-point division operations actually resulted in error.

Any miscalculations are most likely to occur in scientific and high-level applications that require division. It only affects the first Pentiums, and the 75-MHz Pentiums that were produced after the error was corrected are completely free from this bug. As 75- and 90-MHz Pentiums became common, Intel came out with the 120-MHz Pentium, followed by 133- and 150-MHz Pentiums.

RISC and CISC

RISC (reduced instruction-set computing) is the architecture used in the PowerPC. The CISC (complex instruction-set computing) architecture is used in Intel 80 × 86 machines. CISC chips recognize a large number of complicated instructions and compute them efficiently. This causes a slightly slower performance rate than RISC chips, which execute simple instructions. The CISC architecture makes high-performance processors harder to design and build, but its main appeal lies in the large installed software base that runs on the Intel microprocessors, such as the 386 or 486.

Intel and other suppliers of its chips such as Advanced Micro Devices (AMD) and Cyrix are staying with the ability to run existing PC software. Their chip designers believe that any deficiencies can be overcome without converting to full-RISC technology. Also, the next-generation processors may further blur the line between the two technologies.

The changes in microprocessor technology such as RISC-like architectures, are making speed ratings in megahertz less meaningful. When Intel was virtually the only source, the general rule was that the bigger the processor number and megahertz speed, the more powerful the processor was. A 25-MHz 386 was faster than a 16-MHz 386, but not as fast as a 25-MHz 486. Intel began to confuse things with the DX and SX versions and by abandoning numbers altogether with the Pentium. The increased presence of other chip vendors, coupled with technological advances, has complicated all of the processor issues even more. Intel competitors have come through on their claims of chip compatibility and performance, and users should not detect any difference between one type of microprocessor and another.

Intel competitors

Starting with the 286 chip, other chip manufacturers produced Intel clones or variations. These include AMD, Cyrix, IBM, and NexGen. Clone chip makers initially followed Intel's design to create 386 and 486 chips that are compatible with the hardware and software that runs on an Intel-based machine. Each manufacturer has added a few variations to its product.

Cyrix

Cyrix makes both 5- and 3-volt versions of the Cx486DX2 chip. The Cyrix Pentium clone is called the M1 chip. This chip, unlike the Pentium, does not require software to be recompiled for optimization.

The M1 differs from the Pentium in that the Pentium uses branch prediction, while the M1 uses speculative execution. Unlike branch prediction, which guesses whether or not a program instruction will branch and can result in a speed boost, *speculative execution* guesses what the program will do next, while going ahead with the execution. There is no waste of execution time.

The M1 chip has a Pentium-compatible pinout. Both the Pentium and M1 are superscalar and send one part of a pair of instructions sent to each pipeline. The Pentium can issue instructions to both pipelines only under certain conditions, while the M1's design and seven-stage pipeline allow it to increase the number of times where instructions can be paired, which increases throughput.

One limiting factor in superscalar architectures is that one of the paired instructions may require data from the other instruction. This produces a delay, called a *read-after-write* (RAW) *dependency,* where one instruction waits for the other to write the data it needs. Data forwarding techniques allow the M1 to forward the result from the leading instruction to the following one without waiting for the first instruction to be completed. The M1 also uses data bypassing and out-of-order completion capabilities to reduce the effects of data dependencies and has 32 general-purpose registers compared to the Intel 86 architecture.

The M1 initially has a large die size which is twice that of the 90-and 100-MHz Pentiums. This means fewer chips can be produced from a silicon wafer and makes it more expensive to produce.

The M1's architecture allows it to run 30 to 100 percent faster than 100-MHz Pentium processors, depending upon the benchmark used. The Intel 133-MHz P6 is expected to process data at double the speed of the 100-MHz Pentium.

IBM SLC and Blue Lightning

IBM manufactured the 386SLC chip for its own systems and has two 486 chips, the SLC and the Blue Lightning, which are used in IBM systems and on system boards (which are also sold under other names, such as Alaris). The 486SLC2 is a clock-doubled chip, similar to Intel's DX2.

Unlike Intel's 32-bit 486 chips, IBM's have 16-bit external buses, which IBM claims do not slow performance for most applications, yet minimize the cost of manufacturing. The Blue Lightning chip is a clock-tripled 486SLC chip that can provide speeds of up to 100 MHz.

AMD

AMD's 486 chips are found in many desktop units and the K5 chip is AMD's Pentium clone. These are 100-MHz chips that have an 8K cache, compared to the Pentium's 16K. Systems with the K5 chip can cost less since the chips cost the manufacturer about half the price of Pentiums to produce.

NexGen Nx586

NexGen calls its Pentium-type chip the Nx586 which has different pin sockets than the Intel chips. Systems using the NexGen chips need a different system board than those used for the other chips. NexGen provides a 32K cache, which is twice the size of Intel's 16K cache and four times more than AMD's cache. Figure 1-12(A) shows the Nx586 architecture with its separate floating-point processor and Fig. 1-12(B) shows the Pentium architecture with its separate cache controller. Figure 1-12(C) shows an Nx586 local bus system and Fig. 1-12(D) illustrates an Nx586 PCI bus system.

PowerPC

In 1991 Apple, Motorola, and IBM joined up and created the PowerPC chip, which was released in 1993. This is a RISC processor that lets you run Mac and Windows applications on the same system. The Macintosh and Windows applications run under software emulation, which reduces performance greatly.

The only applications that run without emulation are those designed for the PowerPC chip, called *native applications.* Several hundred of these native applications are avail-

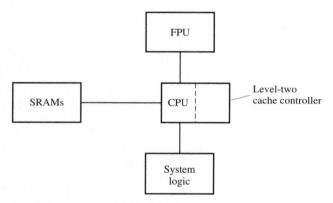

1-12(A) Nx586 with on-chip level-two cache controller and separate floating point processor.

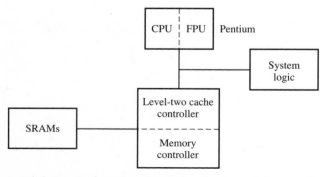

1-12(B) Pentium with separate level-two cache controller.

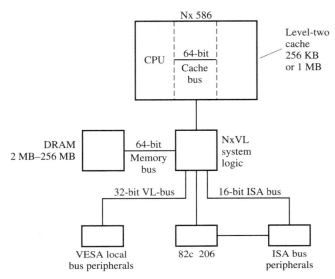

1-12(C) Nx586 local bus system.

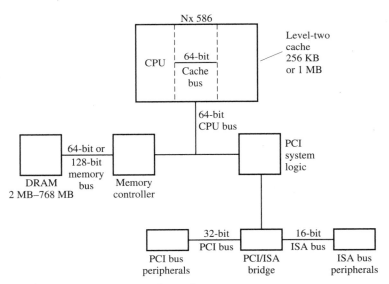

1-12(D) Nx586 system with PCI bus.

able, with more being developed. Figure 1-12(E) shows a block diagram of the PowerPC and Fig. 1-12(F) shows a PowerPC system board.

Other chips include Digital's Alpha 21164 and the MIPS R4000 chips. These do not run DOS, Windows 3.11, or OS/2 applications in native mode. Although these are powerful chips, when they run most graphics applications in emulation mode, the performance is below that of a Pentium. PowerPC-based desktop systems are available from

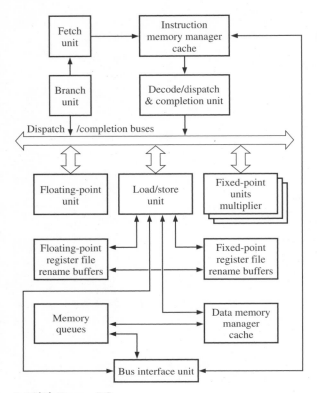

1-12(E) Power PC.

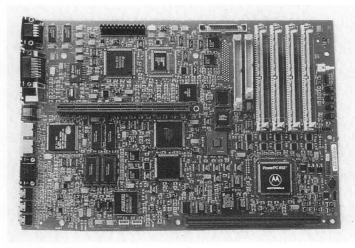

1-12(F) PowerPC system board.

Apple, and IBM has workstations and network servers with the PowerPC chip. The Apple PowerMac and Performa are desktop systems with the PowerPC chip.

Intel P6

Two years after the first Pentiums appeared on the market, Intel had its P6 processor chip ready, which adds another stage to the evolution of personal computing power. The P6 chip will execute about 300 MIPS (millions of instructions per second) at an initial clock speed of 133 megahertz (MHz).

Its speed is about three times faster than the 100 MIPS of a 60-MHz Pentium and about twice the speed of a 100-MHz Pentium. If you go back 20 years to Intel's 8080, it ran at 1 MIPS. In the few years since the Pentium was introduced, we have gone from 60 to 120 MHz.

The P6 uses a power supply of 2.9 V (volts) and has four integer units, compared to two integer units for the Pentium and three for Motorola's PowerPC. The P6 design uses a concept called *Dynamic Execution* which is the next step beyond the superscalar technology in the Pentium processor. *Superscalar technology* allows the processor to move information through two parallel pipelines instead of one.

Dynamic Execution is a combination of technologies, such as multiple branch execution, data flow analysis, and speculative execution, which are designed to keep up a constant flow of data, increasing the efficiency and speed of the processor.

Multiple branch execution increases the amount of work available for the processor to execute, while *data flow analysis* schedules instructions to be executed when ready, independent of the original program order. The P6 is kept as busy as possible with the use of *speculative execution*, which anticipates and executes the instructions that are most likely to be needed. Figure 1-13 shows a block diagram of the P6 chip.

P7 chip

The P6 could be Intel's last pure 86-based chip. Intel and Hewlett-Packard have a joint research and development agreement that could result in the P7 chip, a microprocessor that provides compatibility with the 386, 486, and Pentium architecture and HP's own PA-RISC architecture. The P7 is expected to be a RISC-like chip with Intel 86 emulation, allowing downward compatibility with 86 machines but moving Intel closer to full-RISC technology.

Upgrading and multiprocessing

If high-power graphics and video are pushing the limits of your computer, there are several ways to move up to higher performance. Adding more random-access memory (RAM) is probably the easiest. A graphics accelerator, with 64, 128, or 192 bits, that plugs into the PCI or VL bus is another way. Improvements to the storage subsystem include a larger, faster hard drive, a SCSI drive and interface instead of the standard AT-IDE type, or a connection via the PCI or VL bus.

Some tasks such as 3D renderings require more processing power. This doesn't always mean jumping up to a new computer or moving from a 386 to a 486 or even to a

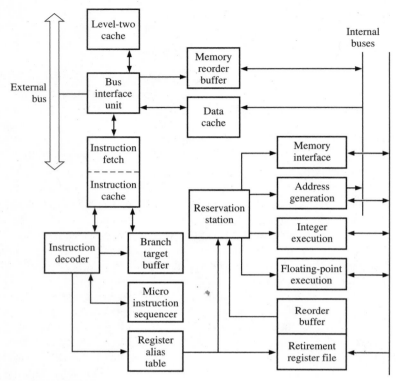

1-13 Intel P6.

Pentium. Systems with built-in sockets on the motherboard allow you to install new CPUs. Intel's Overdrive chips, as well as chips from companies such as Cyrix and Weitek, are designed for upgradable systems. But, once you install the replacement CPU, the original one becomes inactive.

Another approach is *multiprocessing,* where the power of two or more CPUs is harnessed simultaneously. Although it was used effectively in large mainframes and minicomputers, multiprocessing was not available in most desktop computers. This was due to the lack of operating systems that can take advantage of more than one CPU at a time.

You can buy a system with one CPU (a *uniprocessor*) and then add a second or third CPU and get a nearly two- or threefold performance boost. This is called *symmetrical multiprocessing,* or SMP. Figure 1-14 shows a typical multiprocessor CPU card.

Types of multiprocessing

Asymmetrical multiprocessing means a dedicated processor is used for an activity such as communications, graphics, or hardware monitoring. It is called *asymmetrical* since the dedicated processor is not able to perform the same work as the master processor. SMP systems share the total workload among similar or identical CPUs.

SMP has to be implemented at the operating system level and must be transparent to software programs. The applications do not have to be written specially to take

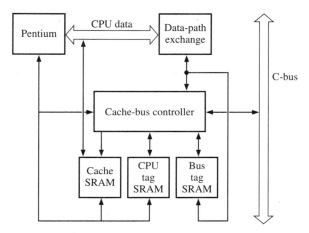

1-14 Pentium multiprocessor system, CPU card.

advantage of multiple processors, since the operating system doles out tasks to an arbitrary number of CPUs and the software programs are unaware that this is occurring. The amount of performance increase from adding CPUs is not linear. The law of diminishing returns starts after you get above four to six processors because of the overhead required to parcel out tasks.

Multiprocessing Specification

Intel has created a standard, called the *Multiprocessor Specification,* that defines a system for two Pentium chips. This allows systems to start out as uniprocessors and be upgraded to dual processing for better performance.

SMP operating systems

A number of operating systems support SMP. SCO UNIX was one of the early options for Intel x86 PCs. Microsoft Windows NT also had this capability, but its usefulness was limited by the small number of compatible applications. IBM has an SMP-capable version of OS/2. But, the DOS-based versions of Windows, including Windows 95, cannot support SMP.

Threads

SMP hardware does not require specially written applications, but for best results programs should be written to take advantage of an operating system feature found in Windows NT, OS/2, and UNIX called *threads.*

Threads are separate, loosely related paths of execution, such as the part of a program that draws an image on a screen or the part that sends it to a printer. SMP-type operating systems can send different threads to different CPUs to greatly boost performance. Not all 32-bit programs are multithreaded.

2

CHAPTER

System Components

A thorough understanding of what is going on in the parts of your computer can help you with troubleshooting and repair. Read this chapter for specific descriptions of the components that make up your PC.

The system unit

The system unit, shown in Fig. 2-1, contains the power supply, the system board, disk drives, a fan, and the system power switch. You can place the unit horizontally on a desk or vertically in a floor stand. Placing the system unit in a floor stand decreases the amount of desk space needed by the personal computer. The floor stand also keeps the unit fixed and allows it enough airflow for proper cooling.

The component design makes installation of options and maintenance of components easy. The system unit cover is secured by screws at the rear of the system box (Fig. 2-2). You can remove the disk drives and power supply by disconnecting their cables and removing their mounting screws. The system module or chassis slides out the back of the system unit (Figs. 2-3 to 2-10). This module has connectors in it for mounting the disk controller, memory extension options, and other options. The connectors for the peripheral devices are at the back of the system unit, as shown in Fig. 2-2.

The system module

The system module, or chassis, is located inside the system unit and is made up of electrical components and circuits. Its major components are the microprocessor, memory chips, power supply, and related hardware.

Mounted on the system chassis is the drive controller board as shown in Fig. 2-11. It controls reading and writing on the disk drives. The system chassis has connectors for mounting memory extension options and other expansion board options. You can expand the system memory by adding a memory extension board. The system chassis

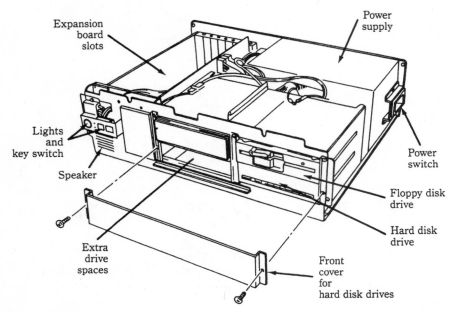

2-1 Typical system unit.

also has a ROM section, which contains diagnostic tests and a bootstrap program for starting the computer.

The microprocessor controls the monitor, the keyboard, and the printer if one is connected. It also controls any additional options that you add to the system unit.

ROM and RAM

ROM (read-only memory) and RAM (random-access memory) provide the basic electronic memory for the computer. ROM and RAM are alike in some ways and different in others. Both are fabricated on computer chips and both are measured in kilobytes (K) or megabytes (MB).

A ROM chip allows reading only (read-only) so you can read its contents but not change them. The information is permanently burned into the chip. The ROM chips contain the fixed instructions that allow the PC to boot following the application of power, and they contain the instructions needed for the specific hardware of that machine.

A RAM chip is reusable. RAM provides the temporary storage that the computer needs to process program instructions and data. The RAM chips hold the data and program instructions only while you work with them. When you turn the power off, RAM chips lose their contents.

RAM disks

You can use a program included on the DOS diskette (DOS version 3.1 or later) to create a RAM disk in your extended memory. A RAM disk behaves like an extra floppy or hard disk installed in the system, but because there is actually no disk mechanically attached, access time is extremely fast.

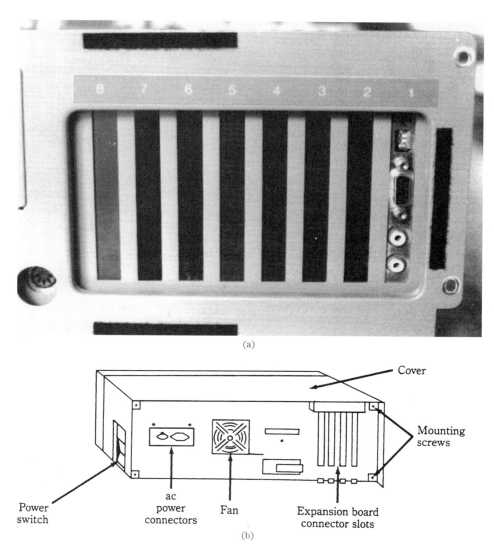

(a)

(b)

2-2(A and B) Rear views of a system unit.

Crystals

The crystal provides the timing for all computer functions. Suppose your computer comes with a 20-MHz crystal. Because computers generally run at half their crystal speed, the computer will run at 10 MHz. If the crystal is dead, the rest of the circuitry will not run at all, and you will have to change the crystal.

You might be able to change to a faster crystal, such as a 24-MHz crystal. Switching to this crystal speeds the system up to 12 MHz.

The crystal looks like a little tin pellet on two wires (Fig. 2-12). One side is usually attached to the system board by an adhesive pad. To change crystals, you pull the old

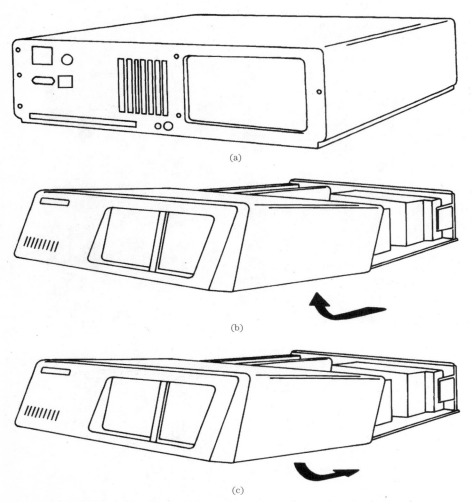

2-3 The classic XT cover design is used in many clones. First, remove the screws from the rear (A). Then slide the cover off and lift up (B). To replace, slide the cover down and then back. Then replace the screws at the rear (C).

crystal loose from the adhesive pad and slide it off the holder. Then install the new crystal on the holder, with the printing side faceup, and stick it down on the adhesive pad.

Memory, I/O, and multifunction cards

The AT computer, for example, is capable of addressing a maximum of 16MB of memory. You might have add-in memory cards that occupy the expansion slots of the unit to upgrade the memory all the way to this limit. If you use your personal computer with a printer, a modem, or another external device, you will use a serial or parallel port (depending on the device). These ports also come with add-in cards. Because many users are

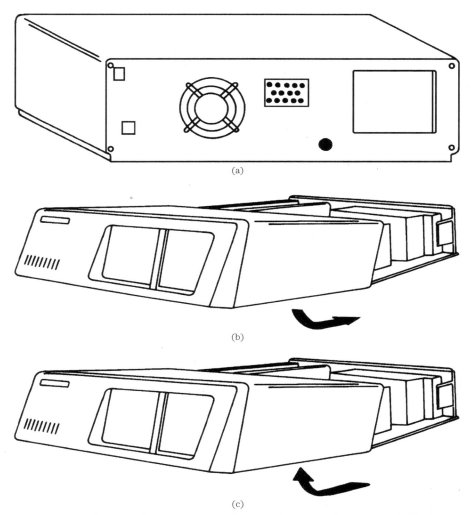

2-4 Some Tandy units have screws at the rear that must be removed (like many clones) (A). To remove, slide the cover down and then back and replace the cover holding screws (B). Then slide the cover forward and up (C).

interested in both of these options and because the number of expansion slots inside each computer is limited, some manufacturers offer multifunction cards. Multifunction cards combine additional memory with serial and/or parallel ports, and offer additional features, on a single card. As with all add-in cards, the card must run on the system clock speed.

Other possible peripherals that you might have in your personal computer include an internal or external modem, a mouse, a light pen, or more floppy or hard disk drives.

The AT system was the first IBM PC to use a 16-bit bus. However, in many units a few of the expansion slots can accommodate an 8-bit card. The left rear section of the system chassis houses the expansion slots.

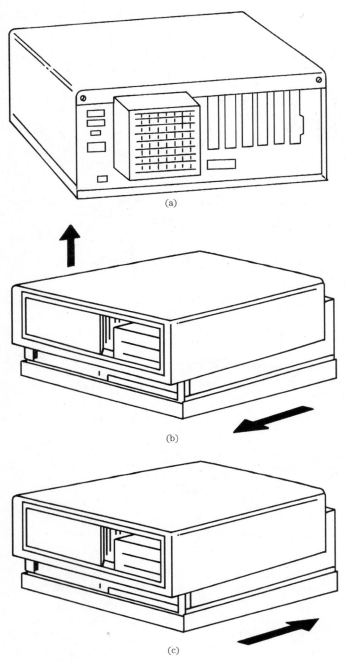

(a)

(b)

(c)

2-5 To remove the cover from some AT&T units, remove the screws from the back of the computer (A). Slide the cover forward to release it; then lift it off (B). To replace the cover, place it on the chassis and slide back. Then replace the screws at the rear (C).

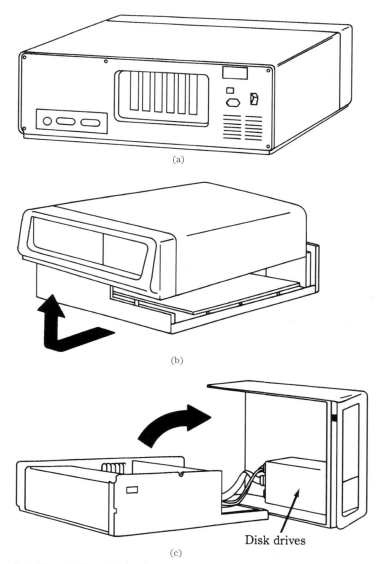

(a)

(b)

Disk drives

(c)

2-6 The ADDs PC also has its cover screws at the rear. First, remove those screws (A). Then, slide the cover back slightly and lift up carefully—the disk drive cables are attached to the cover (B). Slide the cover on its side when it is clear of the chassis (C).

Expansion slots

Expansion slots hold the other circuit boards (the terms *board* and *card* are used interchangeably) that operate the system. In most AT systems, the expansion slots are located in the left-rear section of the system box (Fig. 2-13). Each slot has a rectangular hole in the back of the chassis. Narrow slots, called *slot covers*, cover the slots

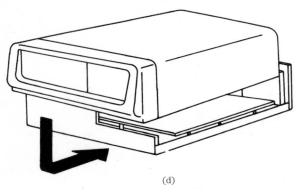

(d)

2-6 (*Continued*) The ADDs PC also has its cover screws at the rear. To replace the cover, lift the cover onto the chassis and push it back (D).

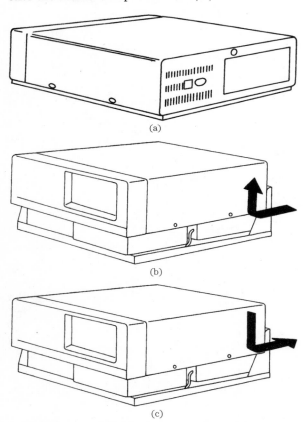

(a)

(b)

(c)

2-7 Some computers such as the Leading Edge computer have some of their cover screws on the sides. Remove the screws (A). Then slide the cover forward and up to remove it (B). To replace the cover, slide it back on the chassis and replace the cover screws (C).

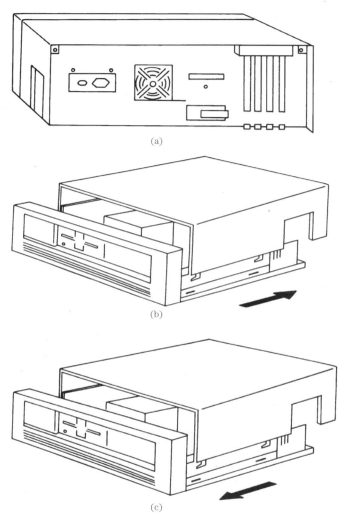

(a)

(b)

(c)

2-8 The Texas Instruments Professional Computer has two cover screws at the rear. First, you must remove those screws (A). Then slide the cover back until it is released; then lift it off (B). To replace the cover, lift it onto the chassis, putting the metal tabs on the cover into the slots, and slide the cover forward. Then replace the screws (C).

when they are empty, and the endplates of the expansion cards cover them when they are occupied.

When you install a card in an expansion slot, the slot cover is removed and the board inserted into the data bus connector. The slot cover screw is used to secure the endplate of the card to the back of the chassis.

You can install some 8-bit cards in a 16-bit slot because there are some 8-bit cards that are physically compatible with a 16-bit slot. The difference is in the bottom edge of the

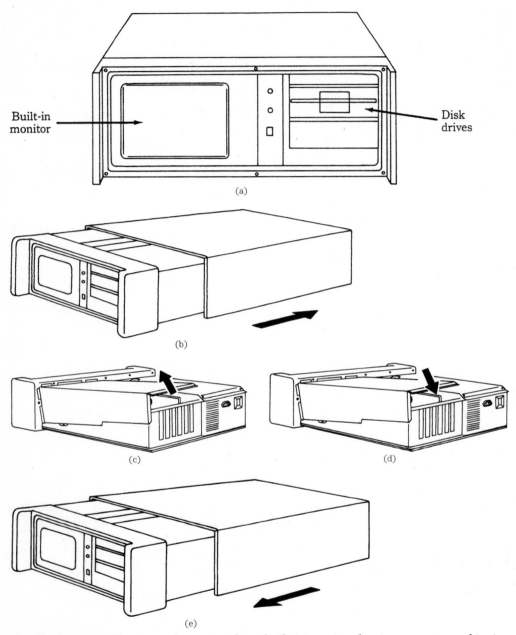

2-9 The IBM portable personal computer has a built-in monitor, but its cover removal is similar to that for most desktop systems (A). To remove the cover, remove the screws from the back of the computer, and slide the cover back and up (B). Remove the screws from the shield on the right side of the computer to get at the expansion slots (C). To replace the cover, replace the shield and the shield screws (D). Slide the cover on and replace the screws (E).

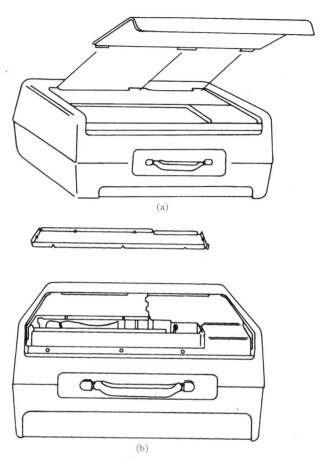

(a)

(b)

2-10 The Compaq portable computer has a lid that opens by pushing inward on the cover and then lifting up. When you close the cover, insert the tabs on the cover into the slots on the back and push down until the cover snaps closed (A). You must remove a metal cover to get at the expansion slots. There are seven screws holding the cover (B).

card next to the 8-bit connector pins. If there is a wide cutout on the card next to the 8-bit tab connector, or if the edge goes straight out from the tab, it is physically compatible.

If the edge of the card dips down against the 8-bit tab connector, it is physically incompatible. You cannot install this card in a 16-bit slot because this part will interfere with the second connector on the system board.

The endplate of the expansion card provides space for a rear connector so that a monitor or a printer can be plugged into the card. The endplate bracket also anchors the card to the system chassis and completes the metallic shield to minimize the entry of EMI (electromagnetic interference).

(a)

Hard-drive data
cable connectors

Hard-drive control
cable connector

Floppy drive control
cable connector

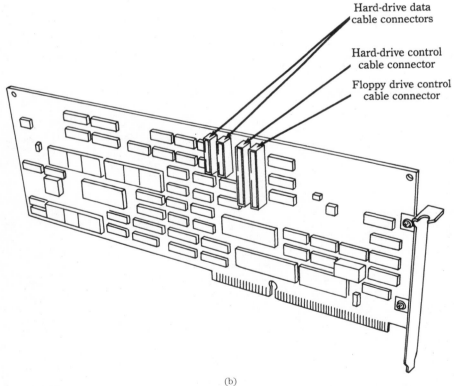

(b)

2-11 Drive controller board. Floppy and hard disk controller used in XT computers (A). Floppy and hard disk controller used in AT computers (B).

2-12 Typical crystal package.

Short cards are less than half the length of standard boards. Short cards were designed for the PC-XT and compatibles, which have one or more expansion slots behind the left-hand disk drive, where only about half the usual space is available. These short slots work the same as long slots, but they require a card that fits physically into a small space.

Many 286 computers and above have no short slots. But you can use short cards in the 286. They are all 8-bit cards and require the same criteria (speed, configurability, and physical compatibility with 16-bit slots) required to use any 8-bit card. To install an expansion card with a 16-bit bus, you must use a 16-bit slot. Some, but not all, 8-bit cards will run in a 16-bit slot.

The primary source of information when replacing peripheral cards is the operator's manual that accompanies each product. However, there are a few general rules that apply.

1. Always remember that circuit boards are very sensitive to static electricity. One discharge can permanently damage some electronic chips. You should rid your

2-13(A) Expansion slots are located in the left rear section of the AT system box.

Expansion
slot
area

2-13(B) Close-up of expansion slot area showing connectors on system board and metal covers at rear of system chassis. There are five long (16-bit) slot connectors available.

Expansion slots

SIMMs   Battery holder

2-13(C) Expansion slots inside a 486 tower system.

hands of static electricity by touching the system chassis every time before you touch a circuit board.

2. Do not eat, drink, or smoke while you are working over an open computer.

3. Remember to screw down the endplate brackets of your cards and keep slot covers in place over every unused slot. The covers minimize the possible entry of radio interference.

4. Usually, install cards that attach to ribbon cables, such as drive-controller cards, to the right of cards without cables. This arrangement helps keep the cables out of the way of other expansion slots.

5. Be careful not to let metal parts such as screws get loose in the computer. If you drop a screw on the system board, you must find it and remove it before you can apply power to the computer or it might cause a damaging short circuit.

The actual replacement of cards in your expansion slots is simple (Fig. 2-14). Choose an empty slot and remove the screw holding the slot cover to the back of the chassis. Slide the card into place, with its tab(s) meeting the grooves in the expansion slot. The endplate of the card should be in the same place that the slot cover just occupied. When the tab meets the groove, press carefully on the top edge of the card. The tab will snap into place.

The PC bus

The original PC uses a clock of 4.77 MHz with the Intel 8088 microprocessor. The expansion board connections are essentially the same as those found on the microprocessor pins. In addition to the 8-bit bidirectional data bus and the 20 address lines,

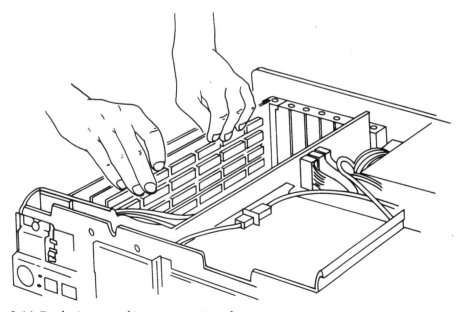

2-14 Replacing a card in an expansion slot.

there are six interrupt lines, three sets of direct-memory access-control lines, and a number of data control and status lines. The total of 62 pins that make up the IBM PC bus is divided into two rows (A1 through A31 and B1 through B31) in the edge connectors. The IBM PC is a single-board computer. The board is commonly called the *motherboard,* or *system board.* The processor, some of the I/O circuits, and memory reside on this board along with the five edge connectors for expansion boards. Data is transferred on the PC bus over the data line pins A2 through A9. Addresses for bus transfers are specified on the 20 address pins A12 through A31. The PC and XT use the 8-bit version of the Intel 8086 16-bit processor. The 8-bit version simplifies the bus by reducing the number of lines required and avoids the problem of byte transfers in 16-bit systems.

The PC uses the 8088 processor in the so-called *maximum mode,* which requires an Intel 8288 bus controller. The 8288 control signals are brought out to the bus, so the two signals ALE (address latch enable) and AEN (address enable) are on the bus. Pins B28 and A11, ALE indicates that a valid address is on the bus address lines and AEN signals if the processor or the DMA controller is driving the bus during a DMA transaction. Other 8288 signals that can also be found on the bus include the following:

I/O read (IOR)	B14	I/O write	(IOW)	B13
MEMory Read (MEMR)	B12	MEMory Write	(MENW)	B11

A bus handshake line, I/O CH RDY (A10), can increase the current bus cycle. This line can only be asserted for a few microseconds so that the dynamic memory is always refreshed. RAM refresh in the PC is handled by one channel of the system DMA controller, which requires the bus.

The six interrupt pins B21 through B25 and B4 are connected to an interrupt controller on the main board that automatically generates vectors for interrupt servicing. There is no interrupt acknowledge signal on the PC bus.

The three pairs of DMA handshake lines include the DRQ1–3 lines (B-18, B-6, and B-16 pins) that handle DMA requests and $\overline{\text{DACK1-3}}$ (B-17, B-26, and B-15 pins) that are the acknowledge lines. $\overline{\text{DACK0}}$ (pin B-19) is used to refresh dynamic RAM boards that can be plugged into the bus. T/C (B-27) is used to indicate when the correct number of DMA bus cycles has occurred during a DMA transfer. OSC (B-30) is used for a 14.31818-MHz clock, and CLK(B-20) is the 4.77-MHz clock that runs the processor. RESET DRV (B-2) is a reset signal for all cards on the bus. Power supplies available to the bus cards include +5 V (B-3), –5 V (B-5), +12 V (B-9), and –12 V (B-7). There are three ground pins (B-1, B-10, and B-31).

Bus cycles take four clock cycles, or 840 ns, and DNA cycles take five clock cycles, or 1.05 ms (microseconds). The cycles are controlled by an 8288 bus controller running at 4.77 MHz.

The bus card has a metal plate attached to one end. This plate is used as both a card guide for the back of the card and a support for I/O connectors that might be attached to the card.

Although it never evolved into an actual industry standard, the IBM PC bus became a popular microprocessor backplane bus. Thousands of boards from hundreds of companies can plug into the PC bus.

The PC/AT bus

The AT is a full 16-bit computer based on the INTEL 80286 microprocessor (Fig. 2-15). The 80286 uses a 16-bit data bus, and the AT expansion bus has a wider data path, more interrupt lines, and more DMA signals. Similar to the PC bus, the AT bus signals resemble the microprocessor signals on which the computer is based. To maintain compatibility with expansion boards designed for the PC, the original 62-pin connector and pin definitions remained the same. A second connector with 36 pins was added to carry the additional signals. Because the second connector is in front of the 62-pin connector, some older boards designed for the IBM PC will physically interfere with the AT expansion connector.

Because there was never an actual standard board size and shape for the PC expansion boards, some manufacturers made use of the available space by dropping the bottom edge of the board just in front of the PC edge connector.

Most of the signals on the AT 62-pin connector retain the same names they had on the PC bus. A few signals have new names, but similar functions. For example, $\overline{\text{DACK}}$ 4K0 on the PC was renamed $\overline{\text{REFRESH}}$ for the AT bus. B-8 on the PC bus was not used; it became 0WS (zero wait state) which allows an expansion board to signal that it does

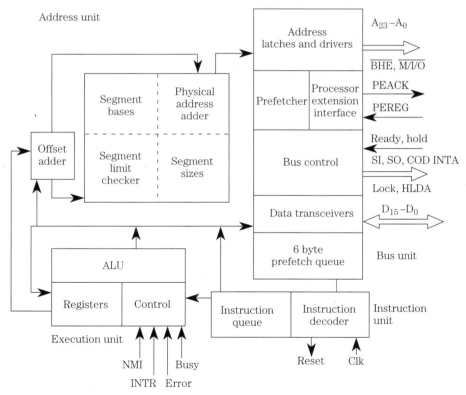

2-15 Block diagram of Intel 80286 microprocessor.

not require the main to insert wait states in the bus cycle. The $\overline{\text{MEMCS16}}$ (D-1) and $\overline{\text{IOCS16}}$ (D-2) signals allow an expansion board to indicate that it can accept a 16-bit, 1-wait-state transfer. These signals are added signals on the 36-pin connector.

Some of the address lines (C-2 through C-8) on the 36-pin connector partially replicate the addresses on the 62-pin connector. Unlike the PC original address lines, the AT 36-pin address lines are not latched on the computer motherboard. Expansion boards that use these lines must latch the address values on the falling edge of the ALE signal.

Since the introduction of the original AT, the clock speeds of compatible computers have increased as Intel and other microprocessor vendors have improved their manufacturing processes. The manufacturers of compatible computers have adopted the AT bus for their 80286-based machines. Chip manufacturers such as Chips and Technologies and Western Digital developed ICs that reduce the motherboard size. In addition to machines based on the 80286 microprocessor, several 80386-based machines also use the AT bus, adding extensions for 32-bit memory boards. However, vendors of 80386-based computers started using different techniques for extending the AT bus to 32 bits so memory boards for these computers are not compatible.

Some vendors offered extensions to the AT bus. AST Research offered an AT bus extension called Smartslot that adds an additional eight pins to the bus. These pins allow multiple processors on several expansion cards to share the bus using an arbitration scheme. A central arbiter for all Smartslot cards grants the bus to one of the requesting cards.

The IEEE (International Association of Electrical and Electronics Engineers) created the P996 Bus Committee to study the feasibility of standardizing the AT bus, but before the committee could produce a standard, IBM introduced its PS/2 line of personal computers that use a completely different and incompatible bus.

PS/2 Micro Channel bus

In 1987, IBM brought out the PS/2 computer line and the Micro Channel bus. IBM patented several aspects of the PS/2 bus so manufacturers need a license to use the Micro Channel. Similarities and differences exist between the older PC and newer PS/2 buses. The Micro Channel uses more power and ground pins than the earlier PC and AT buses. These additional power and ground pins allow expansion cards to draw more power from the computer because the extra pins provide a path with lower impedance to the computer power supply. The ground and power pins also provide a lower impedance path to ac ground for radio frequency interference (RFI). This path tends to reduce interference and improve the data integrity by reducing noise.

The Micro Channel supports three types of cards: 16-bit, 16-bit with a video extension, and 32-bit. The 16-bit version uses 116 pins and the extension adds another 20 pins. The Micro Channel bus is designed to support multiple bus masters. The processor or DMA controller on the PS/2 motherboard usually controls the bus, but the Micro Channel has a set of signals to allow expansion cards to take over as bus masters. The Micro Channel allows up to 15 masters to share the bus with the main board. The 32-bit address bus width supports 4Gb of memory or memory-mapped I/O addressing. The 24-bit subset of the bus permits the addressing of up to 16MB of memory or memory-mapped I/O.

The data bus can also be used as a 24-bit data bus, 16-bit data bus, or an 8-bit data bus. Data can be transferred to system memory or system memory–mapped I/O devices using the matched-memory signals and the matched-memory procedure.

Audio subsystem

The Micro Channel architecture has an audio subsystem feature. An analog audio signal and analog ground signal are used. The bandwidth of the audio signal is 50 Hz to 10 kHz. The subsystem provides high-quality audio capability between devices and output over the system speaker. This subsystem eliminates the need for duplicate audio circuitry on devices added to a system. The Micro Channel bus uses the AUDIO (B-2) and AUDIO GND (B-1) signals. This arrangement allows expansion cards to use the PS/2 audio amplifier and speaker.

In a similar fashion, the video expansion connector allows an expansion card to override the video circuits on the PS/2 motherboard. Refer to Table 2-1 for pin assignments for the 16-bit card. For pin assignments for the video extension to the 16-bit card, see Table 2-2; for pin assignments for the 32-bit card see Table 2-3. A bar over the signal means a signal is low-true.

The data bus is made up of signals D0 through D15 on the 16-bit Micro Channel version and D0 through D31 is used in the 32-channel version. A0 through A23 make up the address bus for the 16-bit Micro Channel bus. The 32-bit bus includes A24 through A31.

Some of the signals on the Micro Channel bus are the same or similar as used in the original PC bus. These signals include the following:

$\overline{\text{REFRESH}}$	Memory refresh
OSC	Oscillator
$\overline{\text{SBHE}}$	Byte high enable
CD CHRDY	Channel ready
CD DS 16	Card data size 16 bits (combination of the PC/AT MEM CS16 and IO CS16 identification signals)
CHRESET	Channel reset
TC	Indicates the last bus cycle of a DMA transfer

The Micro Channel does not use the PC/AT memory and I/O read and write control lines. There are three negative true lines: M/IO, S0, and S1 that work like those in the 82288 bus controller. The state of these lines is used to indicate the type of bus transfers as follows:

M/IO	S0	S1	
0	0	1	I/O read
0	1	0	I/O write
1	0	1	Memory read
1	1	0	Memory write

Table 2-1. 16-bit Micro Channel signals

Pin	Signal	Pin	Signal	Pin	Signal	Pin	Signal
B1	AUDIO GND	A1	CD SETUP	B30	RESERVED	A30	TC
B2	AUDIO	A2	MADE 24	B31	RESERVED	A31	+6V
B3	GND	A3	GND	B32	$\overline{\text{CHCK}}$	A32	$\overline{\text{S0}}$
B4	OSC	A4	A11	B33	GND	A33	S1
B5	GND	A5	A10	B34	CMD	A34	$\overline{\text{M/IO}}$
B6	A23	A6	A9	B35	CHRDYRTN	A35	+12V
B7	A22	A7	+5V	B36	CD SFDBK	A36	CD CHRDY
B8	A21	A8	A8	B37	GND	A37	D0
B9	GND	A9	A7	B38	D1	A38	D2
B10	A20	A10	A6	B39	D3	A39	+5V
B11	A19	A11	+5V	B40	D4	A40	D5
B12	A18	A12	A5	B41	GND	A41	D6
B13	GND	A13	A4	B42	CHRESET	A42	D7
B14	A17	A14	A3	B43	RESERVED	A43	GND
B15	A16	A15	+5V	B44	RESERVED	A44	D0 16 RTN
B16	A15	A16	A2	B45	GND	A45	REFRESH
B17	GND	A17	A1				
B18	A14	A18	A0	B48	D8	A48	+5V
B19	A13	A19	+12V	B49	D9	A49	D10
B20	A12	A20	$\overline{\text{ADL}}$	B50	GND	A50	D11
B21	GND	A21	PREEMPT	B51	D12	A51	D13
B22	$\overline{\text{IRQ2}}$	A22	BURST	B52	D14	A52	+12V
B23	$\overline{\text{IRQ3}}$	A23	+12V	B53	D15	A53	RESERVED
B24	IRQ4	A24	ARB0	B54	GND	A54	$\overline{\text{SBHE}}$
B25	GND	A25	ARB1	B55	$\overline{\text{IRQ10}}$	A55	CD DB 18
B26	$\overline{\text{IRQ5}}$	A26	ARB2	B56	IRQ11	A56	+5V
B27	IRQ6	A27	+12V	B57	IRQ12	A57	IRQ14
B28	IRQ7	A28	ARB3	B58	GND	A58	IRQ15
B29	GND	A29	ARB/–GNT				

- - - - - - - - - POSITIONING KEY - - - - - - - - - (between pin rows 45 and 48)

Micro Channel setup

The Micro Channel bus does not use addressing and option-configuration switches on the expansion cards. This feature is called the POS (programmable option select). When power is turned on, the system board addresses each expansion card with an individual CD SETUP line. This line is not common across the PS/2 backplane. Each expansion slot has its own negative logic CD SETUP line. When a card is signaled by its CD SETUP line, it issues a code. The processor reads this code from the expansion card. The codes define the following conditions:

- Device not ready
- Bus master
- DMA device

Table 2-2. Video extension signals

Pin	Signal	Pin	Signal
BV10	ESYNC	AV10	VSYNC
BV9	GND	AV9	HSYNC
BV8	P5	AV8	BLANK
BV7	P4	AV7	GND
BV6	P3	AV6	P6
BV5	GND	AV5	EDCLK
BV4	P2	AV4	DCLK
BV3	P1	AV3	GND
BV2	P0	AV2	P7
BV1	GND	AV1	EVIDEO

- - - - - - - - - - POSITIONING KEY - - - - - - - - - - -
16-bit Micro Channel slot

- Direct program control and memory-mapped I/O memory storage
- Video adapter
- No device present

The processor matches the code with the configuration data stored in the computer nonvolatile memory and loads that data into the expansion card. Configuration data can include the card bus-master arbitration level, the range of any on-board I/O ROM, and the I/O address range for the card. Because each type of card from different manufacturers must have a unique POS code, this scheme allows IBM to control the types of cards available for PS/2 computers.

A Micro Channel card is 11.5 inches long and 3.475 inches high, including the edge connector. These cards use a smaller edge connector. The PC and AT cards use edge connectors with pads spaced 0.100 inch apart. The Micro Channel cards use pads that are spaced 0.050 inch apart. Positioning keys align the cards. These keys fit into notches in the edge connectors.

A full-length Micro Channel card is about one-third smaller than a full-length PC/AT card. The smaller cards use denser ICs that require less space.

The MADE 24 and TR32 signals change the use of the address lines. MADE 24 indicates when the address bus carries a 24-bit address. TR32 indicates a 32-bit-wide memory data transfer.

An expansion card can use the CHCK (channel check) to indicate an error. This check includes parity errors and time-outs. Switching CHCK low causes an interrupt. Eleven conventional interrupts are numbered IRQ3-7, IRQ9-12, IRQ-14, and IRQ-15.

ISA and EISA systems

The ISA bus refers to the bus used in ISA-compatible computers. The bus is the same as the IBM AT 16-bit bus. In an EISA system, which is the extended version of ISA with a 32-bit bus, it refers to the ISA subset of the EISA bus. The EISA bus is a superset

Table 2-3. 32-bit Micro Channel signals

Pin	Signal	Pin	Signal	Pin	Signal	Pin	Signal
BM4	GND	AM4	RESERVED	B43	RESERVED	A43	GND
BM3	RESERVED	AM3	$\overline{MMC}$ $\overline{CMD}$	B44	RESERVED	A44	$\overline{DS\ 16\ RTN}$
BM2	MMCR	AM2	GND	B45	GND	A4 5	REFRESH
BM1	RESERVED	AM1	MMC	-------- POSITIONING KEY --------			
B1	AUDIO GND	A1	$\overline{CD\ SETUP}$	D48	D8	A48	+5V
B2	AUDIO	A2	MADE 24	B49	D9	A49	D10
B3	GND	A3	GND	B50	GND	A50	D11
B4	OSC	A4	A11	B51	D12	A51	D13
B5	GND	A5	A10	B52	D14	A52	+12V
B6	A23	A6	A9	B53	D15	A53	RESERVED
B7	A22	A7	+5V	B54	GND	A54	$\overline{SBHE}$
B8	A21	A8	A8	B55	$\overline{IRQ10}$	A55	CD DB 18
B9	GND	A9	A7	B56	$\overline{IRQ11}$	A56	+5V
B10	A20	A10	A6	B57	$\overline{IRQ12}$	A57	$\overline{IRQ14}$
B11	A19	A11	+5V	B58	GND	A58	$\overline{IRQ15}$
B12	A18	A12	A5	B59	RESERVED	A59	RESERVED
B13	GND	A13	A4	B60	RESERVED	A60	RESERVED
B14	A17	A14	A3	B61	RESERVED	A61	GND
B15	A16	A15	+5V	B62	RESERVED	A62	RESERVED
B16	A15	A16	A2	B63	GND	A63	RESERVED
B17	GND	A17	A1	B64	D16	A64	RESERVED
B18	A14	A18	A0	B65	D17	A65	+12V
B19	A13	A19	+12V	B66	D18	A66	D19
B20	A12	A20	$\overline{ADL}$	B67	GND	A67	D20
B21	GND	A21	PREEMPT	B68	D22	A68	D21
B22	$\overline{IRQ2}$	A22	BURST	B69	D23	A69	+5V
B23	$\overline{IRQ3}$	A23	+12V	B70	RESERVED	A70	D24
B24	$\overline{IRQ4}$	A24	ARB0	B71	GND	A71	D25
B25	GND	A25	ARB1	B72	D27	A72	D26
B26	$\overline{IRQ5}$	A26	ARB2	B73	D28	A73	+5V
B27	$\overline{IRQ68}$	A27	+12V	B74	D29	A74	D30
B28	$\overline{IRQ7}$	A28	ARB3	B75	GND	A75	D31
B29	GND	A29	ARB/GNT	B76	$\overline{BE0}$	A76	RESERVED
B30	RESERVED	A30	TC	B77	BE1	A77	+12V
B31	RESERVED	A31	+5V	B78	BE2	A78	$\overline{BE3}$
B32	$\overline{CHCK}$	A32	S0	B79	GND	A79	DS 32 RTN
B33	GND	A33	S1	B80	TR 32	A80	CD DS 32
B34	$\overline{CMD}$	A34	M/IO	B81	A24	A81	+12V
B35	CHRDYRTN	A35	+12V	B82	A25	A82	A26
B36	$\overline{CD}$ $\overline{SFDBK}$	A36	CD CHRDY	B83	GND	A83	A27
B37	GND	A37	D0	B84	A29	A84	A28
B38	D1	A38	D2	B85	A30	A85	+5V
B39	D3	A39	+5V	B86	A31	A86	RESERVED
B40	D4	A40	D5	B87	GND	A87	RESERVED
B41	GND	A41	D6	B88	RESERVED	A88	RESERVED
B42	CHRESET	A42	D7	B89	RESERVED	A89	GND

of the ISA bus. It has all of the ISA bus features, along with some extensions to enhance performance and capabilities.

The Extended Industry Standard Architecture (EISA) is a 32-bit architecture based upon the Industry Standard Architecture (ISA) for the PC-AT. EISA capabilities and 32-bit architecture are needed to get the maximum performance out of the 386 and 486 CPUs.

The EISA consortium defined the *EISA bus* as a 32-bit high-performance ISA-compatible system. This open industry standard allows industry-wide compatibility.

EISA provides 32-bit memory addressing and data transfers for CPU, DMA, and bus masters. It allows a 33MB/s (megabytes per second) transfer rate for DMA and bus masters on the EISA bus. EISA provides automatic configuration of add-in cards that eliminates the need for jumpers and switches.

Interrupts can be shared and are programmable. Figure 2-16 shows a card used in an EISA system. The bus-arbitration scheme allows intelligent bus-master add-in cards.

Because the EISA system is compatible with the ISA 8-bit and 16-bit expansion boards and software, ISA cards plug in to the EISA connector slots. The EISA slots are defined as ISA or EISA for compatibility during configuration. The EISA connector set is a superset of the ISA connector set, so there is full compatibility with ISA expansion cards and software. The simultaneous use of EISA and ISA add-in boards is allowed with the automatic system and expansion board configuration scheme.

80386 systems

The Intel 386 DX microprocessor is a true 32-bit microprocessor, and the 386 SX is a 32-bit processor with a 16-bit input-output bus. Multitasking support, memory management, pipelining, address translation caches, and a high-speed bus interface are on one chip. The integration of these features on one chip improves performance and reduces the overall cost of the system. Both paging and dynamic data bus sizing are used. Although the 386 microprocessor is a significant improvement over earlier generations of microprocessors, there is still compatibility with existing 8088 and 80286 software. Hardware compatibility is also preserved through a dynamic bus-sizing feature.

2-16 32-bit EISA video graphics card.

386 characteristics

A 33-MHz 386 DX microprocessor can execute over 16 million instructions per second. This speed is equivalent to 8 million VAX instructions per second, so it operates at speeds comparable to that of a super minicomputer. Speed of this magnitude is possible because of the pipelined internal architecture, address translation caches, and high-performance bus.

The 386 microprocessor has a 32-bit wide internal and external data paths and eight general-purpose, 32-bit registers. The instruction set allows 8-, 16-, and 32-bit data types, and the processor outputs 32-bit addresses for a memory capacity of 4 gigabytes. Separate 32-bit data and address paths are used and a 32-bit memory access takes two clock cycles, providing the bus with a throughput of 40 megabytes per second at 20 MHz.

The pipelined architecture allows the 386 to perform instruction fetching, decoding, execution, and memory management functions in parallel. The 386 prefetches instructions and queues them internally so the pipeline absorbs instruction fetch and decode times, and the processor does not have to wait for an instruction to execute.

Pipelining was used in other microprocessors but including the MMU (memory management unit) in the on-chip pipeline was a unique feature of the 386. By performing the memory management on-chip, the 386 eliminated the access delays that occur with off-chip memory management.

Cache functions

A 386 microprocessor running at 33 MHz can complete a bus cycle in only 60 ns. This speed provides a bandwidth of 66 megabytes per second. At these higher speeds, you must match the 386 microprocessor with a high-speed memory system. It must be fast enough to complete bus cycles without wait states.

Most memory systems use dynamic RAMs (DRAMs), which give you a large amount of memory in a small space. DRAMs that can complete random read-write cycles in 60 ns are not typically available. Faster static RAMs (SRAMs) can meet the bus timing requirement, but they are smaller chips that are available at a higher cost.

A *cache memory system* uses a small amount of fast memory (SRAM) with a large amount of slower memory (DRAM). The system acts like a large amount of fast memory. The cache memory approaches the performance of SRAMs at the cost of DRAMs. The cache places the fast SRAMs between the processor and the slower main memory with the DRAMs. A cache controller contains the logic to implement the cache. In a cache memory system, all the data is stored in the main memory, and some data is duplicated in the cache. When the processor accesses the memory, it checks the cache first. If the desired data is in the cache, the processor can access it quickly, because the cache is a fast memory. If the data is not in the cache, it must be fetched from the main memory.

A cache reduces average memory access time if organized so that code and data that the processor needs most often is in the cache. Programs execute faster when most operations are transfers to and from the faster cache memory.

If the requested data is found in the cache, the memory access is called a *cache hit;* if not, it is called a *cache miss.* The *hit rate* is the percentage of accesses that are hits. It depends on the size and organization of the cache, the cache algorithm, and the program being run. Programs usually access memory in the area of locations accessed most recently. This process is known as *program locality,* or *locality of reference.*

Cache controller

A cache memory subsystem provides faster storage for frequently accessed instructions and data. The faster storage results in faster memory access for the microprocessor and reduces the traffic on the system bus. The 82385 cache controller supports a 32K cache memory and has an integrated cache directory with management logic.

The cache controller partitions the main memory into blocks. Typical block sizes are 2, 4, 8, or 16 bytes. A 32-bit processor usually uses two or four words per block. When a desired word is not in the cache, the cache controller moves the block that contains the needed word.

A 386 running at 33 MHz can perform a bus cycle in 60 ns, for a bandwidth of 66MB/s. The memory system must be fast enough to complete bus cycles with no wait states. Dynamic RAMs (DRAMs) can provide a large amount of memory in a small space. These low-cost DRAMs cannot usually complete random read-write cycles in 60 ns. The faster static RAMs (SRAMs) can meet these bus timing requirements, but they are available in smaller packages at a higher cost.

A cache memory system uses a small amount of fast memory (SRAM) with a larger amount of slower memory (DRAM). The system acts like a large amount of fast memory because the cache memory approaches the performance of SRAMs at a lower cost. A cache memory (Fig. 2-17) has the faster SRAMs between the processor and the slower main memory made up of DRAMs. A cache controller is needed with the logic circuits to operate the cache.

Coprocessor

The performance of the system is improved by the use of specialized coprocessors. A *coprocessor* provides the hardware to perform functions that would otherwise be performed in software. The coprocessor extends the instruction set of the 386 microprocessor. The 386 DX microprocessor has a numeric coprocessor interface designed for the 387 math coprocessor. In applications that need high-precision integer and floating-point calculations, the numeric coprocessor provides support for these operations. The 387 DX coprocessor is software-compatible with the 80287 and 8087 earlier numeric coprocessors.

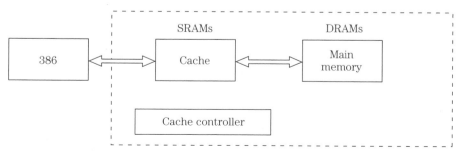

2-17 386 cache memory system.

Peripheral chips

A DMA (direct memory access) controller performs DMA transfers between main memory and an I/O device. The device is typically a hard or floppy disk or a communications channel. In a DMA transfer, a large block of data can be copied from one location to another without the intervention of the CPU.

The 82380 peripheral chip has a 32-bit DMA controller. This chip provides a high data throughput with more efficient bus operation. The 32-bit DMA controller provides eight independent channels that can transfer data at the full bandwidth of the 386 microprocessor bus. A 40MB/s data transfer rate is possible at 20 MHz. It also has a 20-source interrupt controller that will handle 15 external and 5 internal interrupt requests. The built-in DRAM refresh controller is where the refresh request always has the highest priority among the DMA requests.

EISA chips

EISA (extended industry-standard architecture) expands the 32-bit capability of the 386 microprocessor to the I/O expansion bus. The 82350 chip set consists of three components: 82358 EISA bus controller, 82357 integrated system peripheral, and 82352 EISA bus buffer (Fig. 2-18).

A 82355 BMIC (bus master interface controller) is used for add-in board support. The BMIC provides all of the necessary control signals, address lines, and data lines for an EISA bus master to interface to the EISA bus. The EISA specification and the 82350 chip set are both compatible with the ISA (Industry Standard Architecture) AT bus. So, software and expansion boards designed for the ISA bus can also be used in the higher-performance EISA systems. The 82350 can also be used with the 486 DX and 386 SX microprocessors.

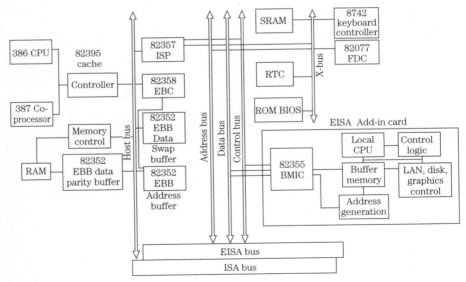

2-18 386 system with 82350 EISA chip set.

MCA chips

The 82311 chip set consists of peripheral components for IBM PS/2–compatible system boards. This chip set supports the Micro Channel architecture and includes the following 82303 and 82304 local I/O support chips: 82307 DMA/CACP controller, 82308 Micro Channel bus controller, 82309 address bus controller, 82706 VGA graphics controller, and 82077 floppy disk controller. The 82311 chip set has all the peripheral functions needed to interface to the CPU, Micro Channel bus, I/O peripheral bus, and the graphics channel. Table 2-4 lists the 386 system components, and Fig. 2-19 shows how they fit into the 386 computer system.

Clock generation

A clock-generator circuit generates timing for the 386 microprocessor and its supporting components. The circuit provides the 386 microprocessor clock (CLK2) and a half-frequency clock (CLK) to indicate the internal phase of the microprocessor. The half-frequency clock operates 80286 devices that might be in the system. It can also generate the RESET signal for the 386 microprocessors.

With the appropriate interface, the 386 microprocessor can use 8086/80286 family components. The 8259A programmable interrupt controller manages interrupts for the 386 microprocessor system. Interrupts from up to eight external sources are handled by one 8259A. The 8259A resolves priority between active interrupts. It then interrupts the processor and passes a code to the processor to identify the interrupting source.

486 microprocessor

The 486 processor is upward binary compatible with the 8086, 8088, 80186, 80286, 386 DX processor, and 386 SX processors. It includes an integer-processing unit, floating-point processing unit, memory-management unit, and cache. With these units on a single chip, more signals remain on-chip, running at higher speeds than those using

Table 2-4. System components

Component	Function
386 DX microprocessor	32-bit microprocessor with on-chip memory management and protection
387 math coprocessor	Performs numeric operations in parallel with 386 microprocessor, expands the instruction set
82380 peripheral chip	Provides 32-bit direct memory access (DMA), interrupt control, and interval timers
82385 cache controller	Provides cache directory and management logic
8259A programmable	Provides interrupt control and management interrupt controller
82350 EISA chip set	Extends the 32-bit transfer capability of the 386 DX microprocessor to the I/O expansion bus
82311 MCA chip set	Provides a Micro Channel–compatible PS/2 system

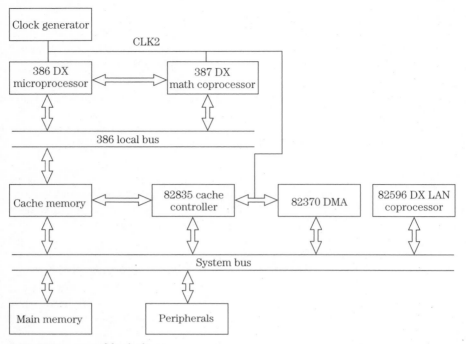

2-19 386 system block diagram.

printed circuit board tracks. The increased level of integration also reduces board space, which lowers the cost.

The 486 can provide two to four times the performance of the 386, depending on the clock speeds used and the application. Similar to the 386, the 486 uses both segment-based and page-based memory protection. Instruction pipelining reduces processing time. The 486 bus is faster than the 386 local bus. Both buses are 32 bits wide, but the 486 bus uses a single-frequency (1×) clock and supports parity checking, burst cycles, cacheable cycles, cache invalidation cycles, and 8-bit data buses.

Burst cycles for read transfers are possible at the rate of one 32-bit (double-word) transfer per clock cycle. In the 386, a data transfer requires at least two clock cycles. The external cache, interleaved memory banks, or DRAMs with static-column addressing help to give 0-wait-state memory performance during a burst.

Instructions also can execute in fewer clock cycles than with the 386. In the 486, streamlined instruction pipelining provides an execution rate of one clock cycle per instruction for most instructions. The internal cache provides a rate of one processor request per clock cycle. There is also a built-in self test.

The 32-bit integrated math processor performs arithmetic and logical operations on 8-, 16-, and 32-bit data types using a full-width ALU (arithmetic logic unit) and eight general-purpose registers. Separate 32-bit address and data paths allow 4Gb of memory to be addressed. An internal write-through cache can hold 8K of data or instructions.

On-chip cache

The 8K cache stores recently accessed information on the processor chip, including instructions and data. When the processor needs to read data that is available in the cache, it uses the cache and avoids the time needed for an external memory cycle. The shorter access time speeds up transfers and reduces traffic on the bus.

Floating-point unit

The internal floating-point unit performs floating-point operations on the 32-, 64-, and 80-bit arithmetic formats. Floating-point instructions execute fastest when they are internal to the processor. The instructions are internal when all operands are in the internal registers or cache. Bus signals monitor errors in floating-point operations and control the processor response to these errors.

System components

The 82320 32-bit MCA system peripherals provide interfacing to Micro Channel expansion buses for PS/2 systems, and the 82350 32-bit EISA system peripherals provide interfacing to EISA expansion buses.

Turbocache module

The turbocache module is a second-level cache for the 486 microprocessor. The module consists of the 82485 cache controller and four to eight SRAMs. The Turbocache Module provides 64 or 128K of external cache memory. Up to four modules can be used for up to 512K of external cache memory. The module typically provides a 5 to 30 percent performance improvement.

486 SX

The first 486 chips were the DX variety, with the built-in math coprocessor. Then, Intel brought out the 486 SX that did not contain the math coprocessor. For those who wanted the math capabilities, the 80487/SX math coprocessor was offered. The 80487SX is actually a complete CPU, with a math unit, which disables the 486SX CPU.

486 DX2 and DX4

Intel's DX2 is a speed-doubler, or clock-doubler, processor. The DX2 CPUs are essentially 25-MHz 486 units, but they execute internal instructions at 50 MHz (Fig. 2-20).

The DX4 is an energy-saving processor that works with 486 boards running at 25, 33, and 50 MHz. It can operate as a clock doubler (50/100 MHz), a clock tripler (25/75 MHz), or at 2½ times the clock speed (33/83). The DX4 has twice the cache of other 486 chips with 16K of on-board cache memory. It also runs on 3.3 volts which reduces the power required to operate the chip as well as the cooling required.

There is also a built-in energy management system which powers the chip down during idle periods. This is Intel's SL-enhanced technology which is used in all Intel processors after the DX4 and allows these chips to meet the Environmental Protection Agency's (EPA) Energy Star guidelines.

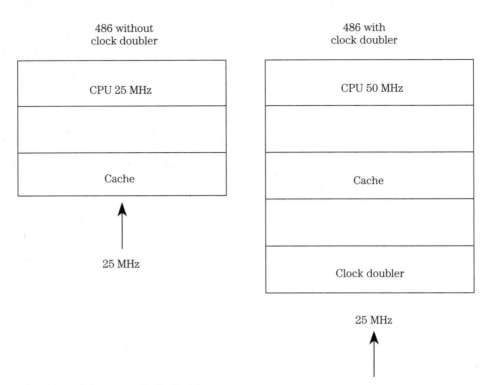

2-20 Use of the DX2 clock doubler.

A close relative to the DX chips is Intel's OverDrive CPU. The main difference between these two chips is that the DX CPUs are factory-installed, clock-doubled CPUs, while the OverDrive chips are add-on clock-doubling units.

OverDrive

If you have a 16-, 20-, or 25-MHz 486 SX PC, it probably has an empty OverDrive socket. This socket was once called a *processor upgrade socket,* changed to a *processor performance enhancement socket,* and then was given the name *OverDrive.* The earliest 486 SX systems had an empty 80487SX math coprocessor socket, and a few low systems had only the main CPU socket. In all cases, you can still plug in an OverDrive chip.

The OverDrive chip does not exactly double the speed; when the OverDrive chip plugs in, it disables the original CPU and adds its own floating-point capability. It doubles the on-chip logic processing to 50 MHz, and it takes over as the central processor. The local system bus remains running at the original speed.

Although the OverDrive internal cache and other components run double speed, the external communications, such as memory transfer, do not. The slower speed is caused by the slower system bus, but some of the speed reduction is a function of memory. For maximum performance gain with an OverDrive processor, the SX motherboard should have a secondary external SRAM cache of at least 128K. Because the SRAM runs at around 20 ns instead of the DRAM 70 ns, it will slow the 50-MHz CPU down much less than the main memory. Also, some boards use a memory controller that is capable of burst mode. This mode is a high-speed transfer rate not used by most older 25-MHz 486 SXs, and use of the burst will improve performance.

The OverDrive chip, such as the manufacturer-installed DX2 chip, contains both the main CPU and the math unit. There are a number of different OverDrive processors, and they fit a variety of sockets including the newer ZIF (zero-insertion force) sockets, which make it easy to drop in the chip (Fig. 2-21).

OverDrive chips exist for the sockets of 16-, 20-, and 25-MHz 486 SX systems, making them 33-, 40-, and 50-MHz systems. There are also OverDrive chips for systems with no OverDrive or 80487SX sockets. You pull the 486 SX CPU out and put in the OverDrive version. OverDrive chips are also available for 33-MHz 486 DX machines that turn them into 66-MHz DX2 systems.

Another 66-MHz DX2 chip has a 240-in socket for a Pentium OverDrive chip (Fig. 2-22). Although a Pentium version of the OverDrive CPU can significantly increase your PC performance, it cannot match the speed of a true Pentium because a 486 runs on a 32-bit bus, and a Pentium is a 64-bit processor.

486 DX2 operation

The DX2 is like other 486 DX chips, except that it runs twice as fast internally. The bus interface of the CPU chip produces a 2-to-1 reduction action. When the DX2 CPU accesses its internal registers, it refers to a memory location already mapped into its internal cache or performs a floating-point operation, the CPU works at the faster rate.

When the CPU has to access main memory, perform I/O instructions to an adapter card, or access one of the other chips on the motherboard, the DX2 signals that move over the bus occur at half speed (25 MHz for a 50-MHz DX2). The DX2 waits for the currently executing instruction to do its off-chip work before continuing with the next instruction.

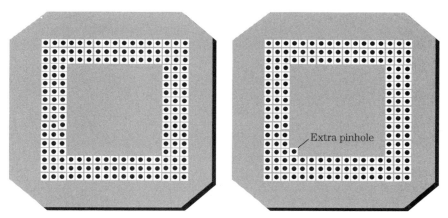

2-21 A standard 486/486 SX socket is shown on the left. The socket shown on the right has an extra pin hold for a 487 SX OverDrive processor. These sockets are ZIF (zero-insertion force) sockets.

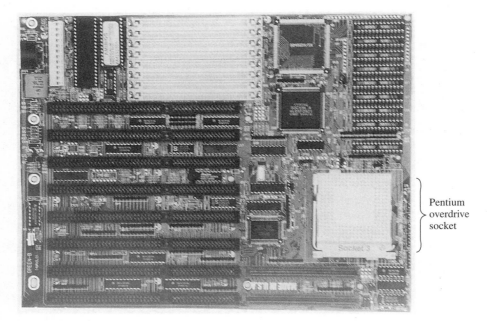

Pentium overdrive socket

2-22 This 486 board has an OverDrive socket for a Pentium processor.

Figure 2-23 shows the DX2 components. The keyboard controller, 8259 programmable interrupt controller, external cache, DMA controller, RAM chips, and the adapter cards operate at the slower rate. The RAM chips, video adapter memory, and unshadowed ROM BIOS memory might insert additional wait states. The high level of integration of a 486 allows clock doubling. The 50-MHz DX2 consumes about 40 percent more power than a 33-MHz 486 DX. Because the 386 uses an external math coprocessor and an external cache, the CPU must go off-chip for most operations. A clock-doubled 386 would only show performance gains for some instructions, such as register-to-register operations.

EISA chip set

The 8235 set of peripherals interfaces the 486 processor to an Extended Industry Standard Architecture (EISA) bus. The chips include three system board peripherals (bus controller, integrated system peripheral, and bus buffers) and one peripheral for EISA-bus expansion boards (bus master interface chip). The EISA standard maintains full compatibility with the existing ISA (IBM-AT) standard. The EISA expansion board connector is a superset of the ISA expansion board connector, allowing installation of existing 8- and 16-bit ISA boards in EISA slots.

486 personal computer structure

In a personal computer system, the processor interacts directly with I/O devices and DRAM memory. Some peripherals are on separate plug-in boards, and others are part of the system board. An industry standard I/O architecture such as MCA or EISA is used. Figure 2-24 shows a typical 486 personal computer configuration.

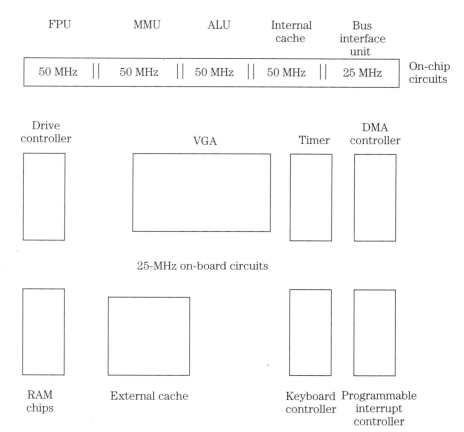

FPU	MMU	ALU	Internal cache	Bus interface unit	
50 MHz	50 MHz	50 MHz	50 MHz	25 MHz	On-chip circuits

Drive controller   VGA   Timer   DMA controller

25-MHz on-board circuits

RAM chips   External cache   Keyboard controller   Programmable interrupt controller

2-23 The bus interface unit of the DX2 processor is the only unit to use the CLK signal from the system board timer. The other units of the CPU use 2 × CLK.

486 bus system

All microprocessor systems include a microprocessor, memory, and I/O devices that are linked by the address, data, and control buses. Figure 2-25 shows the configuration of a typical 486 microprocessor-based system.

The 82596 LAN (local area network) coprocessor is used to provide an interface to a variety of networks. The 82596 is a 32-bit LAN coprocessor that implements the CSMA/CD (carrier sense multiple access with collision detection) link-access protocol. It relieves the processor of all local-network control functions and supports IEEE 802.3 such as Ethernet, Ethernet twisted pair, Cheapernet, StarLAN, and IBM PC networks (baseband and broadband). The 82596 has on-chip DMA and memory management along with network management and diagnostics.

The 82350 EISA chip set provides an interface between the 486 microprocessor and the EISA bus. The chip set includes a bus controller, integrated system peripheral, and a bus buffer. The basic I/O control logic, wait-state generation logic, and the address decode logic needed for EISA implementation is part of the 82350 chip set.

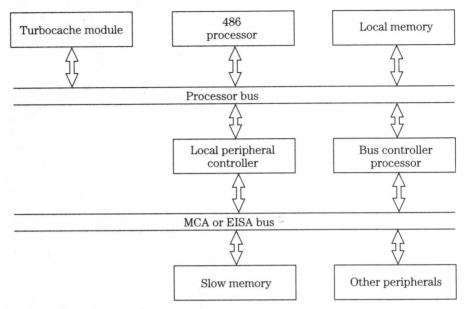

2-24 Typical 486 personal computer configuration.

In most systems, the same control and data logic can access memory as well as I/O devices. The bus interface consists of bus control, data transceiver, byte swap logic, and address decoder. A typical peripheral device has address inputs that the processor uses to select the device internal registers. It also has a chip select (CS#) signal that enables it to read data from and write data to the data bus as controlled by the READ (RD) and WRITE (WR) control signals. If the microprocessor has separate memory and I/O addressing, either memory or I/O read and write signals can be used.

Many peripheral devices also generate an interrupt output asserted when a response is required from the microprocessor. Here, the microprocessor must generate an INTA (low-interrupt acknowledge) signal.

The 486 supports 8-, 16-, and 32-bit I/O devices. The devices can be I/O mapped, memory mapped, or both. The 486 has a 106MB/s memory bandwidth at 33 MHz. I/O-mapped devices reside in the 64K I/O space of the 486. Memory-mapped devices reside in the much bigger memory space of 4GB.

Comparison of 386 and 486

The 486 microprocessor is an integrated chip that comprises a CPU, a math coprocessor, and a cache controller. The 486 is compatible with the 386 microprocessor, but it has several differences (Fig. 2-26). The 486 uses dynamic bus sizing to support 8-, 16-, and 32-bit bus sizes and requires external swapping logic. The 386 DX microprocessor supports only 16- and 32-bit bus sizes and does not require swapping logic.

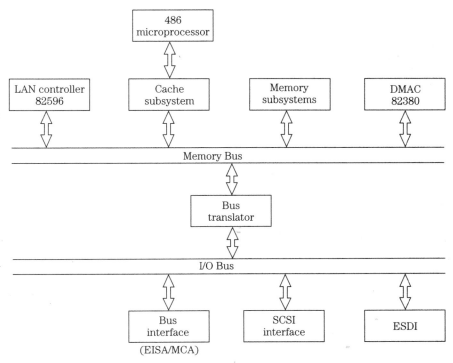

2-25 Typical 486 bus systems.

The 486 has a burst-transfer mode that can transfer four 32-bit words from external memory to the on-chip cache using only five clock cycles. The 386 DX microprocessor needs at least eight clock cycles to transfer the same amount of data.

Pentium

The Pentium is the next generation of the 386 and 486 microprocessor family. The Pentium is binary compatible with the 8086/88, 80286, 386 DX, 386 SX, 486 DX, 486 SX, and 486 DX2. The Pentium processor has all of the features of the 486 with the following enhancements and additions (see Fig. 2-27):

- Superscalar architecture
- Dynamic branch prediction
- Pipelined floating-point unit
- Improved instruction execution
- Separate code and data caches
- Write-back data cache
- 64-bit data bus
- Bus-cycle pipelining
- Address parity
- Internal parity checking

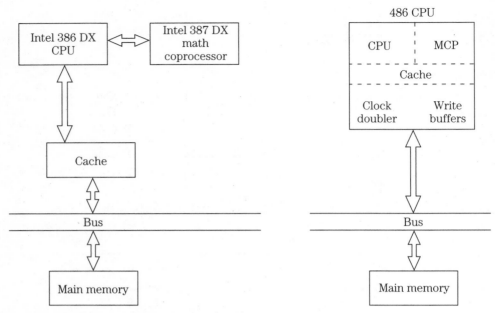

2-26 Comparison of 386 and 486 processors.

The instruction set of the Pentium includes the 486 instruction set with extensions for the additional functions of the Pentium. Software written for the 386 and 486 can run on the Pentium. The on-chip MMU (memory management unit) is also compatible with the 386 and 486.

The Pentium has two instruction pipelines and floating-point units that are capable of independent operation. Each pipeline issues frequently used instructions in a single clock, and the two pipelines can issue two integer instructions in one clock or one to two

Code cache		Instruction fetch	Branch
	Code TLB	Instruction decode	Prediction logic
Bus interface logic	Clock driver		Control logic
	Data TLB	Superscalar integer execution units	Complex instruction support
Data cache			Pipelined floating point

2-27 Layout of Pentium chip showing functional units.

floating-point instructions in one clock. Branch prediction is accomplished in the Pentium with two prefetch buffers. The floating-point unit has faster algorithms to speed some math operations up to 10 times.

Caches

The Pentium processor has separate code and data caches on the chip. Each cache is 8K, with a 32-byte line size. The cache tags two data transfers and an inquire cycle in the same clock. The data bus is 64 bits that improves the data transfer rate. The system supports burst read and write-back cycles as well as bus-cycle pipelining that allows two bus cycles to take place simultaneously.

Test functions

The Pentium processor uses functional redundancy checking for error detection. The checking is done for the processor and the interface to the processor. In functional redundancy checking, a second processor acts as the checker. It runs in parallel with the processor being tested. The checker samples the processor outputs and compares them for a match. It signals an error condition if a match does not occur.

Because more functions have been placed on the chip, board-level testing becomes difficult. So, the Pentium processor has increased test and debug capability. Similar to other 486 CPUs, the Pentium uses IEEE Boundary Scan (Standard 1149). There are four break-point pins for the debug registers. These registers are used for break-point match testing.

Figure 2-28 shows a block diagram of the Pentium processor, which is a 32-bit microprocessor with 32-bit addressing and a 64-bit data bus. Figure 2-29 shows the 273-pin grid array package that is used. Figure 2-30 shows a dual Pentium system that uses both a PCI and ISA bus.

The address lines define the physical area of memory or I/O accessed. When used as outputs, the address lines along with the byte enable signals make up the address bus and define the physical area of memory or I/O accessed. The Pentium can address 4GB of physical memory space and 64K of I/O address space. When they are inputs,

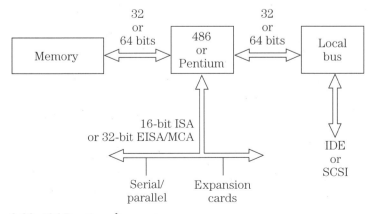

2-28 486 Pentium bus systems.

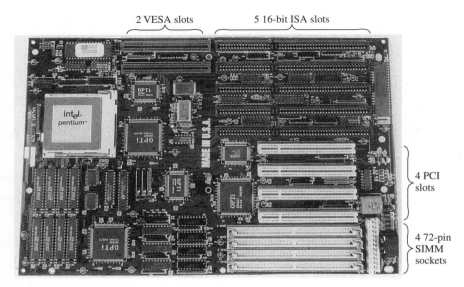

2 VESA slots   5 16-bit ISA slots

4 PCI slots

4 72-pin SIMM sockets

2-29 100 MHz Pentium system board.

the address bus lines drive addresses back into the processor to perform inquire cycles.

There is an address parity check. The status of the address parity check will change when the processor detects a parity error on the A31–A5 during inquire cycles.

Four break-point pins are used for break-point and performance monitoring. The break-point pins (BP3–BP0) correspond to debug registers DR3–DR0. These pins indicate a break-point match of a debug register. BP1 and BP0 also can be used for performance monitoring.

D63 through D0 are the data lines for the 64-bit data bus. Lines D7 through D0 define the least significant byte of the data bus, and lines D63 through D56 define the most significant byte of the data bus. There is one parity pin for each byte of the data bus. DP7 applies to D63 through D56, and DP0 applies to D7 through D0. IERR is an internal parity or functional redundancy check error. When it is low, it alerts the system of these errors.

PCHK is a data parity check. A low indicates the result of a parity check on a data read. Data parity is checked during code reads, memory reads, and I/O reads. Data parity is not checked during the first Interrupt Acknowledge cycle. PCHK indicates the parity status only for the bytes on which valid data is expected. TCK is the test clock input. TCK is a test input that provides the clocking function for the processor boundary scan. TCK is used to clock state information and data in and out during boundary-scan or probe-mode operation. TDI and TDO are the test data inputs and outputs for serial test data and instructions for the boundary-scan and probe-mode test logic.

Bus differences between 486 and Pentium

The Pentium bus is similar to the 486 bus. Enhancements achieve more performance and support for multiprocessing. The differences between the Pentium and the

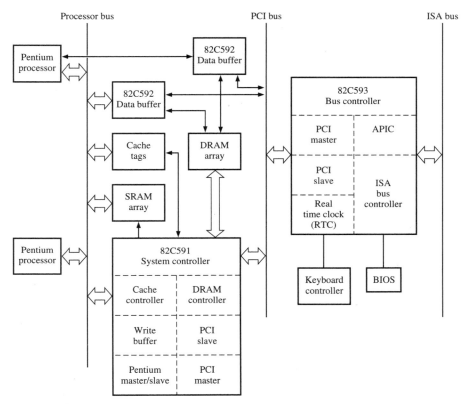

2-30 Dual Pentium system.

486 CPU buses are as follows:

- The Pentium has a 64-bit data bus, but the 486 supports a 32-bit data bus.
- The Pentium has more byte enables (BE7–BE0) and more data parity pins (DP7–DP0) than the 486 to support the larger data bus.
- The Pentium has the capability of driving two cycles concurrently to the bus. It samples the cacheability input KEN only once while the 486 samples KEN twice. Burst-length information is driven in the Pentium with the CACHE pin along with the address. The 486 controls burst length with the BLAST pin.
- The Pentium processor generates 8-byte writes as one bus cycle and does not use the PLOCK pin. It does not change lower-order bits of address and byte enables during the burst.
- The Pentium requires write backs and line fills to be run as burst cycles, and the burst cannot be terminated in the middle because there are no RDY or BLAST pins. Pentium does not support noncacheable burst cycles and nonburst cacheable cycles.
- The Pentium processor supports a write-back cache protocol using the following new pins: CACHE, HIT, HITM, INV, and WB/WT. It does not support the dynamic

bus sizing implemented with BS8 and BS16 or allow invalidations on every clock or invalidations when the Pentium is driving the address bus.

- The Pentium provides an idle clock between consecutive LOCKED cycles and the SCYC pin to indicate a split cycle during locked operations. Noncacheable code prefetches are 8 bytes for the Pentium processor, not 16 bytes.
- The Pentium processor uses an INIT pin in the reset function and holds the states of the internal caches and the floating-point unit.
- The Pentium supports strong store ordering between the processor and the external system along with internal parity error checking, enhanced data parity checking, and address parity error checking. The following new pins implement these features: A PCK, BUSCHK, PEN, IERR, and AP.
- The Pentium implements boundary scan testing with the following pins: TDI, TDO, TMS, TRST, and TCK, which allows a test of the board connections.
- The Pentium processor has IU, IV, and IBT pins and a branch-trace message cycle for execution tracing. The Pentium supports FRC (functional redundancy checking) with the FRCMC and IERR pins and performance monitoring and external break points with the following pins: BP3, BP2, PM1/BP1, and PM0/BP0.
- The Pentium has a system management mode using SMI and SMIACT.

Airspace

Most of the faster processors generate lots of heat, so when you set up and use your computer, keep it on a flat, stable work surface with enough space around it for good air circulation. The following clearances are minimal:

- Rear of system unit 3 inches (8 centimeters)
- Left side of system 6 inches (15 centimeters)
- Right side of system 6 inches (15 centimeters)
- Top of monitor unit 6 inches (15 centimeters)

Other precautions include protecting your equipment from wet environments or liquids. Also avoid dropping, jarring, or shaking your equipment. You also should turn your equipment off and unplug it from the wall outlet or power strip if you move it or open the system unit.

Shutting off the power is also a good idea if you have an accident and expose the equipment to liquid or drop, jar, or bump the equipment.

Display adapters and monitors

If you do not want to use the integrated VGA feature, you must install an appropriate video display adapter. Most 386 or 486 computers work with the other IBM PC or PC AT-compatible display adapters, including the MDA (monochrome display adapter), HCC (Hercules graphics card), CGA (color graphics adapter), EGA (enhanced graphics adapter), VGA (video graphics adapter), SVGA (super VGA), and specialized video adapters.

Most integrated VGA hardware uses a 15-pin port for fixed-frequency (analog) monitors, and they are compatible with the following fixed-frequency and multifrequency monitors:

1. VGA monochrome, IBM 8503 Personal System/2 (PS/2), or compatible displays
2. VGA color, IBM 8514 PS/2, or compatible displays
3. Super VGA or compatible displays
4. Multifrequency displays, such as the NEC MultiSync

To use a multifrequency display in the standard VGA mode, you need to set the monitor display mode to analog and use a 9-to-15-pin adapter to connect the monitor to the integrated VGA. For best performance with the enhanced 800 × 600 graphic display, the multifrequency monitor should be running at a 36 MHz dot rate.

Some 386 computers use a primary video display adapter switch. The switch is sometimes located behind the control console, near the reset button. To set the switch, it is best to use a pointed, plastic object. If you have to change a jumper setting, use tweezers or long-nose pliers as shown in Fig. 2-31.

System setup (CMOS settings)

Most 386 and 486 computers use a built-in system setup program (often called the CMOS, for the chips where it is stored) to configure the system. You set up the system with switches in XTs. ATs use switches and a setup program on the diagnostic disk. You must use the setup program whenever you change or add a hardware component such as a drive. A typical setup or CMOS screen is shown in Fig. 2-32. Figure 2-33 illustrates the system setup flow.

Setup problems

If you are changing the serial ports and Conflict appears next to the serial port address, this indicates that another device (usually an add-on board) already has the I/O

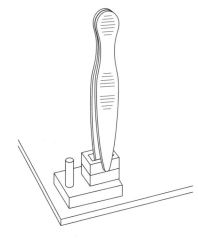

2-31 Use tweezers or long-nose pliers to change jumpers.

```
                              CMOS Table
Current Date & Time: 10/02/1995 15:56:47
   Floppy Drive A: 1.2M (5-1/4")
   Floppy Drive B: 1.44K (3-1/2")
   Base Memory Size: 640K
   Extended Memory Size: 8M
   Primary Display: ECA, PCA, VCA, etc.
                                    WRITE     PARK     STEP    CTRL     TOTAL
DRIVE    TYPE    CYLS    HEROS   SECTS   PRECOMP   PLACE    RATE    BYTE     BYTES
  0:      23     005      4      26      Move      005      0       0     42,054,640
  1:       0     No Drive, or SCSI Drive
```

2-32 Sample setup or CMOS screen.

address. If another device has the address, change the I/O address of the conflicting device, choose a different I/O address for the serial port, or disable the serial port. If you enable only one built-in serial port, it must be serial port 1. You cannot enable serial port 2 if serial port 1 is disabled.

If the system uses the floppy controller located on the system board, you will need to change the field to disable the built-in floppy disk controller and use an add-on floppy controller.

A default speed of high is used most of the time. The low speed might be needed for some older application and game software.

If you add a video adapter board and use System + Video, you might get the following error message:

Cannot shadow the current video BIOS

This message means the BIOS will not shadow this board and you will have to use System. You will need to use None if your software uses timing requests that conflict with those of the BIOS. You can test this by running the software while System or System + Video is enabled. If the system locks up or the software does not run, you will need to change the shadow BIOS setting to None. Some computers do not allow this option; the BIOS is automatically shadowed and you cannot disable it.

In these systems, you might not be able to add other video boards unless they are supplied by the computer manufacturer or compatible with your BIOS.

Cache memory increases the processing speed and might be needed for applications such as desktop publishing and CAD/CAM (computer-aided drafting/computer-aided manufacturing) programs. In most cases, the cache is enabled for optimal performance.

Boot device determines which drive is the boot or startup drive. If you select Hard Drive, the system automatically starts from drive C, if C: is loaded with DOS. This setting causes the system to start faster and is the preferred choice. If drive C is not bootable, for example, DOS becomes corrupted, the system starts from drive A. If you select Floppy Drive, the system boots from drive A if it has a bootable disk, or checks drive C if drive A is empty. You can use this option with software that boots from a floppy disk.

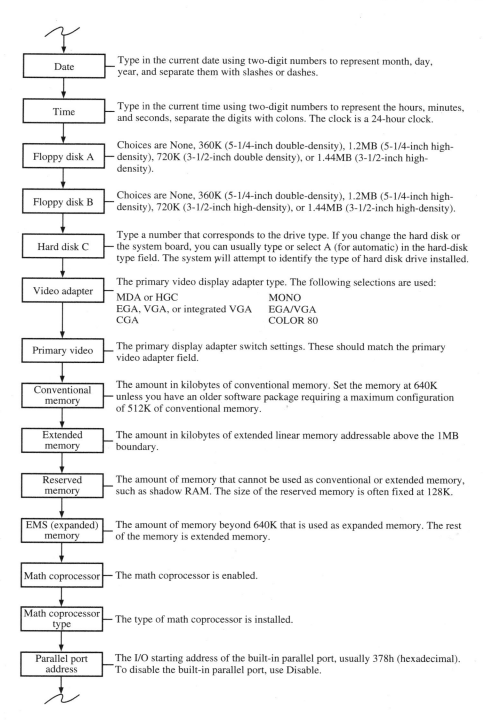

Date	Type in the current date using two-digit numbers to represent month, day, year, and separate them with slashes or dashes.
Time	Type in the current time using two-digit numbers to represent the hours, minutes, and seconds, separate the digits with colons. The clock is a 24-hour clock.
Floppy disk A	Choices are None, 360K (5-1/4-inch double-density), 1.2MB (5-1/4-inch high-density), 720K (3-1/2-inch double density), or 1.44MB (3-1/2-inch high-density).
Floppy disk B	Choices are None, 360K (5-1/4-inch double-density), 1.2MB (5-1/4-inch high-density), 720K (3-1/2-inch high-density), or 1.44MB (3-1/2-inch high-density).
Hard disk C	Type a number that corresponds to the drive type. If you change the hard disk or the system board, you can usually type or select A (for automatic) in the hard-disk type field. The system will attempt to identify the type of hard disk drive installed.

Video adapter — The primary video display adapter type. The following selections are used:

MDA or HGC	MONO
EGA, VGA, or integrated VGA	EGA/VGA
CGA	COLOR 80

Primary video	The primary display adapter switch settings. These should match the primary video adapter field.
Conventional memory	The amount in kilobytes of conventional memory. Set the memory at 640K unless you have an older software package requiring a maximum configuration of 512K of conventional memory.
Extended memory	The amount in kilobytes of extended linear memory addressable above the 1MB boundary.
Reserved memory	The amount of memory that cannot be used as conventional or extended memory, such as shadow RAM. The size of the reserved memory is often fixed at 128K.
EMS (expanded) memory	The amount of memory beyond 640K that is used as expanded memory. The rest of the memory is extended memory.
Math coprocessor	The math coprocessor is enabled.
Math coprocessor type	The type of math coprocessor is installed.
Parallel port address	The I/O starting address of the built-in parallel port, usually 378h (hexadecimal). To disable the built-in parallel port, use Disable.

2-33 System setup flow.

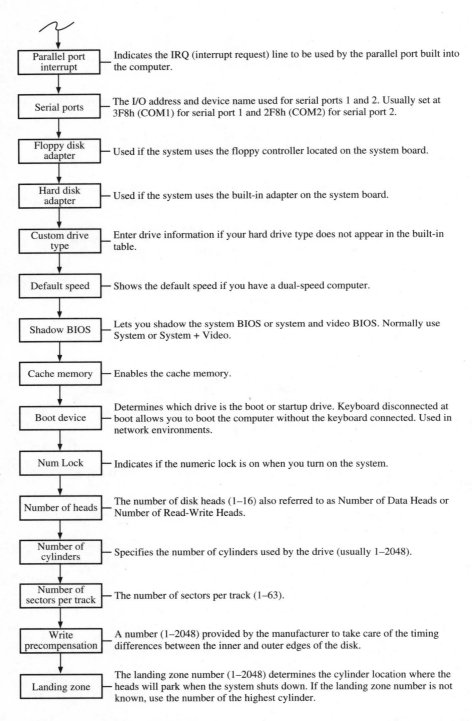

Parallel port interrupt	Indicates the IRQ (interrupt request) line to be used by the parallel port built into the computer.
Serial ports	The I/O address and device name used for serial ports 1 and 2. Usually set at 3F8h (COM1) for serial port 1 and 2F8h (COM2) for serial port 2.
Floppy disk adapter	Used if the system uses the floppy controller located on the system board.
Hard disk adapter	Used if the system uses the built-in adapter on the system board.
Custom drive type	Enter drive information if your hard drive type does not appear in the built-in table.
Default speed	Shows the default speed if you have a dual-speed computer.
Shadow BIOS	Lets you shadow the system BIOS or system and video BIOS. Normally use System or System + Video.
Cache memory	Enables the cache memory.
Boot device	Determines which drive is the boot or startup drive. Keyboard disconnected at boot allows you to boot the computer without the keyboard connected. Used in network environments.
Num Lock	Indicates if the numeric lock is on when you turn on the system.
Number of heads	The number of disk heads (1–16) also referred to as Number of Data Heads or Number of Read-Write Heads.
Number of cylinders	Specifies the number of cylinders used by the drive (usually 1–2048).
Number of sectors per track	The number of sectors per track (1–63).
Write precompensation	A number (1–2048) provided by the manufacturer to take care of the timing differences between the inner and outer edges of the disk.
Landing zone	The landing zone number (1–2048) determines the cylinder location where the heads will park when the system shuts down. If the landing zone number is not known, use the number of the highest cylinder.

2-33 (*Continued*) System setup flow.

Normally, the computer does not start successfully unless a keyboard is plugged in. If you change this in system setup, the keyboard check and tests are not performed during the POST (power-on self-test). This feature is useful in networks.

If Num Lock is on at boot, starting the system sets the calculator keys so that you can use them to enter numbers. If this is off at boot, starting the system sets the keys as cursor controls. After the computer is on, you can use the Num Lock key to enable or disable the lock at will.

Disk compatibility

Most 386 and 486 computers include a 3½-inch 1.44MB floppy disk drive. Many also have a 5¼-inch floppy disk drive. The memory capacity of a floppy disk depends on whether it is double density or high density. For a 5¼-inch disk, double density equals 360K, and high density equals 1.2MB; for a 3½-inch disk, double density equals 720K and high density equals 1.44MB.

Floppy disk drives are designed to accommodate double-density or high-density disks, but there are some precautions you must observe. If you use different capacities of disks and drives, be aware of the following: A 360K drive, 5¼-inch DSDD (double density) can read, write to, and format 360K disks but it cannot read, write to, or format 1.2MB disks.

A 1.2MB drive, 5¼-inch high density (DSHD) can read 360K disks and format them, and use the MS-DOS command

FORMAT drive:/4

Data written on 360K disks in a 1.2MB drive might not be readable in a 360K drive. This drive can also read, write to, and format 1.2MB disks.

A 720K drive, 3½-inch double density can read, write to, and format 720K disks but it cannot read, write to, or format 1.44MB disks.

A 1.44MB drive, 3½-inch high density can read and write to 720K disks, and format them, and use the MS-DOS command

FORMAT drive:/N:9/T:80 2

This drive can also read, write to, and format 1.44MB disks. Figure 2-34 depicts disk compatibility in pictorial form.

Video adapters

The following display adapters are used in the PC family:

1. MDA (monochrome display adapter) video cards can display only text characters in one color.
2. HGA (Hercules graphics adapter) cards are popular video cards that are not made by IBM. Because of their popularity, they have become a de facto standard. They emulate MDA cards but they also support high-resolution monochrome graphics.

3. CGA (color graphics adapter) video cards can display text and graphics in any of eight colors.
4. EGA (enhanced graphics adapter) video cards can display text and graphics in any of 16 colors from a palette of 64. It also supports a higher resolution than CGA video cards.
5. MCGA (multicolor graphics adapter) video cards are crosses between CGA and VGA cards. They support all CGA modes and can display graphics in up to 256 simultaneous colors.
6. VGA (video graphics adapter) video cards can display text and graphics in any of 256 colors from a palette of 262,144. They also support a higher resolution than CGA, EGA, or MCGA video cards.
7. SVGA (super VGA) cards are a higher-resolution version of regular VGAs, with 1024 horizontal lines and 768 vertical lines (other resolutions are also called *super*).

Monitor compatibility

You can use the following monitors with 386 and 486 computers with built-in (integrated) VGA adapters: VGA monochrome, VGA color, and super VGA. If you are using integrated VGA, to make sure your computer runs correctly with your monitor, check the following:

1. Make sure the monitor is compatible with integrated VGA.

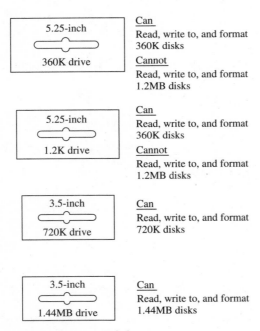

2-34 Disk compatibility.

2. If you are using a multifrequency monitor, you might need to set the multifrequency monitor switch or jumper on the system board to on.
3. Select the primary video display adapter type in the system setup.

If you are using a video display adapter board, to make sure your computer runs correctly with your monitor and adapter board, check the following:

1. The computer primary video display adapter switch or jumper.
2. Set all switches, jumpers, and configuration options on the video adapter board for the proper monitor type and correct video display modes.
3. Indicate the primary video display adapter type in system setup.
4. Make sure the monitor is compatible with the video display adapter.

Power supply

The power supply is the shielded cube in the rear section of the chassis. In 286 machines, a 190- to 200-W power supply was used. Some 386 and 486 machines use a smaller 150- to 160-W supply. The power-on switch is usually part of the power supply, as are the internal cables that are designed to be connected to the drives. A switch on many units lets you select 220-V operation when you use the unit outside the United States. If you need more power cables for additional drives, you can get an inexpensive Y power cable that connects to one of the cables and splits its output in two. You should not use more than one Y cable per system because it is possible to over load the power supply.

The power supply inside the system unit provides power for the system board, adapters, diskette drive(s), hard disk drive(s), monitor, and keyboard. The power supply is designed to operate the maximum number of drives that can be added inside the system unit. Many compatible computers have a total output of 175 to 200 W. A 115/230 Vac selectable switch is usually located at the rear of the power supply enclosure (Fig. 2-35).

Supply characteristics

The power supply is typically designed to operate at a frequency of either 60 $\pm$3 Hz or 50 $\pm$2 Hz, and at 100 to 130 Vac, 5.0 A (amperes) or 220/260 Vac, 2.5 A. The voltage is selected by a switch at the rear of the power supply. The input requirements then become: ac input voltage is either 100 to 130 V or 200 to 260 V selectable.

Output

The power supply provides +5, −5, +12, and −12 Vdc. Table 2-5 shows typical load current and regulation tolerance for a 200-W supply. The power supply is a switching oscillator type with the functional blocks shown in Fig. 2-36. Testing starts by checking the regulator outputs. If the outputs are all dead or low, check the fuse or circuit breaker and the rectifier circuits. The problem could be a faulty diode or capacitor. Use the procedures of Figs. 2-37 and 2-38 to remove and replace the power supply.

If only one output is dead or low, the problem is probably in the regulator circuit. Check the regulator capacitors for shorts. Typically, the voltage into the regulator will be about double the output voltage. So the −5-V regulator should have an input voltage of

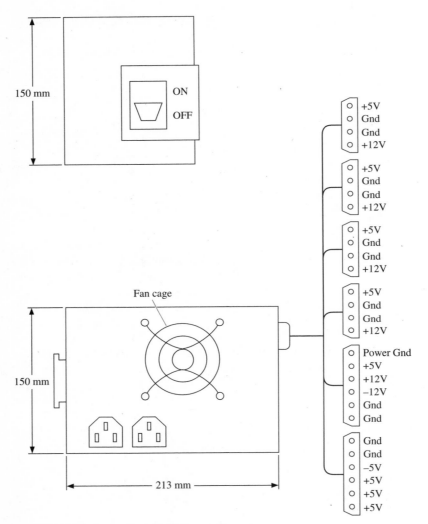

2-35 Typical power supply layout and connections.

about −9 or −10 V, and the +5-V regulator should have an input voltage of about −9 to −10 V. These lines can be traced back if any voltages appear to be in error. You also can run resistive tests to check for shorts to ground. If you trace the problem to a major component such as a transformer, it might be simpler and just as economical to replace the power supply. You can buy power supplies from most computer supply outlets; just make sure the replacement has the proper wattage.

Output protection

If any output becomes overloaded, the power supply will switch off within about 20 ms (milliseconds). This quick shutdown will normally prevent an overcurrent condition from damaging the power supply.

Table 2-5. Typical power supply output characteristics

Output, volts	Load, amperes	Tolerance, percent	Ripple, mV (millivolts)
+5	20	±2	50
+12	7.3	±5	100
−5	0.3	±10	100
−12	0.3	±10	100

Installing add-in boards

Most 386 or 486 computers have 16- or 32-bit IBM PC AT-compatible expansion board slots (Fig. 2-39). You can use these slots for add-on boards such as auxiliary disk or tape drive controllers, printer adapters, network interfaces, modems, and video display adapters (Fig. 2-40).

Before installing any add-in board, it is a good idea to check its electric current rating. If you do not know the rating, you might need to contact the board manufacturer.

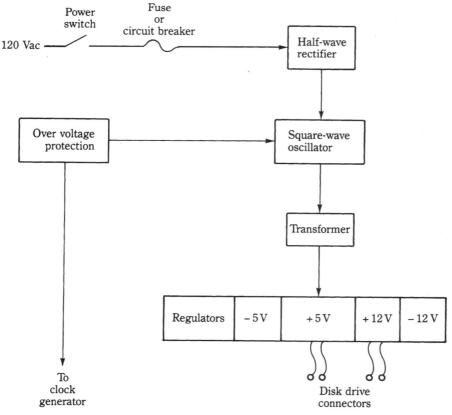

2-36 Typical switching power supply.

Set the Power switch on the system unit to Off.

↓

Unplug the power cord of the system unit.

↓

Remove the cover of the system unit.

↓

Disconnect the system board power connectors by
grasping the connectors and pulling straight up.
Do not pull on the wires when disconnecting connectors.

↓

Disconnect the power connectors from the
fixed drives and floppy disk drives.

↓

Remove the power supply mounting screws.

↓

On some units you need to remove the mounting screws for one
of the drives and slide the disk drive assembly out of the way.

↓

Push the power supply forward, lift and remove.

2-37 Power supply removal.

The power supply provides the +5 and +12 V required for each of the add-on board slots (Fig. 2-41). Below are the typical current loading capacity ratings for 16-bit slots.

Voltage Slot rating, amperes

+5   2.66

+12   0.5

Place the power supply next to the back
plate and slide the supply into position.

↓

Align the screw holes in the power supply with the rear frame.

↓

Install and tighten the power supply mounting screws.

↓

Connect the power connectors to the disk drives.

↓

Plug in the system board power connectors.

↓

Install any drives that had to be moved.

↓

Install the unit cover.

↓

Connect all cables to the unit.

2-38 Power supply replacement.

To find your total slot ratings, multiply the number of slots in your computer by the individual slot rating. The individual rating can be exceeded as long as the total current ratings for all installed boards do not exceed your total slot ratings for the +5-V and the +12-V power supply outputs.

Portable, laptop, notepad, palmtop, and pen computers

These computers will have most of the same functional components as the desktop units, except that the smallest of these will use memory cards for storage and most will not have tube type displays. The early portable computers were basically scaled down versions of desktop units. These included the IBM and Compaq suitcase size units shown in Figs. 2-9 and 2-10 which had small CRT displays. As these units were downsized, the CRT displays were replaced with the smaller lightweight technologies used in calculators and other handheld units.

Working on the older, larger units is similar to working on a desktop system while the smaller units are more like a calculator in both their display and membrane keyboard. Figure 2-42(*a*) and 2-42(*b*) show how parts are changed in a typical laptop. Figure 2-42(*c*) illustrates a typical laptop system board which often has large cutout areas for drives and other components. Figure 2-43(*a*) and 2-43(*b*) show the interior of a typical 486 notebook computer. Figure 2-43(*c*) shows the block diagram of a 486 SLC notebook computer.

Liquid crystal displays

Liquid crystal is an organic material that is liquid in form but it has a crystal structure similar to a solid. This material is placed between light polarizing glass and then a voltage is applied to areas of the crystal to make them appear dark.

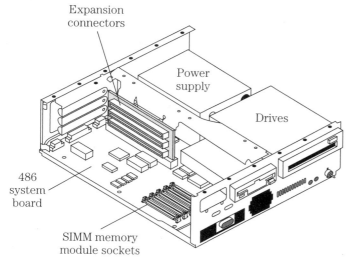

2-39 486 system unit.

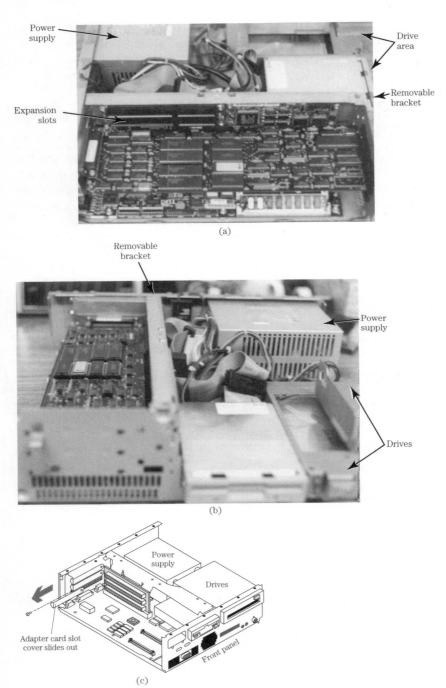

2-40 486 system with riser-card construction. Left side view (A). Front view (B). Removing adapter card slot cover. Replacing cards in a 486 riser-card machine (C).

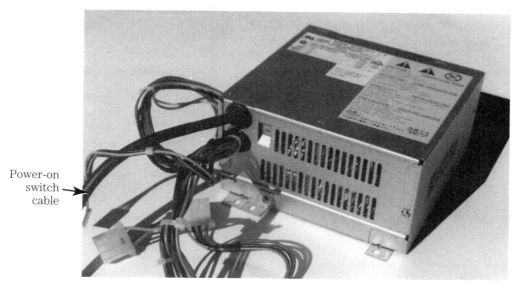

Power-on
switch →
cable

2-41 486 Power supply with power-on switch cable; the power switch is usually
part of the power supply.

The three versions of liquid crystal displays are shown in Fig. 2-44. The first version
is twisted nematic which uses a vertical polarizer in front and a horizontal polarizer in the
rear. The liquid crystal material twists the light by 90 degrees. This version was simple to
make but had a limited viewing angle and poor contrast. The super-twisted nematic uses
an improved liquid crystal material and twists the light by 200 to 270 degrees. This
improves both the viewing angle and the contrast. Although this technology works well
at resolutions up to 1024×800 pixels, it is costly and has a slow pixel response time.

If a compensator sandwich is added after the LCD sandwich to provide a horizontally polarized light output, the viewing angle and contrast are improved even more, but
this adds more weight and cost to the display. It is also hard to backlight this display.

The film-compensated unit solves these problems since it is light and much less
expensive to implement. It is also easily backlighted. There is, however, a slight loss of
viewing angle and contrast due to the use of the film.

Backlighting

This involves the use of a light source to the liquid crystal display to improve visi-
bility in a low-light environment. Three methods are used.

1. Electroluminescent (EL) panels
2. Cold-cathode fluorescent tubes (CCFT)
3. Light-emitting diodes (LED)

EL panels are thin, lightweight, and produce an even light output, but they require an
ac inverter for the 100 or more volts required and have a life of only 2000 to 3000 hours.
LEDs provide more brightness than EL backlighting at low voltages and have a life of more

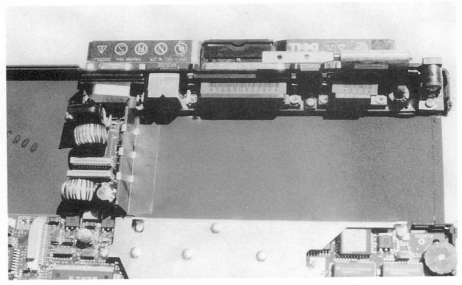

2-42(A) Interior of 486 notebook computer, section of main circuit board is in foreground.

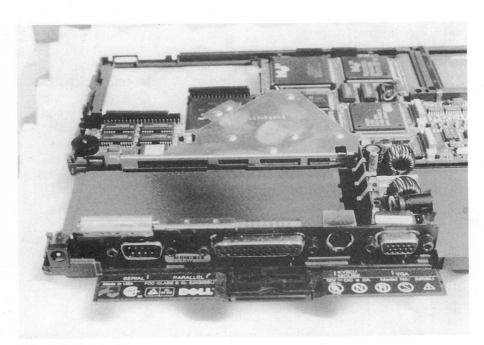

2-42(B) Main assembly of 486 notebook computer showing input-output connectors.

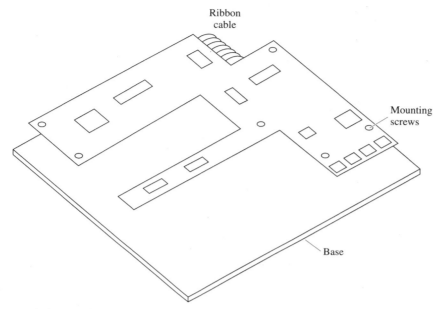

2-42(C) Laptop system board.

than 50,000 hours, but they do not provide the white light preferred for laptops and note-books. These yellow-green displays are used mostly in small character displays such as those found in printers. CCFTs produce a bright white light, consume low power, and have a life of 10,000 to 15,000 hours. They are used for both backlighting and edgelighting with one or two tubes. An inverter is used to supply the 270 to 360 Vac needed by the tubes.

LCD addressing

Passive matrix addressing involves a row and column matrix as shown in Fig. 2-45. Transparent electrodes are deposited on glass sheets, then the two sheets of glass are placed together to form a matrix. The electrodes are driven by small transistors which are controlled by a matrix controller chip. The display is updated about 30 times a second. The need to scan the display makes it too slow for the faster graphics applications including animation.

Active matrix addressing uses individual electrodes for each pixel rather than overlapped rows and columns. Each electrode has its own transistor driver which is built into the rear substrate. A display with 640 × 480 resolution will have over 300,000 thin film transistors. A common electrode is deposited on the upper glass. Since there is no need to update the display, active matrix addressing is much faster. It is also a much more difficult manufacturing process and more expensive to produce.

Color displays

So far, we have been discussing monochrome displays. Color displays require that we have three electrodes for each pixel in a passive matrix, using film compensation.

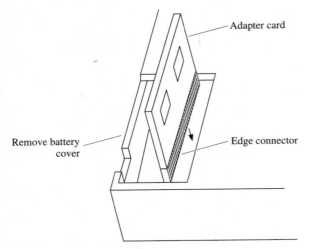

2-43(A) Some portable computers have adapter cards that are installed inside of the battery cover after the battery is removed.

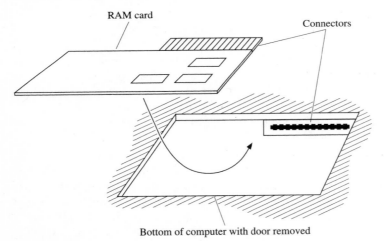

2-43(B) Some portable computers have RAM cards that are installed through an opening in the bottom of the computer.

The front glass is coated with color filter material to block the colors that are not wanted for each red, green, or blue (RGB) pixel. Up to eight primary colors can be produced. Intermediate colors are produced with color hatching. Like monochrome passive matrix addressing, contrast and viewing angle are limited.

Active matrix color involves a red, green, and blue electrode for each pixel. Each electrode has its own transistor, so a 640 × 480 display has almost 1 million transistors on the rear plate. Since the display can closely control the contrast, up to 512 colors are

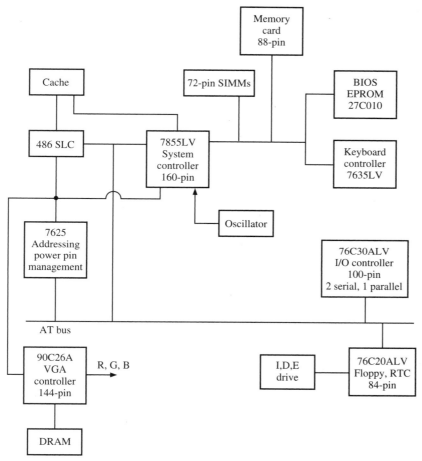

2-43(C) Notebook system.

possible with 256 the usual standard. The contrast ratio is 60 to 1 with a viewing angle of 80 degrees. The response time is about 30 ms providing good performance for fast graphics and animation.

Plasma displays

These displays use neon gas with a small amount of Xenon to improve the light output which is orange-red in color. The contrast is about 50 to 1 with a viewing angle of 120 degrees or more. Two supplies are need to drive the display, 80 to 120 Vdc and 130 to 150 Vdc. Addressing is passive matrix, which was described previously for LCDs. The higher voltage is used for *firing* (writing a pixel) while the lower voltage is used for refreshing. You can use Fig. 2-46 for troubleshooting LCD and plasma displays.

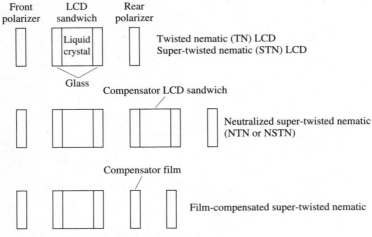

2-44 Liquid crystal displays (LCDs).

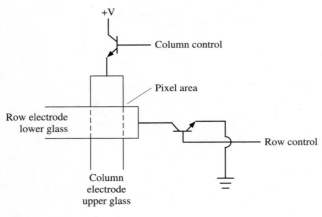

Passive matrix LCD

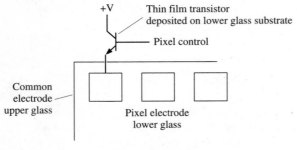

Active matrix LCD

2-45 LCD addressing.

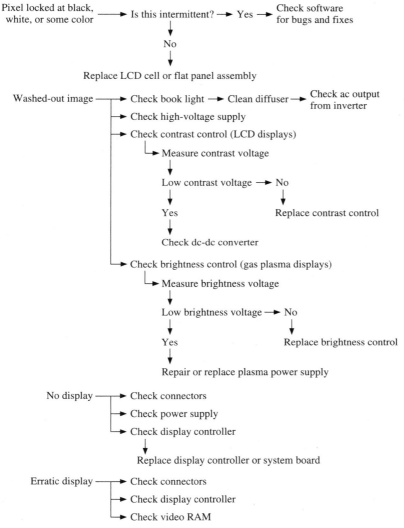

2-46 Troubleshooting LCD and plasma displays.

Memory cards

These credit card–sized units contain memory chips and are used in pen and palm-top computers. There are two basic types of cards.

1. Volatile cards that use static or dynamic RAM (SRAM or DRAM) or some type of erasable ROM
2. Nonvolatile cards that use nonerasable ROM

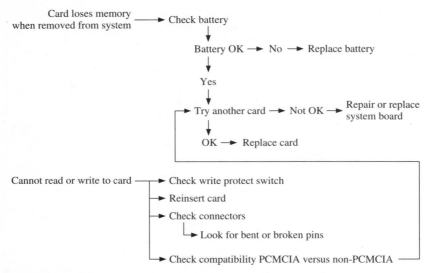

2-47 Memory card troubleshooting.

Static RAM cards use small lithium batteries to maintain the memory when power is off. These cards usually have 32K to 2MB of SRAM.

DRAM cards are about twice as fast as SRAM cards. DRAM cards do not hold their information after power is removed. They are generally used as a convenient expansion memory for portable computers.

Electrically erasable programmable read-only memory (EEPROM) *cards* have a limited capacity of 192K. They can be written to and then erased and rewritten with the proper equipment. They hold the information when power is removed.

Masked ROM cards are programmed by the manufacturer and are used to package software for small computers. They are available with capacities of 16MB. A variation of these is the OTPROM (*one-time programmable read-only memory*) card which are manufactured blank and then programmed by the user or software vendor. These cards are available with up to 4MB.

Flash cards

These are a more recent development in EEPROM technology that can be erased and rewritten quickly. They also have a lower power requirement and more storage capacity than standard EEPROMs. Typical flash cards include 20MB IDE and 14.6MB PCMCIA (Personal Computer Memory Card International Association) solid-state storage cards. Figure 2-47 shows troubleshooting methods for memory cards.

<h1 align="center">3</h1>
CHAPTER

The System Unit

The system unit contains the main printed circuit board, which is called the system board, and the metal shield that contains the power supply and the disk drives (Fig. 3-1). The system board contains chips to handle RAM, support chips to produce clock signals, a set of chips for the ROM programs, and I/O chips to connect the computer to the peripherals.

The older system boards contain about 100 chips as well as the connectors for the expansion boards. Each short connector or slot will accept 62 connection pins. The slots are wired in parallel. They form the output bus for the 62-pin printed circuit boards that will plug into the slots.

The internal program selects the correct expansion board even though they are all wired in parallel. These cards add the peripherals to the computer. For example, the disk controller card connects the disk drives to the system board. A video adapter and a printer card connect the monitor and printer to the system board.

You can use other cards for the expansion of the computer for other options. For example, you can use a modem as well as additional disk drives, additional memory, printers, and other peripherals with the proper card.

Most 386 and above system boards have built-in disk controllers, video adapters, serial/parallel ports for printers, mouse, and modems. The typical connectors found on these boards are shown in Fig. 3-2. Some systems use a separate processor board as shown in Fig. 3-3.

RAM configurations

The 8088 and 8086 chips can only recognize addresses for up to 1MB of memory. Out of this 1MB, DOS can access addresses from 0 to 640K for RAM. This 640K total RAM is the conventional, or working, memory. The remaining 384K handles system functions such as video and ROM instructions. The 1MB limit goes back to PC and XT computers that used the 8088 microprocessor chip because the 8088 can access 1MB of addresses.

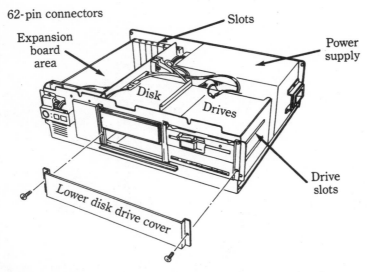

3-1(A) System units and system boards. System unit with cover removed.

Expansion board

3-1(B) XT system board.

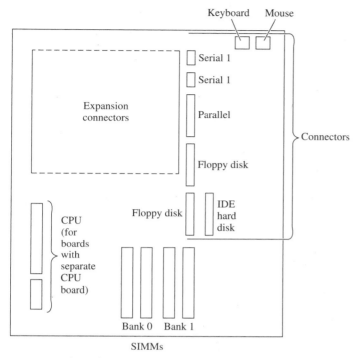

3-2 Typical 386/486 system board connectors.

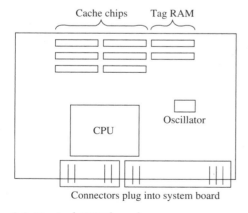

3-3 Typical CPU board.

The AT used the 80286 microprocessor chip that can access 16MB of memory, that is, 16,777,216 storage addresses. The 386s can access 4GB, or more than 4 billion addresses. None of this extra storage space exists as far as DOS is concerned.

Although a 286 system can access 16MB, it might contain only 1MB of RAM. Even this is more memory than DOS can access. DOS can access only 1MB, and out of that

1MB, DOS can use only 640K of RAM to run a program. There are two types of memory that go beyond the DOS limits. These memory types are known as expanded memory and extended memory. Both of these use RAM beyond the 640K limit for DOS.

Expanded memory has no corresponding physical memory addresses. Expanded memory was originally developed to get around the physical memory constraints of the XT. On an XT there are no addresses above 1MB. Lotus, Intel, and Microsoft developed a standard for an add-in memory board called the EMS (expanded-memory specification) board.

Extended memory, in contrast, is standard in many 286 and 386 computers. Extended memory is linear, with its addresses starting at the 1MB limit (Fig. 3-4).

System RAM

A typical 286-compatible system came with 512K to 1MB RAM on the system board. This upgrade can be to 640K or 1MB, depending on the space available on the system board. In addition to its system board RAM, the 286 unit can hold up to 16MB of extended memory on add-in cards. DOS is able to support up to 640K of user-addressable base memory. If you add RAM chips to a 1MB 286 board, you will get a total of 1024K of memory. The extra 384K will become extended memory.

System board RAM chips are often arranged in rows. These rows make up logical banks. For example, as you count from the front of the chassis, the first and third rows might make up bank 1, and the second and fourth rows might make up bank 0.

Each bank must be either completely full or completely empty. You can never have one row or part of a row empty. The 286 can use 64 or 256K RAM chips. The 286 should

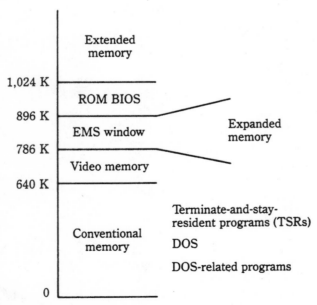

3-4 Memory map showing conventional memory, expanded memory, and extended memory.

use memory chips with a speed of 150 ns or faster. The RAM chip configuration of the 286 is selected by a dip switch on the system board.

Table 3-1 shows typical configurations of system board RAM and the type of chips used in banks 0 and 1 that provide the desired total. Figure 3-5 shows another memory arrangement where an XY memory combination board is used to upgrade from 256K on the main board. Two plug-in modules are used to increase the memory to 640K. Figure 3-6 shows a base memory map obtained from a diagnostic program. The conventional memory is 640K.

Suppose there is a total of 18 chips per bank. Then you need 18 chips, if you are adding one bank, or 36 chips, if you are pulling out the existing 256K chips and populating the board entirely with 64K chips.

Each chip has a pin 1 marked with a notch or a dot. If you look closely at the green PC card, beneath each empty chip socket you will usually see a white printed outline of a notched chip in the proper orientation (pin 1 toward the front of the chassis). You must install each chip in the correct orientation with all the pins fully seated in the socket.

The pins that connect each chip to its socket are easily bent out of shape. You need apply only a little force to install RAM chips. If you have to press hard, you are probably bending a pin. If you make a mistake and must remove a chip from a socket, insert the tip of a small flat-blade screwdriver under one end of the chip and twist gently. When the chip begins to loosen, move the screwdriver to the other end and loosen that side. Work gently back and forth until you free the chip; then straighten the bent pin and start over.

Memory management schemes

Memory management hardware, such as the expanded-memory boards, add memory to the system. Memory management software does not add any chips, but it helps to make more efficient use of existing RAM.

DOS was developed for 8088 and 8086 microprocessors, which cannot work directly with anything over 1MB of RAM (384K of that is set aside for system use, leaving only 640K for programs). Two types of memory, expanded and extended, are available for programs that need more than 640K.

Expanded memory is RAM on an expansion board (Fig. 3-7). This type of memory is accessible only through a window, or page frame, in conventional memory. The window holds different pages of memory that are swapped as needed into the processor

Table 3-1. Typical system board RAM configurations

Total RAM	Chips in bank 0	Chips in bank 1
256K	64K	64K
512K	256K	Empty
640K	256K	64K
1Mb	256K	256K

3-5 XT memory board with plug-in memory module.

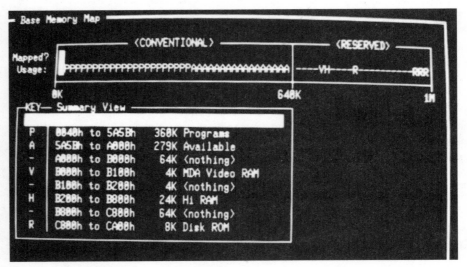

3-6 Base memory map obtained with a diagnostic program. The addresses are hexadecimal.

3-7 An expanded memory with 2MB that supports the EMS standard.

address space. To use expanded memory, a memory board and software that follow the EMS (expanded-memory specification) standard is needed. EMS 4.0 allows you to run programs and store data in up to 32MB of paged RAM. It works on IBM compatibles from XTs to 486 machines.

Extended memory is an extension of RAM, but it is not available on 8086- and 8088-based machines. You can add 15MB of extended RAM at the end of 1MB in an 80286- or 386 SX-based machine. The 386 and 486 machines can handle an additional 4095MB. Some operating systems, such as OS/2 and UNIX, can use extended memory directly; DOS cannot. To run in extended memory, a program must contain a DOS-extender that switches the CPU between the real mode, used by DOS, and the protected mode, which can access memory beyond 1MB. Three standards are used: (1) XMS (extended-memory specifications), (2) VCPI (virtual control program interface), and (3) DPMI (DOS protected-mode interface).

Extended memory is simpler to use than the EMS scheme. However, extended memory will not work in XT-class machines and is newer than EMS for 286s and 386s. EMS is a popular standard for all three classes. Hardware and software products can use either one or a combination of the two memory types.

Expanded memory uses existing addresses within the DOS 1MB address limit that are available. Expanded memory swaps additional blocks of memory into those unused addresses by a process called *bank switching*.

The expanded-memory manager uses a 64K window called a *page frame* to access the memory located outside RAM. The page frame is located within the 1MB that DOS recognizes. The page frame lets DOS access up to four blocks or pages of memory at once. When the program needs data located in expanded memory, the EMM (expanded-memory manager) finds the page or pages the program is looking for and moves it into the 64K page frame so DOS can find it. You use expanded memory by adding an EMS board or installing a software emulator. The emulator mimics an EMS board. Expanded memory can be added to XT, AT, or 386 machines.

Expanded memory results in more memory space for those programs that can take advantage of EMS. These memory expanders commonly take the form of an EMS 4.0 memory board. Software products emulate expanded memory by swapping sections of code using the hard drive or extended RAM to simulate the EMS paged RAM.

An example is Above Disk, which is primarily an EMS emulator, but it also includes utilities for borrowing 96K of EGA or VGA video memory for nongraphics programs and for relocating Novell Netware TSRs. You can use it to simulate the entire EMS 4.0 32MB limit in extended memory or on a hard disk, and it is one of the easiest to install of the memory managers. It begins by asking if this is a first-time installation and which disk and subdirectory to copy files to. Then a configuration screen is used to show the settings for emulating EMS memory in the system. A device driver is added to the CONFIG.SYS file and a memory-resident module to AUTO-EXEC.BAT.

Above Disk will not work with some programs, such as Microsoft Windows/386. Protected mode works only on 286s or 386s with CPUs dated August 1987 and that run DOS 3.3 or later. The package comes with a Lotus 1-2-3 EMS emulator that provides memory management not available in the main program. It provides three memory management functions.

1. Emulating EMS
2. Reclaiming unused video RAM
3. Space for large 1-2-3 worksheets

TC Power supplies EMS emulation only. The installation procedure requires you to create a new hard disk subdirectory, copy the program files, and accept the default settings before rebooting. The program adds a command line to CONFIG.SYS. It can combine extended, expanded, and hard disk memory in any combination up to the 32MB that EMS 4.0 allows. Similar to Above Disk, TC Power will run on an XT, but because XTs do not support extended RAM, the program uses only the machine's hard disk for EMS emulation. The disk-based emulation can provide the full 32MB of EMS 4.0 memory.

Some products make room for the software application by moving TSRs and drivers out of the lower 640K and relocating them to expanded or extended memory, the hard disk, or gaps between 640K and 1MB if your system has memory in this range. The latter occurs with some 286 and 386 compatibles with 1MB on the motherboard.

Other products stretch DOS RAM to 704 or 736K, depending on the type of video card used. Monochrome and CGA cards do not use the memory addresses immediately above 640K, so a memory manager can assign the empty space to DOS. Some other memory-management products are designed for 386s that convert extended memory to expanded memory. These products use the 386 chip memory-mapping capability to substitute for the circuitry on the EMS boards. These products convert extended memory to EMS RAM and use the 386 memory-mapping features to relocate TSRs and drivers.

Extended memory

The MS-DOS (Microsoft Disk Operating System) is able to use only the first 640K of memory for programs. The memory is *linear*. That means that it proceeds (theoretically, not physically) in a straight line from bit 1 through the highest bit in the memory. The memory up to the 640K point is called the *base,* or *conventional, memory.* DOS can use this memory for any purpose. Memory from the 640K point up to the 1MB point is reserved for ROM. This section of memory acts as built-in permanent software for different devices so the system can perform its most basic functions, such as starting up, which also is called *booting,* and testing the system including these devices during this power-up. EMM386.EXE is used to provide access to the memory in the reserved area between 640K and 1MB. Above 640K, extended memory begins. DOS needs a memory manager such as HIMEM.SYS to recognize extended memory.

A common application for extended memory is a RAM disk. DOS version 3.1 and above usually include a program for creating a RAM disk in extended memory. The RAM disk is electronic memory that acts like a fast disk drive. DOS treats it like an extra floppy or hard disk drive connected to the system. Because there is no physical disk involved, the access time to and from the RAM disk depends only on the speed of the memory chips. Even though it acts like storage, a RAM disk is still volatile memory, and the contents of the RAM disk must be saved to a true storage device after a computing session.

Extended memory is different from expanded memory in that only 286s and above can use it. Extended memory is linear. Its addresses begin where the DOS limit leaves off, from 1MB on up to 16MB in a 286 and 4996MB in a 386. Extended memory does not require bank switching as expanded memory does; it is all available simultaneously, instead of being limited to 64K chunks. Extended memory is necessary for *multitasking* (running several applications at once) and for the operating systems that can handle multitasking, including OS/2 (or Operating System 2) and UNIX.

When a PC uses extended memory, it is working in protected mode. Some software programs are written specifically for 286 machines and above, so the program can use the extended memory. ATs and 386s can also run in real mode, the conventional 640K RAM limit, using conventional DOS-compatible software. When running in real mode, ATs and above pretend to be XTs.

DOS works within a 1MB limit. Expanded memory is memory that lies completely outside that limit but is switched into and out of a 64K window so DOS can work with it. Extended memory is a linear extension of that 1MB and can be accessed directly by the CPU. Extended memory is available only with 286 and above computers.

Additional memory

Some 286 units came with 512K of RAM on the system board. This is increased to 640K or 1MB or more by installing more RAM chips on the system board. The RAM chips are located in rows on the system board. Some rows will be filled with chips, and other rows will have empty sockets. The rows are divided into logical banks.

In a 16-bit system, each of the logical banks contains 16 memory chips plus 2 organizer chips for the parity bits. An 8-bit system will use 8 memory chips plus 1 organizer. That way each bank can send 16 bits, one from each memory chip, onto the data bus at one time.

If there are empty rows of sockets on the board, you can upgrade the memory. For example, suppose you have 512K and you want to upgrade to 640K memory. The procedure is determined as follows:

1. Suppose your board has 9 sockets per row.
2. Because 1 chip is used for parity testing, 8 chips of actual memory are used per row.
3. 64K bits times 8 chips equals 64K per row.

4. 64K times 2 rows equals 128K added to the system.

5. 128K plus the original 512K equals 640K.

If the upgrade goes to 1MB of RAM, you need eighteen 256K RAM chips. If you want to downgrade the total system memory to 256K, pull two rows of existing 256K chips and fill all four rows with 64K chips. There is no physical difference between a chip used for parity and a chip used for RAM. Any RAM chip can be the organizer if it is installed in the ninth socket of the bank.

RAM chips are available in different speeds, according to how long it takes the chip to send a bit of information to the central processing unit. Chip speeds are measured in nanoseconds, or billionths of a second. The lower the number of nanoseconds, the faster the chip. In the higher-performance machines, the central processing unit needs chips that can deliver information fast. The CPU cannot be kept waiting for a slow RAM chip. The recommended speed for RAM chips in most 286 machines is 150 ns. The important things to remember about memory additions are the following:

1. *Capacity.*   For instance, in the preceding example you used 64K chips for upgrading to 640K, 256K chips for upgrading to 1MB.

2. *Number.*   Chips must be added in banks; in the preceding example you added 18 chips. You cannot add 9 now and 9 later.

3. *Speed.*   As mentioned, 150 ns or faster is needed for most 286 systems. A lower number of nanoseconds is a faster chip.

Programs are available that swap applications or TSRs in and out of the 640K working area. The swapping lets you switch between programs without exiting one and starting up another. When tasks are switched, the program saves a snapshot of the suspended program, and you work with the new task in the foreground. These products differ from true multitasking environments such as provided by Desqview or Microsoft Windows, which run several programs simultaneously.

System problems and solutions

Even a PC- or XT-class machine can use an EMS expanded-memory board that fits into an 8-bit slot. The board allows some improvement in performance for task-switching programs. You can use a hard disk for a slower but often satisfactory solution with a task switcher or EMS emulator. In most systems, if you use hard disk swapping without adding memory, you might find it too slow. A better solution is to combine these programs with an expanded-memory board. In a 386 system it is best to use as much as possible of the extended RAM, on the motherboard or in a 32-bit memory slot, instead of a slower expansion-board slot. A 386 memory manager will allow EMS access, and a task switcher can be used to make sure all of the RAM is fully used.

Initial checks

When you first turn the power on, check for any indication of power. This check should include the screen display, beep sounds, and disk drive lights. If these seem to be normal, turn off power to the computer, remove the case, and unplug the power cables (on the 5150 PC, these are labeled P8, P9, P10, and P11). Then reapply power and check plug P9 for +5 V on pins 4, 5, and 6; −5 V on pin 3. Check plug P8 for +12 V on pin 3 and −12 V on pin 4. Check plugs P10 and P11 for +12 V on pin 1 and +5 V on pin 4. If all of these voltages are missing, check for an open fuse. The fuse is usually part of the power supply unit.

If one or more voltages are in error, the problem is probably in the power supply or power supply cables. If all the voltages test good at the plug pins, reconnect the power plugs to the system board. Remove all of the expansion cards, turn power back on and recheck the voltages on the same plug pins tested earlier. If the voltages are still present, turn off the power and reinstall one of the expansion cards. Turn power back on and retest the power pins for the proper voltages. If they still appear to be good, turn power off and install another card. Turn power on and test all voltages. If the test passes, continue on with another card. Using the preceding procedure, you can find the card that causes the power failure will most likely have a component or circuit board failure.

Visually check for anything that could cause a short on that adapter card; look for a loose wire or piece of loose solder. Turn the card over and shake it.

System board problems

System board failures can be caused by the loss of the +5 V power or by the loss of clock pulses. An absent, jittery, or noisy clock signal can affect the rest of the system. A faulty clock signal can cause marginal operations or transient problems that can be difficult to find. A faulty clock signal can require the testing of power, clock, ROM, RAM, I/O ports, interrupts, and bus control logic.

The system board (Fig. 3-8) can be divided into two sections or functional areas. One will contain the CPU (central processing unit) circuitry, which includes the microprocessor, the arithmetic processor (if used), the clock generator, bus controller, and buffers (Fig. 3-9). The other section contains the peripheral I/O devices, RAM, and analog circuits.

Figure 3-10 shows the chip layout for the IBM PC system board. Figure 3-11 shows the pins for the 8088 microprocessor with normal voltage levels. Dynamic RAM is typically used in personal computers. Figures 3-12 and 3-13 show the procedures for removing and replacing the system board. Some system boards are fastened with button clips as well as screws. Figure 3-14 shows the type of plastic clip used.

Dynamic RAM chips

Whenever there is a need for RAM of about 4K or more, dynamic RAM (DRAM) is used. It takes up less circuit board area, uses less power, and costs less than static RAM.

Static RAMs use flip-flop circuits that can store a high or low voltage level (1 or 0 bit), and they hold this level as long as power is applied to the chip. Dynamic RAMs use the capacitance on the gates of FETs (field-effect transistors) that are connected together. The logic states are held as a charge or a noncharge in the capacitance between the FET gates and ground. After a logic state is established, a static RAM holds the state as long as it is powered. In a dynamic RAM, the charge on the capacitors will

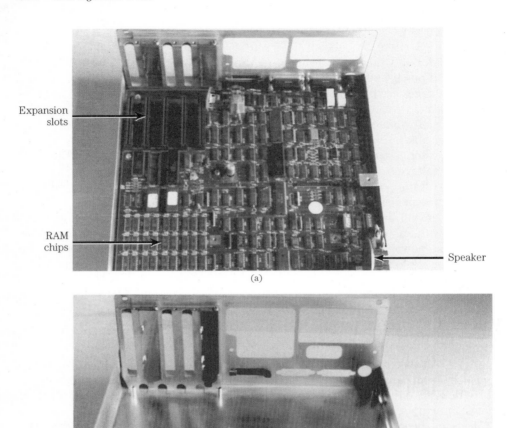

Expansion
slots

RAM
chips

Speaker

(a)

(b)

3-8 An XT system board installed on system chassis (A). A system chassis with system board removed. Notice the speaker mounted to the chassis and the studs that are used to hold system board (B).

leak off in a short time unless it is refreshed. The dynamic bits are recharged every few milliseconds using special circuits such as refresh counters that readdress the storage bits. Refreshing starts at the bottom row of memory and continues to the top row.

The 4116 RAM

The 4116 RAM chip was used in some early PCs (Fig. 3-15) and was a 16Kb chip. The actual memory matrix has 128 rows and 128 columns (Fig. 3-16). The 16 address

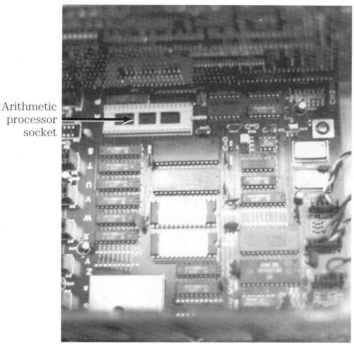

3-9 A close-up of the system board showing arithmetic processor socket.

bits are usually used in the following way. The two most significant bits are used as the chip select. The next seven most significant bits are used to address the 128 rows. The seven least significant bits address the 128 columns. Each bit cell can be addressed by first addressing a row and then addressing a column.

The 4116 chip is used in groups of eight, and these groups are wired in parallel (Fig. 3-17). Each byte is spread over the eight chips, with one bit in a corresponding location in all eight chips. The array of eight chips provides a total of 16,384 total bytes, or 16K. The eight chips are usually numbered 0 to 7.

See Fig. 3-18 for a top view of the chip. Both TTL (transistor-transistor logic) logic circuits and MOS (metal-oxide semiconductor) logic circuits are used on this chip. The TTL circuits are used for input and output functions, and the MOS circuits are used in the memory matrix to store the logic states. The TTL circuits are powered with +5 V at pin 9 and −5 V at pin 1. The MOS circuits are +12 V at pin 8 and ground is pin 16. The seven address lines are A6 to A0. These lines are in parallel with all of the address lines for the rest of the chips in the 16K array. Because a total of 14 address bits are needed to address the memory matrix (seven bits for the 128 rows and seven bits for the 128 columns), a multiplexing scheme is used.

Two signals are used in the multiplexing technique. Pin 4 uses an input called *RAS (row address strobe) and pin 15 uses another input called *CAS (column address

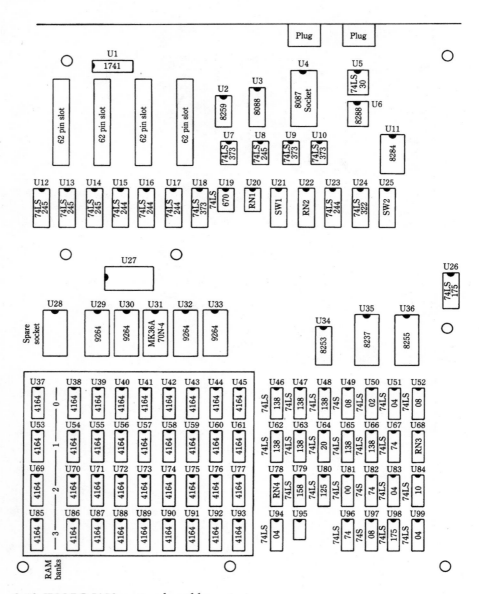

3-10 IBM PC 5150 system board layout.

strobe) (Fig. 3-19). Multiplex chips receive the 14 address bits and separate them into two sets of bits (Fig. 3-20). Then they send the two sets alternately to the array. The multiplexer completes this operation in time sync with the CAS signals. The pin called *WE (write enable) works the read-write function. The contents of the eight bits are either read out or loaded with data.

U3
8088

Top view

L	0 V	1 GND		V_{cc} 40	+5 V	H
P	.8 V ←	2 A14		A15 39	2.9 V →	P
P	1.6 V ←	3 A13		A16/S3 38	1.7 V →	P
P	2.0 V ←	4 A12		A17/S4 37	3.6 V →	P
P	2.0 V ←	5 A11		A18/S5 36	1.4 V →	P
P	2.8 V ←	6 A10		A19/S6 35	1.0 V →	P
P	.1 V ←	7 A9		SS0 34	1.0 V	H
P	4.0 V ←	8 A8		MN/*MX 33	4.0 V ←	L
P	2.7 V ↔	9 A7 – D7		*RD 32	3.5 V →	P
P	2.0 V ↔	10 A6 – D6		HOLD (RQ/GTO) 31	+5 V	H
P	1.8 V ↔	11 A5 – D5		HLDA (RQ/GT1) 30	5.0 V	H
P	2.3 V ↔	12 A4 – D4		*WR (LOCK) 29	4.0 V →	P
P	2.1 V ↔	13 A3-D3		IO/*M (*S2) 28	4.7 V →	P
P	1.5 V ↔	14 A2-D2		DT/*R (*S1) 27	3.2 V →	P
P	2.2 V ↔	15 A1-D1		*DEN (*SO) 26	3.2 V →	P
P	1.5 V ↔	16 A0-D0		(QSO) ALE 25	.4 V →	P
L	.15 V →	17 NMI		(QS1) *INTA 24	.2 V →	P
L	.1 V	18 INTR		*TEST 23	5.0 V	H
P	1.8 V	19 CLK		READY 22	4.0 V ←	P
L	0 V	20 GND		RESET 21	.2 V ←	L

P = Pulse

Notes: Multiplexed data lines are A7 – D7 through A0 – D0, *H* indicates a steady high level and *L* indicates a steady low level. *P* indicates a pulsed condition.

Pinouts for the 8088 microprocessor used in the IBM PC and compatibles. A top view chart such as this can be used for troubleshooting the microprocessor chip.

3-11 An IBM PC 5150. Pinouts for the 8088 microprocessor used in the IBM PC and compatibles. A top-view chart such as the one shown can be used for troubleshooting the microprocessor chip.

Set the Power switch on the system unit to Off.

↓

Set the Power switches on all attached devices to Off.

↓

Unplug the power cord of the system unit from the outlet.

↓

Disconnect all cables from the rear of the system unit.

↓

Remove the cover of the system unit.

↓

Remove all expansion boards.

↓

Disconnect the system board power connectors.

↓

Remove the speaker, keylock, serial, parallel, hard, and floppy disk connectors.

↓

Remove the system board mounting screws.

↓

Slide the system board away from the power supply
until the standoffs can be lifted from the mounting slots.

↓

Lift the system board up and out of the system unit.

3-12 System board removal.

Insert the system board standoffs into the mounting slots.

↓

Slide the system board toward the power supply until
the holes for the mounting screws are aligned.

↓

Install the system board mounting screws.

↓

Install the speaker, keylock, serial, parallel, hard, and floppy disk connectors.

↓

Install the expansion boards.

↓

Install any disk controller cables and
the system board power connectors.

↓

Install the cover of the system unit.

↓

Connect all cables to the rear of the system unit.

3-13 System board replacement.

Push in here to release board

3-14 Button clip used to
hold some system boards.

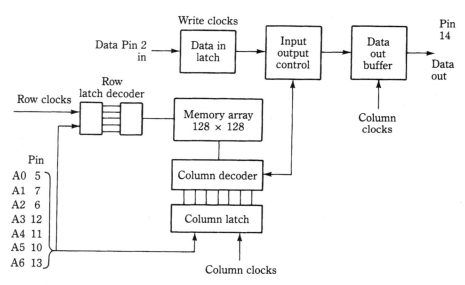

3-15 Block diagram of 4116 RAM.

Multiplexing saves seven pins on the chip. There are only two data pins used on a chip—Data In, which is pin 2, and Data Out, which is pin 14.

RAM chip evolution

The 16K 4116 RAM chip has been replaced by other more dense chips. One replacement is the 64K 4164 that uses the same 16-pin chip as the 4116. The 4164 uses a 256×256 bit (Fig. 3-21) cell matrix and has only two power pins (8 and 16); four power inputs (1, 8, 9, and 160) are used in the 4116. Pin 1 is not connected, and pin 9 is used as an additional address pin, A7 for the 64K bits.

The 41256 chip, shown in Fig. 3-22, has 262,144 bit cells. This fourfold density increase is achieved by doubling the numbers of rows and columns with a matrix of 512 rows and 512 columns. The 41256 is similar to the 4164 and the 4116 in the way they use the *RAS input pin 4, the *CAS input pin 15, and the *WE input pin 3. The main differences are the number of address lines. The 4116 uses A6 through A0 to input 14 multiplexer address bits, 7 at a time. The 4164 uses A7 through A0 to input 16 multiplexed address bits, 8 at a time. The 41256 needs A8 through A0 to input 18 multiplexed address bits, 9 at a time. The 41256 uses pin 1 that was not connected in the 4164, as

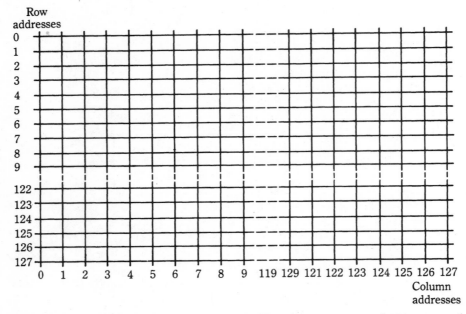

3-16 The 4116 16K RAM chip is made up of a memory matrix of 128 rows and 128 columns of bit locations.

address bit A8 (Fig. 3-23). These RAMs all use the same package, but the 1MB RAMs use a different package.

1MB and larger RAMs

The 1MB RAM uses a matrix of 1024 × 1024 (Table 3-2). A set of eight can provide a million bytes of dynamic memory. To address this set of chips, 20 address bits are needed. The 1MB chips use 10 pins (A9–A0) for multiplexing the 20 address bits. One

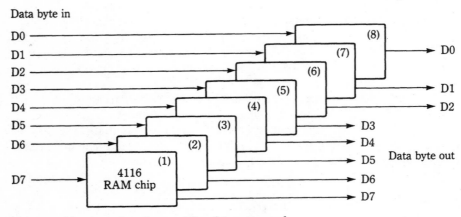

3-17 In order to make a byte, eight chips are used.

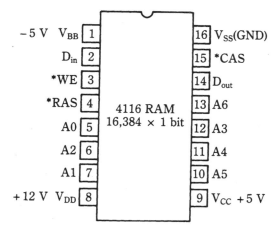

3-18 4116 RAM chip with 16K individual bits.
It uses a 16-pin DIP (dual inline package).

type of package that is used is a 26-pin SMD (surface-mounted device) where three pins on each side of the pin arrangement are removed from the center. The removal of pins provides space for additional components or circuit paths. In the larger chips, the bit matrixes are divided into several sections. The sense amplifiers aid in the refreshing operation that must be performed every few milliseconds.

Dynamic RAM chips have grown to a wide selection of 4 and 16Mb chips and even 256Mb and 1Gb chips are being produced. Figure 3-24 shows how a 1Gb is put together. The chip is built up with 32Mb memory arrays which are connected as shown.

Testing memory chips

Memory chips use MOS circuits for the memory cells and are sensitive to static electricity. Use a wrist strap connected to ground and other precautions to avoid damage due to static electricity. Handle memory chips carefully.

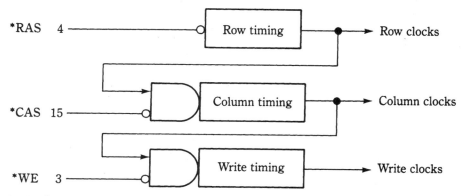

3-19 Three timing signals are applied to each 4116 RAM at pins 4, 15, and 3.

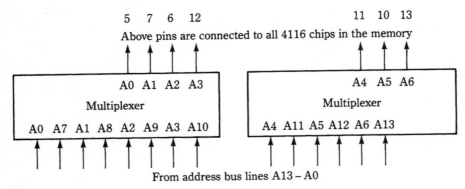

5   7   6   12   11   10   13

Above pins are connected to all 4116 chips in the memory

A0 A1 A2 A3   A4 A5 A6

Multiplexer   Multiplexer

A0 A7 A1 A8 A2 A9 A3 A10   A4 A11 A5 A12 A6 A13

From address bus lines A13 – A0

3-20 The multiplexer chips receive 14 bits from the address bus. During the 4116 *RAS time, they send 7 bits (A6–A0) to the 4116s. During the 4116 *CAS time, they send the other 7 bits A13–A7 to the RAM chips.

Figure 3-25 shows a top view of a 4164 chip with the typical voltages or logic states present at each pin. Use this drawing as a test-point chart. You can use a logic probe or VOM (volt-ohm-milliammeter) to check at each pin.

A bad reading will usually indicate a problem with the chip if the signal is an output. If a bad reading is found at an input, it is more likely that the trouble is due to the circuit providing the input, unless the signal is being shorted by the memory chip. Eight chips are usually in a set to provide a byte, but there might be a ninth chip that is used as a

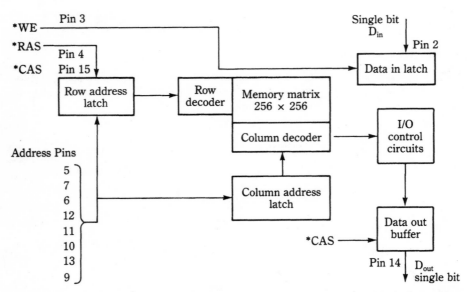

3-21 In the 4164 memory chip, the eight-row and eight-column address bits alternately enter through the eight address pins. *RAS is used to strobe the row address into a latch, and *CAS will strobe the column address into another latch.

4116 RAM
64 × 128 cell array
128 sense-refresh amps
64 × 128 cell array

4164 RAM
128 × 256 cell array
256 sense-refresh amps
128 × 256 cell array

41256 RAM	
128 × 256	128 × 256
256 sense amps	256 sense amps
128 × 256	128 × 256
128 × 256	128 × 256
256 sense amps	256 sense amps
128 × 256	128 × 256

3-22 The RAM cell arrays in the dynamic chips use amplifiers for refreshing. Note that the 41256 is like four 4164 chips.

		4164			
NC	1		16	V_{ss}	
D_{in}	2		15	*CAS	
*WE	3		1	D_{out}	
*RAS	4		13	A6	
A0	5		12	A3	
A2	6		11	A4	
A1	7		10	A5	
V_{DD}	8		9	A7	

		41256			
A8	1		16	V_{ss}	
D_{in}	2		15	*CAS	
*WE	3		14	D_{out}	
*RAS	4		13	A6	
A0	5		12	A3	
A2	6		11	A4	
A1	7		10	A5	
V_{DD}	8		9	A7	

3-23 4164 and 41256 pinout. The only pin difference is the extra address bit on the 41256.

controller of the set or as a parity-checking bit. *Parity checking* involves counting the bit states and determining if the total is odd or even. This total is then compared with a stored total to determine if a bit was lost during an operation.

When a RAM or ROM fails, there is usually a short or open somewhere in one of the internal circuits. The short or open causes a problem in storing data when a program is being run and you must locate the bad chip and change it to restore proper operation. In some cases, a short might produce some smoke from the chip and the chip will appear charred or visually damaged, but most of the time the bad chip looks the same as the other chips. Usually only one chip at a time is defective, although multiple-chip failures can happen if there is a chain reaction from a problem such as a power supply problem.

Table 3-2. Memory chip differences

Chip number	4116	4164	41256	411024
Total bits	16K	64K	256K	1024K
Bit array	128 × 128	256 × 256	512 × 512	1024 × 1024

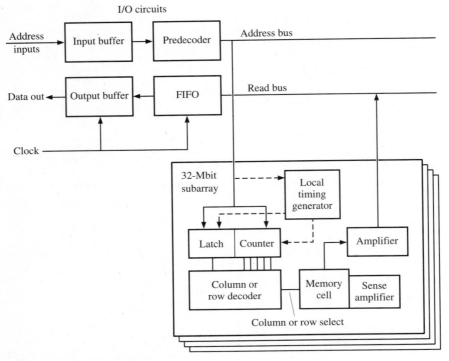

3-24 1Gb memory chip, 64M words by 16 bits.

A defective memory chip will usually cause a problem in running part of a program. A shorted cell location could cause faulty data or addressing to occur. The results could be minor, such as a slight error in calculations, or the program might not run at all.

Diagnostic programs

Many diagnostic programs exist for testing memory because memory problems are common failures. Most computers use an automatic memory diagnostic run whenever

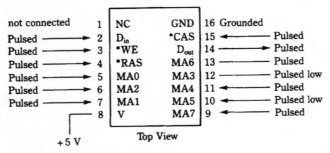

3-25 Pin diagram of 4164 RAM chip with typical voltage states that can be used for troubleshooting.

the computer is booted up. This type of test program will often identify a bad memory chip and display some sort of memory location number for the bad chip on the screen (Fig. 3-26).

The following diagnostic scheme is typical. The microprocessor will write to all of the RAM locations; then it will read all the locations to check that the data was properly loaded. If the read check is okay, the memory location passes the test. (See Fig. 3-27.) If the read check indicates a bad bit location, then the chip should be replaced as shown in Fig. 3-28.

RAM chip testers

RAM chip testers use test algorithms similar to those used in advanced diagnostic software. One design uses an 8088 processor to run a program that includes routines to test the chip peripheral circuitry in addition to a routine that writes, reads, and refreshes every memory cell several times.

The chip to be tested is placed in a ZIF (zero-insertion force) socket. The test results are displayed and indicate the type of chip and its condition. There are also current limiters to protect the chip and prevent any damage if the chip is placed in backward.

A speed verifier test can be used for sorting chips according to their true speeds. When a bank of memory chips fails, the speed test can be used to find a slow chip that might be causing the failure.

The auto loop testing option is useful for detecting intermittent temperature and time-related problems in memory chips. It automatically retests the chip, using different data patterns, until the chip is removed. Detected errors are stored on the display.

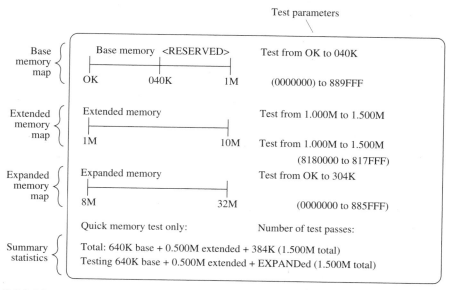

3-26 Memory test screen.

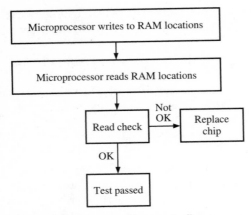

3-27 Basic memory diagnostic flow.

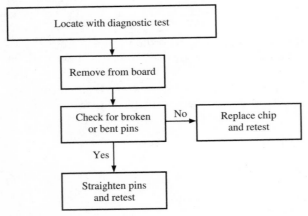

3-28 Replacing a bad chip.

The clock

The computer clock acts as the timekeeper for all processing. It runs at an assigned frequency, and all operations are done in step with the clock. The clock consists of a crystal-controlled oscillator circuit. A crystal oscillator produces a continuous sine-wave output. This sine wave is converted to a square wave for the digital circuits that need to use it. The square-wave pulses provide the quickly rising and falling edges needed to trigger events. The higher the clock frequency, the faster the data processing. The processing frequency derives from the clock frequency.

In the older IBM PCs, the clock components are part of the clock generator chip (U11-8284) (Fig. 3-29). This chip divides the crystal frequency to provide the frequencies needed.

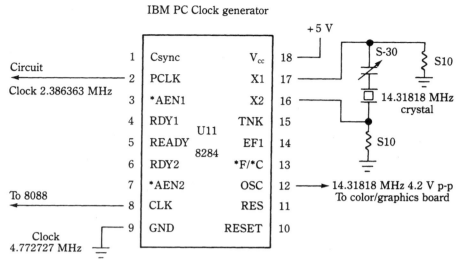

3-29 Clock generation.

The 8284 clock generator has the crystal connected across pins 16 and 17. The crystal used in the PC is cut to run at 14.31818 MHz. When power is applied to the crystal, the effect of the voltage across the crystal causes it to oscillate at this frequency, which is called the *master frequency*. The clock generator circuitry divides this master frequency by 3 to produce the system operating frequency of 4.772727 MHz. Computers that run at a high frequency use a faster crystal.

The 4.772727-MHz signal is sent to the processor, which is an 8088 in the older IBM PC. It is also available on the expansion connectors. The 8284 also divides the master frequency by 6 to provide a frequency of 2.386363 MHz. This signal is sent to a 74LS175 that divides this frequency by 2. This 1.1931817-MHz frequency is used to drive the 8253 programmable interrupt timer chip.

In newer systems, the clock is usually part of the floppy and hard disk controller chip which is mounted on the system board. An example of this chip is the Western Digital 76C20. The operation of the clock circuits will be similar to that previously described but at the higher speeds that these chips use.

The keyboard

The IBM PC family and its clones use a separate encoded keyboard connected to the system unit. The encoded keyboard for the IBM personal computer has five connections on the output plug (Fig. 3-30). Two of these provide the power (+5 V and ground). The other three provide the interface between the keyboard and the system board.

In the IBM keyboard, pressing a key causes the encoded circuits to generate the ASCII (American Standard Code for Information Interchange) code for the key. The

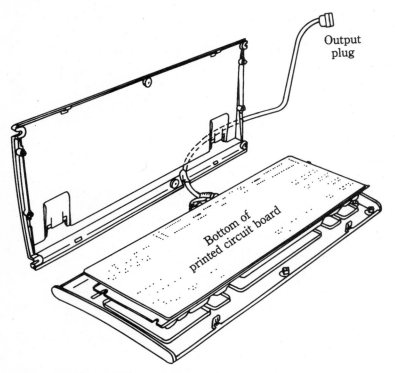

Output
plug

Bottom of
printed circuit board

3-30 Keyboard with bottom removed.

keyboard feeds its ASCII output to the system unit. The keyboard uses a keyboard processor, an 8048 microprocessor chip. The 8048 chip is an 8-bit processor and contains 2K of ROM. The ROM is preloaded with a character code known as a *scan code.*

The processor uses a row-scanning technique to monitor the keyboard matrix. Each key makes a connection at one of the row-column intersections when depressed. The 8048 processor scans the rows for key strikes by sending a high-level logic signal to each of the columns, one at a time. It scans the matrix once every 5 ms (milliseconds).

The 8048 will receive a high-level logic signal from each row if a key in that row has not been pressed. The signals are stored in the scanning buffer resistor in the 8048.

If a key is pressed, then the intersection connection is made and a low is received. The 8048 matches the column that is being scanned with the row that changed state, which sets the intersection point. The 8048 then looks up the character for this key in its character ROM. The coded-bit pattern for the character is then sent out through the keyboard cable to the system board. Inside the keyboard is a printed circuit board with the row-column matrix along with some electronic components including the IC chips and supporting discrete parts (Fig. 3-31). The main circuit chip is the 8048 processor that has internal clock circuits. The clock crystal generates the timing for the processor, which is also sent to the system board. The clock output synchronizes the keyboard timing with the system board.

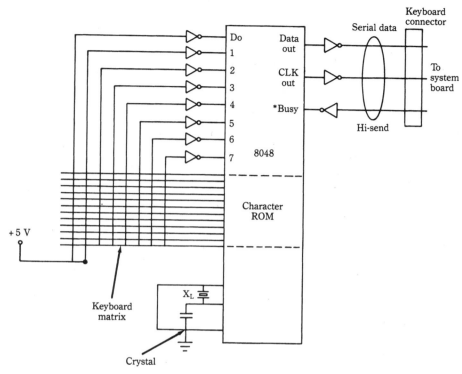

3-31 IBM PC keyboard.

The matrix is divided into rows and columns. The rows are held in the high state by +5 V through a pull-up resistor. The columns use inverter amplifiers to couple the outputs to the 8048 buffer register. The rows are constantly scanned by the 8048 internal circuits. If a key is not pressed, the column outputs are all high. The set of bits leaves the 8048 and is input to the main board in a serial form.

The data output line and the clock output line are sent to a NOT gate before going to the main board. The gate inverts the output and also amplifies it so it can drive the system board circuits.

A BUSY line goes from the system board to the keyboard. It also uses an inverter. The BUSY signal tells the 8048 when it can send data because the system board might be busy and not able to accept data at that time.

Debouncing

The mechanical contact (Fig. 3-32) that occurs when you strike a key is not perfect. As you press the key and the key closes the metallic connection, there is a condition of oscillation for a few milliseconds until the connection is finalized. During this time, the key-switch voltage is unstable and bounces between the two switching voltages. The same type of oscillations occur when you release the key.

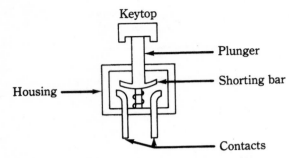

3-32 Typical key-switch construction.

In nonencoded keyboards, a resistor and capacitor are connected as a filter to reduce the oscillations and bouncing effect. In the encoded keyboards, the IBM PC's and its clones, a delay of a few milliseconds is used before the key strike is encoded. The delay is accomplished with a programmed loop that inserts the delay. This inhibiting of the key action during the switch bouncing is called *debouncing.* The 8048 micro-processor performs this debouncing by generating an interrupt during the time the key-board voltage is bouncing.

Keyboard/system board operation

The encoded keyboard signals are sent to the system board as shown in Figs. 3-33 and 3-34. The keyboard output is a serial data signal that is sent to the system board circuits. A busy signal is used to control when the keyboard can send keyboard bits to the system board. The keyboard bits are sent in a serial format with the least significant bit sent first and the most significant bit of the data byte sent last.

The serial data is sent to a serial-to-parallel 74LS322 register that changes the serial format to parallel. The 74LS322 also connects to a dual-D flip-flop, the 74LS74. The latched clock signal from the keyboard is sent from the 74LS175 to the serial-parallel register and the 74LS74 to synchronize these chips with the keyboard.

The 74LS74 flip-flop is used to generate an interrupt request to the 8259 program-mable interrupt controller. This chip generates an output signal that interrupts the main processor (the 8088). The 74LS322 shift register sends its parallel bits to one of the ports of the 8255 I/O chip. The parallel bits are then sent to the system data bus.

These bits, which hold the keyboard characters, are then read by the 8088 proces-sor and stored in the video RAM section of memory. They can then be used by the video display system and sent to the monitor or to the printer for hard copy output.

Audio outputs

Several types of audio outputs are available from personal computers. The sounds are usually created in software. The IBM PCs and most clones have their own speaker and audio circuits (Fig. 3-35). The speaker is usually located on or close to the front panel as shown in Fig. 3-36.

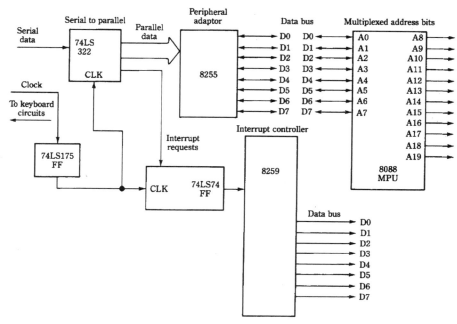

3-33 Keyboard/system board processing.

3-34 End view of 486 board showing keyboard connector.

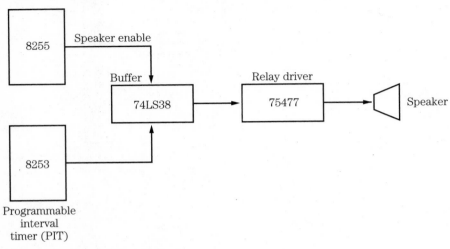

Programmable
peripheral
interface (PPI)

8255

Speaker enable

Buffer

74LS38

Relay driver

75477

Speaker

8253

Programmable
interval
timer (PIT)

3-35 Audio driver circuit.

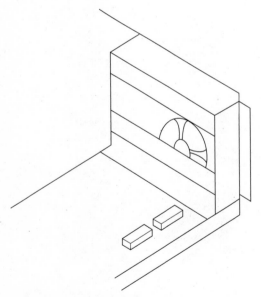

3-36(A) Speaker location on front panel.

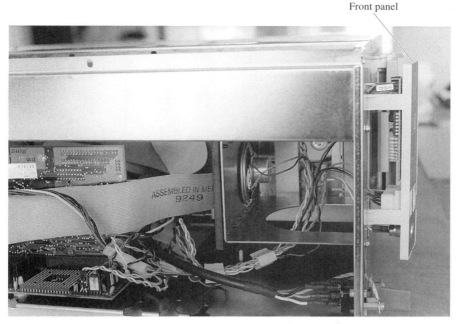

Front panel

3-36(B) Speaker location in 486 tower system.

The audio circuit that responds to the program usually uses four chips. The speaker is typically driven by a 75477 relay driver chip. This chip amplifies the incoming bit signals so the signals can be applied to the speaker cone. Figure 3-37 shows the procedure for removing the speaker. By controlling the frequency of the movement you can produce a range of sounds. Basic can be used to produce sounds up to about 1000 Hz, and machine language can be used to produce sounds up to 3000 Hz.

An 8255 PPI (programmable peripheral interface) chip provides one of its output port pins (pin 1) for switching the audio on and off. A high-level signal turns the speaker system on and a low turns it off. The signal acts under software control, and it is called the *speaker enable.* This signal is connected to a 74LS38 NAND buffer.

Another signal from an 8253 PIT (programmable interval timer) also is sent to the NAND buffer. This signal is also under software control. If the two signals are both true, the buffer will provide an output to the relay driver. The speaker then responds to the buffer output. The audio frequencies generated will be a result of the signals from the PPI and the output of the PIT.

Sound cards

Add-on sound cards allow PCs to speak and provide sound effects as well as play music. Cards with basic capabilities are available for a few hundred dollars and this can double for those with advanced capabilities. Generally, 16-bit sound cards have replaced the older 8-bit models. These bits refer to the size of each digital sample used when the

Set the system unit Power switch to Off.

↓

Remove the system unit power cord from the outlet.

↓

Remove the cover of the system unit.

↓

Disconnect the speaker leads.

↓

Remove the speaker mounting screws.

↓

Remove the speaker.

3-37 Speaker removal.

analog voltages of sound are turned into digital signals the PC can understand and then back to analog when you need to hear them.

Cache memory

Caches are high-speed buffer memories that hold the most frequently used instructions and data for quick access by the microprocessor. They are used in 386, 486, and Pentium systems. Caches operate on the locality of memory references. Computer programs tend to execute instructions stored in close proximity to each other. Programs also exhibit a locality in that they tend to access a small subset of the entire data set a number of times in any time period.

The cache hardware tracks the data accessed by the processor and saves it with the likelihood that it will be requested again. Typically, the cache memory is 20 to 1000 times smaller in size than the system memory and 5 to 20 times faster.

Cache memories have been used in many computers. A cache memory was used in the IBM System 360 as well as the DEC PDP-11/70. They are now used in 386, 486, and Pentium systems.

The cache memory is made up of a number of lines or blocks that can hold the contents of the corresponding elements of the system memory. When the processor issues a memory reference, it is checked with the contents of the cache. If the data is already in the cache because of a previous access to system memory, it is sent back to the processor in a process called a *cache hit*. A *cache miss* requires that the data be fetched from the system memory and sent to the cache.

The cache is made up of two parts. One memory array is for the cached data, and each element in the array is a cache line or block. The other array is used for the cache directory. The memory addresses from the processor have fields: tag, index, and byte number. The index allows access to both the directory and data arrays.

The contents of a previously stored tag are compared with the present tag. A match indicates a hit, and a nonmatch indicates a miss. In a miss, the address is forwarded to the system memory and the data returned from memory overwrites the data in the cache. The tag in the directory is also updated.

SIMM memory

Most 386 and 486 systems have at least 2MB of factory-installed memory. (See Fig. 3-38 and Table 3-3.) By adding single inline memory modules (SIMMs) (Fig. 3-39), you can usually increase the system board memory to at least 16MB. In a 16MB system the amount of memory on the system board and any memory add-in boards must total 16MB or less. If you have the maximum of 16MB on the system board, you cannot add a memory add-in board.

Most systems treat all system board memory above 1MB as extended memory. If you install a memory board, you need to allocate its memory as extended or expanded, depending on the board type.

By default, the system uses 640K of conventional (base) memory. You can reset the conventional memory to 512K if the application software requires it. To do this, use the System Setup program.

Installing SIMM memory

A 386 or 486 system board has sets of sockets called *banks* (Figs. 3-40 and 3-41). Each bank has sockets for the SIMMs. Bank 0 is always the first bank. Each bank can hold 256K, 1MB, 4MB, 8MB, 16MB, or 32MB SIMMs. Table 3-4 shows some typical valid

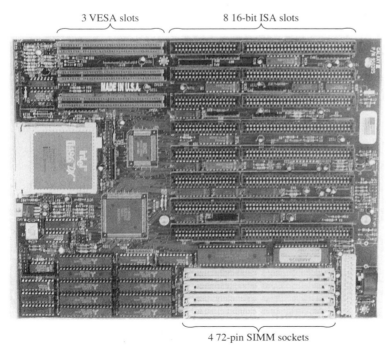

3-38 A 486 system board with room for 1 to 128MB of memory.

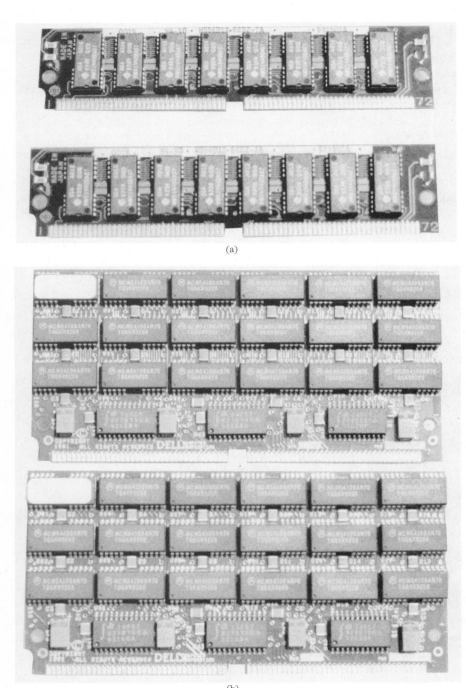

(a)

(b)

3-39 SIMM memory. MB module (A). 8MB module (B).

Table 3-3. Typical 486 memory module requirements

RAM	Module type	Memory modules	Speed, nanoseconds
System	72-pin SIMM	2Mb	70
		4Mb	
		8Mb	
	30-pin SIMM*	1Mb	80
		4Mb	
Video	20-pin DRAM	256K × 4	80

*Some 30-pin SIMMs are taller than others and can interface with the lower adapter card slot. Be sure that the lower adapter card does not touch the SIMM modules.

SIMM configurations for a system with two SIMMs in each bank. Table 3-5 shows a two-bank system for a total memory of up to 32MB. Sockets are available for user-upgradable video memory as shown in Fig. 3-42.

Changing SIMMs

Before handling SIMMs or other components, discharge any static electricity by touching a ground surface, such as a metal portion of your computer chassis. You must fill the banks in sequence: first install SIMMs in bank 0, then bank 1, and then bank 2. Do not mix SIMMs; you cannot put a 1MB SIMM in one socket of a bank and a 4MB SIMM in the other. Also, both sockets of a bank must be either full or empty.

To remove existing SIMMs and replace them, turn off the system and remove the system-unit cover, locate the SIMMs (Fig. 3-43), and carefully pull the retaining clips away from the edge of the last SIMM installed (Fig. 3-44). You might need a small pencil-type screwdriver to grasp the edges. Then, push the SIMM slightly forward and pull the SIMM out of its socket.

To install SIMMs, slide the SIMM into the empty socket on the system board. Push carefully until it is fully seated. Sometimes, you have to work one end in and then the other end of the SIMM. Then, push the SIMM back until it snaps into place (Fig. 3-45).

Changing the math coprocessor

A math coprocessor is a specialized chip that performs processor-intensive functions, allowing the main system processor to handle system functions, and the coprocessor performs these functions. Not all application software programs support a math coprocessor, and you might need to configure some programs to support the coprocessor.

Most XT, AT, and 386 computers provide a socket for a math coprocessor. The socket for the coprocessor chip is on the main board, usually next to or close to the main processor.

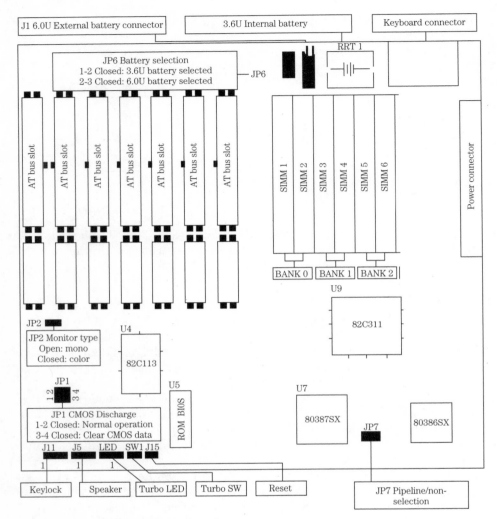

3-40(A) Layout of typical 386 board.

To install a coprocessor, you need to turn off the system and remove the system-unit cover. Discharge static electricity from yourself by touching a grounded surface such as the power supply. Locate the coprocessor socket on the system board. Align the coprocessor with the socket. Match pin 1 of the coprocessor (indicated by a dot or beveled corner) with the beveled-corner marking etched on the processor board.

Carefully insert the coprocessor into the socket. Do not bend any of the pins during insertion. Push down on the coprocessor until it is fully inserted in the socket.

To reinstall a board, line up the board with its slot. Lower the board until each of its edge connectors rests on an expansion-slot receptacle. Using evenly distributed pressure, push the board straight down until it is fully inserted in the slot.

3-40(B) SIMM banks in 486 tower system.

3-41 The video memory chips are in the left center on this 486 board.

3-42 Memory module sockets of SIMMs are used in the 486 system.

Changing video RAM

Many 386 and 486 computers come with 256K of video RAM. You can add RAM chips to the system board to upgrade the video RAM. The computer will support more video modes with more video RAM. In most computers, you will need 256K × 4, 70 or 80 ns, dynamic RAM (DRAM) chips, or SIMMs.

Table 3-4. SIMM configurations

	Bank 0		Bank 1		Bank 2	
Total memory, MB	SIMM0	SIMM1	SIMM2	SIMM3	SIMM4	SIMM5
2	1MB	1MB	Empty	Empty	Empty	Empty
3	256K	256K	256K	256K	1MB	1MB
4	1MB	1MB	1MB	1MB	Empty	Empty
4.5	1MB	1MB	1MB	1MB	256K	256K
6	1MB	1MB	1MB	1MB	1MB	2MB
8	4MB	4MB	Empty	Empty	Empty	Empty
9	256K	256K	256K	256K	4MB	4MB
12	1MB	2MB	1MB	1MB	4MB	4MB

Table 3-5. 1 to 32MB SIMMs (two-bank system)

Bank 0	Bank 1	Total memory, MB
256 × 9, 4 pieces	None	1
256K × 9, 4 pieces	256K × 9, 4 pieces	2
1M × 9, 4 pieces	None	4
256K × 9, 4 pieces	1M × 9, 4 pieces	5
1M × 9, 4 pieces	1M × 9, 4 pieces	8
4M × 9, 4 pieces	None	16
1M × 9, 4 pieces	4M × 9, 4 pieces	20
4M × 9, 4 pieces	4M × 9, 4 pieces	32

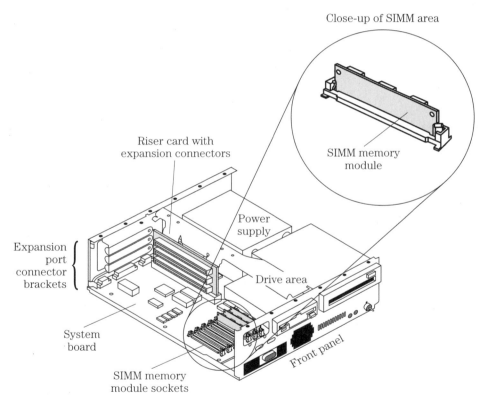

3-43 486 riser card–type system.

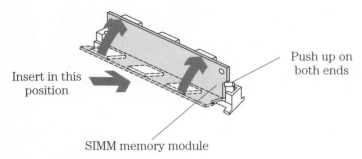

Insert in this
position

Push up on
both ends

SIMM memory module

3-44 Replacing a SIMM.

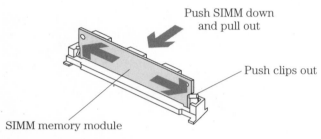

Push SIMM down
and pull out

Push clips out

SIMM memory module

3-45 Removing a SIMM.

To install the video RAM, turn off the system and remove the system-unit cover. Discharge yourself by touching a grounded surface on the computer. Locate the video RAM sockets on the system board (Fig. 3-46). Some sockets are partially obscured by the power supply, but removing the power supply is not necessary to install the RAM.

If you are installing chips on the system board, orient each chip so that the notched end of the chip aligns to the notched end of the socket.

Check that the new chips are fully seated, making certain that no pins are bent underneath the chips and that all the pins are inserted in the socket. To install SIMMs, slide the SIMM into the empty socket on the system board. Push carefully until it is fully

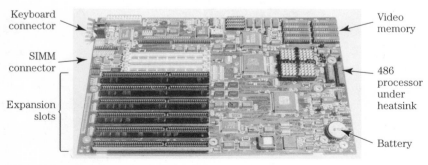

Keyboard
connector

SIMM
connector

Expansion
slots

Video
memory

486
processor
under
heatsink

Battery

3-46 486 system board.

seated. Sometimes, you have to work one end in and then the other end of the SIMM. Then, push the SIMM back until it snaps into place.

DOS will not run in high-memory area

If your computer has extended memory, the setup program should be set so DOS runs in the HMA (high-memory area). The HMA is the first 64K of extended memory. This arrangement conserves conventional memory for use by other programs. You can check that MS-DOS is running in the HMA by using the mem command in DOS 5.0 and up. If DOS is in the HMA, mem gives you the following message:

MS-DOS resident in High Memory Area

If your computer has extended memory, but DOS is not running in the HMA, the problem could be that your CONFIG.SYS file does not contain the correct commands, or that HIMEM is not correctly installed. HIMEM is the DOS extended-memory manager. Either HIMEM or another extended-memory manager is needed for DOS to use the HMA. To run DOS in the HMA you need the following:

1. The CONFIG.SYS file must contain a dos-high command.
2. The CONFIG.SYS file must contain a device command for the HIMEM memory manager (or another extended-memory manager), as shown in the following example:

   device=c:\dos\himem.sys

3. The device command must appear before the device commands for other memory managers.
4. The HIMEM.SYS file must be in the location specified by the device command in your CONFIG.SYS file.
5. HIMEM must be properly installed on your computer.

The setup program will install HIMEM and make any necessary changes. But, there are some hardware components that Setup cannot detect. Check your README.TXT file for information about installing any special hardware components. You can find the README.TXT file in the directory containing your DOS files, or, in 5.0, it is on Disk 5 (5¼-inch disks) or Disk 3 (3½-inch disks).

If your CONFIG.SYS file contains the correct commands, HIMEM is properly installed, and if DOS still does not run in the HMA, the memory configuration of your computer might not permit use of the HMA.

Shadow RAM

For the efficient execution of BIOS, it is better to execute the BIOS code through RAM rather than through the slower EPROMs. Many 486 systems provide a shadow RAM feature which, if enabled, allows the BIOS code to be executed from RAM instead of the BIOS EPROM. The software will transfer code stored in the BIOS EPROMs to the system RAM, before enabling the shadow RAM feature. This feature significantly improves the performance of BIOS-call-intensive applications. Performance improvements as high as 300 to 400 percent have been observed in benchmark tests on the shadow RAM. The shadow RAM feature is invoked by enabling the corresponding bits in the ROM enable register and the RAM mapping register.

When the shadow RAM feature is being utilized, then the RAM is mapped as shown in Fig. 3-47, overlapping or shadowing the EPROM area. In both cases, for accesses beyond the 1MB address range, the process is switched from real to protected mode from BIOS.

Adding cache memory

Many 486 personal computers come with 64K of secondary cache memory, on eight static RAM chips. The chips are located on the CPU board or the system board. You can replace these chips with four or eight chips to increase the amount of cache to 128 or 256K (Fig. 3-48).

Replacing the TAG RAM chip

TAG RAM is the part of cache that keeps track of the memory address stored in cache. This information is stored in its own chip. If the CPU is upgraded with a chip that generally runs at more than 50 MHz, the TAG RAM must be upgraded with a chip that has a 12 ns access time. Also, if you are upgrading to a 256K cache, you will need two TAG RAM chips. The TAG RAM can be removed and replaced in the same manner as the cache chips.

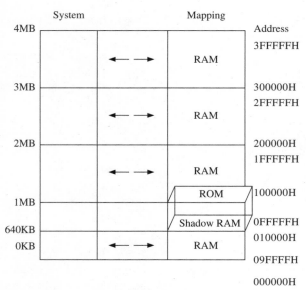

3-47 Memory map with shadow RAM.

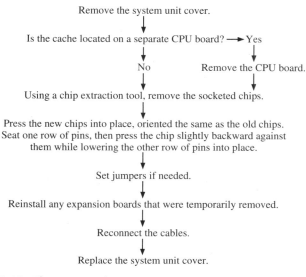

Remove the system unit cover.

Is the cache located on a separate CPU board? ⟶ Yes

No   Remove the CPU board.

Using a chip extraction tool, remove the socketed chips.

Press the new chips into place, oriented the same as the old chips.
Seat one row of pins, then press the chip slightly backward against
them while lowering the other row of pins into place.

Set jumpers if needed.

Reinstall any expansion boards that were temporarily removed.

Reconnect the cables.

Replace the system unit cover.

3-48 Changing cache memory.

EISA chips

The Intel 82350 EISA chip set is an EISA/ISA-compatible chip set used with the 386 or 486 CPU, 82385 cache controller, and 80387 numerics coprocessor. The 82350 chip set was designed for PCs and PC-compatible workstations. The chip set also supports a buffered configuration for extended architectures with SCSI and LAN functions on the system board. The chip set includes the 82352 EBB (EISA bus buffers), 82357 ISP (integrated system peripheral), and 82358 EISA EBC bus controller (Fig. 3-49).

The EBB supports three buses when used in an EISA system. The ISP handles the DMA functions of the system. It has seven 32-bit DMA channels, five 16-bit timer/counters, two 8-channel interrupt controllers, and provides the NMI (nonmaskable interrupt) control and generation. It also provides refresh address generation and keeps track of the refresh requests when the bus is not available.

The EBC acts as the EISA engine, because it works as an intelligent bus controller for the 8-, 16-, and 32-bit bus masters and slaves. It provides the state machine interface to host, ISA/EISA buses, and the other ICs in the chip set.

The EBC provides the interface to the 386/486 CPUs and the EISA bus. The EBC acts as a bridge between the EISA and ISA devices. The data bus size differences are handled by the EBC including byte assembly and disassembly. The 82355 BMIC (bus master interface chip) is a device for add-in cards that makes use of the EISA bus master capabilities.

ICs such as these support the EISA bus in 386 and 486 processors at various clock speeds. These chips use a CPU-to-memory protocol that allows the memory subsection to operate independently of the CPU clock. The CPU protocol is translated to this CPU speed independent of the protocol.

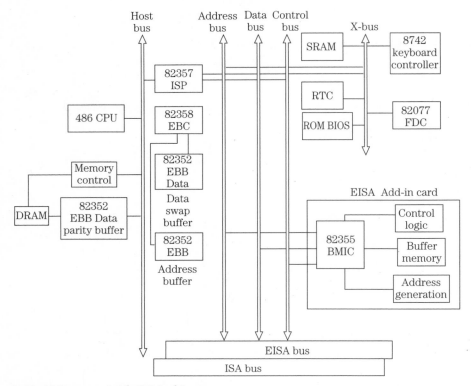

3-49 486 system with EISA chip set.

System components

A typical EISA system consists of the following components. The CPU will be either 386 or 486. A 386 system will use an external cache, usually a 82385 or 82395. The 486 CPU can be used by itself or with a second-level cache, usually a 485 turbocache. Both serial (two-bus) and parallel (single-bus) write-through cache configurations are supported. The 82359 DRAM controller provides the system address path and memory configuration registers and drives the EISA bus without any additional components. The 82353 ADP (advanced data path) chip provides the system data path and also drives the EISA bus directly. The data path is important to system performance. Each 82353 provides a 16-bit slice, and two 82353s are used in 32-bit systems.

The PST (programmable state tracker) is contained in two programmable logic devices. It monitors the CPU bus cycles and starts the memory read-write cycles when needed. The 82359 DRAM controller tells the PST how many wait states are needed and the PST generates a READY signal at the end of the cycle. Different PLDs are used for the different CPU/cache combinations.

The 82351 EISA LIOE (local I/O) chip provides a bidirectional parallel port, chip selects, reset, and other logic. The 82358 EISA bus controller (EBC) translates the

82359, EISA, and ISA protocols. It controls data steering in the 82353 and the address latches in the 82359.

The 82357 ISP (integrated system peripheral) provides EISA input-output functions such as DMA, timers, and interrupt controllers. The 82352 EISA bus buffer (EBB) buffers and latches the DMA address. An 82077 floppy disk controller provides a single chip implementation of the floppy disk interface. It uses a FIFO (first-in, first-out) to make up any differences in bus latencies, and it includes tape-drive support. An 8742 keyboard controller provides both keyboard and mouse support.

The EISA bus connects the masters to memory and acts as a path for CPU accesses to system resources. When the CPU accesses the system, the EBC converts the 82359 handshake into the EISA protocol. The EBC performs any required cycle control for byte assembly/disassembly and controls the latches and transceivers of the 82359 DRAM controller and the 82353 data path chip.

Memory control

Main memory is a critical resource in the system and is used by CPU and bus masters, which do not want to wait for memory to become available. The memory system needs to be optimized for this type of competitive environment. It should be responsive to the different characteristics of CPU, cache, and EISA bus masters. The 82359 DRAM controller is used with two 82353 advanced data path ICs and DRAM for a complete memory subsystem for 386 and 486 processors. The 82359 DRAM controller has over 100 programmable registers. These registers control memory mapping, cacheability, timing generation, and memory arbitration.

The memory system controls the DRAM address and row/column signal generation. It also controls the DRAM data routing. A dual-ported scheme is used so these components provide a CPU-only path to DRAM and a system bus–only path to DRAM. The memory implementation is based on a 128-bit-wide memory data path, although smaller memory widths can be used.

The 82359 supports 386 or 486 systems from 20 to 50 MHz. The memory width can be 32, 64, or 128 bits with a capacity of 1 to 256MB. The memory can be 64K, 256K, 1MB, or 4MB DRAMs. Typically, four or eight 36-bit SIMM slots are used with single or double density.

Dual porting

The dual-port memory architecture differs from previous implementations because the CPU has its own port to memory that is separate from the EISA port. When the CPU requires access to main memory, it can do so independently of EISA bus activity.

If the main memory is servicing the EISA bus at the time of the CPU memory request, the memory controller will start EISA arbitration on behalf of the CPU. Without dual porting, the CPU would have to go into EISA arbitration that could cause an 8-microsecond wait until memory is available.

3-50 486 processor board used in some 486 systems.

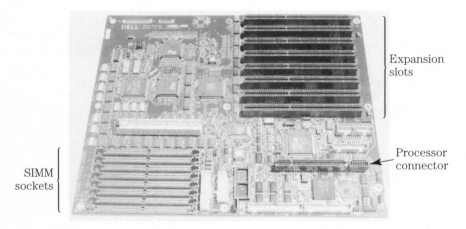

3-51 486 system board.

CPU interface	DRAM controller	Cache controller	VL-bus controller
Miscellaneous logic	AT controller	Local IDE	Keyboard controller
Power management	Clock control		

DMA controller	Interrupt controller	Timers	Real-time clock
Miscellaneous logic			

3-52(A) Chips and Technologies 486 chip set, CS 4041 and CS 4745.

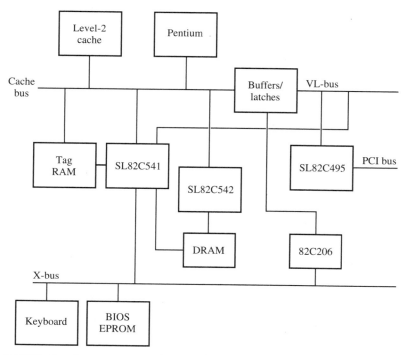

3-52(B) Pentium system with Symphony Labs chip set.

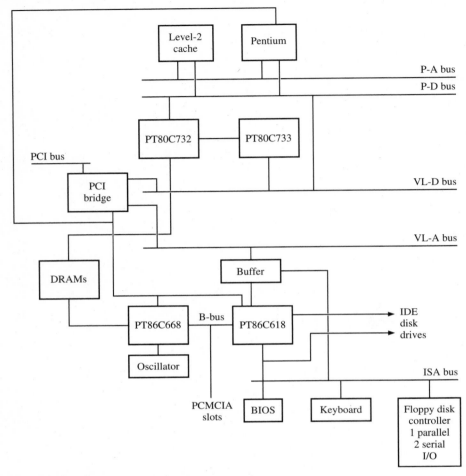

3-52(C) Pentium system with PicoPower chip sets.

The dual-port architecture improves CPU performance when the EISA bus is heavily used. In a single-port system, memory ownership is arbitrated along with EISA bus ownership, which produces a long latency of 8 ms from the time the CPU indicates that it needs memory until the EISA master actually releases the bus.

The dual-port architecture reduces this time by using separate paths to memory for EISA and for the CPU. The 82359 DRAM controller arbitrates the paths and allows the CPU to access memory, and an EISA master still has the EISA bus, which reduces the CPU access time.

Another advantage of the dual-port architecture is that EISA masters that talk to EISA memory do not affect the CPU. The CPU can access main memory concurrently with an EISA master accessing EISA resources, reducing memory latency even further.

Each memory cycle generated by the address controller chip latches 128 bits of memory data in two 82353 chips. Then, with the data latched, the 82353 chips multiplex the four words to the proper destination in a zero wait state. Because of the dual-port architecture, EISA bus activities can occur independent of CPU-to-memory activity.

Most high-performance systems use a memory burst-access scheme. The scheme includes the 486 CPU (Figs. 3-50 and 3-51), the 386 with 82395, and the 486 with 82485. The usual burst is 128 bits wide, and a bus with the same width allows reading the whole burst in one memory cycle, which results in a zero-wait-state burst. Using 1MB technology (256K × 4 DRAMs), a 128-bit memory bus requires a minimum of 4MB of memory in the system. If the memory array is only partially filled, the 82359 generates multiple memory cycles until the burst is completed. The memory controller integrates the state tracking function, accepts the CPU ADS input, and generates a READY output.

Other 486 and Pentium chip sets

In addition to the Intel chip sets, 486 and Pentium systems use integrated circuit chip sets from other manufacturers in order to reduce board space, connections, and cost. Figure 3-52(A) illustrates the functions of the Chips and Technologies two-chip set for the 486. Figure 3-52(B) shows a Pentium system with the Symphony Labs chip set, and Fig. 3-52(C) shows a Pentium system with the PicoPower chip sets.

4
CHAPTER

Diagnostic Hardware and Software

Successful and efficient repair of PCs begins with your knowledge of the diagnostic tools available and your ability to use them. In this chapter, you can learn about many of the tests you can use and about error codes that help you isolate problems.

Diagnostic tests

Two general types of computer-aided diagnostic tests are available to help you detect and isolate problems that might occur in the system.

1. An internal diagnostic test that runs power-up, reset, or self-test
2. A diskette diagnostic test that runs a series of test programs from the diskette (Fig. 4-1)

The internal diagnostic test runs automatically on power-up and checks the internal logic of the system. The test is usually known as the *POST* (power-on self-test). If this test runs successfully, a system message appears on the monitor and the system is ready for a command.

Error messages

If an error message appears as discussed in the following examples, one of the computer operational modes is not working. For example, if a disk drive fails, you would get a message number. In most cases you must find the cause of the error before you can continue. The error message should direct you to the problem. Some examples follow.

4-1(A) Typical diagnostics. Test programs on diskette.

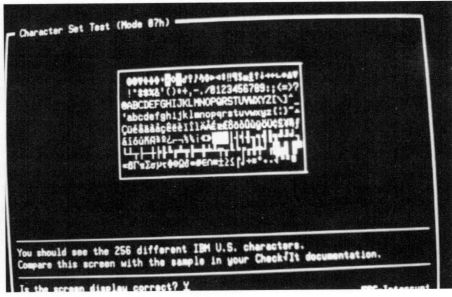

4-1(B) Screen for checking character set.

Self-test errors

In the IBM PC, if you turn off the computer, wait 10 seconds, and turn power back on, the system self-test will run. If no problems occur, the speaker will beep and the computer will try to boot the disk drive. If there is no disk in the floppy drive and no hard drive connected to the PC, the operating system will shift into ROM basic. A failure during the self-test will generate an error code message and there might be a beep.

An error code will appear if the switch settings do not match the installed components. The switch settings for the original IBM PC follow. These were copied by many clone makers during this era.

Switch block 1	*Function*
1, 7, 8	5¼-in disk drive setting
	1 on, 7 on, 8 on = No drives
	1 off, 7 on, 8 on = 1 drive
	1 off, 7 off, 8 on = 2 drives
2	Coprocessor
	2 on = no coprocessor installed
	2 off = coprocessor installed
3, 4	Memory setting
	3 off, 4 off = 64K memory or more
	3 on, 4 off = 48K memory
	3 off, 4 on = 32K memory
	3 on, 4 on = 16K memory
5, 6	Monitor type
	5 on, 6 on = no monitor
	5 off, 6 off = monochrome monitor/printer adapter or more than one monitor
	5 off, 6 on = 40 × 25 color monitor
	5 on, 6 off = 80 × 25 color monitor

Switch Block 2	
1–8	Memory size (used with SW1 3, 4)
	1, 2, 3, 4, 5 on, 6, 7, 8 off = 64K or less
	1, 3, 4, 5 on, 2, 6, 7, 8 off = 128K memory
	1, 2, 4, 5 on, 3, 6, 7, 8 off = 192K memory
	1, 4, 5 on, 2, 3, 6, 7, 8 off = 256K memory

If the system self-test finds a RAM failure, a four-character error code followed by the number 201 will appear in the top-left corner of the screen. The 201 indicates a RAM problem and the four-character code indicates the bank and row of the memory chips where the error occurred. The first two characters show the memory bank in which the failure occurred, and the last two characters show the bit position of the RAM failure in that particular bank of memory, as the following shows for the IBM PC 5150.

System board bank

System board bank	Failed chip	RAM error
00 - Bank 0	00 - parity	201
04 - Bank 1	01 - D0 chip	201
08 - Bank 2	02 - D1 chip	201
0C - Bank 3	04 - D2 chip	201
	08 - D3 chip	201
	10 - D4 chip	201
	20 - D5 chip	201
	40 - D6 chip	201
	80 - D7 chip	201

The preceding chart translates the error codes to malfunctioning bank and bit position. For example, if there is a failure in the bit 2 position of bank 2, a code 0804 201 should appear in the upper-left corner of the screen. If the third and fourth characters in the error code do not match the codes, swap the entire bank of RAM chips and try again. Another technique is to power-down and swap each chip in the bad bank one at a time with the same bit position chip in an adjacent bank. Then power-up and retest. When the error code shifts to the adjacent bank, the last chip swapped was bad.

Power-on checks

If your computer does not work when you try to start it up, go through the troubleshooting chart of Fig. 4-2. You can solve almost 90 percent of the failures that occur by going through this chart.

Error codes

If you see an error code on the screen, look it up on your error code list and follow the accompanying instructions. If the instructions fail to clear up the problem and the error pertains to a peripheral product in the system, such as a monochrome display adapter, check the manual that accompanies that product and try to isolate and correct the problem.

You should always write down the error code that you receive. In the event that the unit requires additional troubleshooting, this information will be valuable.

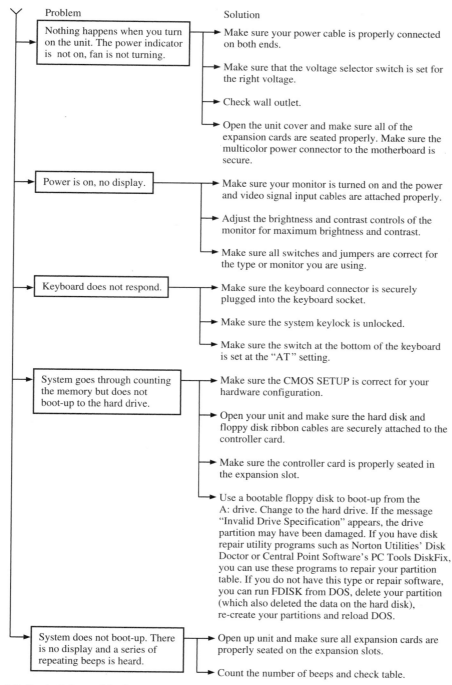

Problem	Solution
Nothing happens when you turn on the unit. The power indicator is not on, fan is not turning.	Make sure your power cable is properly connected on both ends.
	Make sure that the voltage selector switch is set for the right voltage.
	Check wall outlet.
	Open the unit cover and make sure all of the expansion cards are seated properly. Make sure the multicolor power connector to the motherboard is secure.
Power is on, no display.	Make sure your monitor is turned on and the power and video signal input cables are attached properly.
	Adjust the brightness and contrast controls of the monitor for maximum brightness and contrast.
	Make sure all switches and jumpers are correct for the type or monitor you are using.
Keyboard does not respond.	Make sure the keyboard connector is securely plugged into the keyboard socket.
	Make sure the system keylock is unlocked.
	Make sure the switch at the bottom of the keyboard is set at the "AT" setting.
System goes through counting the memory but does not boot-up to the hard drive.	Make sure the CMOS SETUP is correct for your hardware configuration.
	Open your unit and make sure the hard disk and floppy disk ribbon cables are securely attached to the controller card.
	Make sure the controller card is properly seated in the expansion slot.
	Use a bootable floppy disk to boot-up from the A: drive. Change to the hard drive. If the message "Invalid Drive Specification" appears, the drive partition may have been damaged. If you have disk repair utility programs such as Norton Utilities' Disk Doctor or Central Point Software's PC Tools DiskFix, you can use these programs to repair your partition table. If you do not have this type or repair software, you can run FDISK from DOS, delete your partition (which also deleted the data on the hard disk), re-create your partitions and reload DOS.
System does not boot-up. There is no display and a series of repeating beeps is heard.	Open up unit and make sure all expansion cards are properly seated on the expansion slots.
	Count the number of beeps and check table.

4-2 Basic PC troubleshooting.

The following error codes are typical for most clones.

101   *System board error.*   Board requires repair.

201   *Memory error.*   One of the RAM chips might be bad, missing, or incorrectly installed. You need to locate the bad or incorrectly installed chip and replace it.

301   *Keyboard error.*   This code is one of the most common error codes. Usually, the five-pin keyboard cable has pulled out from the system unit. The plug must be in the correct orientation and the bump on the plug must be on top, or the cable will not fit completely into its socket.

401   *Color or monochrome adapter error.*   Check that the monitor is securely plugged in both to an electrical source and to the connector of the display adapter. Check the adapter manual, and verify that any jumpers and/or switches on the adapter are set correctly. If you still get this error code, the monitor needs repair.

501   *Color adapter error.*   Use the same procedure as previously described.

601/602   *Floppy drive or controller error.*   The cables between the floppy drive and its controller might have disconnected or are connected backward. Check that the cables between the floppy and hard disk controller and the floppy drive are properly connected.

701   *Math coprocessor error.*   Check that the math coprocessor is completely pushed into its socket. The math chip might be defective, or if it was installed backward, it has probably been damaged.

901   *Printer adapter error.*   Check that the printer cable is correctly attached to the adapter. If you have two or more printer adapters in the system, such as one port on a display adapter and one on a multifunction card, check that they are not configured for the same LPT (parallel port).

1101/1201   *Asynchronous communications adapter (serial port) failure.* I/O adapter cards, multifunction cards, and some display adapters might include serial ports. Identify the serial ports in the system and check the cabling attached to each. Check for COM port conflicts using the manual or documentation for each serial port adapter. You will need to determine the factory default COM port setting and whether that COM port setting can be reconfigured or, if not needed, disabled. The proper procedure for reconfiguring/disabling that COM port should be indicated in the documentation. You must reconfigure or disable conflicting serial ports. You can check each port by disconnecting each one at a time and rebooting. If you do not get the error code when one of the serial port adapters is disconnected, that adapter is the problem.

1301   *Game port adapter error.*   Check the cabling and if you have more than one game-control device, such as a game paddle and a joystick, test each one in turn to isolate the problem.

1401   *Graphics printer error.*   Check the cabling of the printer to the system unit and to electrical power. (See Chap. 7 for printer troubleshooting.)

1501   *SDLC (synchronous data link control) error.*   Check the attachment of the modem to the system. Reboot system without the modem installed. If the error does not repeat, there is a problem in the modem.

1701   *Fixed-disk error.*   This error code will occur, and it can be ignored the first time you boot up with a new hard disk (if the disk is formatted). If the error still exists after the disk has been formatted, repeat the format procedure. This process can take up to 40 minutes for a 20MB drive, so you should not interrupt the procedure before it is complete. (See Chap. 5 on disks for more information.)

Power-on self-tests

When the power to your computer is first turned on, it automatically runs the internal power-on self-test (POST) program. The POST program is part of the BIOS (basic input-output system) software in read-only memory (ROM) chips on the computer system board. The POST program tests the critical system components, one after the other. As each component is tested, the POST program generates a test number code and sends it to an output port (usually number 80). If all of the tests confirm proper operation, the system boots normally.

A problem detected during these tests will stop the POST program, and the system boot is aborted. Depending on when this happens, an error code might appear on the screen or the screen might just go blank. Diagnostic cards allow the missing codes to be captured.

POST diagnostic cards

A card such as the POST-IT ISA card can be placed in an expansion slot of an ISA (industry standard architecture) bus computer to monitor the code numbers being sent by the POST to output port 80. The code numbers appear on a seven-segment digital LED display during the test.

If POST detects a problem, the number shown on the POST-IT ISA display indicates that component test failed. The BIOS manufacturer's POST codes can then be used to identify the problem.

To troubleshoot, repair, or maintain PCs a number of tools are available to aid these tasks. The diagnostic card verifies that the correct power is being supplied to the expansion bus with a series of green and red LEDs (light-emitting diodes). Information about critical internal bus lines and clocks can be checked with the clock test function.

The POST-IT ISA card fits in a short XT slot and runs in an IBM PC, XT, AT, or a compatible computer using an 8-bit bus and ISA. A dual-hexadecimal LED digital display shows POST codes. Four light-emitting diodes monitor +5 V, −5 V, +12 V, and −12 V. A single LED and jumper block monitor signals from the Address Latch Enable, Input-Output Read, and clock systems.

KickStart 1 is another card designed for engineers, technicians, and advanced PC users who want to identify the cause of motherboard and other system failures.

Because many computer failures can cause the screen to be blank, it makes software diagnostics difficult. With a POST card installed in a slot, when the power comes on, the CPU executes the POST program built into BIOS in the ROM chips on the main circuit board. The LEDs on the card show whether power is applied to the board.

Before running each step in the POST program, BIOS sends test number codes to output port 80 that light up LEDs on the card. If the computer hangs up, stops, or runs in a loop during the test, it is because it detected an error.

The last test number sent to port 80 signals the problem that caused the system to fail. You might be able to find the number in the BIOS manufacturer's POST code list in the manual and know which circuit to repair.

KickStart

KickStart 2 is a multifunction diagnostics card designed for service technicians; it performs both low-level and advanced diagnostics for the motherboard, memory, and peripherals.

This card relays low-level POST failure codes using a digital display. A series of tests in a 522K page EPROM performs advanced diagnostics and measures the power supply voltage.

System tests include CPU, math chip, real memory, extended memory, interrupt control, DMA control, clock, timer, and CMOS RAM. Peripheral tests include serial port, parallel port, floppy disk drive, hard disk drive, keyboard, and video (MONO, CGA, EGA, VGA). You also can run tests from a remote terminal.

Errors can be logged to either a remote terminal (via on-board serial and parallel I/O) or printer. The board includes an 8K CMOS battery-backed RAM for storing configurations and password information, a real-time clock, an Ethernet BNC Terminator, a serial cable assembly and loopback plugs (9-pin serial, 25-pin serial, 25-pin parallel) for communication port testing, and special ROMs to replace BIOS ROMs that do not send POST code errors.

PC Probe diagnostic software

PC Probe is an example of a disk that offers advanced diagnostics and provides system information, utilities, and benchmark testing. It is suitable for the advanced end user and service technician. It uses pull-down menus that can be keyboard or mouse driven along with on-screen help. You also can run the program remotely with programs such as CoSession.

Typically, these tests can run in single pass, multiple pass, or batch mode for isolating intermittent errors. Results can be logged to a disk file, display, serial port, or printer. Tested components include the system board, RAM, video board and display, keyboard and mouse, parallel ports, serial ports, floppy controller and drive, and hard drive (see Figs. 4-3 to 4-7). A number of built-in utilities for fixing common operating

```
                        Loading

            Investigating system configuration

       Local  –  Check for remote operation
  (Standard)  –  Identify BIOS manufacturer
    Complete  –  Determine system components
    Complete  –  Look for RAM (base, extended, expanded)
 Not present  –  Look for math co-processor
 Not present  –  Look for mouse


         System configuration checks complete.

              Press any key to continue
```

4-3 A system configuration display.

problems are also available. You can reformat your hard drive, revitalize hard disk data, list and edit bad-track tables, display and edit CMOS RAM, and locate a bad RAM chip. Serial and parallel port loopback plugs are included in some utilities for communications port testing. A speed test is also built in to test the CPU, FPU (math coprocessor), and video speeds.

There can be displays of CPU, FPU, BIOS, video, RAM, EMS, IRQ, DMA, I/O, CMOS RAM, and cache information.

IBM Advanced Diagnostics

Diagnostic programs such as IBM Advanced Diagnostics are useful for troubleshooting not only the IBM machines but for compatibles as well. However, because the IBM AT keyboard and most compatible keyboards are not identical in their electronics, this program might sometimes generate a keyboard error when none exists. If you use IBM Advanced Diagnostics, be prepared for this problem.

Extended self-test

Many compatibles come with an extended self-test program that runs an extensive internal diagnostic. The diagnostic runs on power-up or reset. The extended self-tests are usually menu driven.

You can run the extended self-test when you suspect a problem in the disk drive, a diskette, or any option added to the system board. To run the extended self-test, you bypass DOS in some compatibles by loading the diagnostic disk and then turning on the computer (see Figs. 4-8 through 4-10).

The diagnostic test will typically run the following types of programs.

1. Floppy or hard disk tests check each hard or floppy disk drive.
2. Extended tests include the previously mentioned drive tests, a memory test, and a video, printer, and communications test.

Program flow   **Remarks**

Diagnostic menu screen appears
    ↓

Select test desired   Selects desired test
    ↓

System Board   Yes ⟶   Go to System Board Test
Test
  ↓ No

Memory Test   Yes ⟶   Go to Memory Test
  ↓ No

Keyboard Test   Yes ⟶   Go to Keyboard Test
   ↓ No

CRT
Display   Yes ⟶   Go to CRT Display Test
Test
  ↓ No

Printer   Yes ⟶   Go to Printer Test
Test
  ↓ No

RS232C   Yes ⟶   Go to RS232C Test
Test
  ↓ No

Floppy Disk   Yes ⟶   Go to Floppy Disk Drive
Drive
Test
  ↓ No

Hard   Yes ⟶   Go to Hard Disk Drive Test
Disk Drive
Test
  ↓ No

Serial/   Yes ⟶   Go to Serial/Parallel
Parallel   Adapter Test
Adapter Test
  ↓ No

End diagnostic

4-4 Typical diagnostic program.

1. All tests	7. RS232C
2. System board	8. Floppy disk drive
3. Memory	9. Hard disk drive
4. Keyboard	10. Serial/parallel adapter
5. CRT display	11. End diagnostics
6. Printer	Select option number__

4-5 Typical diagnostic menu.

Program flow   **Remarks**

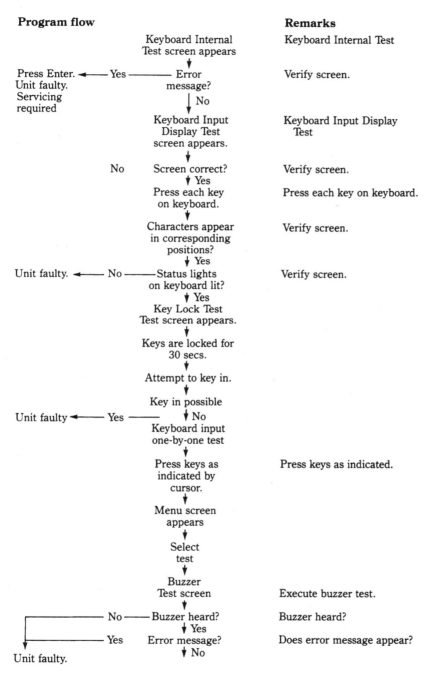

Keyboard Internal Test screen appears	Keyboard Internal Test
Press Enter. ◄── Yes ──── Error message? Unit faulty. Servicing required	Verify screen.
│ No	
Keyboard Input Display Test screen appears.	Keyboard Input Display Test
No Screen correct?	Verify screen.
↓ Yes	
Press each key on keyboard.	Press each key on keyboard.
Characters appear in corresponding positions?	Verify screen.
↓ Yes	
Unit faulty. ◄── No ──── Status lights on keyboard lit?	Verify screen.
↓ Yes	
Key Lock Test Test screen appears.	
Keys are locked for 30 secs.	
Attempt to key in.	
Key in possible	
Unit faulty ◄── Yes ──── ↓ No	
Keyboard input one-by-one test	
Press keys as indicated by cursor.	Press keys as indicated.
Menu screen appears	
Select test	
Buzzer Test screen	Execute buzzer test.
── No ── Buzzer heard?	Buzzer heard?
↓ Yes	
── Yes ── Error message?	Does error message appear?
Unit faulty. ↓ No	

4-6 Typical keyboard tests.

```
TESTING – KEYBOARD INTERNAL
END KEYBOARD TEST
PRESS "ENTER" . . .
```

(a)

```
TESTING – KEYBOARD INTERNAL
XX:XX:XX LOOP COUNT = XX
3XX XXXXXX
END KEYBOARD TEST
PRESS "ENTER" . . .
```

(b)

```
PRESS EACH KEY, HOLD FOR TYPEMATIC TEST
IF OK PRESS "Y THEN ENTER"
IF NOT OK PRESS "N THEN ENTER"
```

(c)

4-7 Typical displays of keyboard tests. **4-7(A)** Normal end. **4-7(B)** Error message. **4-7(C)** Typematic test menu.

Typical diagnostic operation flow	**Action**
Start	
↓	
Load diagnostic floppy disk	
↓	
Diagnostic Utility Menu appears	Activate Diagnostic Utility Menu
↓	
Input desired item and Enter	Select desired item
↓	
Floppy Disk Utility	Go to Floppy Disk Utility
↓	
LOG Utility	Go to Log Utility
↓	
Setup Utility	Go to Setup Utility
↓	
Hard Disk Utility	Go to Hard Disk Utility
↓	
End Diagnostic Menu	

4-8 Main diagnostic program.

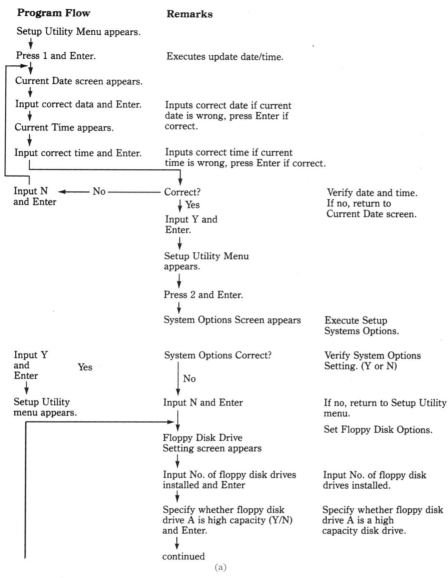

Program Flow

Setup Utility Menu appears.

Press 1 and Enter.

Current Date screen appears.

Input correct data and Enter.

Current Time appears.

Input correct time and Enter.

Input N and Enter ◄— No ——— Correct?

↓ Yes

Input Y and Enter.

Setup Utility Menu appears.

Press 2 and Enter.

System Options Screen appears

Input Y and Enter   Yes

System Options Correct?

↓ No

Setup Utility menu appears.

Input N and Enter

Floppy Disk Drive Setting screen appears

Input No. of floppy disk drives installed and Enter

Specify whether floppy disk drive A is high capacity (Y/N) and Enter.

continued

Remarks

Executes update date/time.

Inputs correct date if current date is wrong, press Enter if correct.

Inputs correct time if current time is wrong, press Enter if correct.

Verify date and time. If no, return to Current Date screen.

Execute Setup Systems Options.

Verify System Options Setting. (Y or N)

If no, return to Setup Utility menu.

Set Floppy Disk Options.

Input No. of floppy disk drives installed.

Specify whether floppy disk drive A is a high capacity disk drive.

(a)

4-9 Typical setup program.

3. New diagnostic test selection allows you to run the tests one at a time. It might allow you to run tests that check the communications port and the printer. The selection can help isolate a problem to a specific device (Fig. 4-11).

4. This selection allows you to install new diagnostic tests to the diskette.

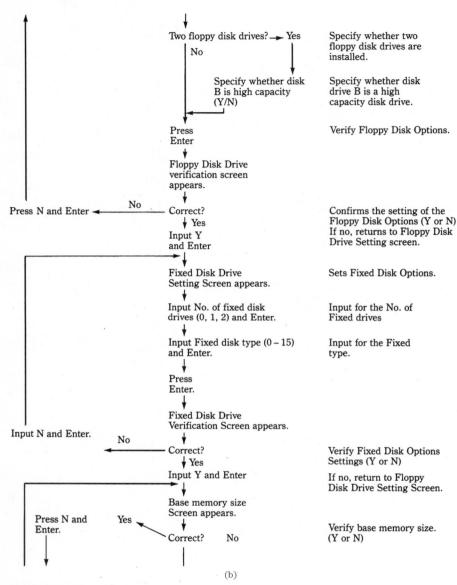

4-9 *(Continued)* Typical setup program.

Extended tests

An extended test checks each disk drive, tests the memory, and checks the communications and printer connectors. The message PASS is displayed on the monitor as each test is completed without error, as shown in Fig. 4-12. After successful completion of the extended test, the message TEST PASSED or something similar appears on the monitor.

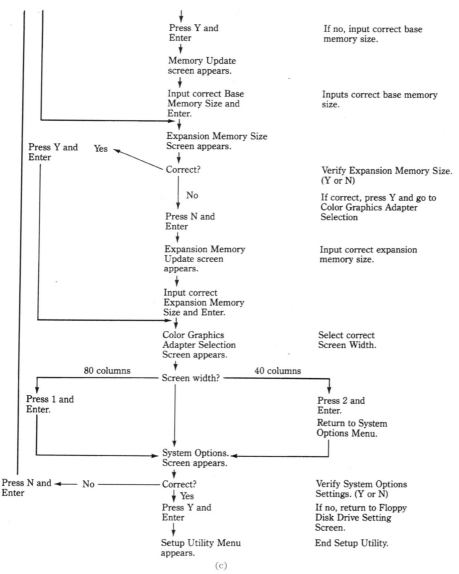

Press Y and
Enter

Memory Update
screen appears.

If no, input correct base
memory size.

Input correct Base
Memory Size and
Enter.

Inputs correct base memory
size.

Expansion Memory Size
Screen appears.

Press Y and   Yes
Enter

Correct?

Verify Expansion Memory Size.
(Y or N)

No

If correct, press Y and go to
Color Graphics Adapter
Selection

Press N and
Enter

Expansion Memory
Update screen
appears.

Input correct expansion
memory size.

Input correct
Expansion Memory
Size and Enter.

Color Graphics
Adapter Selection
Screen appears.

Select correct
Screen Width.

80 columns   Screen width?   40 columns

Press 1 and
Enter.

Press 2 and
Enter.
Return to System
Options Menu.

System Options.
Screen appears.

Press N and   No   Correct?
Enter
↓ Yes

Verify System Options
Settings. (Y or N)

Press Y and
Enter

If no, return to Floppy
Disk Drive Setting
Screen.

Setup Utility Menu
appears.

End Setup Utility.

(c)

4-9 (*Continued*) Typical setup program.

Proceeding from an error

If an error is detected during a diagnostic test, a message similar to the following
might appear after the error message.

```
ERROR
PERCENT FAILURE XXX%
```

```
SETUP UTILITY
1  UPDATE CURRENT DATE/TIME
2  SETUP SYSTEM OPTIONS
3  END SETUP UTILITY
   SELECT OPTION NUMBER __
```
A. Main Menu

```
CURRENT DATE IS: XX-XX-XXXX
ENTER NEW DATE:
CURRENT TIME IS: XX-XX-XXXX
ENTER NEW TIME:
```
B. Option 1

```
CURRENT DATE IS: XX-XX-XXXX
CURRENT TIME IS: XX-XX-XXXX
IS THIS CORRECT (Y/N)?
```

```
ENTER NUMBER OF FLOPPY DISK DRIVES (1 or 2) INSTALLED ? 1
IS FLOPPY DISK A
A HIGH CAPACITY DRIVE (Y/N) ? Y
```
C. Floppy Disk Drives

```
FLOPPY DISK DRIVE A—HIGH CAPACITY
FLOPPY DISK DRIVE B—NOT INSTALLED
IS THIS CORRECT (Y/N)?
```
D. Floppy Disk Drive
   Configuration

```
ENTER NUMBER OF FIXED DISK DRIVES (0, 1, OR 2)
ENTER FIXED DISK TYPE (1 – 15) FOR DRIVE C
PRESS ENTER TO CONTINUE . . .
```
E. Fixed Disks

```
FIXED DISK DRIVE C—TYPE 2
FIXED DISK DRIVE D—NOT INSTALLED
IS THIS CORRECT (Y/N)?
```
F. Fixed Disk Configuration

```
BASE MEMORY SIZE IS 640KB
IS THIS CORRECT (Y/N)?
```
G. Base Memory

```
BASE MEMORY SIZE IS 640KB
IS THIS CORRECT (Y/N) ?N
ENTER CORRECT BASE MEMORY SIZE (256, 512, or 640).
```
H. Base Memory
   Configuration

```
EXPANSION MEMORY SIZE IS 0KB
IS THIS CORRECT (Y/N)?
```
I. Expansion Memory

```
EXPANSION MEMORY SIZE IS 0KB
IS THIS CORRECT (Y/N) ?N
ENTER CORRECT EXPANSION MEMORY SIZE
```
J. Expansion Memory
   Configuration

```
FLOPPY DISK DRIVE A—HIGH CAPACITY
FLOPPY DISK DRIVE B—NOT INSTALLED
FIXED DISK DRIVE C—TYPE 2
FIXED DISK DRIVE D—NOT INSTALLED
BASE MEMORY SIZE—640KB
EXPANSION MEMORY SIZE—0KB
PRIMARY DISPLAY IS COLOR GRAPHICS ADAPTER (80 COLUMNS)
ARE THESE OPTIONS CORRECT (Y/N)?
```
K. System Options
   Configuration Menu

4-10 Setup utility menus. Main menu.

Individual Test Selection

1. RAM Test
2. RAM Arbitration Test
3. Video Controller Test
4. Floppy Diagnostic Test
5. COMM Port Test (no loopback plug)
6. COMM Port Test (loopback plug)
7. Printer Port Test (loopback plug)
8. Printer Confidence Test
9. Synchronous COMM Test
10. System Test
11. Video Alignment Pattern
12. Private RAM Test
13. Keyboard Test
Type Selection Number and < ETR >

4-11 Individual test selection menu.

Test Being Executed   Pass/Fail
Indicator

Floppy Test	Pass	Comm Port Test	Pass
RAM Test	Pass	RAM Arbitration	Pass
RAM Test	Pass	System Test	Pass
Video Test	Pass	Keyboard Self-Test	

Number of drives to be tested? Select 2 or 4
Remove diagnostic disk and insert formatted disks
Warning contents of diskettes are destroyed???
Number of test − 1
Test 1 − Internal Register Test
Test 2 − Head Load Test
Test 3 − Loopback Test
Test 4 − Restore Test
Test 5 − Step Test
Test 6 − Motor Test
Test 7 − Seek Test
Test 8 − Forced Write Errors Test
Test 9 − Write Sectors Test
Test 10 − Forced Read Errors Test

Other messages

Error messages and status

Error: Drive A, failure
Status: testing

4-12 Typical test messages.

After you run the test 10 times, the percent failure is updated. You might be asked to

Type P to exit the loop, and proceed with the next test.

Individual test selection

If you have a printer installed on your computer, you can select the printer tests from the menu. You would type the number of the test needed and follow the instructions that appear on the monitor for that test.

Memory testing

Memory testing involves testing the base memory including memory currently being used by DOS or any other program. If errors occur, a failure indication will appear and the errors might be listed in an activity report. You also can test any extended memory. Like the base memory test, any errors found will result in a failed status on this part of the test, and the specific memory locations might be listed in an activity report.

Next, the expanded memory is tested. Like the other tests, if any errors are found, the specific memory locations will be listed in an activity report.

A test for high-address lines can find problems caused by incorrectly sized chips, bent or broken pins, and other addressing problems where one byte can affect another. The test is similar to a bad address test but generally works on blocks of memory larger than 64K. A high-address line problem can occur when 256K chips are in a 1MB bank or when a pin is broken off a chip.

Most memory tests are nonintrusive. The memory tested during the test will be restored to its original state and the system should run normally afterward. At the end of the memory test, you should have a list of any bad memory locations and bad bits, if any.

Correcting the problem

Most of the time, memory errors are caused by a bad RAM chip. Other times, the problem can be caused by a poorly inserted RAM chip or even a defective memory board.

The first thing to do when a memory problem is reported is to try replacing the chip where the error occurred. Some test programs will locate the bad RAM chips for you on the display to show which RAM chips should be replaced.

Once you have located the defective chip, carefully remove the bad chip from the board. Check to see if any pins have been broken off or are folded under. If this is the case, carefully straighten or correct the damaged pin.

Sometimes it is possible to solder a new section on a broken pin. Then try reinserting the chip making sure all pins are fully inserted in the socket. Then run the memory test again to be sure that you have corrected the problem.

If the bad chip is part of a SIMM (Fig. 4-13), make sure the module is fully inserted on the board. If this does not cure the problem, replace the entire module because the individual chips are soldered into the module.

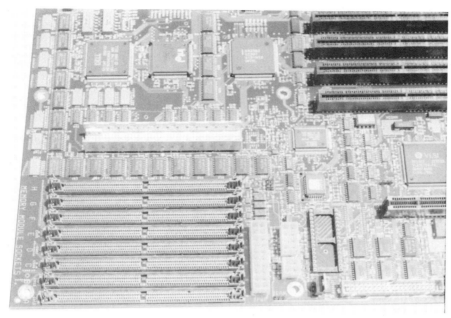

4-13 Section of 486 system board showing SIMM sockets and 486 processor connector; expansion slots are in the upper right-hand corner.

Sometimes other factors cause memory problems. If you have replaced the reported memory chips and the same error appears, the problem might be due to problems on the memory board. For example, a cut or bridged address line on the memory board could cause a memory error. If memory errors occur repeatedly at different locations, the errors might be due to a power supply problem.

Test patterns

The following test patterns are commonly used for testing memory bits. Each pass of the memory test might check the bit being tested several times. Each time, the pattern writes to memory as the following describes; then the inverse of the pattern also can be written. The common patterns used are described as follows:

Pattern used	*Description*
Pseudorandom	The pseudorandom test copies a random pattern into each byte. This test is the most common test and is always run when only a basic test is selected.
Walking bit left	Each memory location is filled with the following initial bit pattern:
	00000001

	On each successive pass through memory, the 1 is moved one position to the left until all the bits are tested.
Walking bit right	Each memory location is filled with the following initial bit pattern:
	10000000
	On each successive pass through memory, the 1 is moved one position to the right until all the bits are tested.
Inverted walking bit left	Each memory location is filled with the following initial bit pattern:
	11111110
	On each successive pass through memory, the 0 is moved one position to the left until all the bits are tested.
Inverted walking bit right	Each memory location is filled with the following bit pattern:
	01111111
	On each successive pass through memory, the 0 is moved one position to the right until all bits are tested.
Checkerboard	The checkerboard test is a test of each memory location with the following bit pattern:
	01010101
Inverted checkerboard	The inverted checkerboard test is a test of each memory location with the following bit pattern:
	01011010
Bit stuck	Bit stuck is a test of each memory location set to all 0s, then set at all 1s.
Lo/hi address	The lo/hi address test is a test that will find memory addressing problems caused by improperly installed chips, those with broken pins, incorrectly sized chips in a bank, such as a 64K chip in a 256K bank, and bad solder traces on a board.

System board test

The system board test is a test of the primary components of the computer such as the processor (central processor unit, CPU), NPU (numerical processing unit) coprocessor,

DMA (direct memory access) controller, and interrupt controller. Figure 4-14 shows a typical test screen. The tests usually have a number of different stages as shown in Fig. 4-15.

CPU testing

The CPU testing might have four stages or steps to check the key functions of the processor. First, there must be a test of the general, math, and logic instructions of the CPU. A failure on one of these tests indicates a major failure in the PC main processor; replace the processor. These tests will check for the following conditions: branching, overflow, two's compliment and BCD (binary-coded decimal) math, shifts and rotates. These functions are necessary for the reliable operation of your PC and a repeated failure indicates a bad processor. You can usually get chip replacements from a well-equipped electronics parts outlet.

Interrupt problems

Interrupt testing will identify CPUs that allow interrupts to occur at the wrong times. This problem occurs in some older 8088 and 8086 chips. If your machine has one of these faulty processors, it could lock up at random times. If this problem shows up on your machine, you need to replace the processor.

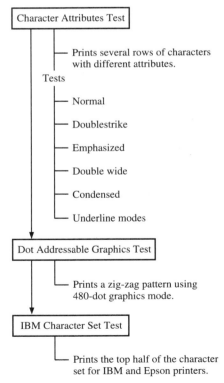

4-14 Typical printer tests.

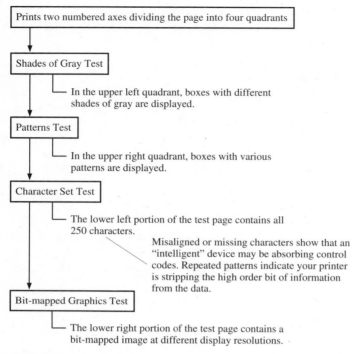

4-15 Laser printer tests.

Protected-mode problems

In PCs with an 80286 or above, you might need to test your processor ability to function in protected mode. When you are using DOS, your CPU is operating in 8086 emulation mode. This mode is called the *real mode.* When your PC is accessing DOS extended memory or running OS/2 or Xenix, your CPU is running under its native mode called the *protected mode.*

A failure of this test only indicates a problem under this mode of operation, and your PC might operate without problems under normal DOS operation. A failure means that your PC will not function correctly if you add extended memory or when you run in an operating system such as OS/2 or Xenix. The test sends the 80286 processor into the protected mode and then back into the real mode. In the protected mode, the processor can access memory above the 1MB address range.

NPU testing

The NPU test will check if the math coprocessor (NPU) is functioning properly. It might be improperly installed or defective. One test will force the NPU to perform a set of floating-point calculations. Then a comparison is made of the actual results with the expected results. If there is not a match, an error is reported. Another test actually verifies that the NPU floating-point comparison operations are working properly. A test might also be available to test the trigonometric functions available on the math coprocessor. The NPU could be asked to compute several tangents, for example. All of these tests will be done with floating-point numbers.

DMA controller testing

The DMS test checks the communication between the CPU and the DMA controller. The DMA controller is responsible for transferring data between the CPU and memory. A failure indicates either the DMA controller or CPU is defective. The AT class of computer uses a second DMA controller that also should be tested.

The DMA test must check each channel and register of the DMA controller. It also must check that the DMA refresh is operating normally. Problems with the DMA refresh cycle can sometimes cause what appear to be memory errors.

Interrupt controller testing

Interrupt testing checks that the PC interrupt controller is operating properly. This controller is responsible for the interrupting that occurs to the CPU when certain events are commanded to happen, such as when a character is about to be received over the serial port. Normally, when an interrupt occurs, the CPU momentarily stops what it was doing, runs a program such as a device driver to handle the cause of the interrupt, and returns to where it was. If this test fails, the problem could be either the interrupt controller or the CPU is bad. If you are using a 286 or above machine, also test the second interrupt controller (Fig. 4-16).

| | (A) | (B) | (C) |
INT	Function	Address	Points to
01h	Single Step	0070:075C	DOS Kernel
03h	Breakpoint	0070:075C	DOS Kernel
04h	Overflow	0070:075C	DOS Kernel
05h	Print Screen Handler	F000:FF54	System ROM

(A) Function

This column describes the normal use for the interrupt. Some interrupts have specified purposes, others are either marked "reserved" or are used by several common applications. This does not mean that they can all work together at the same time but only that the programs listed use these interrupts.

(B) Address

This column shows the address the vector is currently pointing to. The values are in hexadecimal.

(C) Points to

This column displays the location that the vector is pointing toward. In many cases the vector will be pointing to an operating system component like the system ROM, DOS kernel, or COMMAND.COM. Sometimes the vector will be pointing to a TSR or device driver.

4-16 Sample interrupt vectors screen.

The test will set interrupt priority level and interrupt vectors for the 8259 interrupt controller. It will generate an interrupt for each level. It will temporarily reassign any predefined interrupt vector and replace them when the test is completed.

Sometimes if a component has a problem, it can cause the computer to lock up. Usually typical test times are given for each test; make sure you wait at least as long as the times listed for each test step. Then, if the PC still does not respond, copy down the last lines displayed and reboot the PC. The last display will usually indicate the area where the problem lies.

Clock tests

A comparison of the real-time clock time to DOS time is one test you can make. This test checks both times to make sure they are almost the same. Consider differences of as much as 15 seconds close enough. Most systems will show a difference of from 1 to 5 seconds. You can also make a test to compare the real-time clock date to DOS date.

This test will compare the two clocks to make sure the dates are the same (Figs. 4-17 and 4-18). If the real-time clock time or date is incorrect, you must set the time or date.

Most clocks have an alarm feature. The alarm also can be tested. The test will set the alarm to go off in a few seconds. If it does not do this on time, the test fails. A failed test can indicate a problem with the CMOS clock hardware. (Some systems do not support the alarm and will lock up when this feature is used, which can be a potential problem.) If you have this type of problem and wish to correct it, you can usually do this by replacing the BIOS chip with a later version. (See Fig. 4-19.)

You also compare the elapsed time. This test compares the amount of time elapsed on each clock to see if the two are keeping time at the same rate. Any difference here usually means that the real-time clock needs batteries or a component is malfunctioning.

Printer testing

There are also diagnostic programs for testing printers. Figure 4-20 illustrates the types of tests performed on dot matrix and ink-jet printers, and Fig. 4-21 shows the types of tests used for checking laser printers.

386 and 486 error codes

Typical error codes for 386 and 486 systems are shown as follows:

Code	Type	Action needed
111	Parity error	A memory module has failed; turn the system unit off for 10 seconds, then turn the system unit on.
114	Option	Make sure all adapter cards are inserted securely.
161	Bad battery	Make sure the battery is installed correctly. If the error continues, install a new battery.

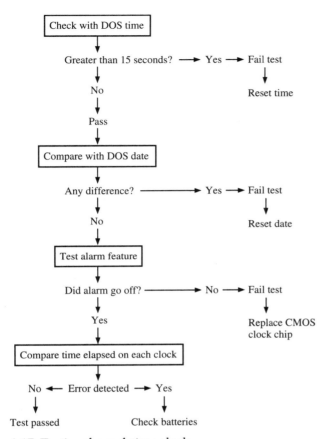

4-17 Testing the real-time clock.

```
        Clock/Calendar Test
        Current Date and Time
        Real-Time Clock:   05/01/1995  19:33:47
        DOS Clock:         05/01/1995  19:33:45
```

(1.88 seconds apart) | Passed | Compare real-time clock time to DOS time.

                      | Passed | Compare real-time clock date to DOS date.

                      | Passed | Test real-time clock alarm.

                      | Passed | Compare elapsed time.

4-18 Real-time clock test screen.

SIMM banks   BIOS chip

4-19 Location of BIOS chip in 486 tower system.

System Board Test Status

| Passed | CPU General Function |

| Passed | CPU Interrupt Bug |

| Passed | CPU 32-bit Multiply |

| Passed | CPU Protected Mode |

| Skipped | NPU Arithmetic Functions |

| Skipped | NPU Trigonometric Functions |

| Skipped | NPU Comparison Functions |

| Passed | DMA Controller(s) |

4-20 System board test screen.

| 162 | Configuration | If you have removed an option, use setup to change your configuration. |
| 163 | Date and time | The clock module on the system board might not be correct. To set the correct date and time, use setup. |

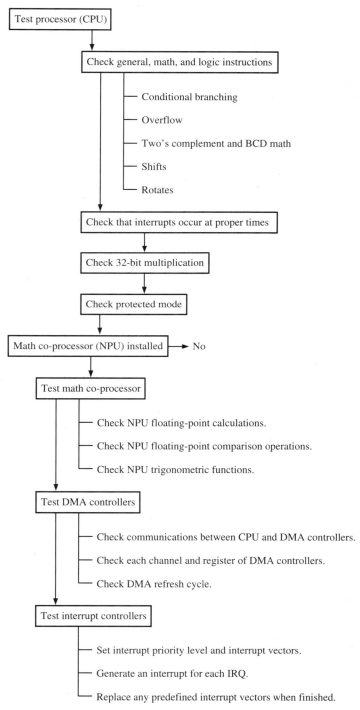

4-21 System board testing.

164	Memory size	If you have removed memory, use setup to check or change the memory size.
1XX	System board	Turn the system off and then on, and be sure the system has adequate cooling.
2XX	SIMM	Turn the system off. Make sure the single inline memory module (SIMM) is installed correctly. Make sure the correct type of SIMM is installed. If the error continues, install a new SIMM.
3XX	Keyboard	Check that the keyboard connector is not loose; check that a key is not stuck. Turn the system unit off, wait 10 seconds, then turn the system unit on.
6XX	Floppy disk drive	Check the cables to the disk drives. Make sure they are secure. If drive A can read and drive B cannot, clean drive B heads. Otherwise, test the controller.
11XX	Serial port	Check setup.
17XX	Hard disk	Check the cables; be sure they are secure. Turn the system off and wait 10 seconds, and then turn the system on.
24XX	Video	Make sure the display cables are firmly connected to the system unit. Make sure the video controller/memory setting is correct; use setup.
		If a video adapter card is installed, make sure it is inserted correctly. If the error continues, remove the video adapter card. If removing the card corrects the error, replace the adapter card. This error is also indicated by one long and two short beeps in some 486 systems and eight beeps in others.
860X	Mouse	Check that the mouse cable is securely attached to the correct port. Check that a key on the keyboard is not stuck.
86XX	Pointing device	Check that the mouse and keyboard cables are securely attached to the correct ports. Check setup.

An X shown as part of the error code represents any number between 0 and 9.

Error beep codes

In many 386 and 486 systems, the BIOS performs various POSTs (power-on self-tests) at the time you power up the system. If any kind of error is encountered during the POST, the system responds by either beeping or displaying the error messages on the monitor. In situations when the display is not working, the system reports the error by giving a number of short beeps. If the error is fatal, the system will halt after reporting the error. If the error is not fatal, the processing will continue. The nonfatal errors allow the system to continue the boot-up process and the error messages normally appear on the screen.

The fatal errors will not allow the system to continue the boot-up procedure. If a fatal error occurs, a repair is usually needed. The fatal errors are usually communicated through a series of audible beeps. The number of beeps for the corresponding fatal error follows. All of these errors are fatal, except for eight beeps, which indicates a video problem.

Number of beeps	*Error*
1	*Refresh failed.* The memory refresh circuits of the system board are faulty.
2	*Parity.* A parity error was detected in the base memory, first block of 64K.
3	*Base memory failed.* A memory failure occurred in the first 64K of memory.
4	*Timer not operating.* Timer 1 on the system board is not functioning properly.
5	*Processor error.* The CPU (central processing unit) on the system board generated an error.
6	*Keyboard controller.* The keyboard controller, usually an 8042, has an A20 gate that allows the CPU to operate in virtual mode. The BIOS was not able to switch the CPU into protected mode.
7	*Exception interrupt.* The CPU generated an exception interrupt.
8	*Video memory read-write.* Video adapter or its memory is faulty. This error is not a fatal error.
9	*ROM checksum.* ROM checksum value does not match the value encoded in the BIOS.
10	*Shutdown register read-write.* Shutdown register for CMOS memory failed.

Nonfatal error messages

If a nonfatal error occurs during the POST routines performed when the system is powered on, the error message is shown on the screen in the following format:

```
ERROR Message Line 1
ERROR Message Line 2
Press <F1> to RESUME
```

You should make a note of the message and press the <F1> key to continue with the boot-up procedure. If the

> Wait for <F1> If Any Error

option in the Advance CMOS Setup has been set to disabled, the <F1> prompt will not appear on the third line. For many of the error messages, there is no error message on line 2. Usually, if there is a message on line 2, it will be

> RUN SETUP UTILITY

Descriptions of the typical error messages are listed as follows:

CH-2 timer error. Most system boards have two timers. An error with timer 1 is a fatal error.

INTR #1 error. The interrupt channel 1 failed the POST routine.

INTR #2 error. The interrupt channel 2 has failed the POST routine.

CMOS battery state low. The battery used for storing the CMOS values appears to be low in power. Replace the battery.

CMOS checksum failure. When the CMOS values are saved, a checksum value is generated for error checking. If the previous value is different from this value, this message appears. To correct this, you should run setup.

CMOS system options not set. The values stored in CMOS are corrupt or missing. Run setup to correct this.

CMOS display type mismatch. The type of video stored in CMOS does not match the type detected by the BIOS. Run setup to correct.

Display switch not correct. Some systems require that a video switch on the system board be set to either color or monochrome, depending upon the type of video being used. To correct, set the switch properly—be sure to shut down the system first.

Keyboard is locked . . . unlock it. The keyboard lock on the system is engaged. The system must be unlocked to continue the boot-up procedure.

Keyboard error. The BIOS has found a timing problem with the keyboard. Be sure you have the correct type of keyboard and keyboard BIOS installed in your system. Most XT keyboards will not work with AT and later systems. You can also set the keyboard option in setup to Not Installed, which will cause the BIOS to skip the keyboard POST routines.

KB/interface error. The BIOS has found an error with the keyboard connector.

CMOS memory size mismatch. The BIOS has found the amount of memory on your system board to be different from the amount stored in CMOS. Run setup to correct this error.

FDD controller failure. The BIOS is not able to communicate with the floppy disk drive controller. Check the connectors after you have powered off the system.

HDD controller failure.   The BIOS is not able to communicate with the hard disk drive controller. Check the connectors after the system is powered off.

C:drive error.   The BIOS is not receiving any response from hard disk drive C:. You might need to run a Hard Disk utility to correct this. Check the type of hard disk selected in setup to see if the correct hard disk drive has been selected.

D:drive error.   The same error as previously described has occurred with hard drive D:. Follow the procedures previously listed to correct this.

C:drive failure.   The BIOS cannot get any response from the hard disk drive C:. You might need to repair or replace the hard disk.

D:drive failure.   The same error as previously described occurred with hard drive D:.

CMOS time & date not set.   Run the setup to set the date and time of the CMOS.

Cache memory bad, do not enable cache!   The BIOS has found the cache memory of the system board to be defective.

8042 gate-A20 error.   The gate-A20 part of the keyboard controller (usually an 8042) has failed to operate properly. The 8042 chip should be replaced.

Address line short!   An error has occurred in the address decoding circuitry of the system board.

DMA #1 error.   An error has occurred with the first DMA channel on the system board.

DMA #2 error.   An error has occurred with the second DMA channel on the system board.

DMA error.   An error has occurred with the DMA controller on the system board. Replace the DMA controller.

No ROM basic.   A no ROM error occurs when a bootable sector cannot be found on either the floppy or hard disk drive. The BIOS tries to run ROM basic, and the message is generated when the BIOS does not find it.

Diskette boot failure.   The floppy disk used to boot up in the floppy drive is corrupt, it will not boot up the system. Use another boot disk.

Invalid boot diskette.   The BIOS can read the disk in the floppy drive, but it cannot boot up the system with it. Use another boot disk.

On board parity error.   The BIOS has found a parity error with some memory installed on the system board. The message will appear with an address line as follows:

```
ON BOARD PARITY ERROR
ADDR (HEX) = (XXXX)
```

XXXX is the address (in hexadecimal) where the error occurred. *On board* means that it is on the system board.

Off board parity error.   The BIOS has found a parity error with some memory installed in an expansion slot. The message will appear with the following address information:

OFF BOARD PARITY ERROR
ADDR (HEX) = (XXXX)

XXXX is the address (in hexadecimal) where the error occurred. *Off board* means that it is part of the memory installed in an expansion card.

Parity error???? The BIOS has found a parity error with some memory in the system, but it is not able to determine the address of the error.

5
CHAPTER

Disks and Disk Drives

This chapter helps you understand how disk drives work and how to diagnose and solve disk drive problems. It also provides you a background in the newer high-capacity storage medium CD-ROM.

Floppy drive operation

The 5¼-inch floppy disk (shown in Fig. 5-1) has been standard for the IBM personal computer family. The 3½-inch floppy is used in the PS-2 and has some advantages. The smaller one is more compact, has a more rugged container, and saves some space.

The floppy disk looks like a small phonograph record. A record uses grooves that a needle travels in while producing mechanical vibrations that are converted into audio frequencies, but computer disks are more like magnetic tape. A layer of iron oxide is coated on the smooth surface of the disk. The coating can be magnetized in small spots on the coating. The spots are microscopic, and each one acts like a very small permanent magnet.

When a spot is magnetized, it can be used to indicate a *true,* or *one state,* by setting the magnetic poles in one orientation. The spots that are magnetized in another orientation or direction are used to indicate a *false,* or *zero state.*

Each line of spots is called a *track.* A floppy disk can have 40 concentric tracks, which are numbered 0 through 39. The outside track is numbered 0, and the inside is numbered 39. The tracks are not a continuous spiral like a phonograph record, but each track is an isolated, closed circle.

Sectors divide the disk into sections that look like pie slices. There could be 10 sectors on each track, and each sector has a unique address. With 40 tracks of 10 sectors each, the 400 sector addresses would be numbered 0 through 399.

When you place the disk in the drive, the mechanism starts rotating the disk to its designed speed, which is usually 300 or 360 rpm (revolutions per minute). The hard disk drive speed is usually 10 times this speed. At a speed of 300 rpm, the floppy disk rotates at a spacing of about 30 microinches from the read-write magnetic head.

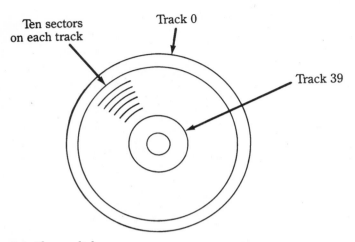

Ten sectors
on each track

Track 0

Track 39

5-1 Floppy disk.

The disk head is on an indexed shaft that moves it from the outer track of the disk to the inner track of the disk. The indexing system allows the head to be positioned over any of the 40 tracks.

Because the disk rotates at 300 rpm, the 10 sectors on each track pass under the head five times a second, and the head positioning takes about a second to locate a sector.

The mechanical system, which is called the *drive* (Figs. 5-2 to 5-5), spins the disks and moves the index arm that holds the magnetic recording head. The drives resemble

5-2(A) Disk drive locations. PC clone showing the floppy disk drive over hard disk drive. Controller board is next to power supply. Note controller cables.

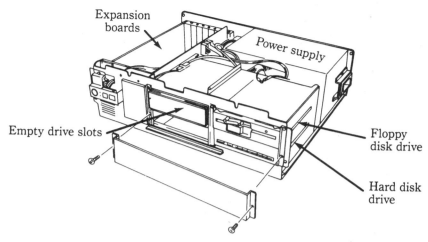

5-2(B) System unit with floppy disk drive over hard drive. Two additional drive slots are available.

5-2(C) Floppy drive location in 486 tower system.

a small record player in some ways, but it is much faster. The mechanical parts can wear out and break down like a record player.

The drive provides the mechanical functions and the electronics required to control the rotation of the disk and access data. The diskette is made of a flexible mylar material. It is coated with magnetic oxide and rotates in a plastic jacket (5¼ inch) or case (3½ inch). A long opening in the jacket or case provides access to the read-write head. The plastic case used to hold the 3½-inch disk has a spring-loaded metal cover that also protects the media.

5-3(A) Disk drive connectors. Rear view of floppy drive over hard drive. The floppy drive motors can be seen as well as the drive power connectors. Note that the sealed hard drive has an additional connector.

5-3(B) Close-up of connectors with floppy drive installed in AT. P1 is the power connector. Controller board is shown at extreme right. Controller connector is shown in lower right corner.

The same head is used for read-write and erase (see Figs. 5-6 to 5-8). The head is moved to the proper track by a positioning motor, usually a stepping motor. The jacket has an index hole that is punched in the disk and marks the beginning of the first sector. The hole is detected by a photosensing circuit (Fig. 5-9). The drive must perform the following functions:

5-4 Top view of floppy disk drive. Note drive spindle in center with photosensor for sectoring next to it. Other photosensor for write-protection table is in lower left corner.

1. Move the head to the track.
2. Use the head to perform either a read or write.
3. Generate or interpret control signals or status information including index hole detection.
4. Drive the spindle motor at a constant speed.

Read and write operations

A read or write operation requires the drive to access the specified track and sector, and to then transfer a block of data. Three operations are needed: (1) head positioning, (2) read-write control, and (3) data transfer.

The head is usually stepped with an incremental stepping motor and takes 3 to 10 ms per step. A head settling delay of 8 to 15 ms is also used to allow for vibrations to die out. The position is verified by reading the track number on the disk and comparing it to a track register. Figure 5-10 summarizes two types of tests used for floppy disk drives, and Fig. 5-11 shows the screen when this test is underway.

Soft sectoring

A hard-sectored disk has a number of holes marking the beginning of every sector. Soft sectoring is used in most PCs, including IBM. In a soft-sectored disk, one pulse is issued per revolution at the beginning of a track. The process is usually repeated every 200 ms. In a soft-sectored disk, sectors must be identified by a header. Less data can be stored compared to hard sectoring but reliability and flexibility are improved.

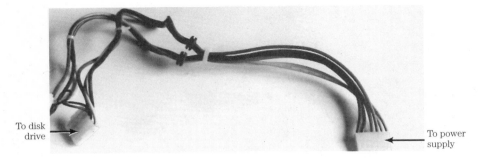

To disk
drive

To power
supply

5-5(A) Drive power cable.

Hard disk power connector

Battery
holder

110/220V
switch

Floppy disk power connector

5-5(B) Drive power connector in 486 tower system.

Recording
head

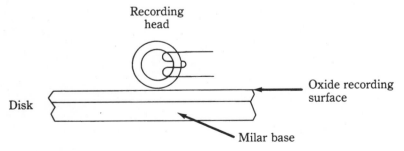

Oxide recording
surface

Disk

Milar base

5-6 Magnetic recording on a magnetic oxide disk.

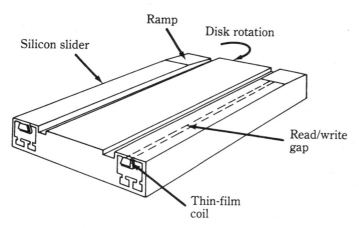

5-7 Thin-film recording head.

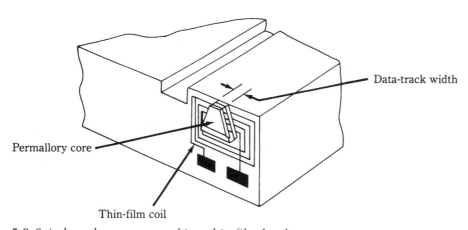

5-8 Spiral conductors are used in a thin-film head.

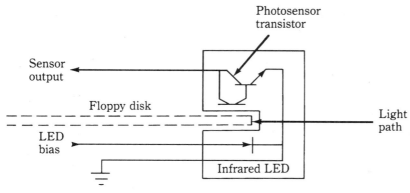

5-9 Photosensing circuit used for indexing.

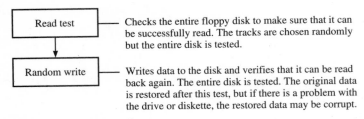

Read test — Checks the entire floppy disk to make sure that it can be successfully read. The tracks are chosen randomly but the entire disk is tested.

Random write — Writes data to the disk and verifies that it can be read back again. The entire disk is tested. The original data is restored after this test, but if there is a problem with the drive or diskette, the restored data may be corrupt.

5-10 Types of floppy drive tests.

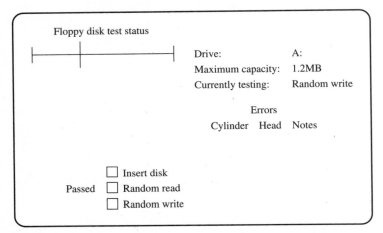

Floppy disk test status

Drive:	A:
Maximum capacity:	1.2MB
Currently testing:	Random write

Errors

Cylinder   Head   Notes

☐ Insert disk
Passed   ☐ Random read
☐ Random write

5-11 Screen for read and write tests.

The INDEX line provides a pulse marking the beginning of sector 0 where the hole in the disk is detected by a photosensitive circuit.

The READY line is true when the diskette has been correctly inserted and is up to speed.

A special tab can be covered on the disk cover. An optical sensor in the drive will detect the covered notch. The tab protects a diskette from accidental writing.

Data recording

Information is recorded on the tracks of the disk in binary format. Usually, an NRZ (not return to zero) technique is used. With NRZ operation, each bit position is magnetized in one direction (1) or the other (0). There is no intermediate state (or true zero), so the process is called NRZ. Frequency modulation (FM) encoding is the basic modulation technique. Each data bit appears exactly halfway between two successive clock pulses.

Other recording methods are used to increase the bit density. The basic idea is to eliminate as many unnecessary clock or data bits as possible. Double-density diskettes use MFM (modified frequency modulation) or M2FM, modified MFM, to increase the recording density. The techniques use a clock bit only if a zero is found in two consecutive frames.

Data on the disk is structured in bytes (groups of eight bits). Each block of information is given a special marker. When the diskette is first used, it is initialized or formatted with these markers.

A serial-to-parallel conversion must be performed to assemble eight bits into a byte. This conversion is usually done by the disk controller.

Density

Two methods can increase the amount of information stored on a floppy disk: increased density and dual heads. *Double density* doubles the number of bits per track by using a packed recording technique, such as modified MFM (M2FM). It requires tight tolerances for reliable operation and is less speed tolerant than regular FM encoding. Dual heads are used for reading and writing both sides of the floppy. The dual heads increase the mechanical complexity of the drive.

Double-density and high-density disks

The main difference between double-density and high-density disks is in the size of the magnetic particles. The difference in particle sizes applies to both 5¼ and 3½ disks. The magnetic particles used in the coating of high-density media are smaller than those found in the double-density media. The smaller the particles, the more data bits you can get on the surface of the disk.

The smaller particles allow the high-density disk to have a higher capacity to hold data. Since the particles are smaller, they emit a lower voltage or signal strength. To allow for this smaller voltage, the read-write head used on a high-density drive must be more sensitive so it can read the signals accurately.

On a double-density diskette, the magnetic particles are larger. These larger particles will send out a stronger voltage or signal strength. The read-write head used in a double-density disk drive is less sensitive than those found in a high-density drive.

You cannot use high-density disks in a low-density drive because the read-write heads will not be able to read the signals clearly. This can result in data errors, problems in retrieving the data, and/or the inability to format the disk properly. You can use low-density disks in a high-density drive if you format the disk properly, but you may have a problem reading a low-density disk (360K) in a 360K drive, if it was formatted and written to in a high-density drive (1.2MB).

High-density drives

Double-density 5¼-inch diskettes use 40 tracks of data with nine 512-byte sectors per track, for a total capacity of 360K. A high-capacity disk such as the 1.44MB 3½-inch disk has 80 tracks and eighteen 512-byte sectors. The larger number of tracks on the 1.44MB disk requires the tracks be placed closer together, and the larger amount of data in a single, smaller circumference track results in the data bits being placed closer together.

When you increase the data density, the magnetic head, which reads the data, must be positioned more accurately over a track. This accuracy is controlled by the positioning motors. Also, since more data exists on the track, the read electronics need to process the data faster because more data moves by the read head in a given time.

Increasing the data density reduces the signal from the magnetic material and it becomes harder for the read electronics to detect the true and false states.

Most media manufacturers refer to an unformatted storage capacity while drive manufacturers specify formatted capacity. A 1.44MB floppy diskette has an unformatted capacity of 2MB. The newer 4MB diskettes have a formatted capacity of 2.88MB.

Higher densities

Higher-density disks (beyond 1.44MB floppies) manufactured by companies such as Toshiba use a different magnetic material. The floppy disk circle of mylar is coated with a thin layer of magnetic material. Typically, disks have a ferric oxide coating, where the magnetic particles are *acicular* (needle-shaped). These particles tend to lie flat so that the needles are in line with the mylar (see Fig. 5-12).

To get the higher data density needed for 4MB diskettes, a different magnetic material, barium ferrite, is used. Barium ferrite particles are *hexagonal platelets* (thin hexagonal disks) as shown in Fig. 5-13. These hexagonal disks lie flat on the mylar.

When you encode data onto a ferric oxide–coated disk, the rodlike particles are magnetized along their length. One end of the rod becomes a north pole and the other a south pole.

When you encode data on a barium ferrite–coated disk, the magnetization axis is through the pill-shaped particles rather than across them. An individual particle will have a north or south pole at the top and a south or north pole at the bottom. This is called *perpendicular,* or *vertical, encoding.*

The read head, which detects the magnetic information stored on the disk, passes over the surface. This head must be able to detect the transition between the areas

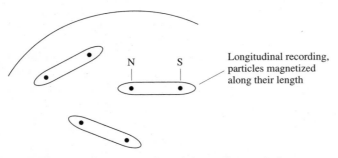

Longitudinal recording, particles magnetized along their length

5-12 Ferric oxide coating, low-density floppy disk.

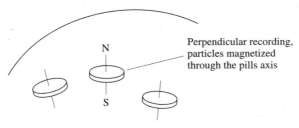

Perpendicular recording, particles magnetized through the pills axis

5-13 Barium ferrite coating, 4MB floppy disk.

where particles are magnetized in one direction and the area where the particles are magnetized in the other direction. On a ferric oxide disk, the transition area is not distinct since the particles may lie in different directions.

In a barium ferrite disk, the distinction is much clearer. This allows the data density to be increased because the edges can still be detected. A 1.44MB floppy disk (ferric oxide) has a density of 17,434 bits per inch while a barium ferrite disk almost doubles this to 34,768 bits per inch.

Disk controllers

In the older PCs, a disk controller card is used that plugs into one of the expansion slots. The disk controller card has a ribbon data cable that connects to the disk drive. A typical controller card can support four disk drives. Many newer PCs have the controller built into the system board.

The data that moves between the disk and the processor is usually controlled by a direct memory access controller such as the 8237 (Fig. 5-14) on the main board. It controls the data transfer operations and is used to move data from the disk to computer memory, from the computer memory to disk, and from one disk drive to another disk drive.

When a disk drive needs to send data, it sends a signal to one of the DREQ (data request) lines of the DMA controller. The chip first turns on one of its DACK (data acknowledge) lines. Then the chip sends a signal to the other I/O devices that puts them into a three-state condition. Next, the starting address and the number of bytes to be transferred are sent to the DMA controller. The data is sent from the disk through the disk controller card onto the data bus and into RAM. After the transfer is complete, control of the data bus is returned to the processor.

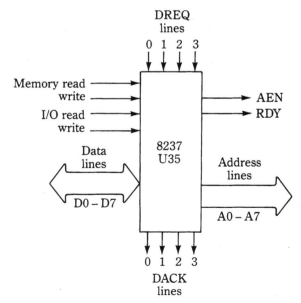

5-14 8237 direct memory access controller.

The floppy disk interface must be able to convert data from serial-to-parallel format and from parallel-to-serial format. The interface must be able to match the data bus in the computer with the disk drive. The data from the bus is converted from parallel to serial and conditioned into the bit pattern format needed by the disk drive circuits.

When data is going the other way, from the floppy disk to the computer, the bits must be also be conditioned. Synchronization bits are used to surround the actual data so that variations in speed of the rotating disk do not cause errors. When the data transfer is complete, the controller turns the operation of the computer back to the processor.

The power connector is a 4-pin, mate-n-lock-type connector. The digital signals use +5.0 Vdc in most desktop systems although +3.3 or +3.0 Vdc are used in some portable computers. The motors normally operate on +12 Vdc. A return, or ground, lead is provided for each supply in the connector. In the 34-pin signal connector, the odd-numbered pins are ground lines, while even-numbered pins are used for the signals. The IBM PC floppy drive connections are shown in Table 5-1 and the signal definitions are shown in Table 5-2.

Floppy disk controller chips

The Intel 82077 is a single-chip floppy disk, and tape drive controller for AT and PS/2 buses. The 82077 uses a 24-MHz crystal, resistor array, and chip select circuits to implement the floppy disk controller. There is an analog data separator for motor speed control and a 16-byte FIFO (first-in-first-out) register. All command parameters and data transfers go through the FIFO.

Table 5-1. Pinlist for IBM PC floppy drive interface

Pin	Function	Pin	Function
2	Normal/high density*	1	Ground
4	In use/head load*	3	"
6	Drive select 3	5	"
8	Index	7	"
10	Drive select 0*	9	"
12	Drive select 1*	11	"
14	Drive select 2*	13	"
16	Motor ON*	15	"
18	Direction*	17	"
20	Step	19	"
22	Write data	21	"
24	Write gate*	23	"
26	Track 00*	25	"
28	Write protect*	27	"
30	Read data	29	"
32	Side select*	32	"
34	Disk change/ready*	33	"

*Indicates a negative true signal.

Table 5-2. Floppy drive signal definitions

DRIVE SELECT 0-3	Determines which drive in the system is active.
MOTOR ON	Starts the drive spindle motor.
DIRECTION SELECT	Head direction.
STEP	Controls the number of steps that the head stepping motor takes.
WRITE DATA	Records information on the disk.
WRITE GATE	Enables the drive to accept data on the WRITE DATA line.
IN USE/HEAD LOAD	Indicates that the read-write head is in use.
WRITE PROTECT	Prevents writing to the disk if the write-protection notch is covered.
READ DATA	When a read takes place, the data is sent on this line.
DISK CHANGE/READY	Tells when the disk is ready for a read or write SIDE.
SELECT	Determines which side of the disk is written or read to.
NORMAL/HIGH-DENSITY	Tells the floppy drive controller what type of media is in use.
INDEX	Negative indexing pulses sent to the floppy drive controller to regulate the spindle speed at the proper value.
TRACK 00	Indicates that the head is at track 00 on the disk.

The main signals that make up the controller interface are shown in Table 5-3.

The chip runs on +5 volts on pins 18, 40, 60, and 68. The ground pins are 9, 12, 16, 21, 36, 50, 54, 59, and 65. AVCC on pin 46 is used for the analog supply and AVCC on pin 45 is used for the analog ground.

Data separation

A data separator is to lock onto the incoming serial read data. When a lock is achieved, the chip's clock is synchronized to the read data. This synchronized clock is called the Data Window and is used to sample the serial data.

One state of the Data Window is used to sample the data portion of the bit cell, and the other state samples the clock portion. Serial to parallel conversion logic separates the read data into clock and data bytes.

For reliable disk/tape reads the data separator tracks changes in the read data frequency. These frequency errors may be caused by motor rotation speed variations and frequency shifts from bit jitter.

The data separator is made up of two analog phase lock loops (PLLs). These are called the *reference PLL* and the *data PLL*. The reference PLL is also called the master PLL since it is used to bias the data PLL. The reference PLL adjusts the data PLL's operating point as a function of the process, junction temperature, and supply voltage. This eliminates the need for external trimming.

Write precompensation

Write precompensation circuits are used to minimize bit shifts in the RDDATA stream from the disk drive. This shifting of bits is due to material changes in the magnetic media. The 82077 monitors the bit stream that is being sent to the drive. The data patterns that require precompensation are adjusted relative to the surrounding bits.

Table 5-3. Floppy disk controller signals

CS	Pin 6	Decodes the base address range
A0, A1, A2	Pins 7, 8, 10	Selects one of the chip's registers
DB0–DB7	Pins 11, 13, 14, 15, 17, 19, 20, 22	Data bus
RD	Pin 4	Read control input
WR	Pin 5	Write control input
RDDATA	Pin 41	Read data input, provides serial data from the disk
WP	Pin 1	Write protect input, indicates if the drive is write protected
DSKCHG	Pin 31	Indicates a DISK CHANGE has occurred, disk ready for a read or write
DRQ	Pin 24	DMA request signal, which is sent out to request service from a DMA controller
DACK	Pin 3	DMA acknowledge control input used in DMA cycles
TC	Pin 25	Terminal count control signal sent from a DMA controller to end the disk transfer
INT	Pin 23	Interrupt output, signals a data transfer in non-DMA mode
DENSEL	Pin 49	Density select, indicates if a low (250/300 Kbps) or high (500 Kbps/1 Mbps) data rate is selected
DRV2	Pin 30	Indicates if a second drive is installed
INDX	Pin 26	Index input, indicates the beginning of the track
TRK0	Pin 2	Track 0 control line, indicates head is on track 0
HIFIL	Pin 38	High filter, analog reference signal used for internal data separator compensation
LOFIL	Pin 37	Low filter, low noise ground return for the reference filter capacitor which is also connected to HIFIL
PLL0	Pin 39	Input used to optimize the data separator for either floppy disks or tape drives
X1, X2	Pins 33, 34	Crystal connections for 24-MHz crystal
MFM	Pin 48	After reset indicates current data encoding/decoding mode
RESET	Pin 32	Places chip in idle state

Read-write operations

A read or write operation takes several steps to complete. The motor is turned on, head positioned to the correct cylinder, DMA controller initialized, the read or write command initiated, and error recovery implemented.

Before data can be transferred to or from the diskette, the disk drive motor must be at full speed. In most 3½-inch disk drives, this spinup takes 300 ms, while the 5¼-inch drive usually requires about 500 ms due to the increased inertia from the larger disk.

One method for minimizing the motor spinup delay for a read involves starting the read operation right after the motor is turned on. If the motor is not up to speed, the internal data separator will not lock onto the incoming data stream. The read operation is repeated until successful. If locking to the data stream takes place when the motor speed variation is significant, errors in reading the disk by some disk controllers can result. The disk drive head is positioned over the correct cylinder by executing a SEEK command. After the seek is complete, there is a head settling time before the read or write operation can begin. For most drives, this delay is more than 15 ms. If the head is already positioned over the correct cylinder, there is no head settling time. Then, the DMA controller is initialized for the data transfer and the read or write command is executed.

Disk formatting

Soft sectoring relates to the division of the disk or track into sectors by software. Soft sectoring is the opposite of hard sectoring, where the beginning of each sector is detected from a hole in the disk. In soft sectoring, each track is marked by a physical index pulse, corresponding to the detection of the index hole on the disk. The disk is marked during the formatting operation.

Every data record is marked by a unique identifier and successive records are separated by gaps. *Gaps* are used to protect the following or the preceding record. Because of speed variations in the disk drive motor, whenever a record has all or some of its contents rewritten, the end of the record might extend beyond the previous record end.

Error detection

A checksum technique is usually used for error detection of any data written on the disk. CRC (cyclic redundancy checking) is one method used. Special CRC bytes are used at the end of a group of data bytes. The data bits are divided by a special equation, usually a polynomial.

The remainder from this division becomes the CRC bytes. When reading data from the diskette, the CRC bytes are checked for errors. The floppy disk controller performs the CRC generation and checking.

Maintenance of disk drives

Some oxide will often build up to form on floppy disks. The oxides form from dust and other contaminates in the air. Because the disk runs so close to the read-write head, some of these oxides will be transferred to the head. If enough oxide collects on the head, the drive will make read or write errors, and if this is allowed to continue there might be damage to the disks or the head.

Cleaning the heads can be done with medical alcohol and a cotton swab that is wrapped in a lint-free material. Use the alcohol sparingly and do not wet any of the components around the head.

A disadvantage with this manual cleaning procedure is that you must remove the system-unit cover and usually the head cover from the disk drive. Each drive manufacturer has its own way to cover or protect the head assembly. Make some notes before you attempt to take it apart. Once you do gain access to the head, then you can clean the oxides off. When the head appears to be clean, let the area dry before you reassemble the head cover and the system unit.

A quicker method is to purchase a head cleaning disk. You can use a special cleaning solvent to clean the head on the disk. Insert the cleaning disk into the disk drive and allow it to rotate. The turning motion of the drive rubs the solvent material against the head and rubs off the oxides.

Floppy disk testing

You can test floppy disk drives with a diagnostic disk. Insert the diagnostic disk and select the floppy tests from the main menu. A message similar to the following will appear on the monitor:

Floppy Tests—Drives A and B
Number of Drives to be Tested? select 1 or 2

You might be asked to remove the diagnostic disk and insert a formatted scratch disk, see Fig. 5-15. Then a selection menu such as that shown in Fig. 5-16 will appear. You select the floppy disk tests you desire from this menu, and your selection will take you to the next menu.

When you remove the diagnostic diskette and insert blank or scratch diskettes into drives A and B, a message such as the following will appear on the monitor:

WARNING CONTENTS OF DISKETTES ARE DESTROYED!!!

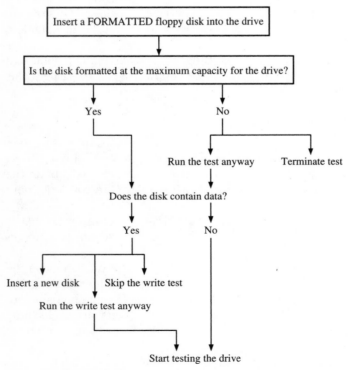

5-15 Beginning floppy disk test menu.

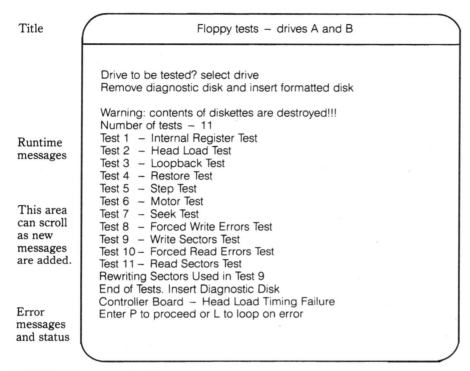

Title

Floppy tests – drives A and B

Runtime
messages

Drive to be tested? select drive
Remove diagnostic disk and insert formatted disk

Warning: contents of diskettes are destroyed!!!
Number of tests – 11
Test 1 – Internal Register Test
Test 2 – Head Load Test
Test 3 – Loopback Test
Test 4 – Restore Test
Test 5 – Step Test
Test 6 – Motor Test

This area
can scroll
as new
messages
are added.

Test 7 – Seek Test
Test 8 – Forced Write Errors Test
Test 9 – Write Sectors Test
Test 10 – Forced Read Errors Test
Test 11 – Read Sectors Test
Rewriting Sectors Used in Test 9
End of Tests. Insert Diagnostic Disk
Controller Board – Head Load Timing Failure

Error
messages
and status

Enter P to proceed or L to loop on error

5-16 Disk drive speed adjustment.

You can usually run the tests automatically, first testing drive A and then testing drive B if desired.

Random read and write tests

The read test will check the entire floppy disk to make sure that it can be successfully read. The tracks read are chosen randomly and this simulates normal operating conditions during the test. The write test will write data to the disk and verify that it can be read back again. Like the read test, the tracks are chosen randomly.

Types of errors

Three basic types of errors can occur during a read-write operation, which are often caused by problems with the disk media.

1. *Write errors.*   Write errors occur when data on the disk is not written correctly. One technique used to verify whether data has been correctly written is to use a write-check. Normally, you will be asked to write the data again repeatedly. If this fails repeatedly, the sector or the track might be damaged and the disk might not be usable. A reformatting can be tried as a further check.
2. *Read errors.*   There are two types of read errors. A *soft error* means the error is not permanent and can usually be corrected by rereading or by moving the

head. Typically, the head is moved one step in its previous direction and then moved back. Usually, this will correct the read errors. If the disk movement fails to correct the problem, it is a *hard error* and unrecoverable. Read errors can occur during the read test or during the write test while reading the data to be compared.

3. *Seek errors.* Seek errors occur when the head does not reach the correct track. When this type of error is detected, the track counter of the disk drive must be reset. The head is moved back to the first track and a new seek order is issued. Seek errors occur when the drive stepper motor is not working properly or when there is an obstruction to the movement of the read-write head on the drive.

The following errors can occur when there is a problem with the drive. Some of these problems can be caused by a bad cable or improperly installed drive. Other possible causes are also discussed.

Comparison errors

Comparison errors occur during the write test if the data read from a disk is not the same as what was written. This type of error is a major problem because it shows that the drive is not properly detecting errors.

Disk changed

Disk-changed errors appear if the disk is changed during the test. Disk-changed errors will also appear if any of the hardware used for the disk-change function, including the drive-door sensors, is malfunctioning on the drive. The error usually aborts the test.

Drive not ready

The drive-not-ready error indicates that the drive motor is not working or the drive door is open or its sensors have malfunctioned during the test.

Write protected

Write-protected errors indicate that there is a write-protect tab on the disk being tested. It can also appear if the write-protect mechanism is malfunctioning on a drive. This error usually aborts the test.

Disk problems

When you get disk errors during tests, run the test again with several different disks to rule out the possibility of bad media. Another probable cause for errors is dirty read-write heads. You can try cleaning the heads and run the test again. If the head cleaning or new media do not correct the problem, the disk drive might have a defective component or need alignment.

Most tests will check the entire disk by using random jumps from track to track. This test helps to test head alignment, the stepping motor, and timing of the drive. More extensive floppy disk tests use a special spiral diskette for timing functions.

Disk drive troubleshooting

When a disk drive fails to boot a system disk, one of several problems might exist: the disk might be bad, there might be a drive electronics or cable failure, the drive mechanics might be out of tolerance, the disk drive controller in the expansion slot might be at fault, or the system board itself might have a failure. Use the procedure of Fig. 5-17 for basic troubleshooting and the procedures in Figs. 5-18 and 5-19 to remove and replace the drive. The drives are usually mounted in a cage on mounting rails as shown in Fig. 5-20. A blank panel is used to cover an empty drive opening.

Check to see if you have the configuration switches set correctly; for example, in the IBM PC, if SW1 switches 1, 7, and 8 are on, this indicates to the system that you do not

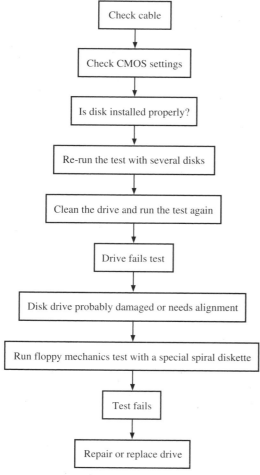

5-17 Floppy drive troubleshooting.

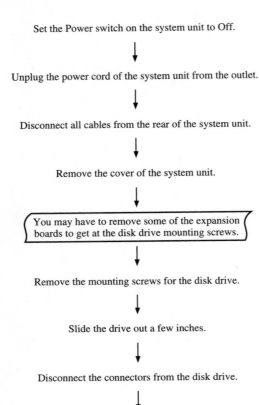

Set the Power switch on the system unit to Off.

↓

Unplug the power cord of the system unit from the outlet.

↓

Disconnect all cables from the rear of the system unit.

↓

Remove the cover of the system unit.

↓

You may have to remove some of the expansion boards to get at the disk drive mounting screws.

↓

Remove the mounting screws for the disk drive.

↓

Slide the drive out a few inches.

↓

Disconnect the connectors from the disk drive.

↓

Remove the disk drive from the system unit.

5-18 Disk drive removal.

have any floppy drives attached. In systems that use a CMOS setup, go into setup and check that the settings match the hardware that is installed.

The boot-up diagnostics usually provide some clues. If you get a short beep and no disk boot, the problem is probably the diskette or in the drive itself. An error display of 601, 606, 607, 608, 611, 612, 613, or 621 through 626 indicates a malfunction in the disk system (disk media, drive, cable, or controller).

When a disk-related malfunction occurs during operation, you must verify that the problem is not in the disk you are using. Reboot with a good copy of the system disk. If the disk seems good, try to reboot with the same disk that you were using when the problem occurred. If a failure occurs, the disk is bad or needs formatting.

Will not boot from drive A

If you cannot boot and run from drive A, power-down, unplug the drive data cable from drive A, and try connecting it to drive B. Also, you can swap the jumper at 1E on the IBM controller card between drives A and B. Power-up again and reboot using drive B. If drive B boots normally, drive A has a malfunction. If not, power-down and check the

Slide the drive in until the front panel is a few inches from the frame.

Connect the cables to the disk drive.

Slide the drive in until the face plate is even with the front panel.

Install the mounting screws.

Adjust the drive for a clearance of 1.0 mm (0.040 in.) between the rear of the front panel and the face plate.

Tighten the mounting screws.

Install the expansion boards.

Install the cover of the system unit.

Connect all cables.

5-19 Disk drive replacement.

Drive cage

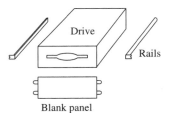

5-20 Drive replacement.

cable for continuity. Clean and examine the cable and the adapter card edge connectors. Check for +5 V on pin 4 and +12 V on pin 1 of the power supply cable. If the power at the plug is normal, check the disk drive controller card.

Both drive lights on

If both drive run lights turn on when reading or writing a disk, check the cables to see if the drive A cable is connected to drive B. An active low signal on either the MOTOR ON, MOTOR ENABLE (A), DRIVE SELECT (A), or DRIVE SELECT (B) lines can cause the LED (CR27 on IBM drives) to turn on. Other possible causes could be failure of the U16 output NAND 7438 or U17 output D flip-flop 74LS273 on the older IBM controller cards. Most cards from this time frame use similar circuits, although the U numbers will differ.

Cannot read data

If you cannot read data from either floppy drive, there could be a failure in the U6 FDC UPD765 or U7 driver MC3487 in the older IBM controllers.

Seek error problems

If you get a SEEK ERROR message displayed, a track is unreadable or head misalignment has occurred. Try to read another disk. If this does not work, it could be the U4 two-input AND gate 74LS08, U6 floppy disk controller D765AC (UPD765), or U18 tristate octal inverter buffer 74LS240 on the IBM controller.

Cannot write-protect data

If you have a problem protecting data on a write-protected disk, it could be a failure in the U6 FDC UPD765, U10 multiplexer 74LS153, U11 D flip-flop 74LS175, or U18 tristate octal inverter buffer 74LS240 in the IBM controller.

Floppy drive diagnostic tests

A number of products are available for diagnosing floppy drives. They can identify most major causes of floppy drive failure without drive removal.

Many of these offer online help and are menu driven. Typical floppy disk drive diagnostic tests include head alignment, head read span, head step linearity, hysteresis, track zero alignment, drive speed, overwrite/read, noise interference, and write protect.

Some products use a separate analog alignment disk and a digital diagnostic disk. Products are available that allow you to diagnose and align 360K, 720K, 1.2Mb, and 1.44Mb MS-DOS–compatible drives.

Most alignment products use a special spiral track disk, and a test and alignment can be done in about 10 minutes. An accuracy to several tenths of a mil is possible on tests such as radial head alignment.

These spiral alignment disks have a limited life and can only be used several hundred times. They are similar to lubricated cleaning disks in that they are good for only about 200 uses.

Adjusting disk speed

Most floppy drives rotate at 300 rpm. If the drive belt is worn or broken, use the procedures in Figs. 5-21 and 5-22 to remove and replace the belt. When the drive speed

Set the Power switch on the system unit to Off.

Unplug the power cord of the system unit from the outlet.

Disconnect all cables from the rear of the system unit.

Remove the cover of the system unit.

Remove the floppy drive.

Place the drive on a work surface, with
the drive belt and pulleys facing up.

Lift the belt off the large pulley,
then off the small pulley.

5-21 Floppy drive belt removal.

Place the drive belt around the small pulley with dark,
shiny side facing the pulleys, then around the large pulley.

Install the disk drive.

Install the cover of the system unit.

Connect all cables.

5-22 Floppy drive belt replacement.

changes due to mechanical wear, the read-write head might not be able to function properly. If the speed is not correct, the head might read a wrong address or write to a wrong sector on the disk. If this occurs, you can adjust the drive speed and make it as close as possible to the designated value.

You can adjust a small resistive control on floppy disk drives with a screwdriver. A method of measuring the drive rpm is needed so the adjustment can be made at the proper speed. You can measure drive speed in one of two ways.

On the bottom of the many drives is a marked pulley with timing marks (Fig. 5-23). The outer marks are designed to be used with a 60-Hz light. To use these timing marks

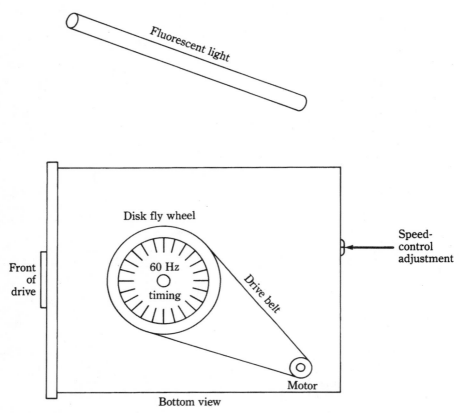

5-23 Disk drive speed adjustment.

you shine a 60-Hz light on them. The timing marks should appear to be stationary when the disk is running at the desired speed.

If the timing marks appear to be rotating during the test, then the resistive control needs adjustment. The marks could be rotating in either one direction or the other. You can stop them by adjusting the speed control until the marks appear stationary. This speed is the one that is desired.

Another technique is to use a disk drive speed program disk. You run the speed test program and the display shows the current speed setting (Fig. 5-24). You can then adjust the speed control until the display shows the speed at 300 rpm. Fluorescent light testing does not allow as fine an adjustment as the drive speed program disk. The procedures for both types of tests are shown in Figs. 5-25 and 5-26.

Hard drives

Hard drives usually require a read-write controller, a head actuator/driver, a spindle motor controller, and a disk interface controller. Data enters and leaves the hard drive through the disk interface controller. This controller is designed for the drive's

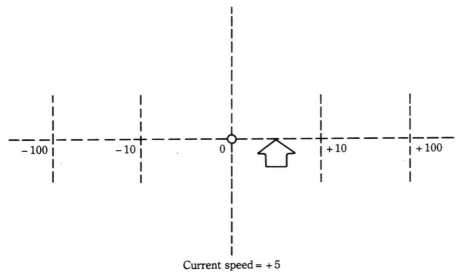

Current speed = + 5

5-24 Typical disk drive test program display—disk drive speed test.

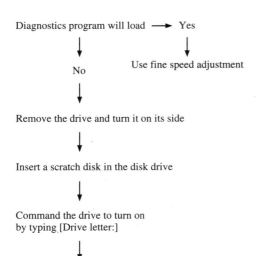

Diagnostics program will load ⟶ Yes

No ↓   ↓ Use fine speed adjustment

Remove the drive and turn it on its side

Insert a scratch disk in the disk drive

Command the drive to turn on
by typing [Drive letter:]

Using fluorescent lighting, adjust the variable resistor on the drive
circuit board until the proper ring of strobe marks appear to stand
still. The outer ring is for 60 hertz, and the inner ring is for 50 hertz.

5-25 Floppy drive motor speed adjustment (coarse).

interface. Most early drives used the Seagate ST-506 for drives which were under
40MB. The ESDI (Enhanced Small Device Interface) doubled the transfer rate to 10MB
per second which allowed more data on the hard disk. Both of these use a 34-pin cable
for the drive control signals, similar to a floppy drive, and a 20-pin cable for the parallel data transfers. The IDE and SCSI interfaces are later standards used in most current

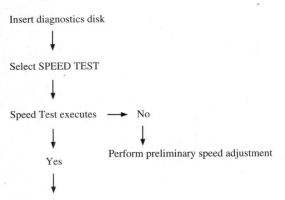

Insert diagnostics disk

Select SPEED TEST

Speed Test executes ⟶ No

Yes

Perform preliminary speed adjustment

Adjust variable resistor until speed is within specification

5-26 Floppy drive motor speed adjustment (fine).

hard drives. The disk interface controller also controls the head actuator driver circuit and spindle motor driver.

Read-Write controller

The Read-Write controller works with the head preamplifier and drive circuits to convert the analog waveforms from the read heads into standard logic levels. The Read-Write controller separates the clock and synchronization signals from the actual binary data. When data is written to the disks, the Read-Write controller generates the write signals that are amplified by the write drive circuits.

Built into the hard drive circuitry is a small microprocessor that coordinates the drive's operations by synchronizing the disk interface controller and the Read-Write controller. This microprocessor is also used for disk spinup and spindown, as well as other safety control features that the drive might have. Some drives use a custom version of a microprocessor called a *microcontroller.* Other hard drives use a standard microprocessor. For the small drives, such as the 1.3-inch units in small portable computers, these circuits are integrated onto one or two complex surface-mount ICs.

Data transfers

A data transfer starts when the main board microprocessor initiates a command to the hard drive controller. In many systems a system controller chip actually drives the hard drive controller. Any parameters that are needed to control the hard drive are taken by the microprocessor from the BIOS ROM.

Hard drive controller

The hard drive controller interfaces the system buses (control, address, and data) to the drive's interface. Data and commands from the drive are converted into computer bus signals by the hard drive controller. The control circuits on the hard drive are used to operate the drive's mechanical functions and to convert the digital information from the interface into magnetic flux patterns that are recorded on the disk. This process of recording and data transfer is reversed for write operation, where the flux patterns are amplified and interpreted for the microprocessor.

IDE drives

IDE, which stands for *Intelligent Drive Electronics* or *Integrated Drive Electronics,* is a popular interface in personal computers for connecting hard drives. It is also known as *ATA,* for AT attachment, which was its original use in the IBM AT PCs. IDE can support two drives of 528MB each. It cannot support external drives or other devices such as CD-ROMs and tape drives.

The circuits needed to operate an IDE drive are on a circuit board which is part of the hard drive assembly. The software routines needed to communicate with the IDE drive are stored in the BIOS ROM on the system board.

The IDE interface connects the hard drive to the system board with a 40-pin connector. The signal cable typically uses a 40-pin insulation displacement connector (IDC). All signals on the IDE interface are TTL-compatible; a logic zero is 0.0 to +0.8 Vdc, and a logic one is +2.0 to Vcc.

There is also a 4-pin power cable in addition to the 40-pin signal cable. The cable pinouts are shown in Table 5-4. The power connector is a 4-pin mate-n-lock-type con-

Table 5-4. Pinlist for IDE hard drive interface

Pin	Function	Pin	Function
2	Ground	1	Reset*
4	DD8	3	DD7
6	DD9	5	DD6
8	DD10	7	DD5
10	DD11	9	DD4
12	DD12	11	DD3
14	DD13	13	DD2
16	DD14	15	DD1
18	DD15	17	DD0
20	Connector Key	19	Ground
22	Ground	21	DMARQ
24	Ground	23	DIOW*
26	Ground	25	DIOR*
28	Reserved	27	IORDY
30	Ground	29	DMACK*
32	IOCS16*	31	INTQ
34	PDIAG*	33	DA1
36	DA2	35	DA0
38	CS3FX*	37	CS1FX*
40	Ground	39	DASP*

nector. IDE hard drives normally use +5 and +12 Vdc. In some low-voltage systems, +3.0 or +3.3 Vdc is used instead of +5.0 Vdc. The return lines for each supply are also part of the power connector. The IDE signals are shown in Table 5-5.

SCSI drives

The Small Computer Systems Interface (SCSI, pronounced *scuzzy*) differs from other disk interfaces in that it is intelligent. Rather than using a hard drive controller that controls the drive, SCSI drives use a host adapter to send commands to the drive. A SCSI drive has an instruction set of commands and up to eight SCSI devices can be connected together on the SCSI bus which uses its own protocol (sequence of events) to communicate between devices. The system microprocessor is not required for the detailed operation of the drive; the SCSI system has enough intelligence to complete each task.

SCSI can be used as a common bus for many types of peripherals, such as CD-ROMs, optical memory devices, modems, and printers. The common bus allows the connection of up to seven other peripherals to one port on the back of the PC.

In a SCSI hard drive, the media defects are mapped out of the usable disk space and when the disk is installed in a system, the defects are recorded so the disk does not use this area. Most hard disks use this feature, but SCSI disk drives can also handle media defects that occur under operating conditions. When the disk develops a bad sector, the drive will prevent data from being written to that sector and redirect the data to another location of the disk.

Connections and terminations

Most of the larger capacity drives are SCSI devices which attach using an SCSI cable supplied with the drive to the PCs SCSI connector. The other SCSI connector on the

Table 5-5. IDE signal functions

DA0 DA2	Address bus lines
CS1FX, CS3FX	Chip select inputs
I/O Read DIOR	Starts a read cycle
I/O Write DIOW	Starts a write cycle
DD0 DD15	Bidirectional data lines, moves data bits in and out of the drive
IORDY	I/O Ready, indicates that a data transfer is needed, the direction of the data transfer is set with DIOR* and DIOW*
IOCS16	16-bit I/O control signal, tells the microprocessor that the drive is ready to send or receive data
DMARQ	Direct memory access, starts the transfer of data to or from the drive
DMACK	DMA acknowledge, sent to the drive from the hard disk controller, when a data transfer is finished
INTQ	Drive interrupt request, used by the drive when there is an interrupt pending
DASP	Drive active, used when the hard drive is busy
PDIAG	Passed diagnostic, indicates the results of a diagnostic command or reset

drive allows you to make a chain of SCSI devices. You can also use other SCSI peripherals, such as scanners and CD-ROM drives. SCSI devices that are connected in a chain require termination and SCSI ID numbers. Termination requires that a special resistor, called a *terminator,* be at both the beginning and the end of a SCSI chain. In many drives, this resistor is built into the electronics. These drives are said to be internally terminated.

Since you need these little black resistor packets to disable the active termination on a device, try one of these tips to keep them from getting lost.

Tape the resistors to the side or top of the device's case. When you need them, you will know where to find them. Remove the resistors from their sockets entirely, and reinsert one of the resistor's legs into its socket. The resistor will be in the right socket, but it will not be connected completely.

In some drives, a separate termination plug is used which you attach to one of the drive's SCSI connectors. Other drives allow you to turn the internal termination on and off with a switch.

If there are two or more SCSI peripherals connected to a PC, an internally terminated drive can be attached only at the beginning or end of the chain. If your PC has an internal hard drive, an internally terminated drive can be attached only at the end of the chain. External and switchable termination are more flexible and a switch is a little more convenient, since there is no terminator plug to lose.

ID numbers

In addition to termination, each peripheral on a SCSI chain must have its own ID number. You set the SCSI ID number with a thumb switch or a rotary dial, a DIP switch, jumpers (usually metal prongs that are covered with a plastic sleeve), or through software. Switches are the most convenient, and they are used on most large-capacity drives. You can usually override the SCSI ID setting with the utility software provided with some drives.

SCSI compatibility problems

Some SCSI command sets have different interpretations which causes one manufacturer's device not to be recognized by another's interface card. Both IBM and Compaq started producing SCSI equipment after many of these different implementations were in use.

There are differences among host adapters and the driver software must be compatible with the host adapter and the other devices. Different SCSI commands may be required by drives manufactured by different vendors. Some manufacturers do not provide SCSI host adapters with their devices and not all host adapters may work with the device. The device driver may need to be installed as part of the setup procedure or it may reside on the host adapter.

Host adapter software

Several variations in host adapters can be found. Adaptec uses a software product that works with its cards called ASPI (Advanced SCSI Programming Interface). Columbia Data Products developed software for cards made by Western Digital called SDLP (Standard Device Level Protocol). These products were developed to resolve the problem of more than one program needing to have access to the same card concurrently.

When ASPI or SDLP are used, the drivers for the disk or tape do not access the hardware directly. They communicate with an ASPI or SDLP driver which coordinates requests and resolves conflicts. A more widely used standard is the Common Access Method (CAM) which allows the same flexibility as ASPI and SDLP.

Software problems

Not every device on your chain requires an ASPI manager. Hard disks, Syquest removable-cartridge drives, and some other types of mass storage can usually be set by your SCSI controller's BIOS as a bootable drive, with no software.

You can remove, or REM out, the ASPI manager in your CONFIG.SYS and try several controller BIOS settings. Check your manual for these settings. If you have other types of devices, such as scanners, connected to your SCSI chain, this will not work. You are going to need the ASPI manager for those drives anyway.

Drivers and memory conflicts

ASPI managers need to reside in the right area in memory. Some ASPI managers cannot be loaded into high memory. If you are installing a set of SCSI drivers, make sure the programs installed by the SCSI package can reside in high memory. If they cannot, specify during a memory optimization which drivers are not to be loaded high. You can use MemMaker for this. Some SCSI packages that support Windows install a new COMM.DRV device in the SYSTEM.INI file, replacing the old one. SCSI packages designed for PCMCIA SCSI adapters use their own COMM.DRV.

Other software, such as communications packages, may be affected. When they do not find the usual COMM.DRV specified in the Windows system configuration, they abort. The SCSI adapter may not work unless the custom driver is present.

Programs that offload existing DRV files for the sake of their own should be avoided. The other solution is to change the communications package.

Controller conflicts

SCSI cards need to coexist with the IDE/floppy/I/O controller that came with your system. These devices can cause conflicts in memory allocation. There are several ways to avoid this problem.

Most SCSI controllers can also work as floppy controllers. When this option is enabled on the board, it will conflict with the floppy controller that is already present. Then, you need to disable the old floppy controller and switch over to the new one or disable the SCSI floppy controller and continue to use the old one. Performance will generally be better with the newer hardware.

Some SCSI controllers support additional parallel and serial ports of their own. You will need to disable these if they are not being used. If they are being used, you need to make sure that they do not conflict with any addresses and ports that already exist.

If you want to disable your native I/O so you can use the SCSI card and your floppy I/O controller is built into the system board, you will need to check your system's ROM

BIOS setup to see if there is a way to disable the functions there. If you cannot find this in CMOS, check your hardware manual to see if there are jumpers or switch settings that change I/O ports.

Scanners

SCSI software packages that come with adapters can include their own TWAIN drivers. These TWAIN drivers are not always compatible with every TWAIN type of scanner. Unless you know your scanner is compatible with one of the models listed in the SCSI documentation, do not load the SCSI package's TWAIN driver. Use the TWAIN driver that came bundled with your scanner.

SCSI cards

A typical card supports the Common Command Set (CCS). Two 128-byte buffers are used for concurrent data transfers on the host bus and the SCSI bus. An on-board BIOS supports bootable devices and automatically configures the system upon power-up. This eliminates the need to run a configuration program or add a driver each time an additional SCSI device is attached to the host adapter. Up to seven SCSI devices and up to four 5¼-inch and 3½-inch floppy disk drives are supported. The card can coreside with hard disk controllers. Board size is 3.8 × 6.0 inches and uses 50-pin Centronics connectors. The current at +5 Vdc is typically 0.58 amps.

SCSI bus

The SCSI bus has 50 pins and 18 signals. Nine are used for an 8-bit data bus with parity and nine are used to coordinate device data transfers. Table 5-6 lists the SCSI bus signals, Fig. 5-27 shows the cable assemblies, and Fig. 5-28 shows the signal flow when a single drive is used.

Table 5-6. SCSI bus signals

Signal	Pin		Signal	Pin
DB0 DATA BUS 0	2		GROUND	30
DB1 DATA BUS 1	4	ATN	ATTENTION	32
DB2 DATA BUS 2	6		GROUND	34
DB3 DATA BUS 3	8	BSY	BUSY	36
DB4 DATA BUS 4	10	ACK	ACKNOWLEDGE	38
DB5 DATA BUS 5	12	RST	RESET	40
DB6 DATA BUS 6	14	MSG	MESSAGE	42
DB7 DATA BUS 7	16	SEL	SELECT	44
DBP BUS PARITY	18	CD	CMD DATA	46
GROUND	20	REQ	REQUEST	48
GROUND	22	I/O	I/O	50
GROUND	24			
TERM PWR	26		Reserved for optional terminator power (plus 5 volts)	

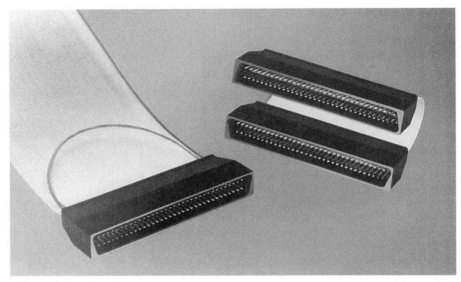

5-27 SCSI cable assemblies.

SCSI system wants to access the hard drive

↓

Drives the SELECT (SEL*) signal to negative true

↓

ATTENTION (ATN*) pin goes true

↓

Drive forces
REQUEST (REQ*) line true.

↓

8-bit message is placed on the bidirectional data bus
(DB0 to DB7)

↓

MESSAGE (MSG*) signal goes true

5-28 SCSI single drive operation.

Hard disk problems

Hard disk drives, as previously discussed, are very similar in concept to floppy disk systems. The main differences are the material the disk is made from and the speed of rotation. The early drives had a rotation speed of 3600 rpm, but some of the larger hard drives have speeds of up to 7200 rpm.

Hard disks are aluminum disks coated with magnetic particles. The drive speed of a hard disk is about 10 times that of a floppy. Because the speed is much higher and the media is rigid, the heads are much closer for read and write operations.

Even though the drive assembly is sealed to prevent dust from getting between the heads and the disk (Fig. 5-29), problems can occur from oxide buildup on the heads and an eventual *head crash* (the head touches the disk and destroys data).

Hard disk utilities

Software known as *disk utilities* can be used to recover after a hard disk crash. Utilities can also help after you have deleted files and want to bring them back. The reason a utility can restore data is that when DOS gets a command to delete a file, it does not actually erase the data off the disk. Instead, it changes the first letter of its name in the directory to a special symbol. Then, when the file is called for by its original name, the operating system will not recognize it.

Unerase and undelete

A utility program with an unerase or undelete function will prompt you for the deleted filename. It will then find it on the disk and rename it, so it can be accessed.

The FAT (file access table) stored by DOS shows the way the files are arranged on the disk. When a disk is accidentally reformatted, the FAT is erased. Some utilities make a copy of the FAT (and other crucial information, such as bindery and trustee rights for a NetWare-formatted disk) and store it at the back of the disk. This copy is not erased during reformatting, and you can replace the original FAT from the copy.

Defragmenting

Another important service that most disk utilities provide is the ability to *defragment* your disk. When DOS writes data to disk, it might not put parts of the same file

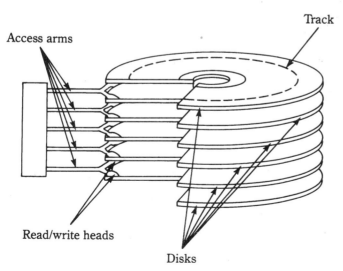

5-29 Sealed components of hard disk drive.

in adjacent sectors. It usually starts from the outside of the disk and moves inward. When it erases a file, it fills up the spaces that erasure creates by moving in a section of a new file. This process causes the fragmentation of files, and it takes the disk heads longer to read a file because they must take extra passes over the disk surface while they are reading the different fragments of the file. A defragmenting utility facility reorganizes the disk surface so that parts of the same file are in adjacent sectors, which saves time when that file is read. Defragmenting also aids in other ways. Accidentally deleted files are easier to recover if they have previously been stored on disk in contiguous clusters.

Instead of using a defragmenting utility to straighten out the disk, you can back up your disk on tape, reformat the disk, and restore the data to the disk. When DOS sends the files to the tape, it collects the bytes for each file from their different locations on disk and sends the file whole. When this data is copied back onto the disk, it comes off the tape in whole files. In this way, it gets back on the disk with all the bytes belonging to individual files in adjacent sectors.

If you use disk utilities, you should make a complete backup of the disk before you even put the utility software diskette in. It is good insurance even if the software vendor guarantees that the program will not damage your data, and not all of them do. The power could fail while the utility is performing the defragmentation and you could permanently lose your data.

Norton Utilities

You can use the Norton Utilities for file recovery and to provide system information. But, like all DOS-based disk utilities, Norton will not work on a NetWare server disk. You can use it with DOS-based network operating systems, including 3Com's 3+.

Norton Utilities runs from a command post program called the Norton Integrator, which also provides online help for each utility. The advanced versions use a program called Speed Disk that arranges the logical structure of the disk. You can use it to optimize the seek time and improve the disk performance.

The Format Recover utility is used to unformat an accidentally reformatted hard disk. A special maintenance mode, can be used for badly damaged disks. It bypasses the DOS logical organization to work at the cluster or sector level. There is a File Al location Table Editor as well as a Partition Table Editor for adding and removing partitions and a Directory Editor. There is also an Absolute Sector mode, for absolute physical sector access and verification.

Golden Bow Utilities

Golden Bow is another set of DOS-based disk utilities. Vopt is a disk organizer package that defragments files, does benchmark timing, and allows you to do system maintenance such as flagging bad clusters. You can run it in under one minute and use a best-fit algorithm.

Vcache is a disk-caching program that can be used to cache up to 15MB of hard disk data in RAM. Vcache is a write-through cache, and all written data is recorded immediately onto the hard disk, unlike a RAM disk. Changes will not be lost if a power failure occurs.

Vfeature Deluxe provides hard disk partitioning for bootable DOS partitions up to 1GB. It supports nonstandard drives, can span two drives into a partition, and includes formatting and security options.

Vtools is a set of tools to display and sort directories and files, delete files or directories, modify them in ASCII or hex format, walk the directory tree, find and display all copies of a file, and compare/update similar files in different directories or disks.

Mace Utilities

Mace Utilities has three programs for DOS-based disks: Recovery, HotRod, and dbFix. Recovery is an unformat utility that you can use if you accidentally reformat your disk. It saves a copy of the index tables at the back end of the disk. If the DOS index tables get deleted during an accidental format, Recovery uses this copy to restore the tables.

Even if you do not have Mace Utilities installed before an accidental format, you can still use the program to restore those files not in the root directory that are relatively continuous on the disk. If the data is subdirectories, you can get back the names of the subdirectories from the names of the files in them. DOS CD command is used to move to the subdirectories where you can find the files. An undelete facility allows you to restore deleted files and subdirectories.

HotRod is a utility for speeding up disk operations by defragmenting your files, providing RAM cache, and sorting directories. dbFix is designed for users of dBase, FoxBase, and Clipper. Files that are lost, unreadable, corrupted, or overwritten can be located, repaired, and recovered. See Fig. 5-30 for basic hard drive troubleshooting techniques.

Disk crashes

Disk utilities can restore a disk when you have accidentally deleted a file or cross-linked files in the same clusters. But they cannot rebuild a destroyed master boot record or get data back after a hardware problem. If this happens and you do not have a backup of the data, or if the backup system fails along with the drive, data from a crashed disk can often be recovered using an outside service. These firms generally perform data recovery along with rebuilding disks in a clean room facility. See Table 5-7 for a list of service firms.

Common hardware problems include controller card failure, where the card might write data improperly to the drive. Other hardware problems can be solved by replacing the circuit board in the drive. If the stepper motor has burned out, it must be repaired or replaced before the data can be retrieved. You can use a diagnostic program such as that shown in Fig. 5-31 to test the controller as well as the hard drive.

If the heads have truly crashed and touched the surface of the platter, iron oxide particles will be removed from the platter, physically destroying data. If a crashed drive is quickly put out of service, it is still possible that some or most of the data can be retrieved.

Drive mounting screws

Four mounting brackets on the side of your disk drive allow you to secure the disk drive to the drive housing. If the screws you use are too long, the threaded end of the

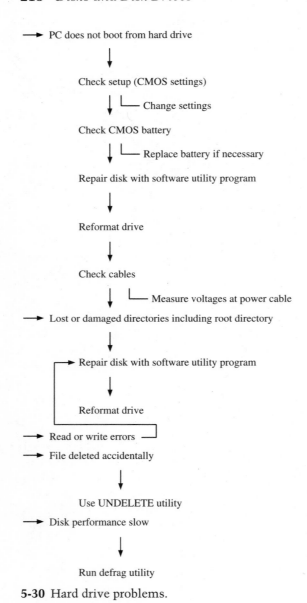

PC does not boot from hard drive

Check setup (CMOS settings)

Change settings

Check CMOS battery

Replace battery if necessary

Repair disk with software utility program

Reformat drive

Check cables

Measure voltages at power cable

Lost or damaged directories including root directory

Repair disk with software utility program

Reformat drive

Read or write errors

File deleted accidentally

Use UNDELETE utility

Disk performance slow

Run defrag utility

5-30 Hard drive problems.

screw can go through the bracket and touch the disk drive housing. When this happens, it is possible for the disk drive housing to become distorted and not work at all. If you back out the screws, the disk drive will work. The screw size for mounting the disk drive to the housing is usually a 6-32 × ⅛ phillips pan-head machine screw. The ⅛-inch length is critical.

Table 5-7. Commercial sources for disk drive repair

ACI Depot Repair Inc.
550 E. Thornton Parkway, Suite 100
Denver, CO 80229
1-800-231-0743

Bell Atlantic Computer Technology Services
4700 Calle Bolero
Camarillo, CA 93012
(805) 987-8628

JB Technologies, Inc.
5105 Maureen Lane
Moorpark, CA 93021
(805) 529-0908

Peripheral Repair Corporation
9233 Eton Avenue
Chatsworth, CA 91311
1-800-627-DISK

Peripherals Unlimited
240 Mayfield Drive, Suite 103
Smyrna, TN 37167
(615) 459-3639

Sprague Magnetics, Inc.
15720 Stagg Street
Van Nuys, CA 91406
1-800-553-8712

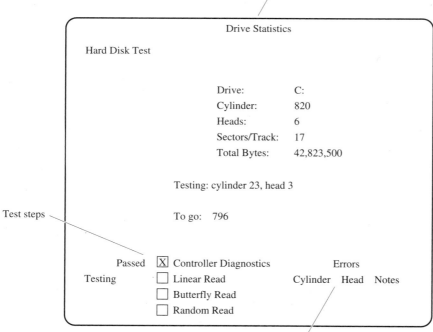

The drive statistics show the physical
characteristics of the drive including its total capacity.

Drive Statistics

Hard Disk Test

Drive:	C:
Cylinder:	820
Heads:	6
Sectors/Track:	17
Total Bytes:	42,823,500

Testing: cylinder 23, head 3

To go: 796

Test steps

Passed   [X] Controller Diagnostics   Errors
Testing   [ ] Linear Read   Cylinder   Head   Notes
                    [ ] Butterfly Read
                    [ ] Random Read

As errors are found, they are
displayed with a short description of the problem.

5-31 Hard disk test screen.

Stiction problems

Stiction is the bonding together of the read-write heads and the media (disks) of a hard disk drive. It occurs primarily with plated (thin-film) media, but it has also occurred on oxide media.

The most common cause of stiction is caused by the read-write heads becoming contaminated with the lubricant used on the media. The lubricant is a fluorocarbon. Fluorocarbons are similar in chemical structure, but not exactly the same, as Teflon. Fluorocarbon is selected because of its lubricity and ability to bond securely to whatever it is applied. Because the spin motor rotates at 3600 rpm or greater, the fluorocarbon needs to bond to the media or it will be lost. If a new disk is measured at various points on the surface, the lubricant will measure between 70 and 110 angstroms, about 2 molecules thick. The thickness of the lubricant after three years of use is more consistent over the surface of the disk than a brand new disk.

Even though the lubricants are selected for their ability to bond securely to a high-speed rotating device, some of the material does spin off. Over time, the material evens out over the disk. The excess lubricant flies off the disk, and some lands on the read-write heads.

Contamination and bonding

Although contamination can occur on all parts of the head assembly, it is the contamination located on the ABS (air-bearing surface) that causes the stiction.

Bonding of the head to the disk can begin the first time the ABS gets contaminated. When the contamination is minor, the torque action of the disk drive spin motor (the motor that rotates the media) during power-up is stronger than the bonding of the heads to the disk. As the contamination increases, the bonding strength can become equal to the spin motor torque. At some point, the bond will exceed the motor torque, preventing the drive from spinning.

In addition to the amount of contaminant, the strength of the bond increases with the amount of time in which the head is in direct contact with the disk. Thus, stiction might not occur when the drive is turned off for a short time, but it will occur when the drive is off for a longer time.

Head parking

Many disk drives park the heads on the disk recording surface. Then, when the disk spins up, the heads drag across the disk until an air bearing is formed. This can cause two types of drive failure: stiction where the heads stick to the media and head slap where the heads actually touch the media. Parking utility software has always been available for moving the heads to the outer edge of the disks to prevent media damage. This is done when the unit is power down. Some drives have this feature built-in.

Head-cleaning fluids

To break the adhesive bond that the fluorocarbon adds to the heads, you must break down the chemical structure of the fluorocarbon. Alcohol and freon, which are generally used for head cleaning, do not break down the chemical structures of fluorocarbons.

Some chemicals will break down the fluorocarbon structure, but they can also cause damage to the other parts of the head assembly, such as the epoxy adhesive on the head, copper wires, wire coatings, plastic wire covers, and stainless steel suspension.

Some special chemical mixtures can be used to remove the fluorocarbon contamination from the read-write heads. These mixtures, if applied correctly, will clean the heads and not damage any of the other head components.

The use of nonlubricated disks will eliminate stiction but will eventually cause a failure by the heads wearing down against the surface of the disk. This type of failure is worse than those caused by stiction, and the failures will occur much quicker.

Some disk drive repair companies are replacing the plated media in the drive with oxide disks. Oxide media does not provide the long-term data integrity and reliability in drives that were originally designed for plated media.

Oxide media

Oxide media begins with a blank, high-precision aluminum disk. The plain disk is then plated with aluminum alloy 5086. The purpose of this alloy is to give the next layer of material, which is a resin mixture, better adhesion to the raw disk.

After this alloy is applied, the resin mixture (an organic polymer with oxide particles mixed in) is applied using a method called *sputtering*. With the disk spinning at 2400 rpm, starting at the inside of the disk, the thick resin mixture (which is almost like a slush or slurry) is sprayed onto the disk at a thickness of about 30 microinches. The spray moves outward until the entire disk is covered. Then the disk is baked to cure and harden the resin mixture.

After baking, the disk is burnished to remove the high spots and surface irregularities. A lubricant is then applied and a second burnishing might be done.

The actual magnetic recording of data occurs with the orientation of the oxide particles in the resin mixture. The movement of these particles creates the north-south magnetic poles.

A problem with oxide media is that you cannot store large amounts of data on the disk because of the nature of the oxide particles in the resin mixture. These particles cannot be produced in a consistent size or shape. So, there are large, medium, and small particles mixed together. The larger particles require greater amounts of magnetic force for polarization. The smaller particles require less magnetic force.

Also, when the oxide particles are mixed into the resin slurry, they do not always mix evenly. In one part of the slurry, there might be a high concentration of particles while another part might have almost no oxide particles. Even under the best of conditions, there is an uneven distribution of oxide.

The resin mixture is essentially a plastic type of paint that is sprayed onto the disk. Over time, sections of the resin might become harder or softer spots depending upon temperature changes and read-write activity. As the texture of the resin changes, the integrity of the disk deteriorates, and you might lose data.

Thin-film disks

Like an oxide disk, a plated or thin-film disk is built up in layers, starting with a high-precision aluminum disk. The first two layers are nickel and chromium. These materials provide greater adhesion and a flatter, smoother surface for the next material that is cobalt phosphorous. This material allows the actual magnetic recording of the data to take place. This layer has a thickness of 2 to 3 microinches compared to 20 to 40 microinches for oxide.

On top of the chromium phosphorous, some disks use a layer of chromium for corrosion resistance and a layer of carbon graphite with diamond particles. The carbon graphite acts as a lubricant, and the diamond particles tend to keep the heads clean. A lubricant is always the last layer because it provides the heads with a smoother lift and landing during power-up and -down. As the drive is powered-up, the heads float at 5 to 25 microinches above the surface of disk. The variation depends on the design of the drive.

Write frequency and drive density

A low frequency used for writing data will penetrate deeper into the media than a higher frequency. A lower frequency is used for oxide disks so it can penetrate through the resin mixture of 40 microinches and manipulate the oxide particles.

A lower frequency produces a wider and taller data bit, which requires wider data tracks that reduces the number of tracks that can be physically placed on the disk. As the write frequency is increased, the data bit becomes smaller. At some point, you won't be able to read the smaller data bit on an oxide disk because of the limitations of oxide in particle size, their distribution, and the resin thickness. The width and the height of the data bit can be adjusted slightly by changing the write current, but this is a minor adjustment primarily used for precompensation.

Thin-film disks use a cobalt phosphorus thickness of only 2 to 3 microinches, which allows a higher frequency to be used for writing data. The higher frequency produces a narrower data bit and allows more bits on a single track. Because the data track does not have to be as wide, there can be more tracks.

The standard MFM and RLL disk drives use frequencies of 5.0 and 7.5 MHz, respectively. The frequencies are close to ideal for oxide disks, but some newer drives write data with frequencies of 10 to 15 MHz.

Some newer controller cards are able to write data at frequencies as high as 100 MHz. They will have be used with disk drive technology that allows frequencies that high. Newer drives may also have several operating modes as shown in Fig. 5-32. Most

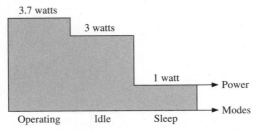

5-32 Some hard drives switch to idle and sleep modes to save power.

486 systems use integrated controllers as shown in Fig. 5-33. Some of these use a drive bracket for the 3½-inch drive as shown in Fig. 5-34(A).

Stepper motor operation

Many older drives use a stepper motor for moving the heads from track to track (see Figs. 5-35 to 5-37). The stepper motor circuit is an open loop, which means there is not a type of signal indicating that the stepper motor has reached the track to which it was sent.

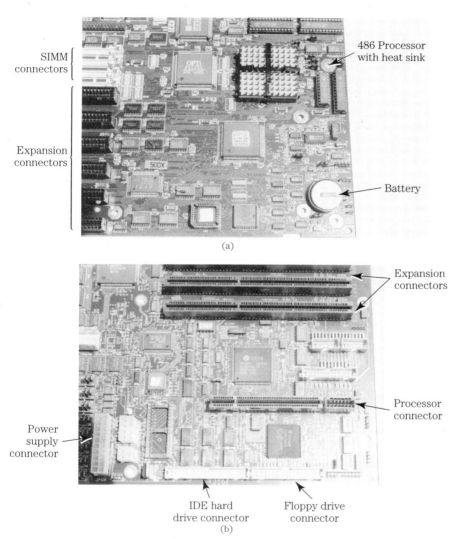

SIMM connectors

486 Processor with heat sink

Expansion connectors

Battery

(a)

Expansion connectors

Processor connector

Power supply connector

IDE hard drive connector

Floppy drive connector

(b)

5-33 Section of 50-MHz 486 DX system board showing battery, on-board battery, on-board processor, SIMM connectors, and expansion connectors (A). Section of 486 board (B).

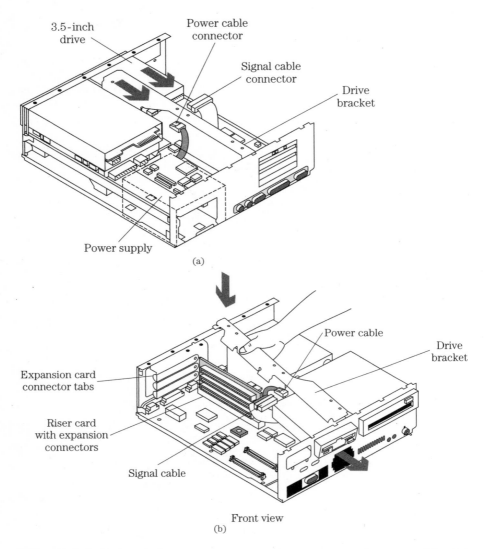

5-34 Changing 32-inch drive in 486 riser card–type system. Remove cables (A). Remove drive bracket; then remove drive (B).

Instead, a calculation is made by the processor to determine the amount of time that the stepper motor needs to position the read-write heads above the proper track. When this time is reached, the processor will send out a SEEK COMPLETE signal, from pin 8 on the 34-pin cable from your drive out to the controller card. This signal will issue a WRITE DATA command to the disk drive or to begin reading the data already on the disk.

The calculation for the SEEK COMPLETE signal depends mainly on the distance that the heads must travel, combined with the amount of torque the stepper motor needs to accomplish this along with the amount of head settling time needed. Head set-

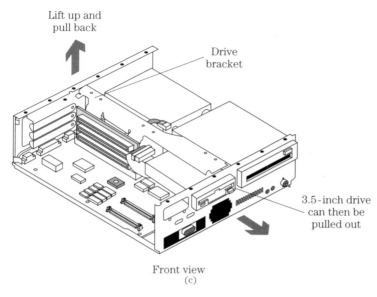

Lift up and
pull back

Drive
bracket

3.5-inch drive
can then be
pulled out

Front view
(c)

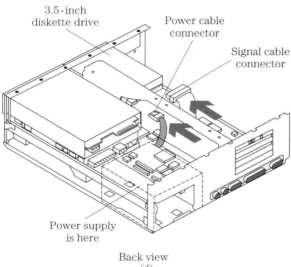

3.5-inch
diskette drive

Power cable
connector

Signal cable
connector

Power supply
is here

Back view
(d)

5-34 (*Continued*) Changing 32-inch drive in 486 riser card–type
system. Remove drive bracket from 486 riser card systems (C). To
replace, first replace drive, then replace bracket and cable connector (D).

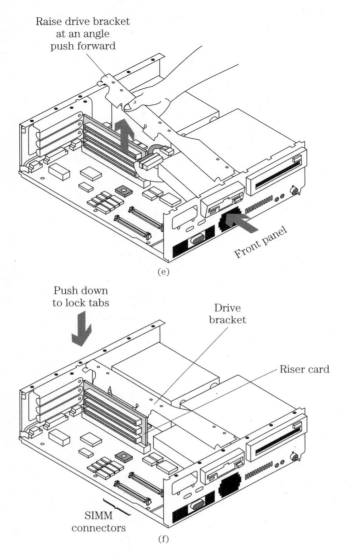

Raise drive bracket
at an angle
push forward

Front panel

(e)

Push down
to lock tabs

Drive
bracket

Riser card

SIMM
connectors

(f)

5-34 (*Continued*) Changing 32-inch drive in 486 riser card–type system. Replace drive bracket from 486 riser card systems (E). Secure drive bracket by aligning tubs with the riser card. Push down to lock in place (F).

tling time is a back and forth action that occurs with the read-write heads as the energy is dissipated before coming to a complete stop.

In the open-loop circuit, the SEEK COMPLETE signal is sent as soon as the calculated time is reached even though the head movement has not stabilized. High or low voltages will increase this head positioning error, tends to be a common problem.

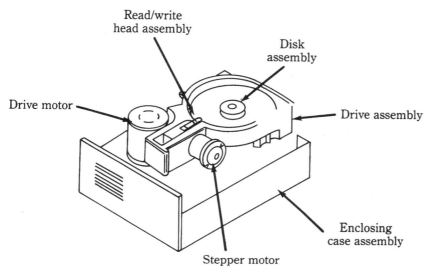

5-35 Typical hard disk drive.

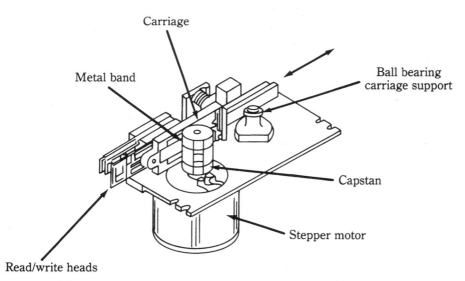

5-36 Hard drive components.

Disk drive voltage-comparator problems

Disk drives use a *voltage comparator* built into the circuit board on the drive, which helps to maintain the integrity of the data on the disk in case the voltage levels going into the disk drive fall below predefined levels.

If the voltage drops below 9.60 V for the 12-V line or 4.25 V for the 5-V line, then the comparator circuit will shut down the disk drive.

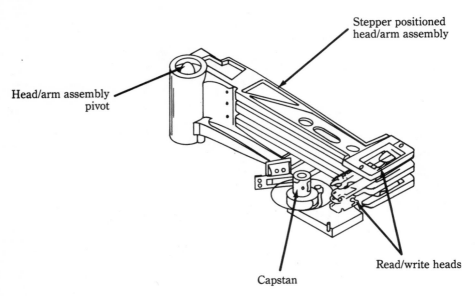

5-37 Radial arm of hard disk drive.

As soon as both voltage levels (5 V and 12 V) are at or above the minimum range, the voltage compare circuit sends out a voltage safe signal and the processor will reset all of the circuits on the disk drive and the drive will begin its power-up sequence. If the voltage drop is long enough, the comparator will shutdown the drive; otherwise, the low voltage will not be detected but it can still cause problems with your system.

Power supplies and data loss

Power supplies can be defective and still supply power to the system, given that they are working properly. A properly working power supply must be able to control the output voltage within 5 percent of the expected voltage levels (including leveling out power-on spikes). This 5 percent tolerance is on the power supply itself. So the 12-V output range becomes 11.40 to 12.60 V, and the 5-V output range becomes 4.75 to 5.25 V.

Leaky inductors and diodes in the power supply can cause problems in two ways: spiking and rippling. *Rippling* can cause an output to fluctuate outside of the acceptable range of the disk drive voltage comparator.

The voltage comparator in the disk drive allows the 12-V line on a disk drive to drop to 9.6 V. If the power supply drops that low, then the system will shut down and you could easily diagnose a defective power supply. If the power supply produces a ripple or momentary change in voltage, the change in voltage might not be long enough to cause a complete disk drive shutdown. Instead, the individual functions of the drive won't work properly. The stepper motor might not be able to step completely to the desired track, which would cause a write or a read failure.

The constant changing of the voltage might cause the spin motor to speed up or slow down. There might not be a large speed difference, but to read the data bit properly, the drive motor spin rate must be stable at 3600 rpm with a 1 percent or 36 rpm tolerance. Some newer drives must maintain the spin speed to a tolerance of ⅒ percent or 3.6 rpm.

The typical disk drive read-write circuitry uses 5 V at the head center tap for a read, and a write function is accomplished by applying 12 V to the center tap. If the drive is writing data to a sector, the voltage drop might not be enough to shut down the drive, but some data might be lost during the low-voltage excursion.

The operation of a disk drive is accomplished by the precise timing of motors spinning, the heads stepping, read or circuit activation, and other timed events. If a circuit chip is malfunctioning and providing inconsistent voltage outputs, a problem can develop. If the main source of power for the drive (the power supply) is failing, you can expect problems in the disk drive, along with the system memory and even the refreshing of characters on the monitor.

Hard disk tests

Many diagnostic programs are available for testing hard disks. Typical of these is CheckIt, which is a general PC diagnostic with hard disk tests, and Spinrite, which is a set of hard disk utilities. As errors are found during the tests, they are displayed on the screen, usually with a short explanation of the problem.

Controller card tests

Normally run the controller card tests at the beginning of the hard disk tests. The operation of the hard disk controller must be checked because a malfunctioning controller card can cause errors and corrupt data, and it will make a good fixed disk act badly or even damage it. If the controller does not pass, the test should be aborted to avoid the possibility of losing data or damaging the hard drive. Controller card testing is summarized in Fig. 5-38.

Read tests

Use read tests to verify each track to make sure that the data on the hard disk can be read. During the test, the cylinder and head currently being tested will be displayed. There are several different types of read tests. Each is designed to find a different type of problem. These procedures are shown in Fig. 5-39.

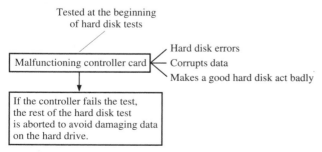

5-38 Hard disk controller card testing.

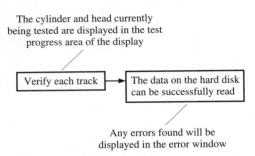

The cylinder and head currently being tested are displayed in the test progress area of the display

Any errors found will be displayed in the error window

5-39 Hard disk read testing.

Linear read test

In the linear read test, each cylinder is checked starting at cylinder 0 and continuing to the last cylinder on the disk. This test makes sure that all of the data can be read under the most basic conditions.

Butterfly read test

In the butterfly read test, each cylinder is read—first the outer cylinders and then the inner cylinders. This test is a worst-case test for the hard disk seeking operation.

Random read test

The random read test is useful for finding problems related to head movement. The tests above represent a more orderly progressive movement for the heads. The random read test is more realistic of the actual head movement. The read tests are summarized in Fig. 5-40.

Error messages

A single error can be reported by several of the preceding tests. The following types of errors are typical. The first types of errors on this list are the least critical, and the errors become more critical as you move down the list.

MARKED BY LOW LEVEL FORMAT.   This message is not considered a problem. It indicates that the error has already been identified by the system. The message

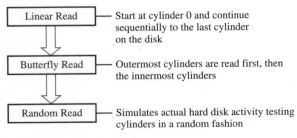

5-40 Types of read tests.

tells you that there is a bad spot on the hard disk. When you run a low-level format on the disk, you should treat this track as bad.

MARKED BY DOS.   This message shows that DOS already knows that this track is bad and the bad spot will not be used by DOS.

SOFT ERROR.   Soft error indicates that a minor type of error occurred. It means that the drive might have had some trouble reading the data. But it was either able to reconstruct the data using ECC (error-correction codes) or by rereading the track. This error also indicates a potential problem track that is starting to fail.

NOT IN A PARTITION.   This message indicates that the bad track is outside the limits of any partition, for any operating system, on the hard disk. This error can occur if you have not assigned all tracks of your hard disk to partitions. Although it might not be a problem now, it might become one when you use FDISK to change the partitions of the hard disk.

NON-DOS PARTITION.   This message indicates that the error occurred in a partition on the hard disk assigned to Xenix or another operating system. You will need to use utilities for that operating system to determine the status of the bad track.

DOS FREE SPACE.   The DOS free space error is caused by a defect on the disk area that is not allocated to DOS. This error can cause data to be lost. If you get this error, always back up your data and reformat the drive. The DOS FORMAT command can be used to identify the bad track and mark it as unusable.

DOS FILE.   The DOS file error occurs when one of your files on the named volume is written on a bad part of the disk. If this occurs, back up your data and reformat the drive. The DOS FORMAT command can identify this bad track and mark it as unusable.

DOS BOOT RECORD.   DOS FILE ALLOCATION TABLE.   DOS ROOT DIRECTORY.   These three DOS types of errors can occur when one of the required sections of the DOS partition is bad. If this occurs, the entire volume might be unusable. Depending on the number of defects and where they are located, you might be able to map out these sectors using the DOS FDISK utility. If you cannot map them out, you might have to get the disk repaired at a disk drive repair facility or it might have to be replaced. Repair or replacement is especially probable if the defects are on the first volume of the disk.

PARTITION TABLE BAD.   This message indicates a major problem. The master boot record (logical sector 0) on the hard disk is bad. If this occurs, you might need to replace your disk because you normally cannot reformat.

EXTENSIVE DAMAGE.   An extensive damage message indicates a serious problem with the hard disk. As the test program was attempting to report the status of a bad sector, it found more bad sectors on critical areas of the disk. You can try reformatting and if this does not work, the drive must usually be sent to a repair facility or replaced. The different types of hard disk errors are summarized in Fig. 5-41.

When a hard drive has many failures, the test will usually be aborted to avoid damaging the drive any further. If the drive is failing badly, copy all your important data.

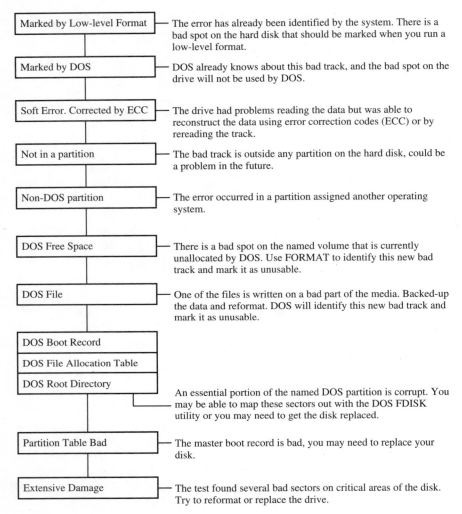

Marked by Low-level Format	— The error has already been identified by the system. There is a bad spot on the hard disk that should be marked when you run a low-level format.
Marked by DOS	— DOS already knows about this bad track, and the bad spot on the drive will not be used by DOS.
Soft Error. Corrected by ECC	— The drive had problems reading the data but was able to reconstruct the data using error correction codes (ECC) or by rereading the track.
Not in a partition	— The bad track is outside any partition on the hard disk, could be a problem in the future.
Non-DOS partition	— The error occurred in a partition assigned another operating system.
DOS Free Space	— There is a bad spot on the named volume that is currently unallocated by DOS. Use FORMAT to identify this new bad track and mark it as unusable.
DOS File	— One of the files is written on a bad part of the media. Backed-up the data and reformat. DOS will identify this new bad track and mark it as unusable.
DOS Boot Record / DOS File Allocation Table / DOS Root Directory	— An essential portion of the named DOS partition is corrupt. You may be able to map these sectors out with the DOS FDISK utility or you may need to get the disk replaced.
Partition Table Bad	— The master boot record is bad, you may need to replace your disk.
Extensive Damage	— The test found several bad sectors on critical areas of the disk. Try to reformat or replace the drive.

5-41 Types of hard disk errors.

Normally the program will read through the partition table until it finds a partition that contains the bad track. Then, if the partition contains DOS data, it will look through the file allocation table (FAT) for information on how the space is used. Errors are reported at the track level while DOS stores files at the sector level so the FAT is used for each sector on the track.

Backup

Although hard disks are a reliable form of data storage, they do fail and valuable information can also be erased by an operator error. Because the volume of information contained on a hard disk is large, the failure of a hard disk that is not backed up can be a major loss. There are several possible ways to back up a hard disk. One method is to copy files onto floppy disks using the DOS backup and retrieve commands. However, floppy disk backup tends to be time-consuming and tedious and many users fail to do it often enough. When the hard disk fails, they can find themselves without the backup of critical files. Also, the quantity of floppy disks needed to back up a high-capacity hard disk can quickly become unmanageable. At first, floppy disk backup appears to be inexpensive, because it requires no special hardware or training. But the cost of the time spent backing up on floppies grows quickly.

The other popular method of hard disk backup involves using a tape drive. There are two basic types of tape drives: floppy tape and streaming tape. *Floppy tape backup* runs directly from the floppy disk controller, so it does not take up an extra expansion slot.

Streaming tape has the advantages of being very fast, standardized, and reliable. Streaming tape drives can be activated automatically at a specified time of day, freeing you from backup operations. Because streaming tape is easy to use, people tend to perform backups more regularly.

The industry standard QIC (quarter-inch cartridge) units allow tapes to be interchanged among drives, which is required for archival storage. The disadvantage of streaming tape is cost, which can exceed the cost of the hard disk drive. The cost difference must be weighed against the cost of regenerating lost data after a disk failure.

Another backup method that is sometimes considered is a second hard disk that is used for backup. This choice is an unreliable one because the reason that causes the main hard first disk to fail, such as an unexpected physical shock to the system chassis, will damage the backup disk at the same time.

An external tape drive requires that you install a controller card that will use the drive. Internal tape drives are available in half-height packages; you can install one under the floppy drive in the right drive bank of an AT PC. The plastic or metal bezel covering the opening is removed.

Install the controller card in a suitable slot that is close to the drive, because there will be a ribbon cable connected from the card to the tape drive. You will also need to connect power cables to power the tape drive.

Floppy drive alignment testers

Floppy drive alignment devices are designed to perform on-site realignment of floppy disk drives. They provide all of the standard alignment testing and exercising functions.

One design digitizes the analog signal from an alignment diskette and does not require an oscilloscope. It is portable and designed not to lose calibration during travel.

Problems with radial, index, sector, amplitude, skew, track 0, and head load are identified by LEDs. The disk drive is adjusted until the proper lights are shown.

Hard disk drive testers

You can use disk drive testers for field testing and repair of hard disk drives. One design uses a small keyboard for single key commands and a 64-character LCD display.

It can be used to test stepper motors, index assemblies, circuit boards, spindle motors, track 0 sensors, and wiring harnesses. This portability lets you run tests on site. A 20MB drive takes about 10 minutes to test. The test provides track and head error counts, maximum step rate, rotation speed (rpm), index speed, and other reports. It can be pre-programmed to perform a series of tests while unattended. Errors flash on the LCD display and an audible tone signals test completion.

CD-ROMs

CD-ROMs (compact disc read-only memory) are a newer way of getting information into a PC. CD-ROM drives are not fast, but they hold over 600MB. Some software products such as Microsoft's multimedia extensions for Windows are available only on CD-ROM. There are also multimedia discs that combine video and synchronized sound. The third-generation drives are faster with an average access time of about 350 ms.

CD-ROM technology

Compact disc read-only memory came from CD audio. A single 4.7-inch plastic CD-ROM disc can hold 660MB of information; you cannot write on the disc or erase any portion of its contents. Information is held on the disc using microscopic pits and lands that are formed into the disc surface. A beam from a small laser in the CD-ROM player illuminates this ridged surface and reflects the stored information to a light-detecting photodiode, which interprets the surface irregularities. No part physically touches the disc.

CD-ROM players can read both CD-ROM and CD audio discs. Both discs have the same appearance; however, the coding standards for the CD-ROM discs are more stringent to ensure the integrity of the stored information.

Formats

CD-ROM drives are standardized. The drives meet the same specifications, and most units are similar. CD-ROM drives support the High Sierra and ISO 9660 standards, which document the basic rules for storing data. This conformance to standards allows you to play most newer discs in almost any CD-ROM drive. The High Sierra data format is a subset of ISO 9660.

Although a CD-ROM can theoretically hold 680MB of data, most commercial discs do not exceed 600MB. Some drives can read the maximum possible amount of data.

Characteristics

Drive characteristics include the average access time, throughput, and the size of the drive buffer. The faster drives have an access time of 350 ms, with 64K buffers and a throughput of 150 kilobytes per second. The speed is about three times slower than a floppy drive.

A key performance feature is a continuous-read facility, which ensures that the maximum amount of data at the bus gets to the drive. Rather than fetching a sector and then waiting for a software command to get the next sector, continuous-read drives take the next few sectors and move them to the drive's cache, which results in a more even flow of data between the CD-ROM drive and the PC. Without continuous read, scrolling on the screen can appear to jump, and animated sequences will not appear to be continuous. If you run multimedia, the CD-ROM drive needs to have a continuous-read facility.

The newer drives reduce dust errors. If the read head is dirty, it cannot decode the light reflected by the lands and pits on the disc surface, and the data becomes garbled. This problem is reduced with self-cleaning lenses and double-seal drive enclosures. Drives can also fail from a bad power supply, faulty lens assemblies, and other problems.

CD-ROM packaging

CD-ROMs are usually packaged inside protective plastic boxes called *jewel cases.* The case provides protection for the disc during shipment and storage. Some CD-ROM drives use the disc directly from the jewel case, requiring that it be replaced in the case the moment that it is removed from the drive. Other drives use a caddy.

The CD-ROM is placed in a plastic disc case, called a *caddy,* which has a built-in metal shutter. When you insert the caddy in the drive, the shutter slides to the side to reveal the disc to the drive optical read head. The caddy provides protection for the disc until it can be returned to its jewel case.

Most CD-ROM drives come with a mounting kit (if the unit is internal), cables, adapter, a caddy for holding discs in the drive, and Microsoft's MS-DOS CD-ROM Extensions version 2.2. To use the drive with DOS, you need the Microsoft extensions. MSCDEX uses the network interrupt for communications between the device driver and DOS.

Changing CD-ROM drives is relatively easy. You plug the drive into the adapter, and you can even daisy chain multiple drives off of the first unit.

Most new drives connect to standard SCSI (Small Computer Systems Interface) adapters. Earlier drives used proprietary SCSI adapters, and you could not daisy chain standard SCSI peripherals to these adapters or operate drives by different manufacturers from the same interface.

Most of these drives can also be used to play music. Equipped with phone and audio jacks and a remote control, they can play audio CDs. Some drives only play audio CDs via software control.

Commercial CD-ROM drives

A typical CD-ROM drive is the Chinon CDC-431 which has an access time of 350 ms, an SCSI interface, a disc caddy, and a remote control unit. It does not have continuous-read, and animation might not flow smoothly.

The Hitachi CDR-1750S drive has a standard SCSI adapter, but a proprietary bus is used in the CDR-1700S. This unit is also much slower because it uses a 32K cache buffer and the proprietary parallel interface used was developed earlier for XT machines.

The CDR-1700S shows animations that appear jerky and unrealistic. The device driver first reads the data, turns off an interrupt, and then waits for the next command. The faster drivers used in the CDR-1750S do not use this procedure. Both the smaller cache size and the use of the Hitachi bus affect the playback in the CDR-1700S; the drive is not faulty when this is noticeable, but cleaning can sometimes help.

The CDR-1750S has a SCSI card, a disc caddy and cables, several audio utilities, and Microsoft MSCDEX. It uses continuous reads and provides better animation even when dirty.

The same drive is used in both models. The case is sealed to keep dust out and it has an automatic lens-cleaning mechanism and a double-door system to reduce dust in the caddy area.

Like an audio compact disc (CD), the CD-ROM holds large amounts of information on an inexpensive medium. The plastic discs store data using microscopic pits on the disc surface. The pits are pressed into the CD media by a glass master using equipment similar to that used to make plastic LP (long-playing) records. The pressed CDs cost only a few dollars to make. After pressing, they receive a protective plastic coating.

The data is read by sensing the change in reflectivity between the pits and the non-pit areas called the *lands*. The light source is a semiconductor laser diode, similar to the type used in laser printers. The laser provides the small, highly focused light source that is needed. CD audio discs work the same way, and many CD-ROM players can also play audio CDs with the proper software. Audio CD players cannot read CD-ROMs, because they do not have needed accuracy or software to interpret the digital data, which sounds like a hiss or noise.

The discs used to press CD-ROMs are called *masters,* or *master discs.* These discs are glass discs with light-sensitive photoresist coatings. The master is created by a device called a *CD burner* that uses a more powerful laser than the type used in drives and printers to cut holes in the master's photoresist coating. The tiny holes are cut along a spiral track like a phonograph record, except the tracks and pits are smaller and closer together. Each pit averages about 0.12 micrometers deep with a width of about 0.6 micrometers. There are about 1.6 micrometers between tracks and about 16,000 tpi (tracks per inch). A 360K floppy disk has 48 tpi.

The master disc is developed like a photograph, and the areas of photoresist exposed by the laser are removed, leaving the pits. The developed master is used to produce negative discs. A negative of the master is needed for pressing the final discs. The negative has raised pits and is produced using an electroplating or photopolymer process.

The actual production duplicates are made by hot injection–molding with a polycarbonate plastic. The finished polycarbonate discs are clear so they are given a silvered reflective coating so that they can reflect light. The silvering coats the lands and pits with the reflective coating. This coating is protected with a scratch-resistant lacquer. The label is usually silk-screened on the disc before it is packaged. The final product is 4.72 inches (12.0 centimeters) in diameter and about 1.2 millimeters thick. The spindle hole has a diameter of 1.5 centimeters. The construction of a cross section of a completed disc is shown in Fig. 5-42.

Reading the discs

The CD drive contains a small laser and sensor to detect the patterns of pits and lands. The combination laser/detector head is mounted in slides or rails so it follows the spiral track of the CD.

When the laser beam hits a land, the light is reflected back at the detector, producing a strong output signal. When the laser beam hits a pit, the reflected light is much

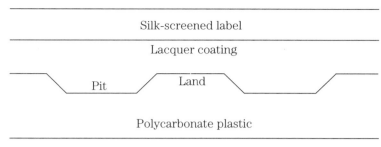

5-42 CD-ROM construction.

smaller, because much of it is scattered. The output signal generated by the detector is much smaller. The difference in these signals is interpreted as binary levels.

The binary information is encoded using EFM (eight-to-fourteen modulation). A binary 1 is represented by transition from pit-to-land or land-to-pit. The length of a pit or land represents the number of binary 0s.

Because the CD-ROM has a continuous spiral track, sector and track labels cannot be used. The disc is divided up from 0 to 59 minutes, and 0 to 59 seconds are recorded at the beginning of each block. A block has 2048 bytes of data, error correction moves the block up to 2352 bytes. The disc can hold up to 79 minutes of data. But, most CD-ROMs limit the data to 60 minutes because the last 14 minutes of data take the outer 5 millimeters of the disc. This area is the most difficult to manufacture and keep clean, so most CD-ROMs hold about 600MB.

The ISO 9660 format is an update of the High Sierra data format standard of 1985. A drive designed to operate with the High Sierra format might not read an ISO 9660 disc, but a drive designed for the ISO 9660 standard should read discs written in the High Sierra format.

Because DOS does not support CD-ROMs directly, a device driver is needed to run the drive. Each drive has its own driver that is used along with a DOS CD-ROM extension drive such as Microsoft's MSCDEX. After these are installed, the CD-ROM is used like any DOS drive, except you cannot save any information on it. You can check the CD-ROM directory and run executable files on the disc.

CD-ROM drives

The drive must turn the disc at a constant linear velocity so the disc speed changes inversely with the head tracking radius. At the outer edge, the disc speed is slower and as the head moves toward the center, the speed increases.

The drive head must follow the spiral path on a moving disc within 1 micrometer or less along the disc radius. The drive electronics must detect and correct data errors during operation. The CD-ROM uses a cast aluminum or stainless steel frame like other drives. The other components are mounted to this frame. There is a front bezel or door along with a drive-in-use LED and an eject button. Most drives use a sliding tray, so the front bezel or door assembly differs among manufacturers.

Most drives have two circuit boards: a larger board contains the drive control and interface circuits, and a smaller board holds the audio circuits, if the drive is equipped for audio. The main mechanical assembly is called a *caddy,* or *engine.* Like laser printers, most drives use the same type of engine to hold, spin, read, and eject the disc. Sony, Phillips, and Toshiba are the main producers of CD-ROM engines. IBM and Ikka also make caddies.

The top of the drive contains the mechanisms to accept, hold, and eject the disc. Below this is a frame that holds the head and head positioning rails along with the positioning motors. This frame is shock mounted for protection from handling.

A slider unit and a loading assembly take the disc and position it onto the drive spindle and remove the disc and eject it. Dampening levers and oil-filled dampers are used to slow down and smooth out these operations. The motor for these operations is on the load/unload assembly.

The spindle motor uses a thrust retainer to keep the discs turning smoothly. The optical device contains the 780-nm (nanometer), 0.6-mW gallium aluminum arsenide (GaAlAs) laser diode and detector, along with the optical components. The optical head slides on guide rails that act as linear positioning encoders. This part of the unit is called a *sled.*

The sled is controlled by a linear motor, which works like the voice-coil motor used to control hard drive read-write heads. The linear motor operates in a closed loop where the signal driving the motor is constantly checked and adjusted as a function of sled position from the linear position encoders, allowing the sled to follow the track on the disc smoothly and accurately. Some older CD drives use stepping motors with a fine-pitch lead screw to position the sled, but most drives use a linear encoder and motor. Figure 5-43 shows a typical sled motor and linear encoder arrangement.

Optical heads

Components of a typical optical head are shown in Fig. 5-44. A laser diode provides about 600 watts of light energy. The beam from the diode passes through the beam-

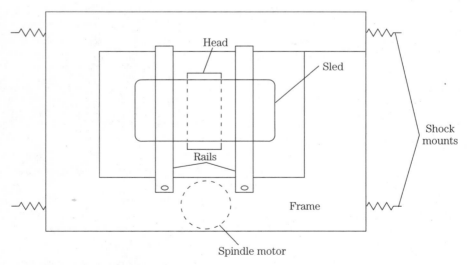

5-43 Optical head mounting.

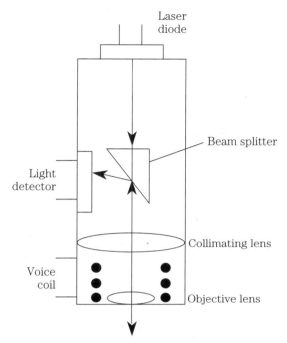

5-44 Optical head construction.

splitting lens. The collimating lens sends the light to the objective lens so it can be focused on the disc surface. The focal point is designed to be at the land area. The voice coil acts as a sensor for the lens position and allows a precise focus. The drive circuits on the main circuit board control the focusing.

When the focused light hits a land area, maximum reflection occurs. The return beam goes through the objective and collimating lenses and hits the reflecting side of the beam splitter where it is reflected into the photodetector, which produces the strong signal needed to define ones and zeros. When the focused light hits a pit, the light is scattered, and only a small signal is produced by the photodetector. The optical head is completely sealed because dust can affect the operation of the head.

Drive control

The circuit blocks in the drive are shown in Fig. 5-45. The controller section provides the SCSI interface, which is an intelligent drive controller. This interface handles most of the needed functions in reading the disc.

The drive control portion of the drive electronics handles the drive's mechanical operations. The data decoding uses extended frequency modulation (EFM) and error correction. The EFM signal is converted into binary data and CIRC (Cross-Interleaved Reed-Solomon-Code) information for error correction. If the drive has an audio output, a digital-to-analog converter translates the binary information to an audio signal that is filtered and amplified.

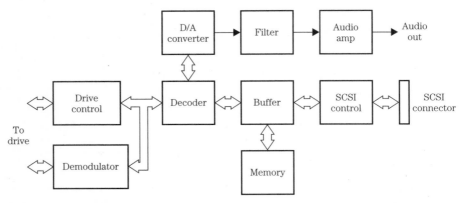

5-45 CD-ROM electronics.

Although most newer drives use SCSI interfaces, some use proprietary interfaces and others use an IDE interface. There are also nonstandard implementations of the SCSI system, especially among older units. These nonstandard interfaces require a drive built by the same manufacturer. The SCSI (Small Computer Systems Interface) is a standard device interface that can be used for different types of peripheral devices (Fig. 5-46), mainly used for SCSI drives. The interface uses a 50-pin cable and a single controller board can handle up to eight SCSI devices.

The proprietary interfaces that are used by some manufacturers are generally provided with any special cables and connectors needed. In most cases, the manufacturer also supplies the driver software that you need to install to control the drive. If this software becomes corrupted or lost due to a hard drive error or failure, you will have to reinstall it to get the CD-ROM going again. This is one of the first things to check, if you have a proprietary CD drive system. You should also check the proprietary controller board because it only runs the CD-ROM drive. Many of these boards have DIP switches that must be set properly during configuration.

CD-ROM drive problems

In a CD-ROM drive, the optical tracking systems are delicate and are factory aligned for optimum performance, replacement. User adjustment can affect this alignment and make the drive unusable. Remember you are dealing with a very delicate mechanism. Isolate the problem and get the suspected part before you tear down the drive. If you cannot get the part, it often means that disassembly must be done at a service center.

Disc handling

Disc-handling problems might be caused by a foreign object getting into the disc slot or tray. Before any disassembly, check these areas for obstructions. Then remove any cover plates to expose the assembly and check each mechanical linkage. Slowly remove or free any obstruction. Use extreme care around the load/unload assembly. Disconnect the motor assembly and try moving the load/unload mechanism by hand. If you feel any resistance check for obstructions. Replace any worn or damaged part of the mechanism, or replace the entire load/unload assembly. Check the motor teeth for any

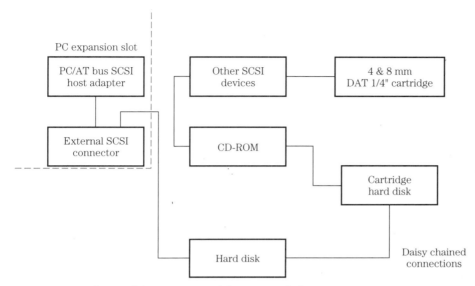

5-46 SCSI can be used for a variety of devices including CD-ROM.

damage or obstruction. Broken or slipping gear teeth can affect the operation of this mechanism. Replace any damaged gears or the entire geared assembly.

If the load/unload mechanism does not work at all, the drive motor might be at fault. Check the dc voltage across the dc motor. When a load or unload occurs, you should measure a voltage across the motor. If there is a voltage, but the motor does not turn, replace the motor. If there is no voltage, the problem is in the drive circuits and you might need to repair or replace the drive circuit board.

Read heads do not move

The optical head must follow the spiral track through the disc. The head must move properly for accurate encoding. The head movement should look smooth and continuous and not jerky. Examine the sled rails for contamination or foreign objects.

If the rails appear clean, check the voltage across the linear actuator. If there is no voltage at the linear motor, the drive circuits might not be functioning, this could be a driver or controller IC. Trace the motor signal back to the drive circuit board. Check all components the signal goes to. If there is voltage across the motor, but the motor does not turn, the linear motor is at fault. Linear motor replacement should be done by an experienced technician.

Disc does not read

If the disc does not read, the problem is indicated by a message

DOS LEVEL SECTOR NOT FOUND

or

DRIVE NOT READY

Possible causes of the problem include the wrong format, disc not inserted properly, and damaged or dirty discs. The disc is sensitive to dust and other surface problems. Dust or other contamination can prevent the head from reading the disc properly. Test this with a known good disc. If this disc works properly, the problem is in the disc itself or the jewel case or caddy.

CD-ROM drives are similar to conventional CD players with some extra circuitry. They fall prey to dust and dirt. Try a cleaning disc, but do not use it often, in the long run it can do more harm than good.

The problem could be dust or dirt affecting the head optics. Check this assembly for dust or dirt and gently dust or clean the head optics.

Has your system configuration changed since the last time you used your CD-ROM drive? New software or hardware you installed could be interfering with your CD-ROM's setup.

Make sure none of the connections on the CD-ROM drive or controller are loose. Reroute the ribbon cables away from the power supply. Try another ribbon cable with the same number of wires. Ribbon cables do get fatigued and can suffer internal breakdowns.

Most newer drives use SCSI interfaces; older drives and some newer ones use proprietary interfaces. If you are using other SCSI devices from the same host controller card and the other SCSI devices are operating properly, the problem must be in the CD-ROM drive. If other SCSI devices are also malfunctioning, try a new SCSI host controller board.

You can use an oscilloscope to view the analog signal from the optical head. If an analog signal is present, a disc is turning, the problem is likely to be in the drive electronics. Trace the signal to a defective component on the board if possible or replace the drive circuit board.

If there is no signal from the optical read head, you need to replace the optical head, be sure you can get one first. Head replacement might need to be done at a service center.

Jammed CD-ROM disks

CD-ROM drives are equipped for the event of a jammed disk. You can get your disc out if there is no physical eject button. There should be a small hole, about the diameter of a pencil lead, in the drive's front panel. Straighten a small paper clip and push the end of it into the hole. The jammed disc should pop out.

Disc does not rotate

Be sure that the drive is properly configured and that the drive Busy LED comes on when a drive access is attempted. You might also get a DOS error message indicating that the computer does not recognize the CD drive. If you get a message similar to the following:

INVALID DRIVE SPECIFICATION

there is probably a setup or configuration error. If the optical head aperture is clean, sometimes recleaning can get the drive turning again. A dirty optical head can inhibit the disc spindle operation.

Measure the voltage across the spindle motor. If there is a voltage across the motor but the motor does not rotate, the spindle motor is probably defective and should be replaced. If there is no motor voltage, trace the signal lines to the spindle motor driver or controller chip. You might have to replace these if possible or replace the drive circuit board.

Focus problems

If the drive cannot focus its laser beam properly, then it cannot read the data on the disc. The optical head has a built-in focusing mechanism that operates from a small voice coil actuator. If this mechanism is not working properly, you can get DOS drive error messages. First, try a new or different disc, if this makes a difference, for better or worse than the original disc, the focus is probably defective. If there is no difference between different discs, the focus is probably working properly. Use an oscilloscope to measure the focus signal going to the voice coil. If there is a signal present, you probably need to replace the optical head. Be sure you can get this part because you might need to have it replaced at a service center. If there is no focus signal going to the voice coil, trace the signal leads to the drive circuit board. The focus signal driver or focus controller might be the problem. Try tracing the signal to a defective component and replace it if possible. You might have to replace the drive circuit board.

No audio

Start by checking your headphones or speakers. Test the headphones or speakers with another sound source. Check the drive volume control, which is usually found on the front bezel. Test the volume control with an ohmmeter. Be sure any software needed to operate the drive audio output is installed and loaded properly. Check that any needed audio drivers are installed properly.

Trace the audio signal back from the output connector. If a signal is present into the amplifier, but is not available at the connector, the amplifier or connector might be defective and need to be replaced. If audio is present into the audio amplifier, but there is no signal out of the audio amplifier, try to trace it to a defective component or replace the defective audio amplifier. If there is a signal into the audio amplifier, work back, check the filter and then the D/A (digital-to-analog) converter. Try to trace the problem to a defective component, or you will have to replace the board these parts are on. Figure 5-47 summarizes CD-ROM drive problems.

Playing audio CDs

If you want to play audio CDs in your CD-ROM drive, you may get an error if the [MCI] CD Audio driver is not installed. You can solve this by opening Control Panel, selecting the Drivers icon, clicking on the Add button, and selecting the [MCI] CD Audio driver. If the driver has not been installed on the system, Windows will prompt you for the installation disk.

If you are using a MIDI device, you will need to set an option to redirect the output signals to your MIDI device. Open Windows' Control Panel, then click on the icon called

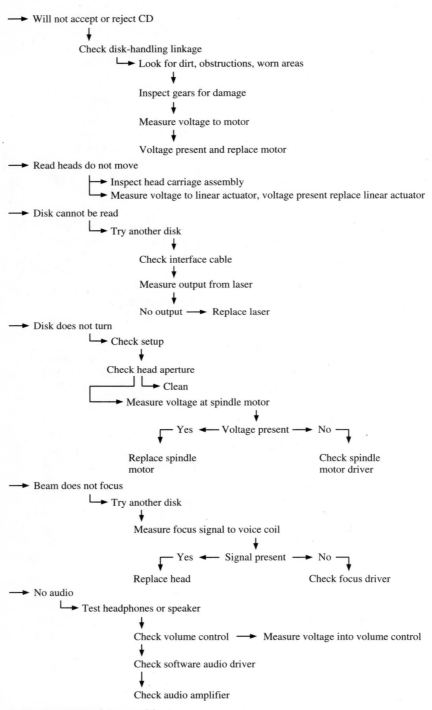

5-47 CD-ROM drive problems.

MIDI Mapper from the MIDI Mapper dialog box, open the Name list, and choose the setup you want to use. Then close the MIDI Mapper window.

Repairing scratched discs

If you have a skipping CD and you determine that there is not a problem in the drive, you can try a product such as CD Miracle Mender. It consists of cloth abrasives, abrasive cream, cleaning fluid, and lint-free polishing pads for removing scratches, smudges, and imperfections.

6
CHAPTER

Video and Sound Systems

Much of the operating information you need when using your computer comes to you through the video display adapter and the monitor. This chapter describes the various components for you and provides the detailed information you need to be sure your video system operates correctly. Sound cards are another output that are being used along with video more and more.

Displays and adapters

A *video display adapter* is a card that controls the computer monitor. It takes up one of the expansion slots (Fig. 6-1). Most 386 and 486 systems have an integrated adapter on the system board. The display adapter and the monitor must be compatible. You cannot use a monochrome monitor with a display adapter that is designed only for color monitors.

Some display adapters will run two or more monitors. Others offer features such as 132-column extended display, dual displays, and the ability to run color graphics software on a monochrome monitor.

The display adapter installs in one of the expansion slots (Fig. 6-2). Use the procedures shown in Fig. 6-3 to remove an adapter. Most are designed for 8-bit slots but there are some 16-bit display adapter cards. Many older display adapters are not designed to run reliably at the higher-megahertz speeds, so this can be a problem if you run at high-megahertz speeds.

Some computers have a slide switch on the system board. It determines whether the system boots up in color or monochrome mode, and you must refer to the manual for the correct switch setting. Often a display adapter will have several different display modes, which are set by jumpers or DIP switches (Fig. 6-4). Be sure to use the correct switch settings for the system board because you can damage some monitors by attaching them to a display adapter configured for the wrong mode.

(a)

6-1 An early monochrome full slot display adapter (A).

Monochrome monitors

A monochrome monitor runs at a horizontal frequency of 18.432 kHz (kilohertz) and a vertical frequency of 50 Hz (hertz). It is usually available in amber or green. A monochrome monitor will display a 16-pixel text character with 25 rows of 80 characters.

Pixel is short for *picture element.* Pixels are the individual points of light that make up the patterns on the screen. The resolution of a display is defined by the numbers of pixels across and up and down on the screen.

A standard monochrome video adapter displays 720 × 348 pixel graphics. Some adapters can emulate color/graphics (CGA), enhanced graphics (EGA), or video graphics array (VGA) displays. These color emulation boards display the colors as varying tones of amber or green. Often you can adjust external vertical and horizontal sync (synchronization) controls. It might be necessary to adjust the sync frequencies to change the monitor resolution for different video modes, allowing all modes to operate properly on the monitor.

In some cases, a temperature change can cause the monitor to alter its sync characteristics, which might cause a monitor to roll vertically.

The monitor case might be exposed to direct sunlight, which warms the monitor and changes its vertical sync frequency. A small adjustment of the vertical sync control can correct this problem. The original IBM monochrome display did not have external sync controls and even minor adjustments of the sync frequency required removing the case.

The more expensive monochrome monitors use PLL (phase-locked loop) circuitry to track drifting of the input sync signal. Many color emulation boards will not work properly unless the monochrome monitor is equipped with PLL.

To display clean, clear text free of interference from external sources, some monitors filter the input signal to remove noise. Color emulation boards alter the signal characteristics to produce gray shades. The filter circuit can interpret this alteration as noise and convert it back to a clean monochrome signal. This filtering can reduce the scaling and allow just a few shades. Monitors that use only a shielded cable for filtering will not have this problem.

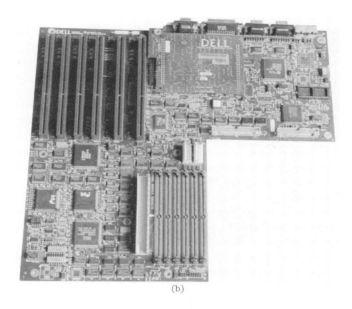

(b)

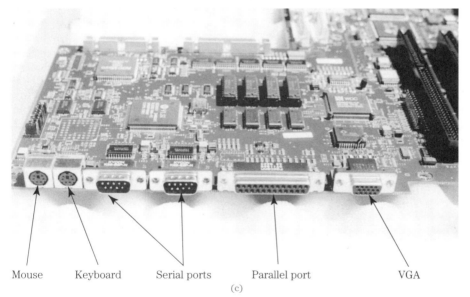

Mouse   Keyboard   Serial ports   Parallel port   VGA

(c)

6-1 (*Continued*) 486 L-type board. Output connectors are in the upper left, SIMM connectors are in the upper right, and the processor is in lower right (B). 486 system board showing output connectors (C).

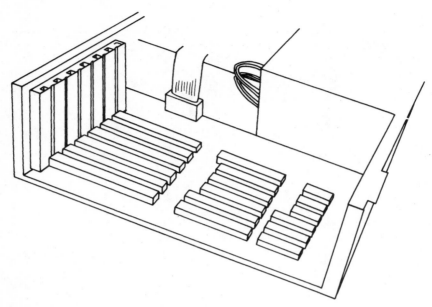

6-2 Expansion slots in typical AT computer. The display adapter will take up one of these slots.

RGB monitors

An RGB (red, green, blue) monitor, often called a CGA monitor (see Table 6-1) has an input frequency of 15.75 kHz horizontal and 60 Hz vertical. Separate red, green, blue, and intensity inputs (RGBI format) allow a total of 16 colors to be displayed. The characters are 8 pixels high by 8 pixels deep on an 80 by 25 character display. Graphics can be displayed to a maximum of 640×200 pixels.

Multivideo adapters allow an RGB monitor to display monochrome and EGA graphics. Because the maximum vertical resolution of an RGB monitor is 200 pixels, these adapters use an interlacing technique to produce the 350 lines required for EGA or monochrome graphics.

Set the power switch on the system unit to off.

↓

Disconnect all cables from the rear of the units.

↓

Remove the cover of the system unit.

↓

Remove the adapter board mounting screw.

↓

Grasp the adapter board by the top corners and lift straight up.

6-3 Adapter board removal.

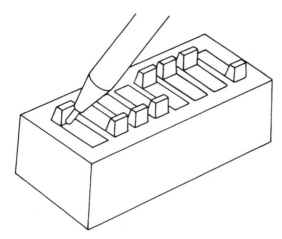

6-4 DIP switch setting, always change the switch positions with a ballpoint pen or equivalent instrument. Never use a lead pencil because the lead can break and jam the switch.

Interlacing involves creating a virtual screen in memory and forming the display with two alternating 200-line segments. The result is a screen with 400 lines. Interlacing does not change the vertical frequency, but it does change the screen refresh rate to 30 Hz and can produce flicker. When interlacing is used, the RGB monitor should have a high-persistence phosphor to reduce the flicker.

You usually need external sync controls if you want to use EGA or monochrome emulation boards with an RGB monitor. Changes in vertical sync characteristics can distort screen images and make the text characters difficult to read.

Dual-frequency monitors

A dual-frequency monitor is a display that can operate at either monochrome or color sync frequencies. These monitors usually have a monochrome screen and produce shades when operating as a color display. You might see dual-frequency monitors in many computers, and they are also available as stand-alone units. These monitors can switch from monochrome sync frequencies (18.432 kHz horizontal, 50 Hz vertical) to color sync frequencies (15.75 kHz horizontal, 60 Hz vertical) by analyzing the input sync frequency. Some monitors check the pin configuration (usually pins 3, 4, and 5) to determine if a color adapter is connected.

When using a dual-frequency monitor with a multivideo board, operate the monitor as a monochrome display. This operation allows the highest resolution and eliminates the need for interlacing. However, an adapter with the capability to display video on a color monitor will have circuit connections for pins 3, 4, and 5. To use monochrome operation, you need a special cable between the monitor and the video board to disconnect these pins.

Table 6-1. Color display systems

Display name	Resolution	Bandwidth, MHz	Input	Horizontal sweep	Vertical sweep
		Typical characteristics			
CGA color graphics adapter	300 × 200 16 colors	35	Digital	15.6 Hz	60 Hz
EGA enhanced graphics adapter	640 × 350 16 of 64 colors	35	Digital	21.8 Hz	60 Hz
VGA video graphics array	320 × 200 256 of 256,000 colors	35	Analog	31.5 kHz	60 Hz
Macintosh II	16 million colors		Analog	35 kHz	60 Hz
NEC multisynch	1024 × 768 and lower	65	Analog Digital	Variable 15.75–35.5 kHz	60 Hz

EGA monitors

An EGA monitor displays an 8 × 14 pixel character on an 80 × 25 display. It can be driven by a CGA adapter (15.75 kHz) or by an EGA adapter (21.8 kHz) to deliver graphic resolutions from 320 × 200 pixels to 640 × 350 pixels. The vertical sync frequency is constant at 60 Hz. A total of 16 colors from a choice of 64 can be displayed at any one time. Colors are generated through primary and secondary red, green, and blue inputs (RGB format). Special programs allow an EGA monitor to support character fonts that can be downloaded.

Most EGA adapters also emulate monochrome text and graphics on the EGA display. Some EGA monitors do not support the 15.75-kHz horizontal scan frequency. This scan limits the monitor to EGA resolution (640 × 350). These monitors can be recognized by the absence of the 15.75-kHz frequency from the monitor specifications. Some video adapters double scan CGA graphics to produce better graphics. Most EGA monitors can handle these frequency changes, but some monitors will lose vertical sync.

25-kHz 400-line monitors

The 25-kHz monitor was designed to produce better CGA graphics by double scanning each of the 200 lines used on a CGA graphic screen. Some adapters are only CGA-compatible, but others can emulate EGA and provide their own 640 × 400 and 752 × 410 pixel graphics modes on the 25-kHz monitor. These monitors do not have an established standard. Many manufacturers use their own specifications for video frequencies and color format. Horizontal frequencies can vary from 23 to 27 kHz. Some 25-kHz monitors use a combined horizontal and vertical (composite) sync signal instead of the separate horizontal and vertical signals used in the standard RGB monitor. An important consideration for matching a 25-kHz monitor to a video adapter is the sync polarity.

A CGA monitor uses a positive sync for the horizontal frequency and a negative sync for the vertical frequency. An EGA monitor uses a negative sync for horizontal and vertical frequencies in high-resolution modes and switches to a positive horizontal/negative vertical sync in CGA resolutions. A 25-kHz monitor might use one of the above formats or it might use its own.

VGA monitors

VGA monitors are the latest in the IBM PC graphics standards. They operate at a horizontal frequency of 31.5 kHz and a vertical frequency of 70 Hz. These monitors provide 640 × 480 pixel resolution. The VGA monitor uses an analog RGB input scheme to achieve the 262,144 different colors available in VGA modes. By switching the vertical and horizontal sync polarity, the VGA adapter signals the monitor to change its vertical sizing characteristics for lower vertical resolution modes.

Multisync and multimode monitors

Multisync monitors adapt themselves to the sync characteristics of the video board. They can operate with most video boards including special purpose and workstation video adapters. Multimode monitors are different from multisync monitors in that they can only match input sync characteristics within one of several frequency ranges. Most of the multisync and multimode monitors support both digital (monochrome, CGA, and EGA) and analog (VGA and graphics workstations).

Some multisync monitors will not synchronize on frequencies below 21 kHz. They cannot be used with CGA adapters, but they can be used with video boards that double scan CGA. With the use of multimode monitors, some multivideo board emulation modes might be within an unsupported frequency range with EGA and VGA boards. Some high-resolution modes might not be supported when using these adapters on multimode monitors. Connecting a multisync or multimode monitor to a VGA adapter requires a special cable to mate the video board connector with the monitor analog input connector.

A VGA adapter can cause a multisync monitor to experience changes in the vertical display size when the video mode changes because the monitor might not sense the sizing signals that are sent by the VGA adapter.

Special monitors

High-resolution graphics are available for other CAD applications. These monitors usually accommodate the monitor manufacturer's proprietary video system. If another video system is used, then it is important to match the monitor's sync characteristics with those of the video adapter. The following characteristics must match:

1. Vertical/horizontal sync frequency
2. Analog/digital signal

3. Sync polarity
4. Color format
5. Composite/separate sync

Dual display

Dual display gives you the ability to run two monitors with different displays on each one, at the same time. This feature is supported by some software packages (such as Lotus 1-2-3 and Symphony). With a dual-display card running one of these packages, you can graph on an enhanced monitor and simultaneously enter text on a monochrome monitor. You could type changes on the monochrome monitor, and the graph on the enhanced monitor would modify itself to show the changes. *Dual-monitor support* means the system supports two different types of monitors, and *dual displays* refers to the dual, simultaneous, independent display on two separate monitors.

Display adapter compatibility

Many graphics display adapters are compatible with several types of monitors. The graphics capabilities available with a particular adapter, including resolution and the number of colors, vary depending on what type of monitor is used and which display adapter you wish to simulate. The capabilities of a particular monitor can be affected when other graphics display adapters are installed in your system.

The following list shows several compatible IBM monitors and display adapters:

1. The 5151 MD1 (monochrome display) is designed to be used with the MDA (monochrome display adapter).
2. The 5153 CD (color display) is designed to be used with the CGA (color/graphics adapter).
3. The 5154 ECD (enhanced color display) is designed to be used with the EGA (enhanced graphics adapter).

Tables 6-2 and 6-3 show the typical compatible modes that are possible.

Descriptions follow for each type of IBM monitor. Information is also included about the type of graphics adapter most often used with that monitor.

Monochrome display monitor, IBM 5151

The IBM 5151 monochrome display was designed to be used with the IBM MDA. This monitor has a screen refresh rate of 50 MHz (noninterlaced), and a maximum bandwidth of 16.257 MHz. The MD monitor is TTL (transistor-transistor logic) compatible and has a horizontal scan frequency of 18.432 kHz.

Color-display monitor, IBM 5153

The IBM 5153 color display was designed to work with the IBM CGA card. This monitor can display 16 different colors by combining digital outputs of red, green, and blue with intensity values. Monitors of this type are sometimes called *digital RGB monitors* because they combine the colors red, green, and blue to create color variations. This

Table 6-2. Typical graphics modes

Adapter	Number of colors	Resolution, h × v	Monitor
EGA	16/64*	640 × 350	ECD
EGA	16	640 × 200	CD, ECD
EGA	16	320 × 200	CD, ECD
EGA	4/64	640 × 350	ECD
EGA	2	640 × 350	MD
CGA	4	320 × 200	CD/ECD
CGA	2	320 × 200	CD/ECD
CGA	2	640 × 200	CD/ECD

*Refers to 16 colors that can be displayed from a 64-color palette. This capability usually requires 256K of graphics memory on the adapter.

Table 6-3. Typical text modes

Adapter type	Number of colors	Character size, pixels	Characters per screen	Monitor needed (2)
EGA	16/64*	8 × 14	80 × 25	ECD
EGA	16/64*	8 × 8	80 × 43	ECD
CGA/EGA	16	8 × 8	80 × 25	CD/ECD
CGA/EGA	16	8 × 8	40 × 25	CD/ECD
CGA/EGA	2	8 × 8	80 × 25	CD/ECD
CGA/EGA	2	8 × 8	40 × 25	CD/ECD
MDA/EGA	2	9 × 8	80 × 43	MD
MDA/EGA	2	9 × 14	80 × 25	MD

*Refers to 16 colors that can be displayed from a 64-color palette. This capability usually requires 256K of graphics memory on the adapter.

monitor has a high-contrast black screen. There are many IBM-compatible digital RGB monitors; some of the older monitors provide only 8 colors instead of 16.

The maximum bandwidth for this type of monitor is 14.318 MHz, and the screen refresh rate is 60 Hz (noninterlaced). The monitor is TTL-compatible and uses a horizontal scan frequency of 15.750 kHz.

Enhanced color display monitor, IBM 5154

The IBM 5154 Enhanced Color Display was designed to be used with the EGA. This type of monitor can usually support software written for either the EGA or the CGA. The ECD monitor has a screen refresh rate of 60 Hz, and the horizontal scan rate can be either 15.75 kHz or 21.850 kHz. This type of monitor can be considered to be an RGBI monitor because each color can be intensified.

Sync adjustments

Some monitors have external vertical and horizontal sync adjustments. It may be necessary to adjust the sync frequencies for different video modes. Sometimes temperature changes will cause the monitor to shift its sync characteristics. This can cause the monitor to roll vertically due to the change in vertical sync frequency. An adjustment of the vertical sync control may be needed to correct this problem.

The early IBM monochrome monitors did not have external sync controls and minor adjustments of the sync frequency required removing the case. Later monochrome monitors used phase-lock loop (PLL) circuitry to control drifting of the input sync signal. Many color emulation boards will not work properly unless the monochrome monitor is equipped with PLL. In order to reduce interference from external sources, some monitors filter the input signal to remove electrical noise. Color emulation boards alter the signal characteristics to produce gray shades. The filter circuit can interpret these changes as noise and convert them to a clean signal. This may modify the shading effects. Monitors that use only a shielded cable for filtering do not cause these problems.

Super VGA

These monitors are an upgrade beyond VGA. A super-VGA graphics board will give you at least 800×600 pixel capability and can go up to 1024×768.

Super-VGA boards may provide 256 colors at the lower resolution, or 16 colors at 1024×768. Multiscan monitors are also compatible with the VGA standard. Most multiscan monitors support interlaced scanning only at 1024×768. This means the electron gun inside the monitor tube is making two passes to create an image instead of one, which can cause some screen flicker. Boards with special graphics coprocessors can speed up performance. If you install a Windows driver for super-VGA resolution, most Windows applications will be able to use it and you will not have to install a separate driver for each application.

Graphics coprocessor boards

The IBM 8514/A was one of the first boards to offer resolution beyond standard VGA boards. The 1024×768 boards available today can be divided into two groups. One group is the clones of IBM's 8514/A board. The other group uses Texas Instruments' 34010 coprocessor.

Most graphics coprocessor boards drive noninterlaced monitors running at 1024×768, but a few will not interlace at this resolution. Most boards use video RAM (VRAM) and have enough VRAM for 1024×768 at 16 colors (see Table 6-4). Figure 6-5 shows the functions of a single-chip SVGA controller that can be used as a motion video accelerator.

PS/2 displays

The PS/2 displays have graphics support integrated into the system and display adapter. Double-scan 200-line modes are used and there is a palette of more than 256K colors. The following monitor types are used.

Table 6-4. Some graphics coprocessor boards

Manufacturer/model	VRAM	VGA colors (Interlaced/Noninterlaced)		
		640 × 480	800 × 600	1024 × 768
Artist Graphics XJi	768K		256	256/256
Compaq 1024	1MB	256		256/256
Hercules	1MB	32,000	256	256/256
HP IGC10	512K	16	16	0/16
IBM 8514/A	1MB			256/0
NEC MultiSync	1MB	256	256	256/256

PS/2 Monochrome Display (8503)

The input signal is analog with a display size of 12 inches (diagonal measurement). The display is white on black or black on white with a palette of 64 shades of gray. Resolution modes of 720 × 400 text and 640 × 480 or 320 × 200 graphics are available. An 8 × 16 character box is used for monochrome and a 9 × 16 character box in the VGA mode. A 31.5-kHz horizontal scan frequency is used for all modes. The monitor is noninterlaced with up to a 70-Hz vertical refresh rate.

PS/2 Color Display (8512)

The input signal is also analog, but the display size is 14 inches diagonal. The user has a palette of 256 out of more than 256K colors. The resolution is 720 × 400 text and 640 × 480 or 320 × 200 graphics. The character size is 8 × 16 pixels for MCGA and 9 × 16 for VGA. A 31.5-kHz horizontal scan frequency is used for all modes. The monitor is noninterlaced with up to a 70-Hz vertical refresh rate. A 0.41-mm stripe format is used on the display screen.

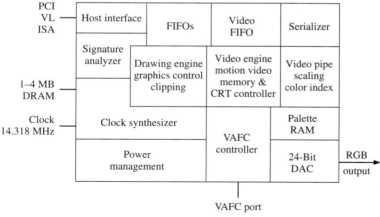

6-5 9710 single chip SVGA motion video accelerator functions.

PS/2 Color Display (8513)

The input signal is analog with a display size of 12 inches diagonal. A color palette of 256 out of more than 256K colors is available. The resolution is 720 × 400 text and 640 × 480 or 320 × 200 graphics. An 8 × 16 character box is used for MCGA and a 9 × 16 character box for VGA.

A 31.5-kHz horizontal scan frequency is used for all modes. Operation is noninterlaced with up to a 70-Hz vertical refresh rate. It is compatible with the PS/2 Display Adapter 8514/A. The screen uses a 0.28-mm dot phosphor pitch.

PS/2 Color Display (8514)

This is another analog monitor but the display size is 16 inches diagonal. The color palette is 256 out of more than 256K colors. If the 8514/A adapter is used, you can get 1024 × 768 graphics for all modes of the 8512 and 8513 displays. This resolution uses either a 12 × 20 character box to provide 85 columns × 38 rows or a 7 × 15 character box for 146 columns × 51 rows. A 35.5-kHz horizontal scan frequency is interlaced at a 43.5-Hz vertical refresh rate. A 0.31-mm dot phosphor pitch is used on the display screen.

Monitor and video board specifications

Pitch is a measurement of the density of the pixels displayed on the screen. Color monitors refer to the *dot pitch* of the display, giving the measurement of the space between pixels, or the *stripe pitch,* which is the measurement between horizontal scans. These measurements are usually in millimeters (mm).

The *horizontal scan frequency* is the rate at which the monitor updates the screen image. Higher horizontal scan frequencies correspond to higher screen resolutions. Monitors that have multiple scan frequencies or can multisync and lock in on a range of horizontal scan frequencies are compatible with multiple video standards. Table 6-5 shows the scan rates for several types of monitors.

Resolution

Screen resolution will be a function of the pixel density (pixels per inch) and the scan rate. The pixel density has already been discussed. The *scan rate* is a measure of the number of horizontal scan lines that the monitor draws each second. This is measured in kHz (kilohertz), with a better monitor having a value of 60 kHz, or 60,000 lines per second, and a standard broadcast television receiver having a value of 15 kHz, or 15,000 lines per second.

High-resolution monitors generally have more than 700,000 pixels displayable on the screen. The number of pixels is determined by multiplying the horizontal and vertical pixel densities. A monitor with a 1024 × 768 resolution, for example, would display 768,432 pixels.

The *dots-per-inch* (dpi) measurement is a gauge of the number of pixels contained in one linear inch, either horizontally or vertically. The higher the dpi value, the greater the appearance of image sharpness, and the smaller the image will appear relative to the

Table 6-5. Monitor scan frequencies

Manufacturer/model	Screen size, inches	Maximum resolution	Scan frequencies	
			Horizontal, kHz	Vertical, Hz
Packard Bell PB1272	12	720 × 350	18.43	50
Goldstar 2195G	12	720 × 350	18.43	50
Samsung MA2571	12	720 × 350	18.43	50
Packard Bell PB1472	14	720 × 350	15.75–18.43	50/60
Magnavox BM7622	12	900 × 350	15.75	50
NEC Multisync GS/A	14	720 × 480	15.7/18.4/21.8	49.6/59.9/60
Tatung MM-1233	12	640 × 480	31.5	50–70
Princeton MAX-15	14	1024 × 768	15–36	45–120
Packard Bell PB1518DT	15	1006 × 1048	62.75	59.88
Micro Display Genius MC	15	736 × 1008	62.76	60
NANAO 7030H	12	640 × 200	15.75	49–61
Princeton HX-12E	12	640 × 350	15.75/21.85	60
AMDEK 722	13	640 × 350	15.75/21.85	60
AST Research	14	720 × 480	21.85/31.47	60/70
Princeton UltraSync	12	800 × 600	15–35	45–120
IDEK SpectraSync	15	800 × 600	15.75–37	50–90
Princeton SR-12	12	640 × 400	31.5	60
NEC Multisync 2A	14	800 × 600	31.5/35.2	56/60/70
NEC MultiSync 30	14	1024 × 768	15.5–38	50–90
Toshiba P20CU00	21	1280 × 1024	30–70	50–70

screen it was designed for, assuming that it was not originally designed for a high-resolution display. When the computer uses a 72-dpi screen display, then a large screen monitor that also utilizes 72 dpi will maintain the same proportional relationship and provide a WYSIWYG (what-you-see-is-what-you-get) view. A monitor that has a greater dpi value than the computer system it supports will produce sharper screen images, but each image will be smaller.

Flicker and brightness

The refresh rate can be significant, since a refresh rate of less than 60 Hz (hertz) will produce a visible flicker. Screen flicker can be a real problem, resulting in eyestrain, headaches, and fatigue. In general, a high-quality monitor will have a refresh rate of 63 to 66 Hz. Once the problem of flicker is eliminated there is no need to increase the refresh rate.

An unacceptable refresh rate can produce undesirable screen movement. Screen flicker is best observed by viewing the screen from the corner of the eye, since peripheral vision is more sensitive to it.

Evaluating monitors

Image clarity is a characteristic that has a number of elements. The *spot,* or pixel shape, should be square so that graphic images and typographic characters are properly rendered. When the pixel shape is not square, the images that are displayed will be distorted relative to the deviation from a true square. The pixel aspect ratio should be 1:1.

The spot size should be as small as possible to make the image sharp and clean. The screen clarity should be free of electronic noise, which can appear as breaks or fuzzy images on the screen; this condition is similar to snow on a regular television set. A good indication of acceptable clarity can be determined by drawing a large circle on the screen using a CAD or paint program. The circle should be round and not oval. Also important in a desktop publishing environment is the display of small type, which should appear crisp and sharp.

The range of brightness setting of the monitor should be wide enough so that the setting is not on maximum for sufficient contrast and clarity. A monitor that needs to be set on maximum brightness will generally have a reduced life. The range of screen brightness settings should be able to meet the direct and ambient lighting conditions normally encountered. *Linearity* refers to the correct representation of lines, circles, and squares on any part of the entire screen surface. Lines should seem straight, circles round, and squares equilateral. Lines and shapes should maintain their character even when placed along an outer edge or corner of the screen.

The raster lines should be straight and the screen edges should not be bowed. As images are moved around the screen, they should appear equally well in any area.

Adjusting your video

If your display flickers, be sure the refresh rate is set to the highest value supported by your monitor. Check the video adapter and monitor manuals for the specifications. Many video adapters include DOS utilities for specifying the resolution and some include Windows-based utilities.

If you want higher resolutions and more colors, you may want to add some video memory to your adapter. With additional DRAM or VRAM, depending on what the card uses, you can move up to high, or true, color.

Most cards come with 1MB of video memory and can be expanded to 2 or 4MB. Check your adapter manual to see if your particular card is expandable.

Other adjustments can improve the readability of your monitor. First, set the contrast and brightness to provide an optimal picture, and adjust the height, width, and position of the screen to maximize your display area. Some monitors also allow you to change the color content and convergence to enhance the images.

If your display seems a little dim, change the color temperature to provide brighter whites. If the text looks fuzzy with discolored edges, check the convergence controls to make sure all the colors are correctly aligned. Adjust the color content if your monitor is tinted red, green, or blue.

Phosphors and glare

The *phosphor* is the chemical that determines the color of the screen. It controls a number of screen characteristics. The quality of the phosphor determines the smallest attainable spot size, the *screen persistence* (a measure of the screen's ability to redraw quickly with no ghosts), and the screen grain. *Ghosting* or *smearing*, which leaves an undesirable afterimage, can be checked by moving the cursor around rapidly. The P104 Phosphor provides a high-quality white color that is pleasing to the eye. It is also efficient when comparing the light output against the power input.

Some studies have shown that a screen that uses black characters against a white background is better to read and not fatiguing. Some monitors can switch to a reverse video screen that is activated through hardware or software control. The screen phosphor should be bluish white and the characters should appear black in reverse video.

Glare is due to the reflection of light from overhead illumination, outside windows, highly reflective surfaces, and other sources onto the surface of the monitor screen. Excessive glare can result in eye strain and headaches. The better monitor screens are treated during manufacture with an antiglare coating that not only reduces glare, but also results in improved screen contrast. An antiglare coating such as the OCLI HEA can reduce glare by a factor of 14. Antiglare screens are also available.

Interlacing

Interlacing is the process of alternating the refresh rate of alternate horizontal lines. Interlaced screens produce flicker which can be a real distraction. They use a refresh rate of 30 times per second for every second raster line. Noninterlaced monitors are preferred, since they display all of the raster lines at a constant rate. A noninterlaced monitor will display a single thin, horizontal line as a steady image with no flicker.

Generally, the flatter the screen the better. Curved screens tend to produce more glare and distort the image. The curve of the screen is directly related to the amount of image distortion. Positioning identical images in the corners and the center of the screen will provide you with a good check of curvature distortion.

Smoothing graphics boards

Some graphics boards such as those from ATI use anti-aliasing methods to smooth the jagged edges out of curved and diagonal lines. ATI uses software fonts to smooth the edges while Icon uses a special chip.

8514/Ultra

The ATI 8514/Ultra board can anti-alias text under Windows 3.0 but not for DOS applications. Small text is made legible with ATI's Crystal Fonts. The board uses a proprietary graphics coprocessor to increase the speed of video imaging. The 8514/Ultra includes both super-VGA and 8514/A 1024 × 768 noninterlaced modes, which refresh the screen one line at a time to reduce flicker.

Software/hardware compatibility

If an adapter is compatible with an IBM standard such as EGA, it will also be supported by the VDI (virtual device interface) specification described by IBM and GSS (Graphics Software Systems). Software that is written using the VDI interface will run on most adapters with an EGA driver. Most, but not all, CGA software that runs on IBM's EGA also will run on other EGA adapters.

Using multiple display adapters

Depending on your software applications, you might use your display adapter along with another coexisting display adapter. Most color adapters can only be used with another display adapter if one adapter is operating in a color mode and the other is in a monochrome mode. For example, if a color adapter coexists with a CGA, then one color adapter must be configured in monochrome mode.

When two display adapter cards coexist, you must specify which adapter is primary and which is secondary, accomplished through switch settings. The adapter designated as primary will be the adapter in use when you boot up your system. The secondary card will not be used unless it is activated through a DOS MODE command.

For example, to switch over to a monochrome display adapter designated as secondary, you would enter the following command at the DOS prompt:

```
C> MODE MONO <Enter>
```

Display problems

During system power-up, one of the BIOS routines initializes and starts the CRT controller and tests the video read-write storage. The program causes the CPU to check the video settings. In the XTs, the settings are in the video switch SW1 which is read by port A of the 8255 PPI. This port is connected to the two configuration switches SW1 and SW2. The CPU logically ANDs the port data with the hex value 30H, thus checking the settings of switches SW1-5 and SW1-6. If they are not off, the program jumps to a subroutine that tests to see which type video card is installed. If SW1-5 and SW1-6 are off, the program goes into an I/O memory parity test and then into setting the video mode. If a parity error occurs, a message is displayed. In systems that use CMOS settings, the video information is stored there. If a problem occurs setting the video mode, another error message is displayed.

The program also conducts a test of the video storage memory. If a failure occurs, the speaker is beeped. By reading the CRT controller status port and logically ANDing the reading with binary 1000, a test is made to see if the video/horizontal line changes state. If it does not go low during this timed test, a timer clocks out and an error message is displayed and the speaker is caused to beep. Several times during this power-up testing, the INT 10H video I/O procedure is called.

Display problems: no video

One thing you must do is determine if the failure is in the display unit or the system board. You can do this by connecting a good test monitor with a good cable to the PC and recheck. If the problem is corrected, try the original display unit with the good cable. If this works, replace the cable. If it does not work, the problem is in the display unit.

If there is no video using the test monitor and cable and no cursor appears, check the configuration switches on the system board (these are SW1-5 and SW1-6 in the 5150 PC). These switches are used to configure the system for the particular type of monitor adapter that you are using.

Inspect and wipe clean the pins of the edge connector on the adapter card. On some older adapter cards, the bracket on the adapter must be grounded to the chassis for proper operation.

If there is still a problem, check the +5 V power on the adapter board. If the voltage is incorrect, it could be a power supply problem.

If the system seems to work fine without the color card installed, but shuts down when it is mounted in the expansion slot, check ICs U26, U42, U60, U66, or U67 (these and the following IC numbers apply to the IBM CGA card). If there is a problem with the horizontal or vertical sync, it could be ICs U21, U63, U67, or U101. If the cursor is not blinking or is missing, check U12. Color fading or the wrong color can be caused by U20, U22, U43, U44, U45, U65, or U67. Video RAM problems require checking ICs U50 through U60. Error code 501 will appear when there is a problem in the color/graphics adapter card.

Monochrome display problems

When problems occur on systems that have a monochrome display/printer adapter installed, run the following preliminary checks. Connect the system to a good monitor with a known good cable to eliminate the display unit and cable as the problem cause. A 401 error code will appear if there is a problem.

If there is no video, then check for +5 V on the adapter board. If this voltage is not present on the monochrome video board, troubleshoot from the +5 V power input to the point where there is a loss of power.

If there is no cursor on the screen, check the system board configuration switches (SW1 and SW2 in the IBM PC 5150). Both should be in the off position; check that these have not shorted.

Also clean the pins and reinstall the adapter card. If the cursor is not blinking properly or is missing, check U55 in the IBM PC (DM74LS174N).

Installing the newer video adapters

The newer high-performance video adapters use a 64-bit local bus accelerator and support VESA DPMS (Display Power Management System), with refresh rates of at least 72 Hz at all resolutions. Most of the fast, new graphics accelerators are designed for the PCI or VL-Bus.

Some newer cards accelerate graphics and allow full-motion video at less cost than that of two separate cards. Some accelerators include a feature connector that lets you add motion later. Adapters with the VESA Advanced Feature Connector (VAFC) or VESA Media Channel (VMC) interfaces let you connect to video capture, acceleration, or playback cards.

Some larger monitors support either BNC (with four-colored plugs) or D-SUB (15-pin) connectors. These may require flipping a switch in the rear or pushing a button in the front. These buttons let you switch between two inputs.

Avoiding problems

Use only the latest drivers when you install a new graphics adapter. Drivers are updated to fix bugs and increase performance, and are available on the adapter manufacturer's bulletin board. Also, check the readme files that often accompany the drivers for known incompatibilities or other problems.

Some preparation can make your video card installation go smoother. If you are using Windows, change your video driver back to VGA before exiting Windows. Under Windows Setup in the Main group choose the Option menu, and click on Display.

Select VGA from the list of choices. This will prevent crashing, especially if your system enters Windows when it boots up. This allows you to reenter Windows and specify the new driver once you have installed the adapter.

You should also make a backup copy of your Windows directory and subdirectories before installing a new video adapter. This will let you return to your original setup if you should have problems.

Video interfaces

In many IBM personal computers the video outputs are on plug-in expansion cards; in newer units this capability has been integrated into the system board electronics. The use of a typical VGA controller chip is shown in Fig. 6-6. The outputs are always designed to be displayed on specific types of monochrome or color monitors with various resolutions.

Regardless of the type of monitor used, the output of the video circuits must contain all the elements needed to create an image on the display screen. These circuits must be able to encode a number of different display forms. They must be able to show the alphanumeric characters that are on the keyboard as well as graphics.

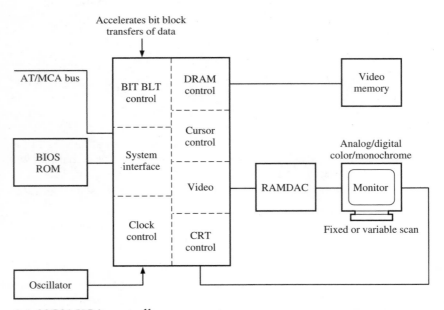

6-6 90C31 VGA controller.

The monitor screen

A monochrome screen has a display face with a single color phosphor, usually green, amber, or white (Fig. 6-7A). At the other end of the cathode-ray tube is the electron gun. It sends a beam of electrons to the face of the tube that lights up the phosphor and causes it to glow. The beam lights up only a small dot on the screen at any one time.

In a color tube (Fig. 6-7B) there are small patterns of color phosphor dots (red, green, and blue) on the face of the screen. Three electron beams are sent from the electron gun (Fig. 6-7C). One beam controls the red dots, another the green dots, and the other controls blue dots. The three colors are additive and produce the colors needed for a color image. In higher-resolution monitors the color dot patterns are made closer to each other and produce a more natural color display. Figures 6-8 and 6-9 show the interior of a typical monitor.

The beams scan the face of the tube, on a line-by-line basis from the top down. As the scanning takes place, each dot is switched either on or off (Fig. 6-10). This scanning is done by the video circuits that control or focus the beam.

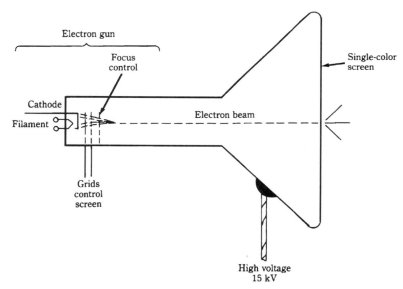

6-7(A) Monochrome cathode-ray tube.

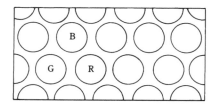

6-7(B) Color-tube screen with alternating red, blue, and green dots over the face of the screen.

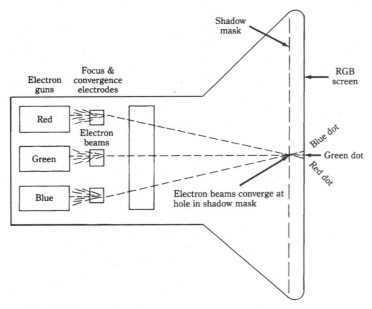

6-7(C) Color-tube operation.

6-8 Interior of typical monitor showing CRT, CRT frame, and main circuit board.

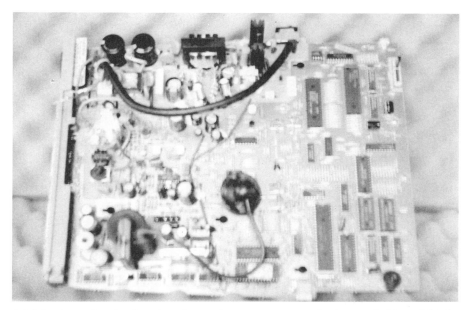

6-9 Monitor circuit showing low-voltage power supply (upper left) and high-voltage power supply (lower left).

Most tubes use electromagnetic focusing. As the beam travels from the gun to the phosphor, it must go through the focusing coils. One coil is used for horizontal focusing and the other for vertical focusing.

The horizontal coil moves or sweeps the beam from side to side at a rate of more than 15,000 times every second. The vertical coil moves the beam up and down about 60 times a second (Fig. 6-11). This scanning operation results in writing 264 lines of light on the screen 60 times a second (Fig. 6-12).

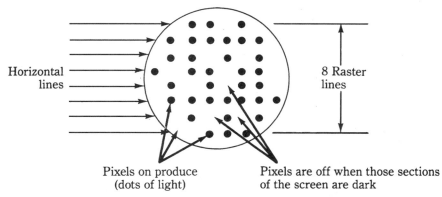

6-10 Close-up view of raster lines and pixels.

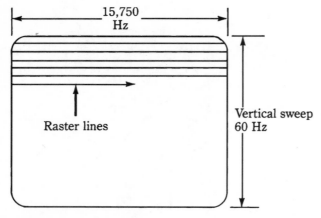

6-11 Horizontal sweep.

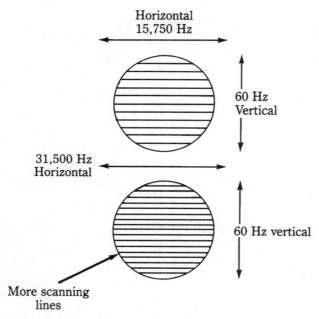

6-12 A high scanning frequency produces more scanning lines and improves the resolution.

The scanning takes place using the timing of the monitor sweep circuits. A higher scanning frequency produces more scanning lines. The scanning must be in sync with the computer clock. The computer sends horizontal and vertical sync signals to the sweep circuits to lock the horizontal and vertical oscillators in step with the computer operating frequencies as shown in Fig. 6-13.

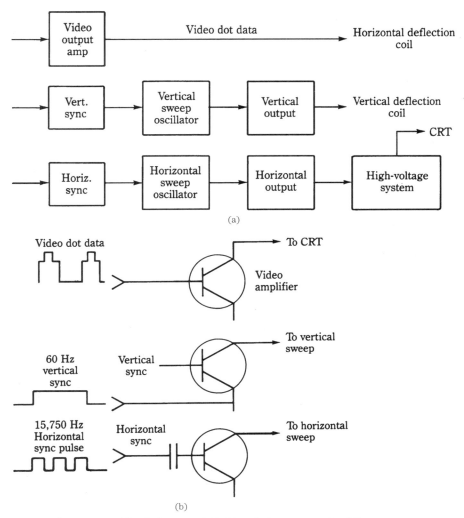

6-13 Video-system block diagram (A). Signal characteristics (B).

The monochrome I/O card

The IBM PC uses a separate adapter card (Fig. 6-14) that plugs into one of the I/O sockets and provides a port on the rear of the system unit for a monochrome display. The modular approach makes it convenient for troubleshooting.

On the card is a video output chip, usually a 6845 CRT controller (Fig. 6-15). It is the main chip for the conversion of digital bits from the computer to the image on the monitor. Other support chips on the board includes 4K of static RAM and an MK-36000 character ROM.

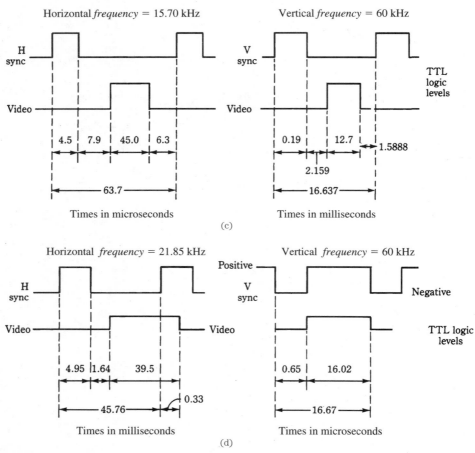

6-13 (*Continued*) Timing chart (horizontal frequency = 15.70 kHz) (C). Timing chart (horizontal frequency = 21.85 kHz) (D).

This RAM is a part of the system memory map. It acts as the video RAM. On the monitor screen of 80 × 25 characters, a total of 2000 characters is present. Each character needs two bytes of RAM to function. One byte contains the ASCII code for the character, and the second contains control bits for features such as blinking of the character, high or normal intensity, and normal or reverse video.

The address of the video RAM ranges from hex B0000 to B0F9F, beginning at the upper left-hand corner of the screen and ending at the lower right-hand corner with the last RAM address. The video RAM is constantly scanned and the contents of each byte are used to turn the dots on and off.

The monochrome adapter uses a 9-pin connector (Fig. 6-16). The functions of the pins are as follows:

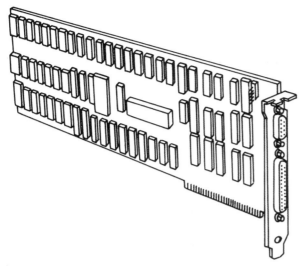

6-14 Display adapter.

Pin 1	Ground
Pin 2	Ground
Pin 3	Not used
Pin 4	Not used
Pin 5	Not used
Pin 6	Intensity
Pin 7	Video
Pin 8	Horizontal sync
Pin 9	Vertical sync

The CRT controller receives address, data, and clock signals from the computer. In the controller chip, the address information is used to access the video RAM and the data bits are sent to the video RAM. The controller uses the system clock information to generate the horizontal and vertical sync signals.

The CRT controller acts as a video processor. It uses the video RAM to update the dot information on the screen. It reads the video RAM data and sends this information to the MK-36000 character-generator ROM. The actual character generation is done in the character ROM. As the ASCII-coded byte arrives at the ROM, it is coded into the proper character byte.

The character bytes are sent to a 74LS166 shift register that converts the parallel byte to serial format. This signal is conditioned and sent to the video output (pin 7). The CRT controller also provides the horizontal and vertical sync information through pins 8 and 9.

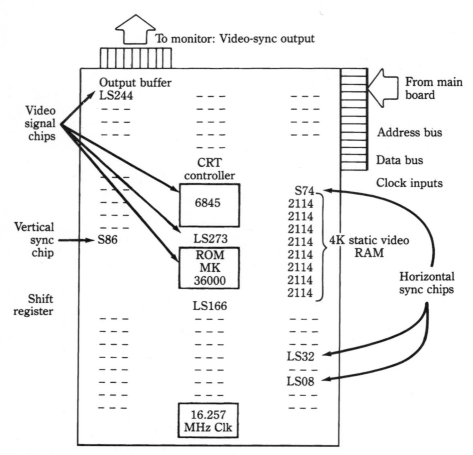

6-15 IBM monochrome adapter layout.

The output signals of the card can be checked with a TV servicing scope. Figure 6-17 shows the typical signals that should be present. Differences from these signals indicate problems with that particular function.

Color/graphics cards

A color/graphics card requires the same type of circuits as a monochrome card, plus the color and graphics circuits needed. Various cards are made for the IBM PCs from other manufacturers. These cards might have different features but the basic operation is the same. The card that IBM provides uses the circuits shown in Fig. 6-18.

A 6845 CRT video processor is used to control the input from the computer. The video RAM is dynamic rather than static and it holds 16K. It uses 14 address lines, A13–A0, with a starting address of B8000. The locations are accessed through four multiplex chips.

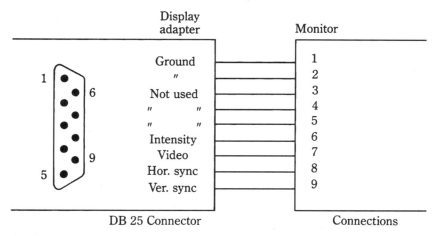

6-16 Monochrome monitor connections.

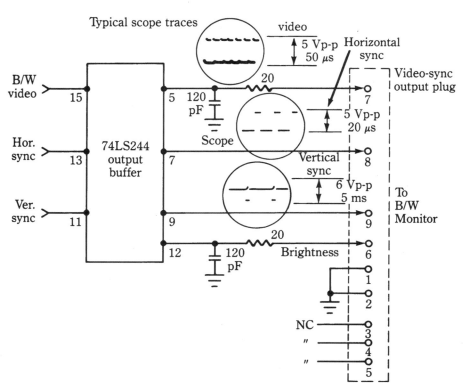

6-17 Troubleshooting monochrome card video-sync outputs.

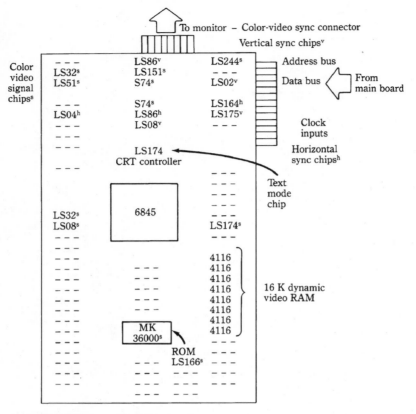

6-18 IBM color graphics adapter layout.

The dynamic RAM sends its contents to an MK-36000 character ROM. The ROM outputs are conditioned and sent to the 9-pin DIN adapter connector. The following pin functions are used.

Pin 1	Ground
Pin 2	Ground
Pin 3	Red
Pin 4	Green
Pin 5	Blue
Pin 6	Intensity or brightness
Pin 7	Unused
Pin 8	Horizontal sync
Pin 9	Vertical sync

In addition to these signals for the monitor, the color/graphics adapter might have additional output connectors. Sometimes an RCA-type jack provides a composite video signal. The three color outputs, the color burst, and clock signals are combined using a

74LS151 multiplexer chip, buffered with a 74LS244 or similar chip, and then sent to the RCA jack (see Fig. 6-19).

Another optional output found on some older adapters is on a 4-pin Berg-type strip. The Berg strip provides the same outputs as the RCA jack plus a connection to the +12-V power supply. This jack can be used to connect the PC to a television. An RF (radio frequency) modulator is also required.

It will use channel 3 or 4 of the commercial broadcast band. The RF modulator provides the modulation frequencies for channel 3 or 4, and the +12 V is used to power the modulator that modulates the composite signal for a color television.

Troubleshooting color adapters

You can use a television service scope to check the output signals of the adapter. Figure 6-20 shows the typical output traces that should be observed under normal operating conditions.

System shuts down with monochrome card installed

If the system shuts down, one of the following ICs on the monochrome monitor/printer adapter could be bad.

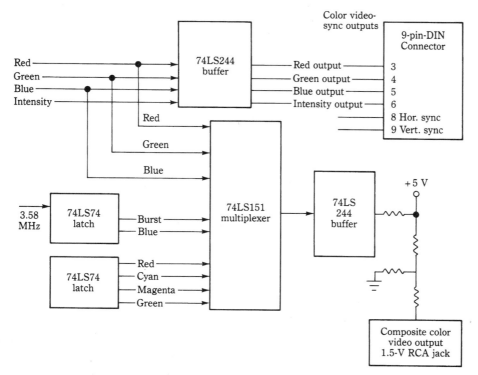

6-19 Color/graphics card block diagram.

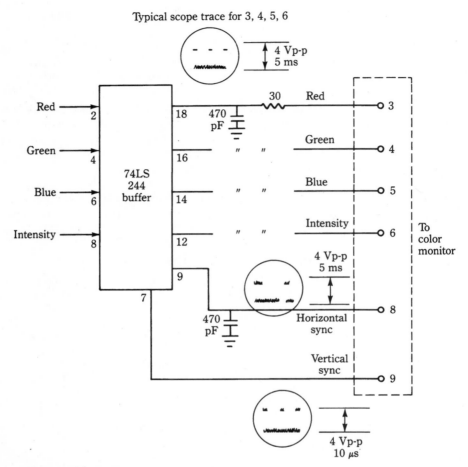

6-20 Troubleshooting color/graphics card video-sync outputs.

U3	DM74LS08N
U35	MC6845P
U45	74LS74APC
U54	DM74S86N
U64	DM74LS244N
U100	74LS32N
U101	74LS74PC

Monitor testing

Special testing units designed as monitor testers are available. Most of these testers are able to test a wide range of monitors. You can use them to test, align, and repair monitors in the field because many are handheld. They can be especially useful for troubleshooting LANs because they eliminate the need to disconnect and carry the monitors to a service depot for testing.Fig. 6-21 shows a typical tester.

To use these testers, you plug the monitor under test into the tester, select the mode, and start testing. The unit generates video, intensity, RGB and horizontal/vertical sync, and TTL signals in different patterns. Units are available testing color and monochrome monitors.

Sometimes the monitor display will provide characteristic clues to the location of the problem. Figures 6-22 through 6-25 show some typical display symptoms along with their usual causes.

VGA signals

The signals and pins for the VGA video signal cable are shown in Table 6-6, and the VGA type of connector is shown in Fig. 6-26.

Timing VGA/SVGA/8514/A

The differences in timing for VGA, SVGA, and the IBM 8514/A standard are shown in Table 6-7. A typical SVGA adapter uses the Tseng Laboratories ET4000AX chip, 512 or 1Mb of 100-ns memory, and a Samsung RAMDAC; another popular combination is the Western Digital WDC90C11 video controller, 512K of RAM, and a Brooktree RAMDAC. Figure 6-27 shows a typical SVGA monitor and circuit board. See Fig. 6-28 for horizontal and vertical timing and Fig. 6-29 for several common transistors used in monitors.

Timing VESA VGA/USVGA

The differences in timing between VESA, VGA, and USVGA are shown in Table 6-8.

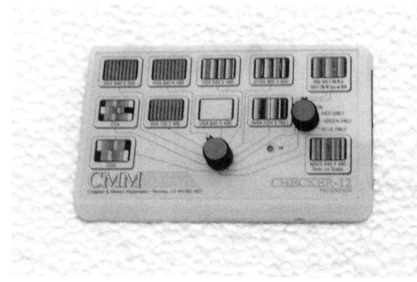

6-21 A color monitor pattern generator.

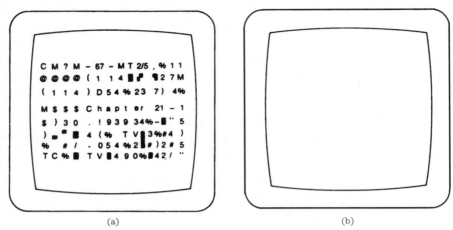

6-22 These types of displays indicate that the video operation is okay and that the problem is in the digital circuits of the computer, processor RAM, ROM, and I/O. Often the screen will appear to lock up and not accept commands. Garbage text, normal borders (A). Blank display, normal borders (B).

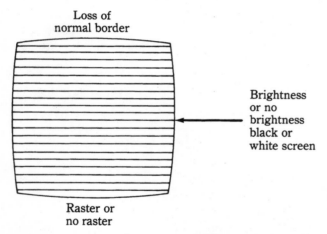

6-23 Loss of border with or without a raster usually indicates a problem in the video circuits.

Sound cards

The first 8-bit boards provided a low-quality sound and the demand for better sounds both in recording, games, and other sound-intensive applications have pushed the move to standardize on 16-bit boards. While the term *sound cards* is a generic term, there are three separate types of sound applications and these have put different demands on the cards.

In games, the most important feature is Sound Blaster Compatibility. Creative Labs is the maker of the Sound Blaster line of cards and was one of the first companies with

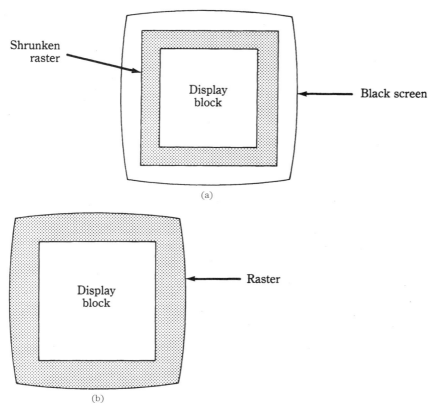

6-24 Typical power-supply failures. Four-sided shrinkage of screen (A). Bends in pictures with some shrinkage (B).

sound cards. Its cards became the standard for game sounds and most, but not all, sound cards are Sound Blaster–compatible.

MIDI

MIDI (Musical Instrument Digital Interface) has become the standard for computer-controlled synthesized music. Most sound cards have MIDI capabilities. Low-end sound cards tend to use *FM synthesis,* an older technology. *Wavetable synthesis* has become the standard for high-quality MIDI. This technology uses digitally sampled recordings of actual instruments.

Wavetable synthesis provides sounds that are much more like the sounds of real instruments than cards that use FM synthesis. FM synthesis employs sounds that are generated through the modulation of different frequency waves, while wavetable synthesis use samples of real sounds and instruments.

Wavetable synthesis cards are compatible with the General MIDI specification, allowing you to connect the card to a keyboard or other MIDI device to create music. The MIDI specification supports 24-note polyphone and 16 MIDI channels, and includes

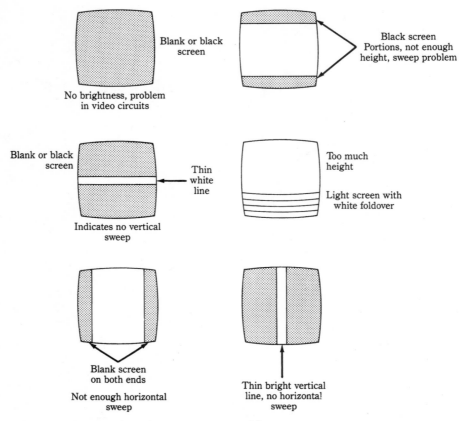

6-25 Several examples of sweep-circuit problems.

128 instruments, 18 drum kits, and 50 sound effects. Figure 6-30 shows a two-chip sound system designed for multimedia audio.

Newer cards use wavetable-based MIDI and synthesizing chips along with software, such as the E-mu Systems Advanced WavEffects found in the Sound Blaster AWE-32. The MIDI boards include external MIDI connectors for connection to MIDI instruments.

Sound cards designed for professionals such as the CardD-Plus from Digital Audio Labs are not Sound Blaster–compatible and do not include any MIDI capabilities. This

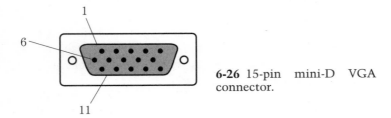

6-26 15-pin mini-D VGA connector.

**Table 6-6. Signals and pins
for VGA video signal cable**

Pin number	Signal
1	Red
2	Green
3	Blue
4	Ground
5	Ground
6	R-ground
7	G-ground
8	B-ground
9	No connection
10	Ground
11	Ground
12	No connection
13	Horizontal sync
14	Vertical sync
15	No connection

Table 6-7. Differences in timing for VGA, SVGA, and IBM 8514/A adapters

	VGA		SVGA		8514/A
	640 × 350	720 × 400	640 × 480	800 × 600	1024 × 768
fH (kHz)	31.468	31.468	31.469	35.156	35.520
Aμs (line time total)	31.778	31.778	31.778	28.44	28.150
Bμs (synch. pulse)	3.813	3.813	3.813	2.00	3.919
Cμs (back porch)	1.907	1.907	1.907	3.556	1.247
Dμs (active)	25.423	25.423	25.422	22.22	22.810
Eμs (front porch)	0.636	0.636	0.636	0.667	0.178
fV (Hz)	70,000	70,000	59.940	58.25	86.960
P ms (frame time total)	14.286	14.28	16.683	17.78	11.500
Q ms (synch pulse)	0.063	0.063	0.064	0.057	0.113
R ms (back porch)	1.937	1.143	1.049	0.626	0.563
S ms (active)	11.111	12.698	15.253	17.01	10.810
T ms (front porch)	1.175	0.381	0.318	0.028	0.014
	Separate sync	Separate sync	Separate sync	Separate sync	Separate sync
H. sync polarity	Positive	Negative	Negative	Negative	Positive
V. sync polarity	Negative	Positive	Negative	Negative	Positive
Interlaced	No	No	No	No	Yes

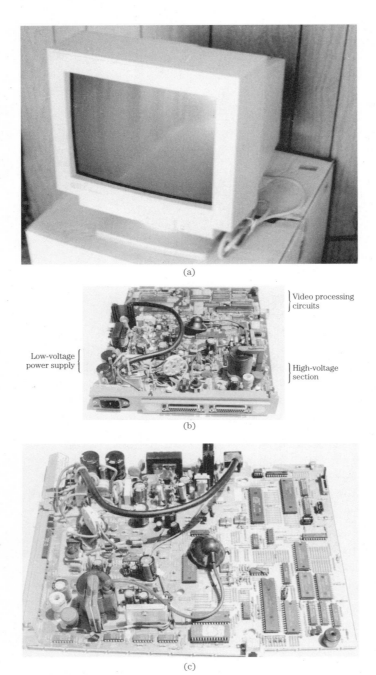

(a)

Video processing circuits

Low-voltage power supply

High-voltage section

(b)

(c)

6-27 Typical SVGA monitor (A) and circuit board (B) and (C).

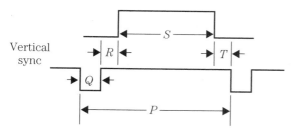

6-28 VGA sync timing.

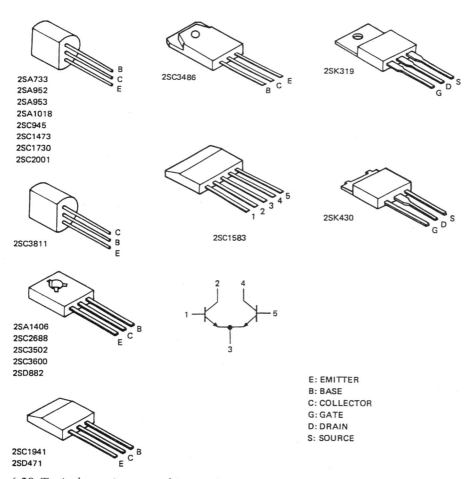

6-29 Typical transistors used in monitors.

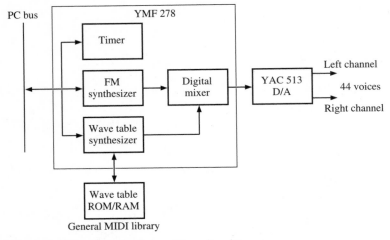

6-30 Intel/Spectron multimedia audio chip set.

card is designed for professional direct-to-disk recording and editing. It uses high-quality components designed to eliminate the clicks, pops, and sound dropouts found in inexpensive cards.

PCMCIA cards

Other sound cards are designed for portable computers. They plug into a standard PCMCIA Type II slot. The New Media Corporation's Multimedia Combo Card is typical of

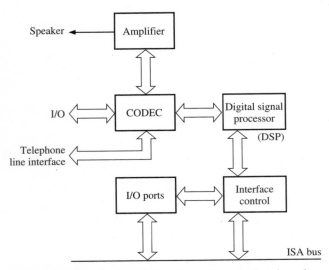

6-31 CODEC chip used for multimedia sound and modem applications.

these. It is a 16-bit sound card in a seven-ounce credit-card-sized package. There is also a SCSI interface for connecting an external CD-ROM drive. Most sound cards use sampling rates of 44.1 kHz and 48 kHz.

Codec chips

These chips are used in most sound and modem applications. The AD1843 is multi-channel codec (coder/decoder) that supports PC-based signal-processing functions, including high-fidelity stereo audio, 28.8-Kbit/s (V.34) modem, and echo-canceling speakerphone. This chip uses a technology called Continuous Time Oversampling which is designed to synchronize audio, communications, and video signals having different sample rates. It can adjust, synchronize, and resample incoming signals at a rate between 4 and 54 kHz in 1-Hz resolution steps, as well as advance or retard the sample clock phase. Figure 6-31 shows how this chip is used.

Installation problems

Sound cards are not always easy to install. You have to deal with the available interrupts, memory I/O ports, and DMA channels in order to get your sound card to work. Sometimes, the default settings of the card will allow you to plug it in and have it run-

Table 6-8. Differences in timing for VESA, VGA, and USVGA adapters

	VESA		VGA		USVGA
	640×350	720×400	640×480	800×800	1024×768
fh (kHz)	37.500	37.500	37.500	48.090	48.363
Aμs (Line time total)	26.667	26.667	26.667	20.794	20.677
Bμs (synch pulse)	1.282	1.282	1.282	2.399	1.000
Cμs (back porch)	4.103	4.103	4.103	1.281	2.977
Dμs (active)	20.513	20.513	20.513	15.995	16.950
Eμs (porch)	0.769	0.769	0.769	1.119	0.750
fV (Hz)	80.333	83.333	72.115	72.010	60.530
P ms (frame time total)	12.000	12.000	13.867	13.887	16.521
Q ms (synch pulse)	0.080	0.080	0.080	0.125	0.080
R ms (back porch)	1.654	1.013	0.747	0.479	0.541
S ms (active)	9.333	10.667	12.800	12.511	15.880
T ms (front porch)	0.933	0.240	0.240	0.772	0.020
	Separate sync	Separate sync	Separate sync	Separate sync	Separate sync
H. sync.	Positive	Negative	Negative	Positive	Positive/ Negative
V. sync.	Negative	Positive	Negative	Positive	Positive/ Negative
Interfaced	No	No	No	No	No

ning in a few minutes. There are software tools such as Touchstone Software's SetUp Advisor. This program checks your computer, figures out what resources are available, and matches them to a database of common add-in cards, including most of the sound cards listed in Table 6-8. You still need to do some work, either changing settings with jumpers on the card or using software that comes with the card.

SCSI sound card problems

When you connect multiple SCSI devices, each device has a different SCSI ID. The SCSI ID allows the host adapter to talk to more than one device and it is possible that neither device will be recognized if both share the same ID.

The SCSI bus must be terminated at both ends for communications between add-on SCSI devices and the SCSI interface. Sound Blaster 16 SCSI-2 is already terminated, so the device farthest away from the audio card must also be terminated. If a closer device is terminated, the card often will not recognize any other devices.

7
CHAPTER

Printers

Printers, like video display adapters and monitors, provide an essential interface between you and your computer. This chapter describes the various types of printers that you commonly see with computers. It provides you information so you can keep your printer running smoothly.

Types of printers

Dot matrix printers: impact type

The dot matrix printer creates the character by selectively moving tiny pins to form a pattern of dots in the shape of the desired character. The dot matrix printing mechanism does not rotate, but it prints using a vertical array of the wire pins. Typically, 7 to 9 pins are used in low-resolution printers, and 18 or 24 pins are used in high-resolution printers. The more wire pins the unit has, the more closely the printing mechanism approximates the print quality of fully formed characters. The characters to be printed are stored in ROM, which determines which pins in the array are to strike the ribbon and imprint the character on the paper.

The impact process used is the traditional way to transfer ink to paper. It involves the compression of paper, type element, and inked ribbon. Impact printers press the character element (or pin) against the inked ribbon, making an impression of the character on the paper.

The serial impact dot matrix printer in Fig. 7-1 consists of a print head with 7, 9, 18, or 24 solenoid-operated print wires. A shoe that engages in the slot of a cylindrical cam moves the print head (Fig. 7-2) across the printing area. A single-groove cam ensures vertical linearity by eliminating the crossover found in a multigroove cam.

Two stepper motors drive the print mechanism: one is used for moving the print head, and the other is used to advance the paper (Fig. 7-3). The two motors operate independently and are controlled by a microprocessor.

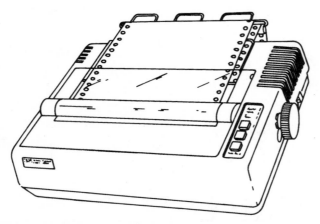

7-1 Dot matrix printer with tractor-folded paper.

Printers use one of two methods of paper feeding. One method is a pressure roller driving the paper with friction, and the other method uses a set of tractors that pull the paper along with pins that mate with holes in the paper. Paper can be fanfold (with or without tractor holes), rolls, or single sheets. Optional roll-paper holders and single-sheet feeder assemblies are available for many machines. The inked ribbon is usually self-contained in a cartridge and is easily replaced by opening a lid on the printer case.

Nonimpact printing

Nonimpact printing can be divided into plain and coated-paper technologies. Among those using plain paper are ink-jet printers, in which tiny droplets of ink are forced onto the paper, and electrophotography, which uses a laser writing on a drum. Coated-paper processes include the following techniques:

1. *Thermal.* Heated elements write on thermally sensitive paper.
2. *Electrosensitive.* Electric charges burn off a thin metallic coating to reveal a black undercoat.
3. *Electrostatic.* The coated paper is selectively charged by a stylus and then passes through a toner that is attracted by the charged area.

Nonimpact printers that create matrix images include the thermal-matrix printer. The print head moves across the print line, forming characters by heating chemically treated paper at the desired locations. Print rates typically range from 20 to 120 cps (characters per second). Figure 7-4 shows thermal printing. With this printer, 5×7 dot matrix characters are printed one at a time, in serial fashion.

Electrosensitive-matrix printers use an aluminum-coated paper that changes color when a voltage is applied. The print head contains electrodes that are pulsed on when a dot is to be formed. The electric charge goes through the paper to a metal plate behind the paper. The plate is at ground potential, and it completes the current path. Figure 7-5 shows the basic operation.

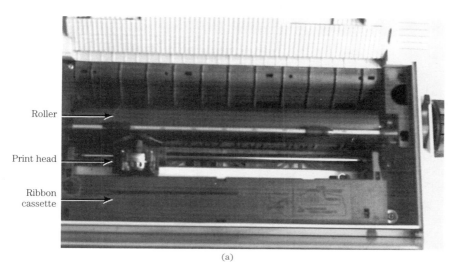

(a)

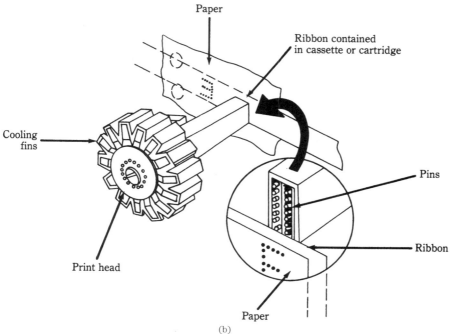

(b)

7-2 Matrix printing. Interior view of a dot matrix printer (A). Print-head operation (B).

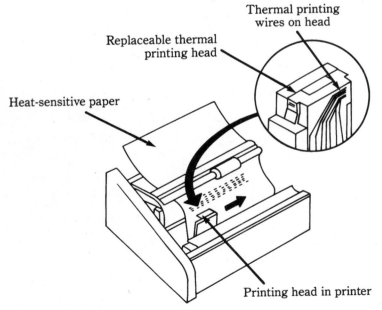

7-3 Typical layout of impact dot matrix printer.

Line printers

Line printers form characters for a complete line, one line at a time, and are rated in lpm (lines per minute). The principle of operation makes these printers much faster than serial printers that generate only one character at a time.

Line printers use a type-element array, such as a drum, chain, train, cylinder, belt, or band (Fig. 7-6). Some line matrix printers use a shuttle comb or bank of print elements. Multihead matrix printers have multiple solenoid-operated print heads.

7-4 Nonimpact thermal printing.

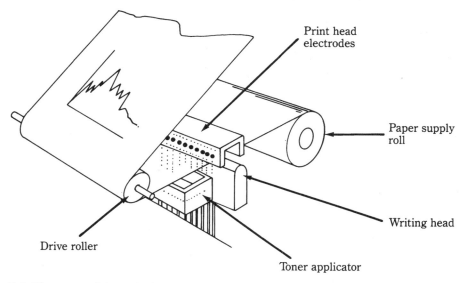

7-5 Electrosensitive printing.

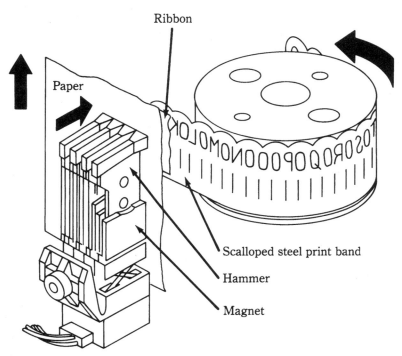

7-6 Solid-line printer using band technology.

Impact line printers include band, drum, and chain types that use a hammer to force the paper from behind against the ribbon and a moving-type element. The drum printer (Fig. 7-7) has a complete set of characters embossed against the circumference of a horizontally rotating steel drum. One full set of characters and one hammer exists for each print position.

Characters to be printed are transferred to a receive-data memory, one line at a time. The data memory is scanned and coupled to the rotating drum. As the character to be printed rotates into position, a hammer-on signal is issued and the hammer strikes the paper, forcing it into the ribbon and drum. The print rate for this type of mechanism is determined by a combination of drum speed, character set size, paper movement time, and data transfer rate.

Figure 7-8 shows a line printer that uses a single-hammer system and a cylinder with a series of raised letters. The carriage movement, the motion of the hammer, and the revolution of the cylinder must be synchronized. The synchronization is done with the mechanical construction of the hammer, platen, cylinder drive, and a dot sensor that counts raised dots on the cylinder. The relationship between the hammer and the position of the raised dots is tracked and controlled by the dot-sensor signal.

Daisy-wheel printers

Solid printing, also called *formed printing,* produces whole, solid images at one time. The character to be printed is selected from an array of type elements that are located on an IBM Selectric type ball, a daisy wheel, or a thimble.

In the daisy-wheel printer, the printing mechanism consists of a steel or plastic disk that rotates in a circle, moving the proper pedal or fingerlike component to the area where the print hammer can strike it. Typical printing speeds for daisy-wheel printers range from 30 to 80 characters per second. The printing mechanism is easily removed to change type styles (see Figs. 7-9 and 7-10).

Printer characteristics

An important characteristic of printers is speed. Several factors are involved: print rate, throughput, and input data rate. The *print rate* is measured in cps and tells how

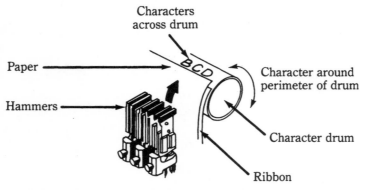

7-7 Line printer using drum technology.

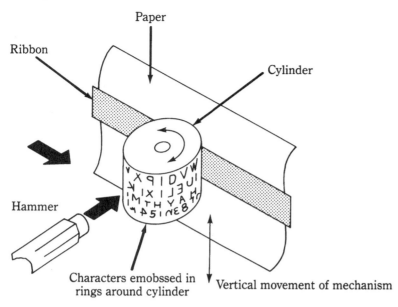

Paper

Ribbon

Cylinder

Hammer

Characters emobssed in
rings around cylinder

Vertical movement of mechanism

7-8 Printer using cylinder technology.

many characters can be placed on the paper in a second. In line printers, it refers to the number of lines printed per minute (lpm).

The *input data rate* depends on the interfacing of the printer with the computer. There are three interfacing methods: 8-bit parallel, RS-232-C, and Centronics-compatible. Regardless of interface type, however, the input data rate means how fast the printer can process characters and therefore determines how frequently the printer and computer must handshake.

Noise is another important consideration. Impact printers generally exhibit noise figures ranging from 50 dBA (adjusted or A-weighted decibels) to as high as 75 dBA. Dot-matrix printer heads make a buzzing sound, but this sound is usually something you can live with. You can always cover the unit with a noise-dampening cover.

Printer problems

Unique problems exist in each of the printing techniques discussed. For example, you must adjust line printers properly, or there will be smear or character misregistration. Vertically moving character sets, such as drums, can produce vertical misregistration or wavy lines. Horizontally moving character sets, such as bands and belts, can cause *horizontal misregistration,* or uneven spacing between the characters on a line.

Printer controls

You will find the following controls in most printers; proper operation is essential to most printer functions.

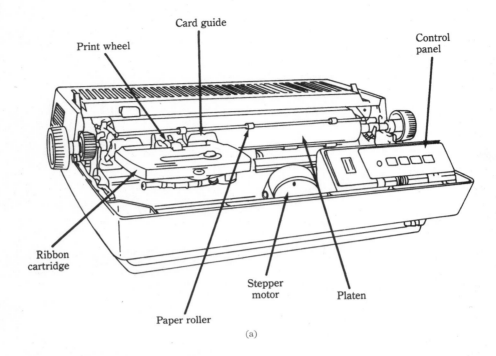

(a)

(b)

7-9 Daisy-wheel printer. Printer with major components (A). View of print wheel and ribbon cartridge area (B).

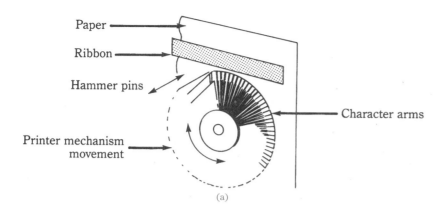

7-10 Daisy-wheel method of serial printing. Hammer and print-wheel method operation (A). View of print-wheel carriage stepper motor with cable drive (B).

Paper bail

The *paper bail* holds the paper against the platen. Marks on the bail help you position paper on the platen and locate the horizontal printing position. The paper thickness lever adjusts the print head position to allow for different printing-form thickness. The lever should be close to the platen for normal printing. The lever should be farther from the platen for thicker sheets and multicopy forms.

Paper-release lever

The *paper-release lever* controls paper-holding tension. In the forward position, paper is held tightly against the platen. In the backward position, the paper is free for positioning or removal. The platen knob allows manual control of the platen for paper insertion and for changing the vertical position of the paper.

Maintaining the printer

Most printers need only a little preventive maintenance. You can clean the surfaces and platen with a damp cloth. Be careful to avoid cleaners with solvents or excessive water.

To help maintain proper operating temperatures inside the printer, keep the printer away from extreme temperatures, such as direct sunlight and direct airflow from room heaters and air conditioners. Keep paper clips, coffee, matches, cold drinks, and other small objects and liquids away from the printer.

Paper loading

Select the right paper for the job and always make sure to position paper squarely and tightly around the platen. Also, make sure the paper thickness lever is in correct position. To remove paper from the printer, use the form feed switch or turn the platen knob.

Print head and ribbon cartridge replacement

Samples of early printouts can help you know when to replace both the print head and ribbon cartridge (see Fig. 7-11). Use only quality ribbon cartridges in your printer. Other cartridges might not give the same performance and might damage your printer.

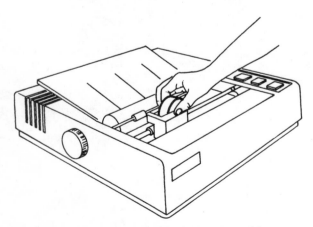

7-11 Removing the print head. Remove ribbon cartridge first. Push print head clips away from head or remove retainer screws. Firmly pull head upward, avoiding bail bar.

Store print heads and ribbon cartridges in their containers and in the same environment as the printer.

Troubleshooting dot matrix printers

The checklist shown in Table 7-1 should be helpful in locating most printer problems. Before trying to correct the trouble, always turn off the printer.

Printer confidence test

A *printer confidence test* allows you to send a message to the printer and verify that the printer received your message. For this test, you must input the following information. You can often check this information using a setup procedure under the printer heading and make a note of the values selected before running the test.

Table 7-1. Dot matrix printer troubleshooting

Trouble	Probable cause	Corrective action
Printer does not start when power is turned on	Power cord not functioning	Check power cord. Check power cord connections; check power cord for damage.
	Power connection fault	Check internal power connections.
	Fuse open	Make sure fuse is in place. Replace fuse if open. (See Fig. 7-12.)
No printout	Printer out of paper	Reload paper and press the paper READY button.
	Access cover open	Close cover and press the READY button.
Light print	Paper thickness lever set incorrectly.	Reset paper thickness. Reset paper thickness lever to a position closer to the platen.
	Ribbon worn	Replace ribbon cartridge.
Carriage moves, but no printing	Paper thickness lever set incorrectly.	Reset paper thickness lever to a position closer to the platen.
	Print-head fault	Replace the print head. Refer to print-head replacement.
Paper jams	Paper path obstructed	Clear paper path.
	Paper thickness	Reset paper thickness lever to a position away from the platen.
Pinfeed paper jams	Tractors set incorrectly	Release and reposition tractors. Avoid pulling or compressing paper.

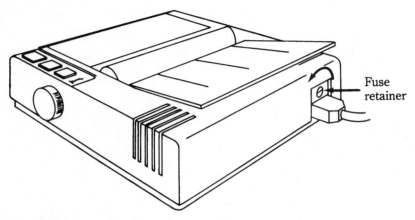

7-12 The fuse is often located next to the power cord.

1. Baud rate
2. Number of stop bits (1 or 2)
3. Number of bits per character (7 or 8)
4. Parity enabled/disabled, even/odd

After you enter the information, the test might request that you input your message. The message is then sent to the printer.

Printer troubleshooting

When printing ceases (or never begins), like the video output, you have three possible sources for the problem: the system board, the adapter card, or the printer itself. One of the few preliminary tests that you can conduct is a printer self-test to see if the printer itself is functioning properly.

Printer self-tests

Most printers provide a self-test to indicate correct operation. This self-test allows you to analyze problems. The self-test is usually invoked by setting a self-test switch or holding one of the printer switches such as LINE FEED or NLQ (near letter quality) down while the printer is switched on.

The printer might execute the self-test by testing ROM, RAM, and the printing capability of unit. Typical self-tests include the following:

SIGN ON.   The sign-on test prints a message such as "Printer Model XXX . . . Self Test . . . ," indicating basic printer function.

ROM TEST.   The ROM test prints the status of the ROM. The result is zero (0) if the ROM is coded correctly and a

ROM BAD

condition might prevent the execution of additional tests.

RAM TEST. The RAM test prints the status of the RAM. If the message is

RAM BAD

the test is aborted.

PRINT TEST. The print test is the basic self-test used in most printers. The printer will print a certain amount of repeated text. This action gives a visible indication of the printing capability of the printer.

Many computer diagnostic programs contain routines for testing different types of printers as shown in Fig. 7-13. Some of the tests that are conducted on nonlaser printers are shown in Figs. 7-14 to 7-17.

Cleaning print wheels

Print wheels used with carbon-film ribbons seldom need cleaning. If you need to clean a print wheel, remove the print wheel and clean with Fantastik, Formula 409, or a similar product. Rinse with water and then dry. Do not soak the print wheel in water.

Dry the print wheel quickly. Be sure that the reflective coded segments on the back or character side of the print wheel are shiny. You can use a soft cloth to clean these. When cleaning a print wheel, be careful not to bend the petals.

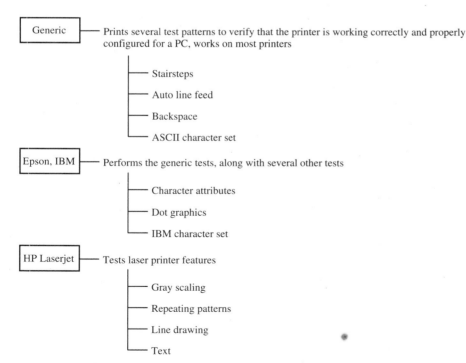

7-13 Printer diagnostics.

Prints every character
in the ASCII character set

ASCII Character Set Test

```
20h – 2Fh:   !  "  #  $  %  &  '  (  )  *  +  ,  -  .  /
30h – 3Fh:  0  1  2  3  4  5  6  7  8  9  :  ;  <  =  >  ?
40h – 4Fh:  @  A  B  C  D  E  F  G  H  I  J  K  L  M  N  O
50h – 5Fh:  P  Q  R  S  T  U  V  W  X  Y  Z  [  \  ]  ^  _
60h – 6Fh:  `  a  b  c  d  e  f  g  h  i  j  k  l  m  n  o
70h – 7Fh:  p  q  r  s  t  u  v  w  x  y  z  {  |  }  ~
```

7-14 ASCII character set test.

Each successive line
shifts the sequence left by one

Checks each element of a print wheel or every
pin of a dot matrix print head

Prints several lines
of the ACSII character

```
! "#$%&'()*+, -. /0123456789: ; <=>?@ABCDEFGHIJKLMNO
! "#$%&'()*+, -. /0123456789: ; <=>?@ABCDEFGHIJKLMNOP
"#$%&'()*+, -. /0123456789: ; <=>?@ABCDEFGHIJKLMNOPQ
#$%&'()*+, -. /0123456789: ; <=>?@ABCDEFGHIJKLMNOPQR
$%&'()*+, -. /0123456789: ; <=>?@ABCDEFGHIJKLMNOPQRS
%&'()*+, -. /0123456789: ; <=>?@ABCDEFGHIJKLMNOPQRST
&'()*+, -. /0123456789: ; <=>?@ABCDEFGHIJKLMNOPQRSTU
'()*+,-. /0123456789: ; <=>?@ABCDEFGHIJKLMNOPQRSTUV
()*+,-. /0123456789: ; <=>?@ABCDEFGHIJKLMNOPQRSTUVW
)*+,-. /0123456789: ; <=>?@ABCDEFGHIJKLMNOPQRSTUVWX
*+,-. /0123456789: ; <=>?@ABCDEFGHIJKLMNOPQRSTUVWXY
+,-. /0123456789: ; <=>?@ABCDEFGHIJKLMNOPQRSTUVWXYZ
```

7-15 Stairsteps test.

Cleaning the platen and roller

The platen and paper rollers are made of rubber. They require periodic cleaning to renew their surfaces for more positive friction drive. You should periodically clean the platen, paper rollers, and pressure rollers (you usually need to remove the platen for access to these). Use soft tissues or cloth wipers and a commercial platen cleaner. Be careful not to get platen cleaner in the unit.

Cleaning the guide

Most printers use a plastic or metal guide to hold paper flat as the print head moves across the paper. The guide moves with the head. Usually, you will have to remove the ribbon cartridge to get at and raise the paper bail. You might be able to grasp the plastic card guide firmly on each end and pull straight up to remove the guide if it is held in place by spring clips. You can clean the guide using soft tissue or a soft cloth, Fantastik, Formula 409, or another commercial product.

Prints a line of text with a word in bold
by printing a character, backspace and
then print the character again

If the printer is not set up
correctly, each character
appears twice

CORRECT TEST
This line tests **BACKSPACE**
INCORRECT TEST
This line tests BBAACCKKSSPPAACCEE

7-16 Backspace test.

Prints one line with bold text

CORRECT RESULT

This line tests **CARRIAGE RETURN** and **LINEFEED**

INCORRECT RESULT

This line tests CARRIAGE RETURN and LINEFEED

CARRIAGE RETURN   LINEFEED

If the printer is set up wrong,
you may have two lines

7-17 Auto line-feed test.

Do not use alcohol to clean plastic print wheels or to clean the platen or other rubber parts because alcohol hardens the surface. Periodic wiping of the exterior of the printer with a soft, damp cloth will keep up its appearance. Periodic wiping and dusting of the interior should be done to remove large accumulations of paper dust and other foreign matter. Lubrication is best done as the printer is reassembled; place a drop of light machine oil on each bearing surface after it has been wiped clean with a soft cloth.

Ink-jet printers

Figure 7-18 shows a Hewlett-Packard DeskJet Plus printer. An ink-jet cartridge used in a printer like this can have 50 or more nozzles. Each of these is about ½ the diameter of a human hair. A resistive heater is switched on to form an ink bubble. This can occur at up to 3600 times a second for each nozzle. As the bubble grows to its maximum size, the ink is ejected out of the nozzle.

Since the ink cartridges also contain print nozzles, they are automatically replaced each time you add a new one. An average cartridge can produce over 120 million drops of ink. It can take up to 25 individual bubbles to make the dot on an *i*. The cartridges require a few special precautions.

1. Always use fresh cartridges.
2. Always keep unused print cartridges sealed in their containers.
3. When replacing print cartridges, install the new print cartridge promptly.

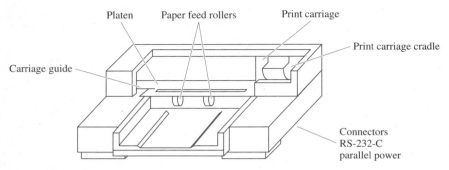

Platen   Paper feed rollers   Print carriage

Print carriage cradle

Carriage guide

Connectors
RS-232-C
parallel power

7-18 Ink-jet printer.

4. Avoid turning the printer off with the print cartridge out of the park or home position (right end of the carriage path).

When in the park position, a cap seals the print cartridge nozzles from exposure to air, preventing the ink from drying in the nozzles. Do not allow the cartridge contacts and nozzles to touch anything, including your fingers. Oils on your skin and dust can affect print quality. Always store print cartridges at room temperature.

Missing dots

Printouts may begin missing one or more rows of dots, when the following problems exist:

1. The print cartridge has passed its expiration date.
2. The cartridge is not pressed firmly against the carriage contacts.
3. The cartridge ink reservoir is low or empty.
4. The contacts on the cartridge or printer carriage are dirty.
5. There are bubbles in the cartridge.

Figure 7-19 shows how to handle paper jams and Fig. 7-20 illustrates basic ink-jet troubleshooting.

HP DeskJet

HP's DeskJet 500 printer produces 300-dpi output like most laser printers. It runs at three pages per minute. The DeskJet has other laserlike features. It is quiet and can handle up to 100 sheets of letter or legal-size paper with its paper tray.

The DeskJet uses a variation of Hewlett-Packard's PCL command language, so it can work with software programs written to drive a LaserJet. The printer has built-in Courier, Gothic, or CG Times fonts and you can add font cartridges or download fonts to a RAM cartridge.

There is a driver that lets Windows programs access scalable Courier, CG Times, Univers, and Symbol typefaces. You can also use the DeskJet 500 with Windows print enhancers, such as Adobe type manager.

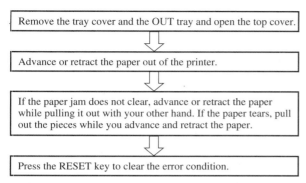

7-19 Paper jams in ink-jet printers.

Lexmark ExecJet

The Lexmark ExecJet printer is a 64-nozzle ink-jet printer. It is designed for low-to-medium usage with tractor, automatic sheet feed, and a front manual-feed slot. It has 360×360 dpi resolution for text and graphics, quality and draft modes, 18 resident fonts as well as font cards. Most applications use about one ink cartridge a month. The cartridges have a shelf life of two years.

Laser printers

The laser has become one of the most widely used technological tools of the present age. *Laser* is an acronym for *light amplification by stimulated emission of radiation.* All lasers share the following features:

- The frequency and phase of light are fixed.
- The beam of light generated is coherent (sharply defined) and intense. The laser might use a gas, liquid, or solid to produce the light beam. The *semiconductor laser* is a type of solid laser used in computer printers. It is driven by simple control signals, has a compact size and consumes less power than other types of lasers. In the laser printer, the laser beam is controlled by the printer signals from the computer. The main components of the laser printer are shown in Figs. 7-21 through 7-24.

Laser problems

Several types of problems are unique to laser printers and, to keep print quality high, it is necessary to clean and maintain the printer as discussed below. If you are having problems with print density, paper curl, or margin widths use the procedures of Figs. 7-25, 7-26, 7-27, and 7-28.

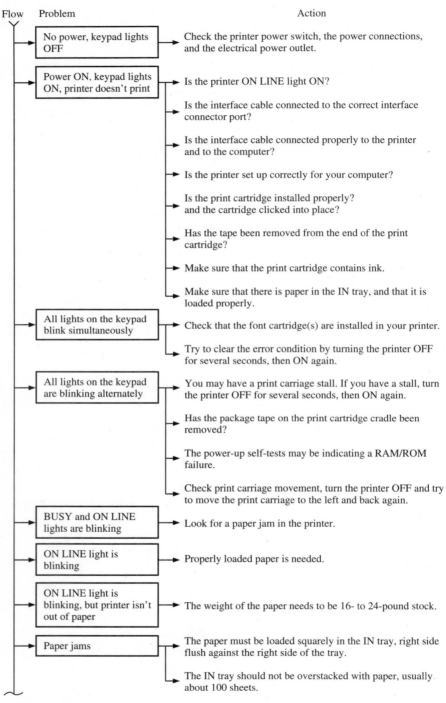

Flow	Problem	Action

No power, keypad lights OFF → Check the printer power switch, the power connections, and the electrical power outlet.

Power ON, keypad lights ON, printer doesn't print →
- Is the printer ON LINE light ON?
- Is the interface cable connected to the correct interface connector port?
- Is the interface cable connected properly to the printer and to the computer?
- Is the printer set up correctly for your computer?
- Is the print cartridge installed properly? and the cartridge clicked into place?
- Has the tape been removed from the end of the print cartridge?
- Make sure that the print cartridge contains ink.
- Make sure that there is paper in the IN tray, and that it is loaded properly.

All lights on the keypad blink simultaneously →
- Check that the font cartridge(s) are installed in your printer.
- Try to clear the error condition by turning the printer OFF for several seconds, then ON again.

All lights on the keypad are blinking alternately →
- You may have a print carriage stall. If you have a stall, turn the printer OFF for several seconds, then ON again.
- Has the package tape on the print cartridge cradle been removed?
- The power-up self-tests may be indicating a RAM/ROM failure.
- Check print carriage movement, turn the printer OFF and try to move the print carriage to the left and back again.

BUSY and ON LINE lights are blinking → Look for a paper jam in the printer.

ON LINE light is blinking → Properly loaded paper is needed.

ON LINE light is blinking, but printer isn't out of paper → The weight of the paper needs to be 16- to 24-pound stock.

Paper jams →
- The paper must be loaded squarely in the IN tray, right side flush against the right side of the tray.
- The IN tray should not be overstacked with paper, usually about 100 sheets.

7-20 Basic ink-jet troubleshooting.

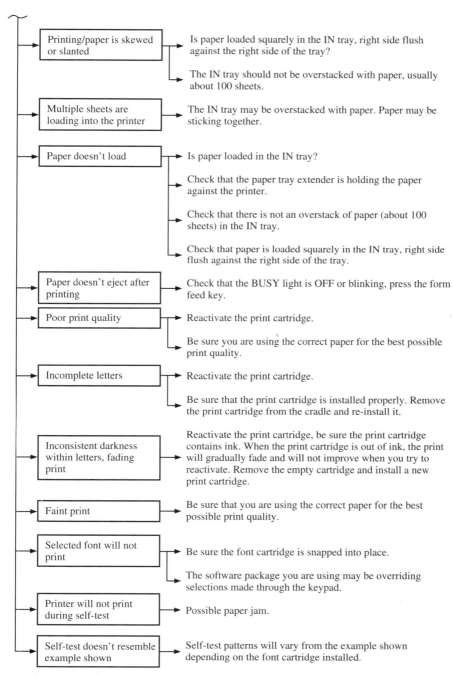

Printing/paper is skewed or slanted	Is paper loaded squarely in the IN tray, right side flush against the right side of the tray?
	The IN tray should not be overstacked with paper, usually about 100 sheets.
Multiple sheets are loading into the printer	The IN tray may be overstacked with paper. Paper may be sticking together.
Paper doesn't load	Is paper loaded in the IN tray?
	Check that the paper tray extender is holding the paper against the printer.
	Check that there is not an overstack of paper (about 100 sheets) in the IN tray.
	Check that paper is loaded squarely in the IN tray, right side flush against the right side of the tray.
Paper doesn't eject after printing	Check that the BUSY light is OFF or blinking, press the form feed key.
Poor print quality	Reactivate the print cartridge.
	Be sure you are using the correct paper for the best possible print quality.
Incomplete letters	Reactivate the print cartridge.
	Be sure that the print cartridge is installed properly. Remove the print cartridge from the cradle and re-install it.
Inconsistent darkness within letters, fading print	Reactivate the print cartridge, be sure the print cartridge contains ink. When the print cartridge is out of ink, the print will gradually fade and will not improve when you try to reactivate. Remove the empty cartridge and install a new print cartridge.
Faint print	Be sure that you are using the correct paper for the best possible print quality.
Selected font will not print	Be sure the font cartridge is snapped into place.
	The software package you are using may be overriding selections made through the keypad.
Printer will not print during self-test	Possible paper jam.
Self-test doesn't resemble example shown	Self-test patterns will vary from the example shown depending on the font cartridge installed.

7-20 *(Continued)*

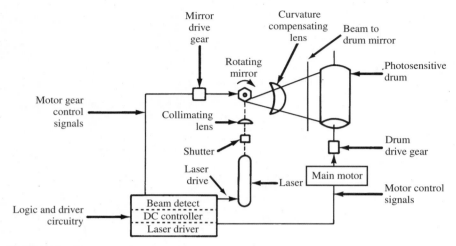

7-21 Laser image system.

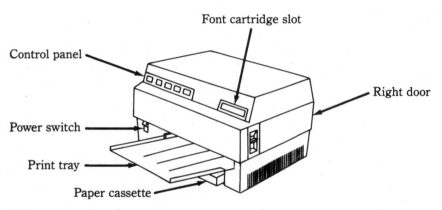

7-22 Laser printer, front view.

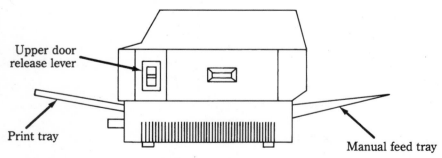

7-23 Laser printer, right side view.

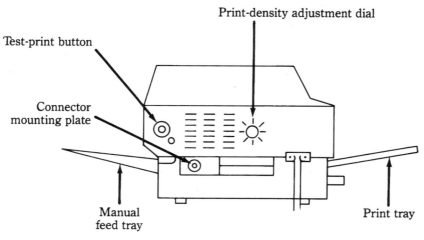

7-24 Laser printer, left side view.

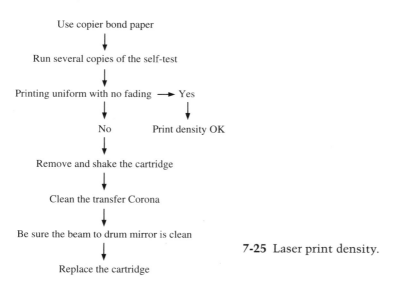

7-25 Laser print density.

Paper jams

When paper jams in the printer, an error code will appear on the status display. Paper moves through the printer from right to left as shown in Fig. 7-29. The printer will have a cassette feed area, a manual feed area, a feeder area, and a fixing assembly area as shown.

When your printer jams, use the following procedure to locate and clear it.

1. Open the unit and search for jammed paper around the fixing assembly area. Remove the paper carefully as shown in Fig. 7-30. If you find no jammed paper, proceed to the feeder area.

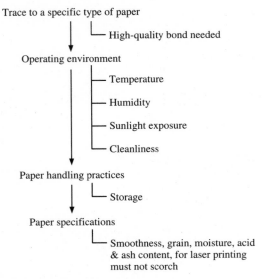

Trace to a specific type of paper

└─ High-quality bond needed

Operating environment

─ Temperature

─ Humidity

─ Sunlight exposure

─ Cleanliness

Paper handling practices

└─ Storage

Paper specifications

└─ Smoothness, grain, moisture, acid
& ash content, for laser printing
must not scorch

7-26 Print quality problems.

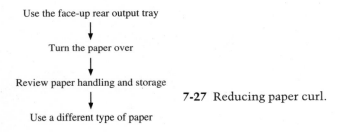

Use the face-up rear output tray

Turn the paper over

Review paper handling and storage

Use a different type of paper

7-27 Reducing paper curl.

2. Search for jammed paper around the feeder area and remove it carefully as shown in Fig. 7-31. If you find none, proceed to the next area.
3. Open the rear door and check for jammed paper. Pull any paper out of the printer and close the rear door as shown in Fig. 7-32. If you find no jammed paper here, proceed to the paper cassette.
4. Remove the paper cassette and check it to see that the paper is placed in it correctly.

After checking these areas, clear the paper jam. If you get a false or undetected paper out message, use the procedures of Fig. 7-33.

Faint printout or white-stripe problems

If white or light lines or stripes appear on the printout, check the print capacity indicator on the toner cartridge. If it indicates a low condition, usually red, replace the cartridge. If the indicator is not completely red, you can distribute the toner by rocking the cartridge as shown in Fig. 7-34.

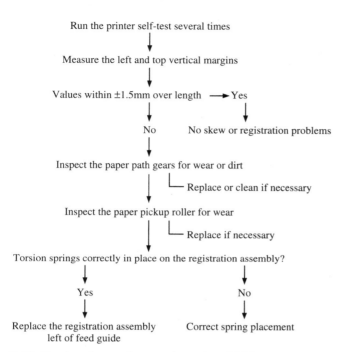

Run the printer self-test several times

Measure the left and top vertical margins

Values within ±1.5mm over length ⟶ Yes

No   No skew or registration problems

Inspect the paper path gears for wear or dirt

└─ Replace or clean if necessary

Inspect the paper pickup roller for wear

└─ Replace if necessary

Torsion springs correctly in place on the registration assembly?

Yes   No

Replace the registration assembly   Correct spring placement
left of feed guide

7-28 Testing skew tolerance (margin width).

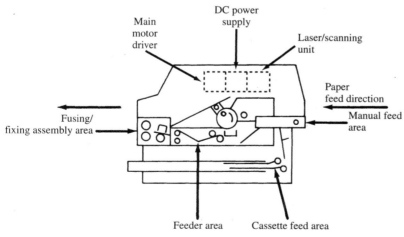

7-29 Paper path through the printer.

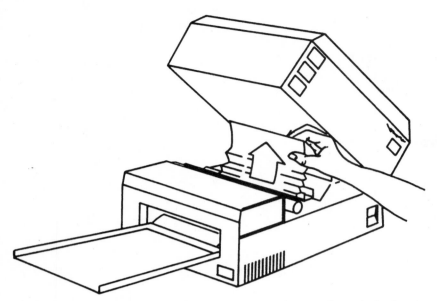

7-30 Open the unit and carefully pull any jammed paper through the fixing assembly area.

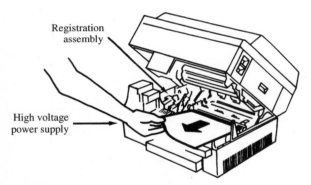

7-31 Carefully pull any jammed paper through the feeder area.

If you move the cartridge too vigorously, the toner can leak and stain the printing. Make a few test printings to check this. If toner stains appear on the printout, the primary corona wire, transfer corona wire, or transfer guide probably need cleaning.

Black-stripe problem

If dirty stripes due to toner stains appear on the printout, it is necessary to clean each of the following parts. Be sure that the power cord is unplugged from the wall outlet before starting these cleaning operations.

To clean the primary corona wire, open the printer and remove the cartridge. The standard Cannon engine uses a special wire cleaner that is inserted into a slot in the cartridge (next to the shutter) (see Fig. 7-35).

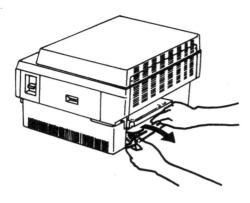

7-32 Open the rear door and pull any jammed paper through slowly.

Paper tray not fully inserted
└ Push the tray until it contacts the microswitches

Tray identifier protrusions broken
└ Replace the tray

Paper sensor arm broken?
└ Replace the arm

Check paper sensor arm movement
└ Free to swing through its full motion?

Check that paper tray identifier microswitches function
└ Observe display

Check that paper-out sensor functions
└ Observe display

7-33 False or undetected paper out.

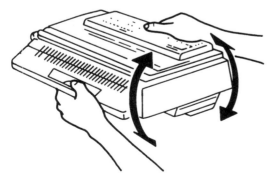

7-34 Grasp the toner cartridge with both hands and rock it gently to distribute the toner.

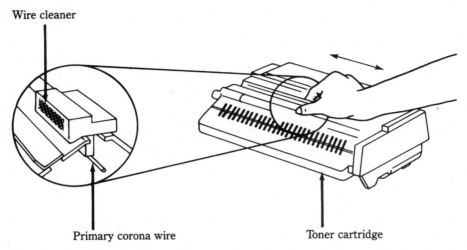

7-35 To clean the primary corona wire, the wire cleaner is inserted in the slot in the toner cartridge and moved back and forth.

Move the wire cleaner back and forth in the slot. The special wire cleaner will displace a thin protective plastic sheet in the cartridge.

To clean the transfer corona wire, remove the cartridge. Then, move a cotton swab up and down the corona wire carefully (Fig. 7-36). Clean the transfer guide using a damp, clean cloth to wipe the transfer guide as shown in Fig. 7-37.

Clean the separation belt in Fig. 7-38 if a black line appears on one side of the printed sheet. If the front or rear of the belt is dirty, you can clean it with a cotton swab or paper towel.

Separation belt replacement

If the separation belt breaks, you can replace it using the following procedure. Open the unit up to get at the separation belt. Open loop A on the separation belt with a

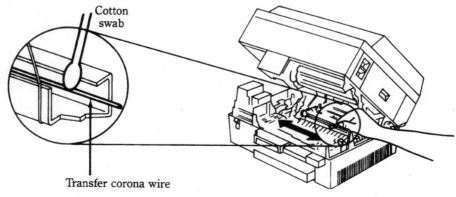

7-36 Clean the transfer corona wire with a cotton swab.

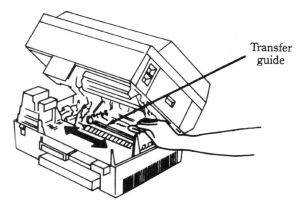

Transfer guide

7-37 Clean the transfer guide with a damp cloth.

screwdriver (Fig. 7-39). Hang loop A on the separation belt from the right side of the upper transfer guide. The indentation on the separation belt should be on the right side.

Then pass the separation belt over the transfer roller, and under the separation pinchroller. Hook loop B on the separation belt to the underside of the spring suspension side of the spring suspender.

Check the following items after installing the separation belt:

1. The indentation should be on the right-hand side.
2. Loop A should be securely hung from the upper transfer guide.
3. The belt should pass over the transfer roller.
4. The belt should pass between the separation roller and the separation pinchroller.
5. The separation belt spring should be hooked securely to the underside of the spring suspension side of the spring suspender (see Fig. 7-40).

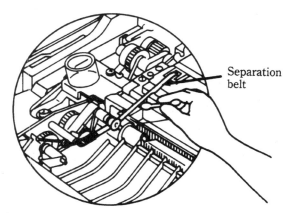

Separation belt

7-38 You can find the separation belt on the left side of the internal mechanism. It can be cleaned with a cotton swab if it is dirty.

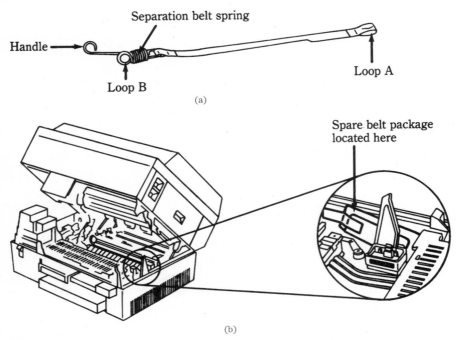

7-39 Separation belts can break, so a spare belt is usually taped inside the printer case separation belt (A). Spare belt location (B).

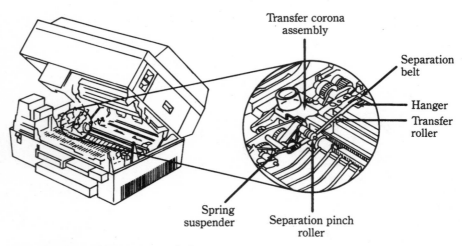

7-40 Installing the separation belt.

Replacing the cartridge

You determine when the cartridge needs replacement by looking at the color of the print capacity indicator, which is visible through the window. As the drum rotates, the color of the indicator will change to indicate the usable service life of the cartridge as shown in Fig. 7-41. Use the procedures of Fig. 7-42 if you get a no cartridge message and the procedures of Fig. 7-43 if you get a low toner message.

Each cartridge contains enough toner to make about 3000 letter-size prints with 5 percent toner image in the effective image area. If many originals with high toner-image ratios are printed, toner is used up more quickly, and white stripes might appear on prints before the printing capacity indicator turns red.

The number of prints is based on an assumed average of 4.5 drum revolutions per print. The fixing roller cleaner felt in the fixing assembly should be replaced and the transfer corona wires cleaned with a cotton swab when the cartridge is replaced.

Storing and handling cartridges

Avoid storing cartridges under the following conditions:

1. Direct sunlight, near windows, or outdoors
2. High temperatures and humidity
3. Areas where the air is dusty
4. Inside a vehicle for an extended time
5. Areas where corrosive gases or salty air is present

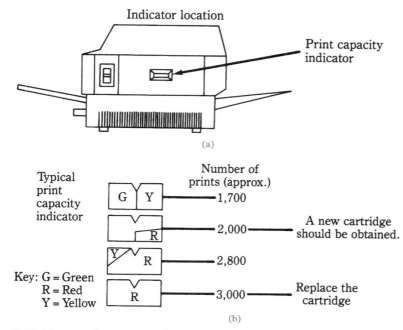

7-41 Toner replacement indicators.

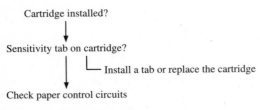

Cartridge installed?

↓

Sensitivity tab on cartridge?

└── Install a tab or replace the cartridge

↓

Check paper control circuits

7-42 No cartridge message.

Do not stand cartridges on end or turn them upside down. Always keep the caution label or the handle facing up. Do not try to modify or disassemble the cartridges or open the drum protective shutter.

Do not expose cartridges to direct sunlight or light of more than 1500 lux. Do not use cartridges for at least an hour after moving them from a cold environment to a warm one. Always use your cartridges before their stated expiration date. Copy quality might deteriorate if you use outdated cartridges.

The following is a list of typical laser printer problems that might occur.

Problem	*Solution or recheck procedure*
Paper out	Install the cassette after refilling it.
Printer power off	Close the unit correctly and press the Online switch.
Paper jam	Remove the paper causing the jam and press the Online switch.

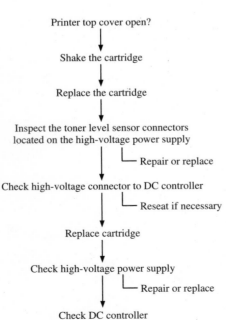

Printer top cover open?

↓

Shake the cartridge

↓

Replace the cartridge

↓

Inspect the toner level sensor connectors located on the high-voltage power supply

└── Repair or replace

↓

Check high-voltage connector to DC controller

└── Reseat if necessary

↓

Replace cartridge

↓

Check high-voltage power supply

└── Repair or replace   **7-43** Toner low message.

↓

Check DC controller

Cartridge not installed	Install the cartridge and press the Online switch.
Request for manual paper feed	Insert the correct size of paper into the manual paper feeder.
Request for font cartridge setting	Reset the font cartridge and press the Online switch.
Page buffer overflow	Reset the error using the Error Skip switch and press the Online switch.
Print overrun	Reset the error using the Error Skip switch and press the Online switch.
Receiving buffer	Press the Error Skip switch and press the Online switch.
Download overflow	Reset using the Error Skip switch and press the Online switch.
Paint memory overflow	Reset using the Error Skip switch and press the Online switch.
Vector graphic reject	Cancel job.
Work memory over	Reset using the Error Skip switch and press the Online switch.
Communication error	Reset using the Error Skip switch and press the Online switch.
Print check request	Reset using the Error Skip switch and press the Online switch.
Fixing assembly	Turn off the power switch, wait for 10 minutes, and turn it on again.
Beam defect fault	Reset using the Error Skip switch.
Laser temperature control fault	Turn off the power switch, wait for 10 minutes, and turn it on again.
Main motor fault	Reset using the Error Skip switch.
Printer control	Reset using the Error Skip switch.
Bus error	Power reset.
Program ROM check	Power reset.
Built-in font ROM	Power reset.
Dynamic RAM error	Power reset.
Scan buffer error	Power reset.
Dynamic RAM control fault	Power reset.

Laser printer troubleshooting

Using the procedures of Fig. 7-44 for isolating the problem to an operation of the printer. The image development check (Fig. 7-45) and the repetitive defect chart (Fig.

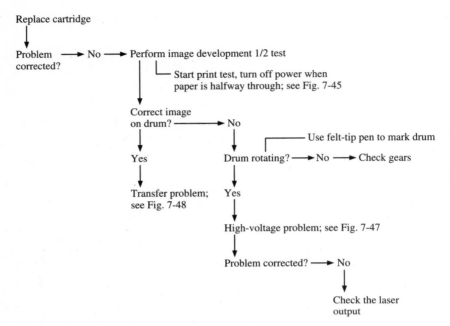

7-44 Image formation troubleshooting.

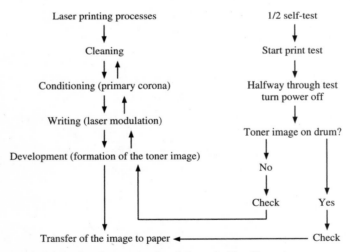

7-45 Image development check (one-half self-test).

7-46) will also aid you in isolating the problem. Use Fig. 7-47 for high-voltage problems and Fig. 7-48 for transfer corona troubleshooting. If you get a beam detect error message or a scanner malfunction on the display, use Figs. 7-49 and 7-50.

Fig. 7-51 illustrates a simple fusing check and Fig. 7-52 shows how to troubleshoot the fuser system.

First occurrence of the print defect

Registration assembly transfer roller	0.5 in (13 mm)
Upper registration roller	1.5 in (38 mm)
Lower registration roller	1.75 in (44 mm)
Cartridge developer roller	2.0 in (51 mm)
Lower fusing assembly roller	2.56 in (65 mm)
Upper fusing assembly roller	3.16 in (80 mm)
Cartridge photoconductive drum	3.75 in (95 mm)

7-46 Repetitive defects.

Printer communications protocols

Communications protocols are needed to prevent print buffer overflow when print data is being received faster than the printer can empty the print buffer. A communications protocol is usually needed at baud rates above 300, and in some cases at 300 baud and below.

RS-232-C printer communications

Three protocols are commonly used for printer control. The protocols are the DC1/DC3, PRINTER READY, and ETX/ACK protocols. In addition to printer buffer control, the DC1/DC3 and PRINTER READY protocols also can be used to respond to error conditions.

ETX/ACK protocol

When the ETX/ACK protocol is used, the computer must transmit a string of data, which is smaller than the printer buffer size, followed by the control code ETX. The computer will then stop transmitting. The printer withdraws the data from the buffer at a rate determined by the print speed of the printer until the last character, which is ETX, is removed.

Then, the printer generates the control code ACK sent back to the computer. The computer will start transmitting data again on receipt of the ACK code. This process is used to protect data from being lost as a result of buffer overflow. When this protocol is used, the computer must keep the data string transmitted from exceeding the capacity of the printer buffer.

DC1/DC3 protocol

In the DC1/DC3 protocol, when the computer begins to transmit a data string, the printer responds with the DC3 character when the printer buffer is almost full (usually within 64 bytes) or when the printer is in check.

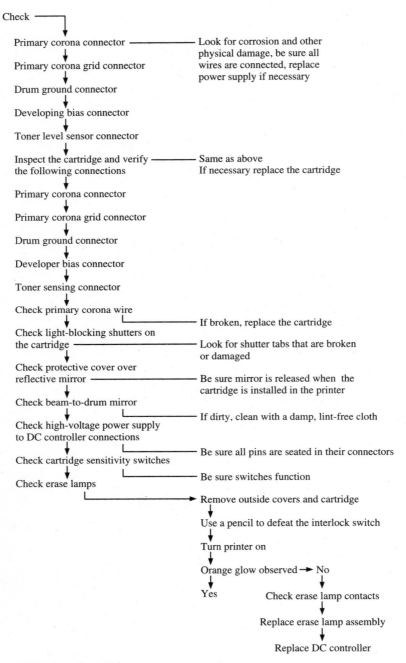

Check

Primary corona connector ——————— Look for corrosion and other
physical damage, be sure all
Primary corona grid connector wires are connected, replace
power supply if necessary
Drum ground connector

Developing bias connector

Toner level sensor connector

Inspect the cartridge and verify ——— Same as above
the following connections If necessary replace the cartridge

Primary corona connector

Primary corona grid connector

Drum ground connector

Developer bias connector

Toner sensing connector

Check primary corona wire
———— If broken, replace the cartridge
Check light-blocking shutters on
the cartridge ——————————— Look for shutter tabs that are broken
or damaged
Check protective cover over
reflective mirror ————————— Be sure mirror is released when the
cartridge is installed in the printer
Check beam-to-drum mirror
———— If dirty, clean with a damp, lint-free cloth
Check high-voltage power supply
to DC controller connections
———— Be sure all pins are seated in their connectors
Check cartridge sensitivity switches
———— Be sure switches function
Check erase lamps
————————→ Remove outside covers and cartridge

Use a pencil to defeat the interlock switch

Turn printer on

Orange glow observed ——→ No

Yes   Check erase lamp contacts

Replace erase lamp assembly

Replace DC controller

7-47 High-voltage system.

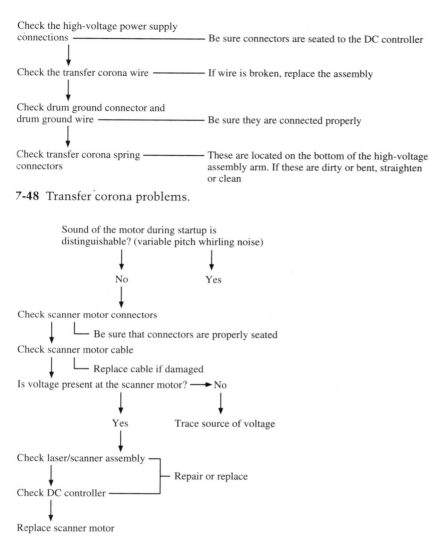

Check the high-voltage power supply
connections ———————————— Be sure connectors are seated to the DC controller

Check the transfer corona wire ————— If wire is broken, replace the assembly

Check drum ground connector and
drum ground wire ————————— Be sure they are connected properly

Check transfer corona spring ————— These are located on the bottom of the high-voltage
connectors   assembly arm. If these are dirty or bent, straighten
                                            or clean

7-48 Transfer corona problems.

Sound of the motor during startup is
distinguishable? (variable pitch whirling noise)

            No   Yes

Check scanner motor connectors
        └── Be sure that connectors are properly seated
Check scanner motor cable
        └── Replace cable if damaged
Is voltage present at the scanner motor? ——▶ No

            Yes   Trace source of voltage

Check laser/scanner assembly ┐
                             ├─ Repair or replace
Check DC controller ─────────┘

Replace scanner motor

7-49 Scanner malfunction message.

    This protocol requires that the computer monitor the printer for an indication of printer status. The printer will transmit the control code DC3 when its buffer is close to being full. The computer will stop transmitting at this point while the printer works on the data in its buffer. When the buffer is almost empty, the printer will transmit a DC1 code asking the computer to resume transmitting data. A DC3 code also will be transmitted if the printer is in check. Either of these conditions will cause a NAK control code to be transmitted following the DC3 code. The printer must be in check or a DC1 will be sent to the computer by the printer when the printer buffer is nearly empty.

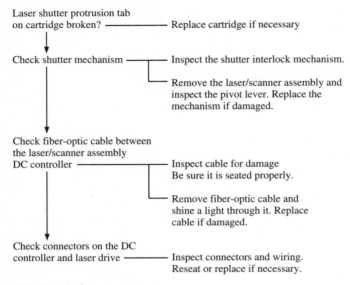

Laser shutter protrusion tab
on cartridge broken? ———————— Replace cartridge if necessary

Check shutter mechanism ———— Inspect the shutter interlock mechanism.

Remove the laser/scanner assembly and
inspect the pivot lever. Replace the
mechanism if damaged.

Check fiber-optic cable between
the laser/scanner assembly
DC controller ———————— Inspect cable for damage
Be sure it is seated properly.

Remove fiber-optic cable and
shine a light through it. Replace
cable if damaged.

Check connectors on the DC
controller and laser drive ———— Inspect connectors and wiring.
Reseat or replace if necessary.

7-50 Beam detect error.

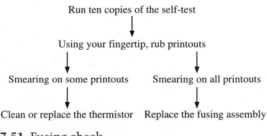

Run ten copies of the self-test

Using your fingertip, rub printouts

Smearing on some printouts   Smearing on all printouts

Clean or replace the thermistor   Replace the fusing assembly

7-51 Fusing check.

Printer-ready protocol

The PTR/RDY protocol uses the +DTR interface line. This line will go low (false) when there is a print head or wheel restore error or when the printer buffer is nearly full. The DTR signal will go high (true) when the printer buffer is nearly empty and all other conditions are corrected. You can use the procedures in Fig. 7-53 to check out serial communication problems. Table 7-2 shows the RS-232-C interface signals typically used for printer operation along with the teclo and CCITT designations and the usual pin assignments for the DB25 connector.

Centronics parallel communications protocol

The Centronics printer interface is an 8-bit parallel connection with relatively simple handshake signals. This interface does not support device addresses so only one device can be connected to the host output port. The typical timing chart shown in Fig.

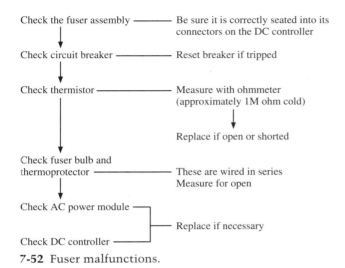

7-52 Fuser malfunctions.

7-54 will help you troubleshoot the timing relationships of the handshake signals that serve as the communications protocol for printers operating with this type of interface.

Typical operation

In operation, when the printer is ready, the BUSY signal is low. The computer places the data on the data bus and sends a pulse to the STROBE line. The BUSY signal goes high and the computer reads in the latched data, places the data in the print queue, and outputs an ACK pulse. The BUSY signal then goes low after the ACK pulse. The DEMAND signal is the inverse of the BUSY signal. The printer will activate the FAULT line if the printer detects a print head or print wheel restore error and is in a check condition.

Following is a description of the Centronics signal lines.

STROBE	Starts the reading of data, it is initiated by the computer.
ACK	Indicates that the printer has received data and it is ready to accept the next data.

Table 7-2. RS-232-C serial interface signals

Signal name	Telephone designation	Pin (DB25)	CCITT designation
Protective ground	AA	1	101
Transmit data	BA	2	103
Receive data	BB	3	104
Request to send	CA	4	105
Data set ready	CC	6	107
Signal ground	AB	7	102
Data terminal ready	CD	20	108

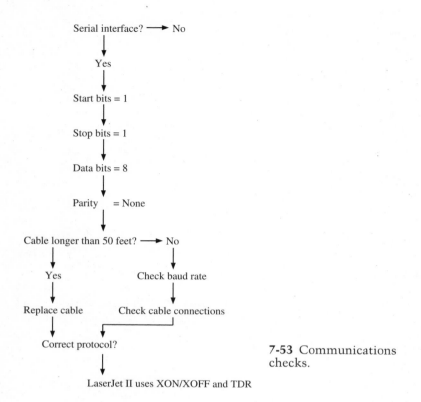

7-53 Communications checks.

BUSY	Indicates that the printer cannot receive data.
PE	Indicates that the printer is out of paper.
SELECT	Indicates that the printer is online.
DEMAND	The inverse of the BUSY signal.
INPUT PRINT	A pulse from the computer that initializes the printer.
FAULT	The fault line indicates that the printer is in the error mode.

Normal data transfer

STROBE is a signal line from the computer that indicates to the printer that the data lines have valid information on them. The data should be valid at least one microsecond before the negative-true STROBE is asserted. Data must be held valid at least one microsecond after STROBE is negated. The length of time STROBE is asserted can range from 1 to 500 microseconds.

The trailing edge of STROBE causes the printer to assert ACK. In Centronics printers, the delay between the negation of STROBE and the assertion of ACK is on the order of 2 to 10 microseconds.

These times are for a normal data transfer. Centronics calls the handshaking sequence Normal-Data-Input timing (Fig. 7-55). For Centronics printers, normal trans-

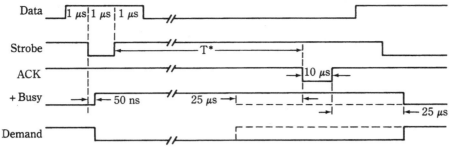

*Depends on the program loop time.

7-54 Typical Centronics timing.

fers take place when the printer is filling an internal line buffer and is not printing or performing some other operation. If one of these operations is being performed, a BUSY condition exists.

Busy-condition timing

A BUSY condition occurs when the printer is given a command to print the line in the print buffer (carriage return), or when a vertical tab, form feed, line feed, delete, bell, select, or deselect character is sent. The receipt of one of these special characters causes the printer to perform some mechanical operation that takes considerably more time than a few microseconds. In these cases, the handshake changes to BUSY condition timing.

The handshake mechanism during a BUSY condition is as follows. After STROBE is negated, BUSY is asserted instead of ACKNOWLEDGE. BUSY indicates that the printer is busy and cannot complete the handshake until it is done. Centronics printers can be busy for durations of 2 to over 300 milliseconds.

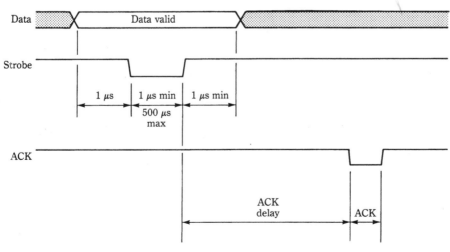

7-55 Centronics interface timing.

After negating BUSY, the printer asserts the negative-true ACK line. This action occurs after a few microseconds and ACK is asserted for a few microseconds. The busy-condition timing ends with this negation of ACK, as does the normal-data-input timing. Figure 7-56 shows the busy-condition timing for the Centronics parallel interface.

Some printers do not use BUSY because both normal and busy protocols end with an ACK. Other printers use a switch to implement either ACK or BUSY. The switch allows the end user to decide which handshake signal is used.

Some printers that use the Centronics interface require the data to be valid for 0.5 microsecond before STROBE is asserted and to be held valid for 0.5 microsecond after STROBE is negated. The STROBE needs only to be asserted for 0.5 microsecond. These times are all half of the original Centronics specification. Any computer interface designed for a Centronics printer can also drive this printer, with some margin. The BUSY and ACK signals might also be a little different.

BUSY can be activated on the falling edge of STROBE instead of the rising edge, and negated after ACK is negated. The original Centronics specification requires that ACK not be asserted until BUSY is negated, if a busy condition exists.

Some interfaces for Centronics printers assume that the rising edge of ACK is the end of the transfer, which is not quite right because the negation of BUSY will follow the negation of ACK by another 5 ms. If the computer responds to the completion of one transfer cycle with another after 5 microseconds, this printer interface will work with Centronics printers, even though the signal timings are different.

Table 7-3 lists the connector signals for Centronics interface printers. All of the signals are not used by all printers, especially the newer printers.

Figure 7-57 shows the Centronics 36-pin connector at the rear of a dot matrix printer. Next to the connector are two DIP switches that are used for setting printer parameters. Figure 7-58 shows a typical parallel printer port card that provides the Centronics interface signals.

Many diagnostic programs allow you to check if the computer's parallel part is working (Figs. 7-59 and 7-60). You will need a loopback connector wired as shown in Fig. 7-61. Some programs also use the data lines test illustrated in Fig. 7-62. Use Fig. 7-63 if you have errors during the parallel port tests.

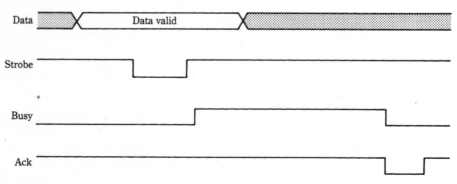

7-56 Timing diagram for the Centronics parallel interface-BUSY-condition timing.

Table 7-3. Pinout for the Centronics parallel interface

Signal name	Positive- or negative-true	Signal pin number	Associated ground wire pin number
Data Strobe	Negative	1	19
Data 1	Positive	2	20
Data 2	Positive	3	21
Data 3	Positive	4	22
Data 4	Positive	5	23
Data 5	Positive	6	24
Data 6	Positive	7	25
Data 7	Positive	8	26
Data 8	Positive	9	27
Acknowledge	Negative	10	28
Busy	Positive	11	29
Paper out	Positive	12	None
Select printer	Positive	13	None
Signal ground	—	14	None
OSCXT (OSC out)	—	15	None
Signal ground	—	16	None
Chassis ground	—	17	None
+5 V supply	—	18	None
Input prime (printer reset)	Negative	31	30
Fault	Negative	32	None
Line count	Negative	34	35

Data meters

Data meters are useful if you are trying to get one computer or peripheral to talk to another. They provide most of the information you need to know about RS-232 data transmission settings but cost less than the more expensive data communications analyzers.

Data meters can be used to test both DCE and DTE devices and some can generate test patterns and receive data transmissions to give you baud rate, word length, parity, and stop bits. A single-button operation lets you select from menu options such as READ, PARAMETER SCAN, PARAMETER SELECTION, and PRINT.

1. READ can be used to determine the serial protocol being sent from the RS-232 device and displays.
2. PARAMETER SCAN sends protocol combinations to the device being tested. It generates random characters until the correct protocol is found. The correct parameter settings are then printed out.
3. PARAMETER SELECTION allows the selection of serial protocol for output.

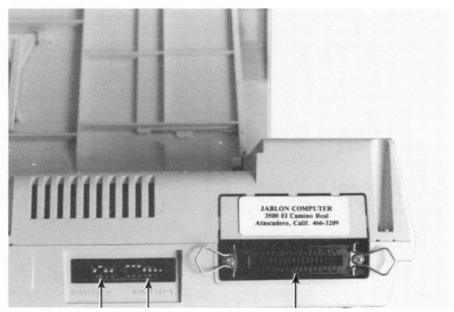

DIP switches
for printer parameters   36-pin Centronics connector

7-57 Rear of dot matrix printer showing 36-inch Centronics connector and DIP switches for changing printer parameters.

7-58 Parallel printer port card for providing Centronics interface signals.

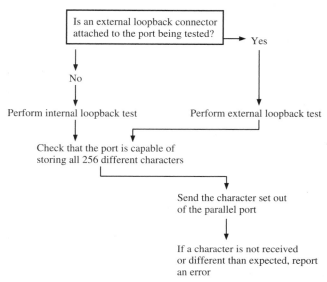

7-59 Parallel port testing.

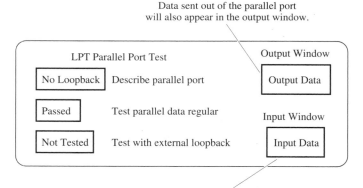

7-60 Parallel port test screen.

Printer exerciser/testers

Exerciser/testers exercise and test parallel printers. They are designed as field diagnostic instruments that go beyond the printer self-test. They can be used to identify problems on site and can be used to test the most popular dot matrix and daisy-wheel printers or any printer that can emulate one of these. Most testers use the parallel (Centronics) interface and work independently, in place of the computer, so the printer does

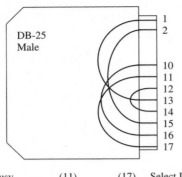

Busy	(11)	——	(17)	Select Input
Acknowledge	(10)	——	(16)	Initialize
Paper End	(12)	——	(14)	Auto Feed
Select	(13)	——	(1)	Strobe
Data Bit 0	(2)	——	(15)	Error

7-61 Parallel loopback connector.

Tests individual data lines of the parallel cable.
Each line should alternate between p and another character.

Data Line 0: pqpqpqpqpqpqpqpqpqpqpqpqpqpqpqpqpqp

Data Line 1: prprprprprprprprprprprprprprprprprpr

Data Line 2: ptptptptptptptptptptptptptptptptptptp

Data Line 3: pxpxpxpxpxpxpxpxpxpxpxpxpxpxpxpxp

Data Line 4: p`p`p`p`p`p`p`p`p`p`p`p`p`p`p`p`p`p`

Data Line 5: pFpFpFpFpFpFpFpFpFpFpFpFpFpFpFpFpFp

Data Line 6: p0p0p0p0p0p0p0p0p0p0p0p0p0p0p0p0p0p

7-62 Parallel data lines test.

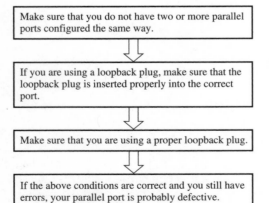

Make sure that you do not have two or more parallel ports configured the same way.

If you are using a loopback plug, make sure that the loopback plug is inserted properly into the correct port.

Make sure that you are using a proper loopback plug.

If the above conditions are correct and you still have errors, your parallel port is probably defective.

7-63 If errors occur in parallel port testing.

not need to be connected to any other device while under test. The ability to test an unconnected printer makes it useful for field testing as well as depot repair.

LED status indicators are used to simulate printer conditions such as busy, paper out, or a fault. A bank of DIP switches is used to set up the configuration of the different printers and for special conditions such as Handshaking, AutoLF, Force Carriage, and Wide Carriage. The following tests can be performed: paper drift; platen roll; carriage movement; form feed; special functions such as underlining, bold, and pitch changes; head movement; daisy-wheel servo motor; daisy-wheel characters; and dot matrix print heads. It also provides the ability to send continuous ASCII characters and tests for dot matrix pin firing with each pin individually.

Other printer problems

If the PAUSE light is on, press the PAUSE button. If the PAUSE light is off and nothing is printed, follow this procedure:

1. Check that the software is installed properly for your printer.
2. Check the software printer settings.
3. Check both ends of the interface cable between the printer and the computer. Make sure your interface cable is secured to the printer and computer.

If the printer sounds like it is printing, but nothing is printed, the ribbon cartridge might not be installed properly. If the printer makes a strange noise, the buzzer sounds several times, and the printer stops. Turn off the printer and check for paper jams or other feed problems.

If the PAUSE light flickers and the printer does not print, or it stops printing abruptly, the print head might be overheated; wait a few minutes and the printer will resume printing when the print head cools.

Print is faint or uneven

If the printed characters have parts missing or are faint, the ribbon cartridge might not be installed properly or the ribbon might be worn out. Reinstall or replace the ribbon cartridge. Also, check that the paper-thickness lever is set correctly for the paper you are using.

A line of dots missing in the printout means the print head is damaged or the pins are sticking. Try lubricating the pins with a light oil; you might have to replace the print head.

When dots are missing in random positions, there might be too much slack in the ribbon or the ribbon might have come loose. Reinstall the ribbon cartridge and make sure the ribbon starts out tight. You might have to replace the ribbon.

If the type style or characters set by your software cannot be printed, check that the software is correctly configured for your printer. If the font selected on the control panel does not print, your software might be overriding the control panel setting. Check the printing style set in your software. When the wrong characters are printed, this usually means the wrong character table or the wrong international character set is selected. Check the DIP-switch settings.

If all the text is printed on the same line, you might have to change a switch setting, so that the printer automatically adds a line-feed code to each carriage return. If the text is printed with an extra blank line in between, this means two line-feed signals are being sent and a switch setting is incorrect.

If regular gaps occur in the printout, you might have a one-inch skip-over-perforation switch set. Check the DIP switches. If vertical printed lines do not align, check the switch settings for unidirectional printing.

Paper handling problems

The following problems can occur in handling single sheets and continuous paper.

When you insert the paper, the platen rotates but paper does not feed. The paper feed might be crooked or the paper is jamming. The push tractors might be slipping and may need to be replaced. Be sure the sprocket units are locked and their covers are closed; also check that the paper-thickness lever is set correctly for the paper you are using.

Be sure the release lever is not slipping out of the push-tractor position.

Position the paper supply within 3 feet of the printer. The paper might be old or creased; try new, clean paper. The paper might be too slack; adjust the position of the sprocket units to take up any slack across the width of the paper.

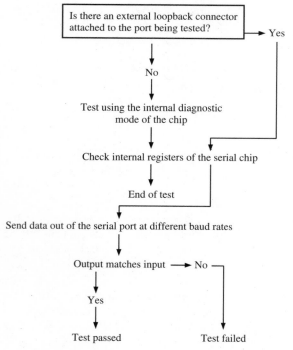

7-64 Serial port testing.

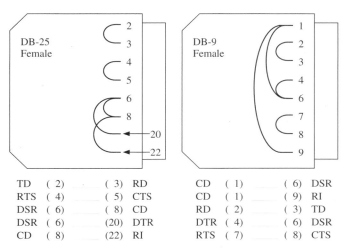

TD (2) (3) RD
RTS (4) (5) CTS
DSR (6) (8) CD
DSR (6) (20) DTR
CD (8) (22) RI

CD (1) (6) DSR
CD (1) (9) RI
RD (2) (3) TD
DTR (4) (6) DSR
RTS (7) (8) CTS

7-65 RS-232 loopback connectors (25 and 9 pin).

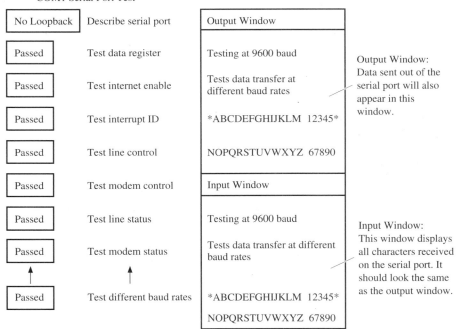

7-66 Serial port test screen.

Cable and interface problems

If the printer does not print or the printout is not what you expected, you might be trying to use a faulty interface or interface cable with the wrong signals. Check the printer interface specifications to make sure you can use the interface with this printer. The computer and printer interface settings might not match; check the settings on the computer and printer. The interface might have been disabled; make sure that the port has been set up properly. If you have a serial interface, you can use a diagnostics program to test it. You can test the interface with or without a loopback connector as shown in Figs. 7-64 and 7-65. A typical test screen is shown in Fig. 7-66.

8
CHAPTER

Network problems

Long before PCs were popular, the most familiar computer was the mainframe computer. Users took for granted the ability to operate on the same data as other users on the system. Stand-alone PCs made this sharing difficult, but now networks provide you the advantages of both the mainframe and PC worlds. This chapter helps you to understand networks and keep them operating.

What is a LAN?

A LAN (local area network) lets you connect PCs and other devices, allowing you to share their resources. With a LAN, you can share files and disk storage and communicate with other users on the LAN.

You can communicate with other people on the LAN by electronic mail and reduce or eliminate the need for letters and memos on paper. You also can share peripherals such as printers and CD-ROM drives.

Local area networks are limited to a confined area, usually a building, although they can run to nearby buildings. LANs generally use electrical or fiber-optic cables, but other wider networks might use microwave, telephone, or satellite communications.

Types of LANs

LANs can be distributed (peer-to-peer) or centralized. Both types can use file servers. *File servers* are PCs that coordinate access to shared files. The file servers store files and process all incoming requests for files.

Centralized LANs generally use dedicated file servers. *Dedicated file servers* are PCs committed to central storage and retrieval. They only perform file-serving tasks and cannot be used for other tasks such as the processing of data. Processing takes place at the local workstation. Dedicated file servers require a fast CPU, a large hard disk, and plenty of RAM.

Distributed networks, in contrast, allow any or all of the networked PCs to share resources. As a user, you can publish your resources for other users to access. In a centralized LAN, the only shared resources are on the server hard disk. For example, suppose you have two PCs, 1 and 2, and file server 3. PC 1 can access the file server 3, but it cannot access PC 2. In a distributed LAN, PC 1 and PC 2 can access each other's hard disk.

Although distributed LANs also can contain dedicated file servers, their file servers are typically nondedicated. A nondedicated file server can be used as both a server and a workstation.

A PC can also be designated to coordinate requests for service to a printer or other device. A PC designated as a *print server* acts as the conduit for all print jobs. Like file servers, print servers can be dedicated or nondedicated. Centralized-server LANs are often used for heavy traffic or security reasons. Distributed LANs are usually less expensive and are used on smaller networks.

LAN components

A LAN requires both hardware and software. The *NOS* (network operating system) coordinates the LAN hardware activity, just as DOS coordinates the hardware activity on an individual PC. The NOS intercepts the data you enter at your PC and passes it along. The NOS does not replace the operating system of the PC. The individual PCs will still use DOS as their operating system to run applications at the local PC. The NOS is the bridge to the local PC to the network.

LANs require additional hardware. Following is a summary of LAN-specific hardware components.

Network interface cards

The *NIC* (network interface card), which is also called a *network adapter* or *LAN board,* installs in one of the PC's expansion slots. The NIC provides the connection between the PC and the cabling system. It works with the network software and allows the PC to communicate on the network. Figure 8-1(A) to 8-1(E) show several types of network interface cards.

The cabling system

Cables are necessary to hook up the *nodes,* which are the individual PCs in most cases, although any device can be a node. The cabling system provides the path for data through the network. Several types of cabling systems are available, which, in turn, depend on the type of network used.

A working LAN is more than hardware and software. Protocols and topologies are other vital LAN components, and they affect how LANs work. *Protocols* are sets of rules that govern how LANs communicate, and *topologies* are the actual physical layouts the way the PCs are hooked up to each other.

Network technologies can be grouped into three basis types: PBX (private branch exchange), cable television broadband, and the baseband types. PBX is most suitable for terminal-computer networking.

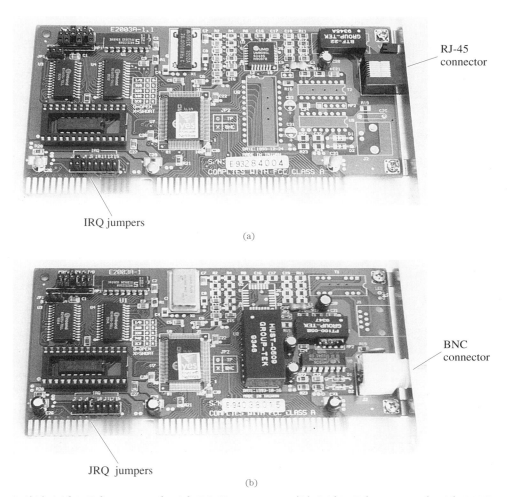

8-1(A) 16-bit Ethernet card with RJ-45 connector. **(B)** 16-bit Ethernet card with BNC connector.

Broadband networks

Broadband networks use cable television technology to provide up to 400 MHz of bandwidth. These different network technologies can coexist, with each serving a different set of needs in the organization. Interfaces are available between the various technologies.

Broadband technology supports tree and bus configurations, and uses single or dual 75-W (ohm) coaxial cable. The different devices or user groups connected to the network are assigned frequency ranges called *bands*.

These networks provide the high bandwidth necessary to support hundreds of voice, video, and data channels within the network. Broadband is especially suitable to

(c)

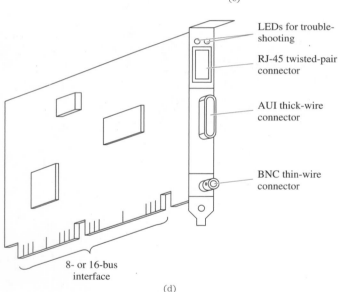

(d)

8-1 *(Continued)* **(C)** 3 Com Ethernet card with AVI and BNC connectors. **(D)** LAN adapter for twisted pair (10BASE-T), thin and thick-wire Ethernet cables.

facilities with a number of buildings in a campuslike environment. The broadband networks, with their large bandwidths and high transfer rates, can support most types of communication and allow multiple data channels for data and video.

Broadband local networks offer the highest bandwidth capacity, but they are also the most costly for initial implementation even though the technology is based on community-antenna television hardware. Broadband networks are cost-effective for

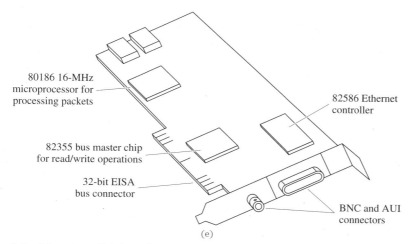

80186 16-MHz microprocessor for processing packets

82586 Ethernet controller

82355 bus master chip for read/write operations

32-bit EISA bus connector

BNC and AUI connectors

(e)

8-1 *(Continued)* **(E)** 32-bit LAN adapter.

users with a high volume of voice, video, and data communications. All broadband local networks require separate transmit and receive paths for bidirectional operation.

PBX networks

PBX-based local networks usually use star or tree configurations while using in-place wiring as the signaling medium. These networks are suitable for installations that have been renting telephone equipment.

The PBX acts like a large automated switching matrix. Time-division sampling techniques are used to sample each conversation and convert the analog signal into a digital representation. By synchronizing the paths of the digital signals from the various extensions, the PBX establishes a virtual circuit connection.

Microcomputers connected in a PBX network can be switched to a local host computer, another local computer acting as a file server, or an outward dial trunk on the public switched telephone network. PBX local networks are best suited to low-speed and low-volume traffic.

Baseband networks

The computers are typically provided with baseband transceivers in the form of expansion boards. Baseband local networks allow a mix of more types of traffic and applications than is possible with PBX networks. The cost of baseband technology is similar to that of broadband technology, depending upon the data rates and station configuration. Baseband networks are limited in maximum cable distances and have less growth capacity than broadband networks.

Baseband local networks use a time-division scheme to apportion the single stream of high-speed digital bits among the users. The network typically uses a ring topology. Telephone wiring supports only a star topology, rarely used for baseband.

Access methods

The different access methods include token passing, and the different versions of CSMA (carrier sense multiple access)—CSMA/CD (CSMA with collision detection) and CSMA/CA (CSMA with collision avoidance).

The CSMA methods are best used for networks with an aggregate network utilization of less than 30 percent, and device utilization of between 10 and 40 percent. Carrier sense multiple access local networks are best for asynchronous applications and should not be used for synchronous communications applications higher than 30 percent or for supporting digitized voice applications mixed with any type of data traffic.

Token-passing access is used for applications with use rates greater than 30 percent. Token passing tends to be inefficient for a small group of devices in a highly used network.

Token-passing origin

The expression *token-passing ring* originated on British railroads in the nineteenth century. On single sections of track in which trains traveled in both directions, a token was needed to switch the track from one direction to the other. The token was a lead block about four inches on a side, with the insignia of the railway company. It had to physically be put into the switch for the direction to be changed.

Once the signal was switched, the person responsible for signaling would put the token in a canvas bag. The bag was then hung from a large brass ring, the token passing ring, which itself hung off a pole next to the track. As the train passed, the driver reached out the window and took the ring and token. Upon reaching the end of the track section, the driver handed the token over to the next signal person, who would reverse the track with the token and then hang it back up on the ring for the next driver.

Peer-to-peer networks

In a peer-to-peer network, machines should be equal, in their operations, but one is usually used for data storage. Each PC still has access to the resources and peripherals of the others. This type of network is often used in smaller offices where it is convenient to tie together several PCs.

Some popular peer-to-peer networking products are Netware Lite and Personal Netware from Novell, LANtastic from Artisoft, and Windows for Workgroups from Microsoft. Both the Artisoft and Microsoft products work with Novell's Netware.

Client-server networks

In this type of network, one PC is dedicated as the server. Each PC can be run independently of the network, just as in peer-to-peer networks. The client-server network can be more powerful and faster, since the server only processes information requests for the PCs and then only delivers the requested information to the workstation. This tends to reduce the overall network traffic and results in a faster network. Banyan's VINES and IBM's LAN Server products are both client-server-oriented.

Topologies

This refers to the physical arrangement of the network and includes bus, ring, and star topologies. In the bus-connected system, the PCs are tied to a single cable called a *backbone.* Ethernet and ARCNET often use this topology. The data travels along the bus and can be sensed by all the PCs, but only the PC that the data is addressed to will actually receive the data.

The ring or token-ring topology operates in a similar way, but the bus curves around and the ends are connected to make a ring. The star topology uses a hub to connect all of the PCs. The data goes through the hub, then to the PC. ARCNET and unshielded twisted-pair Ethernet (or 10BASE-T) are often connected this way.

Cabling

The wiring between the PCs is called the *media.* Unshielded twisted-pair (UTP) cabling, which is used for modular phone lines, is popular because of its low cost. There is a voice grade of this cabling and a data grade. It is also known as 10BASE-T and can transmit data at 10 megabits per second (Mbps). A more expensive version is the faster 100-Mbps UTP cabling, known as 100BASE-T. Fiber-optic cabling is an even more expensive cable, but it has the fastest data transfer speeds.

Two pieces of coax cabling may look the same, but they can have different impedances. A common mistake is to splice together two differently rated cables, such as an RG-58 coaxial cable rated at 50 ohms and an RG-59 coaxial cable rated at 75 ohms. Always check the label on the outside sheath of the cable.

A network adapter card or network interface card (NIC) is placed in one of the expansion slots of the PC and the cable is attached to the connectors on the card.

There are also special adapters for connecting the parallel ports of PCs to the network. These pocket adapters are mainly used for a temporary connection of a portable or laptop computer.

Ethernet

This is the most common network standard. It was developed by Xerox in the mid-1970s, and Xerox, DEC, and Intel made it a standard. About half of the installed base of network nodes use Ethernet. This includes PCs, engineering workstations, and mini-computers.

Ethernet is often used for PC-based LANs, as well as minicomputer and mainframe computer environments. Almost all UNIX networks are Ethernet-based.

Most Ethernet installations use the linear bus topology defined by the Institute of Electrical and Electronics Engineers (IEEE) 802.3 standard. Other IEEE standards are the twisted-pair Ethernet standard designated as 802.3 10BASE-T and 802.5 which defines token ring.

There are three major cabling standards for Ethernet, thick Ethernet, Thin Net or thin Ethernet, and unshielded twisted-pair (UTP). Thick Ethernet cable uses a coaxial cable which is about one-half inch in diameter.

Connection to the network bus cable is made with vampire taps which clamp on to the cable and puncture it, making contact with the center core. If splicing is needed, it is usually done with N-type connectors. The first Ethernet systems used the thicker coaxial cable, called thick Ethernet, thickwire, or thick cable.

Transceivers

These are transmitting and receiving devices, that provide input and output functions to a device on the network. Some transceivers are part of the network adapter cards while others are separate units.

Networks with thick Ethernet usually have separate transceivers that come with transceiver cabling. The transceiver is connected to the adapter with another cable called a *drop cable*.

Thin and thick cabling

Thin Net, or cheapernet, is a less-expensive type of Ethernet cabling. This is a thinner coaxial cable which is also called thin cable or thin wire. The RG-58 coaxial cable used looks like television cable, but it is slightly smaller in diameter.

Devices in a Thin Net system usually connect directly to the cable with a T connector and bayonet-type network connector (BNC) fittings. Most Thin Net interface cards include the transceiver and do not use a drop cable.

In some installations that have been added onto many times, the maximum cable lengths can become close to their limits. This can cause the network problems, since some of the data may not be recognized properly. A thick Ethernet segment can be as long as 1500 feet while a segment of thin Ethernet can only be wired for 600 feet. The total cable length of thick Ethernet can be almost twice that of thin Ethernet—3000 feet compared to thin Ethernet's 1800-foot limit. Another limit is the number of stations. Thick Ethernet can operate with 1024 stations, while thin Ethernet has a limit of 100 stations.

Lattisnet is another cabling method for Ethernet. It allows standard UTP telephone cable to handle the 10 megabyte-per-second (Mbps) Ethernet transmission rate standard. A device called a *concentrator* may be connected to each PC network adapter, which allows Ethernet to function in a star-type network. The IEEE 802.3 10BASE-T standard defines the Ethernet specifications for 10-Mbps twisted-pair wiring.

There are also different voice-grade 10BASE-T and data-grade 10BASE-T cabling. The data-grade cable is designed for networks which provides more reliable performance. The higher cost 100BASE-T UTP cabling can be used to increase data throughput.

Ethernet rules

Based on the cables to be used, an Ethernet network can be built up various ways. The main types of Ethernet networks are described as follows:

1. Thin-cable networks that use thin coaxial cable
2. Thick-cable networks that use thick coaxial cable
3. Unshielded twisted-pair networks that use unshielded twisted-pair cable
4. Linked thin and twisted-pair cable networks
5. Linked thick and twisted-pair cable networks

Ethernet thin-cable and thick-cable networks are made up of a main cable, referred to as *trunk cable,* which is used as a common bus line to link many stations together. The trunk cable can have several segments of cable and each segment must be terminated with a terminator at both ends. Each segment consists of a number of sections, a *section* being defined as the length of cable connecting to any two stations.

The segment has a maximum length and a maximum number of nodes it can accommodate. An Ethernet network can have more than one segment cable device called a *repeater* for connecting each two segments together. The repeater can be positioned at any point on a segment cable as long as it is between the two terminators used to terminate that segment.

An unshielded twisted-pair network uses unshielded twisted-pair cable and hubs/concentrators in a star-wired topology. The wiring hub sits at the center and is connected by unshielded twisted-pair to the LAN adapter in the PC.

An unshielded twisted-pair Ethernet network is flexible and can be linked with an existing thin-cable or thick-cable network using the BNC or AUI port on the Ethernet hub.

Distance limitations of Ethernet

No matter what type of medium and configuration is used in an Ethernet network, distance limitations need to be observed. These are shown in Table 8-1.

Thin-cable networks

A network using thin cable is also called *cheapernet.* A thin-cable network uses this less-expensive thin coaxial cable and BNC-type connectors. A thin-cable network may have the following hardware.

Table 8-1. Ethernet distance limitations

Media	Connection	Maximum distance, meters
Twisted pair	Hub-to-station	100
Twisted pair	Hub-to-hub	100
Twisted pair	Hub-to-AUI	100
RJ45 transceiver		
AUI cable	Hub-to-Ethernet	50
Thin cable	Hub-to-hub	200
Thick cable	Hub-to-hub	500

1. Ethernet card with setting for using BNC connectors
2. Thin coaxial cable (RG-58 A/U)
3. Tee-connector
4. BNC barrel connector
5. BNC terminator
6. Ethernet repeater (optional)

The Ethernet card is installed to the thin cable with a T connector as shown in Fig. 8-2. No other cable is used between the Ethernet card and the thin cable.

A BNC barrel connector is used to connect two lengths of thin cable together. The barrel connector should not be used unless it is necessary, since the fewer connections in the cable, the more reliable the network will be. A BNC terminator should be installed at each end of each segment.

If the network length exceeds the maximum length of a segment, an *Ethernet repeater* is required. Using Ethernet repeaters, a complex multidimensional network can be built up. The following rules need to followed:

1. Minimum distance between T connectors 0.5 meters.
2. Maximum segment cable length 200 meters.
3. Maximum number of segments is 5.
4. Maximum network trunk cable length is 1000 meters.
5. Maximum number of nodes per segment is 30, a repeater counts as one node on the segment.

Thick-cable networks

A thick-cable network is more suitable for a long-distance network. It uses more expensive Ethernet thick coaxial cables, external transceivers, and N-series connectors. A thick-cable network, can have the following hardware.

1. Ethernet card that used N-series connectors
2. Thick RG-11 coaxial cable
3. DIX connector
4. Transceiver and transceiver cable
5. N-series barrel connector
6. N-series terminator and Ethernet repeater

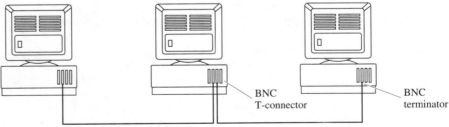

Thin trunk cable RG-58 A/U

8-2 3 PC thin cable network.

There will be a transceiver and a transceiver cable for each station. The transceivers will be linked together with lengths of thick cable using the DIX connectors.

An N-series barrel connector can be used to connect two lengths of thick cable together. The N-series barrel connector should not be used since the fewer connections in the cable, the more reliable the network will be. An N-series terminator must be installed at each end of each segment. If the network length exceeds the maximum length of a segment, an Ethernet repeater is required. The following limitations apply.

1. Minimum distance between transceiver 2.5 meters.
2. Maximum transceiver cable length 50 meters.
3. Maximum segment cable length 500 meters.
4. Maximum number of segments is 5.
5. Maximum network trunk cable length 2500 meters.
6. Maximum number of nodes per segment 100, a repeater counts as one node on the segment.

Unshielded twisted-pair networks

A basic twisted-pair network can have one Ethernet hub that the computers are connected to. Multiple twisted-pair networks can be linked together three ways. Using twisted-pair wire, the Ethernet hub can be linked with other hubs in a daisy chain to extend the network as shown in Fig. 8-3(A).

If the Ethernet hubs have a BNC port, RG-58 thin coaxial cable can be used as the backbone network trunk to link the twisted-pair networks together as shown in Fig. 8-3(B). The maximum length of the twisted-pair wire is 100 meters and the coaxial cable maximum is 1000 meters. If the Ethernet hubs have an AUI port, it can be used to link the twisted-pair networks together. A twisted-pair Ethernet network and thin-cable Ethernet network can also be linked together by using Ethernet hubs.

An Ethernet hub with an AUI port, can be used to link a thick-cable Ethernet to a twisted-pair Ethernet network. A thick-cable to twisted-pair Ethernet link can also be made through the RJ-45 jack in the hub by using the AUI-RJ45 transceiver. AUI-RJ45

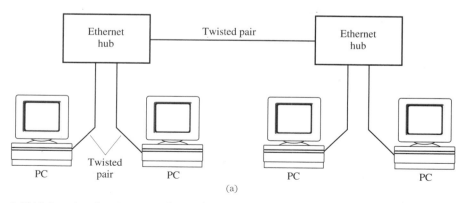

8-3(A) 2 twisted-pair networks tied together.

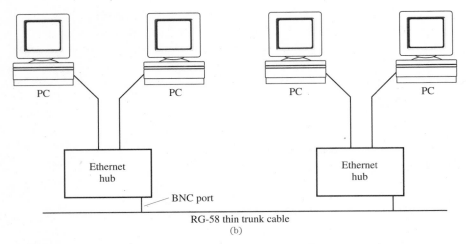

8-3(B) Twisted-pair networks tied together with thin cable.

transceivers have an AUI port and a modular RJ-45 jack for converting Ethernet thick-cable signals into twisted-pair Ethernet signals.

Token Ring

This type of network was introduced by IBM in 1984 to provide connectivity for installations with a mix of computers. The IEEE 802.5 standard defines the token-ring standard and Token Ring has also been adopted as a standard by ANSI and ISO.

The Token Ring passes a packet (also known as a *frame* or *token*) along a cabling loop. Each network adapter card accepts the incoming data and copies it for transmitting, moving the data from one workstation to another. The workstation for whom the token is addressed is the station that acts on the data packet. A disadvantage in this type of network is that failure of one workstation can force the whole network to be inoperative.

The hub of the ring uses a multistation access unit (MAU). Most MAU units have 10 ports. A stand-alone configuration can be formed with eight computers and can be connected to the MAU in an arrangement sometimes called a *canned ring.* The MAU senses which ports are used by workstations, using the remaining two ports to make connections to the ring. If a workstation should go down, the MAU bypasses the defective workstation, allowing the ring to continue running.

Token Ring runs on several types of cables, including shielded twisted-pair (STP), which looks more like lamp cord than telephone wire. IBM Type 2 is the most common, but IBM Types 1, 3, 6, and 9 are also used. The main ring is limited to 1200 feet and the maximum distance from a MAU to a node, called the *lobe length,* is 330 feet.

Environment files

Computers on a network use *environment files* for automating the connection to the network, configuring the workstation to run on the network, and loading drivers to initialize the network adapter card. In Novell's Netware, the environment files are STARTNET.BAT, NET.CFG, and AUTOEXEC.NCF. These are used to load the different drivers and configuration information for the workstation.

Protocols

The rules that the PCs use to communicate on the network is called the *network protocol.* These rules define the packet format of the data and error checking as well as other things. Messages are transferred from one network using routing and e-mail (electronic mail) protocols.

A few of the more common protocols include the Transmission Control Protocol/ Internet Protocol (TCP/IP) used by the Internet, AppleTalk used by Macintosh computers, and Novell Netware Core Protocols (NCP) protocols, Internetwork Packet Exchange (IPX), the Sequenced Packet Exchange (SPX), the Routing Information Protocol (RIP), and the Server Advertising Protocol (SAP).

Gateways

These are connection points or translators between two networks with different protocols. The gateway may be another computer or a special device connected between the networks. The gateway is implemented in software and run on the computer placed between the networks. The gateway performs protocol conversions for the data traveling back and forth. Gateways can also be used to access wide area networks (WANs), such as an electronic mail service for network users that is also connected via a gateway to a larger, public service such as MCI.

Bridges

These are devices used to connect two similar LANs together. The bridge can be implemented in a special hardware unit or it can be another computer connected between the networks. Bridges can improve the performance of the LAN by keeping the data traffic down to smaller segments. While the use of a bridge refers to the connection of networks with similar protocols, bridges may be used to connect networks with different topologies.

Routers

A *router* is like a bridge in that it is used to connect networks, but it does more than a bridge, since it ensures that messages are properly sent from one LAN to another LAN. Routers are often used to balance network traffic loads, finding the best way to send a message even though several networks may be involved. Routers are also used to break up large LANs for security purposes. A *brouter* is a hybrid of a bridge and a router; the brouter will first try to connect the networks as a router. If it is unable to do so, it will connect them as a bridge.

Repeaters

These are used to boost the signal back to its original strength after it travels through a length of cable. This is done to take care of the signal fading as it travels over a distance. In networks, the repeater is the simplest type of LAN interconnection device and its function is to allow for longer lengths of cable between connected PCs.

Network operating systems

The network uses its own operating system, which is different from a single station PC operating system like MS-DOS. The network hardware, including the adapter cards and transmission over the media, is controlled by the network operating system (NOS).

The NOS may be one of the NetWare versions provided by Novell or a NOS such as the 3Plus Open, which runs under OS/2 and uses 3COM's Ethernet network cards. IBM also markets networking software with its Token-Ring cards.

Other NOSs include DECnet, TOPS, and NET/OS. DECnet was one of the first Ethernet-based networks. It was used for connecting Digital Equipment Corporation (DEC) minicomputers. Later versions also allowed DEC VAX minicomputers to act as file servers for PCs on a LAN.

The TOPS network from Sun allows you to connect PCs and Apple Macintosh computers together to share files on the same network. The peer-to-peer configuration provides low-cost and low performance. It can be used for file sharing, but is limited in performance.

NET/OS is another network product that provides a simple, low-cost peer-to-peer network. NET/OS can emulate some of the NetWare low-level network routines such as file locking. Proprietary network operating systems exist that only work with adapter cards from the operating system manufacturer. These include ViaNet, Corvus Omninet, and 10 Net.

Another variation is *slotless LANs* or LANs that use the PC's parallel or serial port. They do not require a network adapter card, but work over standard RS232 serial ports or parallel ports. An example is the PC-Interlink network product. Printer sharing, file exchange, and messaging is available for up to four PCs. The parallel port adapter plugs in and a printer cable can then be plugged into the parallel adapter.

Novell NetWare

NetWare is a proprietary network operating system designed to run on PC-based network file servers using an open architecture. The open architecture allows NetWare to be used with hardware from different vendors.

NetWare works with a wide variety of hardware, but the company will not support any adapter it has not certified to run with its NOS. It is possible to mix adapter hardware brands and topologies. A 386 or 486 computer is often used as a server. The faster the server is the better the performance will be. You can use almost any PC as a workstation. Even the DEC VAX and many UNIX machines can be used as file servers with NetWare for VMS or Portable NetWare.

NetWare has better performance than competing products due to a combination of techniques. These include

1. Turbo FATs (indexed File Allocation Tables).
2. Elevator seeking (which reduces disk head movement).
3. Caching.
4. Split reads (splitting read requests among two mirrored disks). NetWare supports most recognized network standards including NETBIOS as well as gateways to TCP/IP and other standards.

Boot ROM configurations

There is no limitation on the hardware configurations for using Remote Boot ROM under Novell NetWare. The user may use any combination of hardware parameters such as IRQ, I/O Address, and ROM Address for Remote Boot ROM.

Arcnet

Arcnet, which stands for *attached resource computer*, is a token-passing bus network. A token determines who has access to the media. Only the PC holding the token can broadcast onto the cable. Arcnet is usually a physical star, but it can be a physical bus.

Every PC on the network has a sequential number. The token passes incrementally from PC to PC by number. When it reaches the last PC in order, the token returns to the beginning. This action forms a logical ring. To transmit data or a token, each PC broadcasts its data out onto the network. The data moves to every PC. Only the PC that is next to receive the token or to whom the data is addressed can listen to the broadcast.

Arcnet cards

The Arcnet card consists of four sections. The controller implements the Arcnet protocols and controls access to the card packet buffer. It also decodes addresses and acknowledges packet reception. A transceiver retimes the signal so the controller knows when to accept the data. The third component, called the *hybrid*, moves data to and from the cable to the card. It converts the analog signal in the cable to the digital signal in the card. An impedance transceiver is needed for bus topologies. The other component is the packet buffer, which holds 2K. It can hold up to four packets of information at any one time. When data is received by an Arcnet card, the hybrid action converts the analog signal to a digital signal. The signal is retimed and sent to the controller chip.

With these actions completed, the controller can operate on the packet. Arcnet packets are less than 512 bytes of data. The first four or five bytes are overhead. They contain the ID of the sender, the ID of the receiver, the length of the information, and a protocol identifier that indicates the type of network operating system. The controller strips away the preliminary data, leaving the message text. The text is shipped off to the packet buffer for temporary storage.

After storing the data, the controller posts an interrupt to the CPU. The interrupt notifies the host of the packet's reception. It requests permission to move the data from

Table 8-2. LAN technology

	Ethernet (IEEE 802.3) thick net standard Ethernet	ARCnet (802.4 modified)	Token Ring (802.5)
Speed	10 Mbps*	2.5 Mbps	4 Mbps
Media access method	CSMA/CD	Modified token passing	Token passing
Topology	Bus	Star or bus	Ring
Cabling	Standard Ethernet (thick cable)	RG-62/U (coax) or twisted pair	IBM type 1 (AMP) or IBM type 3 (UTP)
Maximum nodes per segment	100	255	
Maximum distance per segment	500 m/segment	2000 ft	300 m station to MAU** 200 m MAU to MAU**
Typical NICs (network interface cards)	8-bit 8K SRAM 16-bit 16K SRAM	Coax star Coax bus Twisted pair	MAU

*Million bits per second.
**Multistation access unit.

the card to the host memory. When permission is granted, the data is moved into the host memory, where it is processed.

Arcnet LANs are easy to install because there are few configuration rules. Workstations need to be within 2000 feet of the hub, but daisy chaining the hubs extends the distance between nodes to four miles. The thin coax (coaxial cable), RG-62, is easy to work with and there are twisted-pair cards making Arcnet even easier to install.

When a cable fault occurs, it is easier to isolate a problem than with a bus or ring topology. Most Arcnet cards come with diagnostic lights. See Table 8-2 for a summary of LAN technologies and characteristics.

Data recovery

You can recover data from a crashed server disk by using an outside service. These firms generally perform data recovery and rebuild disks in a clean-room facility. Many of these firms handle DOS as well as NetWare and other network operating systems.

Typical problems that can occur with NetWare disks include controller card failure, where the card, because of SFT NetWare's disk mirroring feature, writes data improperly to the first drive and the same improper data gets written to the second drive. In this case, you must repair or replace the controller card pair and rebuild the affected directories. If the master boot record is destroyed, the boot record must be rebuilt byte by byte.

In some cases, NetWare's Vrepair utility can attempt to rewrite data improperly. A disk running SFT NetWare will crash because of the redirect area filing. When you run

Vrepair on these disks, in some cases it will destroy the directories and file a location table. Use Vrepair only for small disks of no more than 50Mb.

You can solve other hardware problems by replacing the interface board in the drive or the controller card. If the stepper motor has burned out, it must be repaired or replaced before the data can be retrieved.

If the heads have truly crashed into the surface of the platter, iron oxide particles will be removed from the platter, physically destroying data. However, if a crashed drive is quickly put out of service, it is still possible that some or most of the data can be retrieved.

Ontrack network utilities

Ontrack offers several disk-management utilities. The Disk Manager-N is a disk-installation software package for Novell NetWare-based LANs. It allows you to install a nonstandard disk subsystem under NetWare and to save considerable money over the expense of a Novell-compatible drive.

Using Novell's Compsurf formatting utility, a 117Mb disk can take over 30 hours to format. Using Disk Manager-N, the process can be done in 75 minutes. A 72Mb drive can take NetWare over 20 hours, but Disk Manager-N can complete it in less than an hour because Compsurf does not do retries on soft errors, and it needs to be sure that it has found all of the bad sectors during installation. The Ontrack package uses retries. It also allows you to create custom disk partitions to meet specific requirements and to select an interleave factor that optimizes the performance of the software operating from each partition.

Another Ontrack package for NetWare users is Netutils, which is designed for maintenance and data recovery. The program allows you to scan all data on both a disk and file basis. You can move through the disk partition by partition or scroll through the sectors, head, and cylinders. You can check each byte and get a hexadecimal/ASCII representation of your data, as well as search for specific characters you wish to modify. You can also complete this check file by file. Data on both the hard and floppy disk in a NetWare network can be examined.

Netutils also lets you retrieve data from the server even when it's down due to network hardware failures. As long as the workstation and hard disk continue to function, you can retrieve data from a server that is down.

Netutils prevents the loss of data by locating bad spots on the disk, deallocating them, and moving the data. The directory is rebuilt along with the file allocation tables. Ontrack's Dosutils is the DOS version of these utilities for DOS-based network operating systems like 3+ and PC LAN.

Before your server has a chance to go down, you can run another Ontrack program, Disk Manager Diagnostics, to find potential problems. This program uses diagnostic tests to detect and isolate disk, controller, and media problems. These tests include a controller test, a nondestructive write-read test, and error correction code test, a nondestructive scan test, a random read test, and a seek test.

If you use these programs during installation or reinstallation of the disk drive, they can ferret out problems in cabling and jumper selection.

Cheyenne network utilities

NetBack is a set of utilities for Novell NetWare users. The program allows you to reconstruct the server and its bindery using information previously stored in a storage utility. This utility, called VaultFile, extracts information from the current server and creates a file for storage of bindery data, log-in scripts, system autoexec file, and printer definitions.

You can reconstruct a corrupt server before data files are reloaded. If you need to set up a new network server, you can set up the new server based on information from the VaultFile of another server, regardless of its NetWare version. If you need to restore trustee rights, NetBack can do it even if the directories no longer exist. NetBack also generates reports on system usage, trustee assignments and disk usage reports.

Network errors

Network performance is often a function of error conditions on the network. A frame-check sequence or cyclic redundancy check verifies that the bits in the frame were transferred correctly. A misalign error occurs when a frame is received with a frame-check sequence error showing a total number of bits not divisible by eight. Errors might be due to several conditions.

Illegal-size frame errors can be of two types. Frames of less than minimum or 64 bytes are known as *runts*. They are usually caused by collisions on networks over large distances. This problem occurs on large networks when one node begins transmission and another node physically distant from the first begins transmission and collides with the first. Runts occur because of the propagation delay on the network that allows the first node to transmit enough of its frame onto the network to be recognized as a partial packet.

Frames longer than a maximum of 1514 bytes are sometimes called *jabbers*, which are normally caused by hardware failures. The presence of runts indicates future potential problems. Hosts and file servers tend to be the concentration points for such traffic. In the locating of specific nodes, the suspect nodes are those with high levels of incoming and outgoing traffic. The activity of a particular node can indicate where problems can exist.

Collisions on some types of networks are a part of the access technique. In light traffic situations (under 5 percent) collisions occur as a function of the randomness of the data.

Network loading

Network loading information has several important uses. It facilitates the pinpointing of potential problems. Each frame sent from a given source gives a number at the intersection. The number indicates the frequency of traffic. The important factors are data and error rates as well as frame size activity.

Activity can change rapidly depending on user activity, but often there are a few connections that generate most of the traffic. These sites will usually be the source of any problems.

Network testing

Many protocol and network standards use special commands and responses for testing protocols and software. In addition to loopback testing procedures for the upper-layer protocols, several local area network standards include loopback procedures. Examples of such test facilities are the Ethernet CTP (configuration testing protocol) and the IEEE (Institute of Electrical and Electronic Engineers) 802.2 Test Command and Response.

The Ethernet CTP allows single or multiple-hop loopbacks. With this test facility, a frame can be sent to a node, and then either returned or forwarded to a third node, returning finally to the originating node.

The IEEE 802.2 test facility sends a test command frame to a node. If the command is the proper format, the node will return a TEST RESPONSE that contains an information field identical to the original test command. You can use these facilities to test for the proper functioning of the network interface.

Delay measurements

Delay measurements show how performance varies with network usage and give a good indication of potential performance and capacity problems. To measure the propagation delay, it is necessary to compare the time the message is successfully placed on the network to the time the response message is successfully received.

The remote node processing time is subtracted and the remaining time represents the round-trip propagation delay for the network. Measuring this variation over time under a variety of network loads will indicate the network contribution to transaction response time.

Propagation delay measurements are particularly useful at gateways and bridges. By taking the measurements over long periods of time, it is possible to determine how performance varies with network usage and to flag potential performance and capacity problems.

Network baseline

To measure network characteristics effectively, you must establish a baseline of information about the network. The baseline consists of the network performance information. Baseline characteristics can include ongoing utilization, peaks, and error rates.

The network baseline can serve many purposes. It can provide a basic reference of data to explain the general network characteristics. It can also be used as a reference in troubleshooting performance problems.

One network traffic parameter that can influence errors and waste network capacity is the *burstiness* of the traffic. When a network node receives a large number of packet bursts, it is possible for that node to miss some packets. The miss occurs when the node or its interface is not able to process the incoming packets fast enough. These errors are masked from the user by the upper-layer protocols. Protocols retransmit the data one or more times until it is properly received.

Protocol analyzers

A LAN protocol analyzer is a type of instrument that can be used to provide an independent, controlled network load. Use the analyzer to observe the effects on network performance parameters. Simulating traffic and measuring its effects will provide information on the impact of network changes. Modeling the traffic target for or addressed to specific devices and measuring their response is useful for identifying the limitations of such devices as bridges and gateways.

When a simulated traffic load is used, it should have the same characteristics including the distribution of frame size and burst rate. Adding traffic with representative characteristics makes it possible to predict performance error rates and collisions. Local area network analysis can provide you with the following:

What channels are most active.

What types of errors are occurring.

What the network loads are at any particular time.

Products such as Excelan's LAN analyzer and Hewlett-Packard's HP 4971s provide network performance statistics and can be used to run tests on individual stations and review the results. They can analyze high-level protocols such as Transmission Control Protocol/Internet Protocol and Xerox Network Systems. They cannot simulate a terminal to perform extensive testing, nor is it possible to remove faulty products from the network with this type of analyzer.

Most products of this type interface with the local area network and provide menus that permit the operator to establish test parameters, take measurements, and evaluate the results.

Different packaging approaches allow several alternatives. Controller boards are available that fit into an expansion slot in an IBM Personal Computer, XT, AT, or compatible with at least 512K of random-access memory. Packaged systems might consist of an AT type of personal computer with 640K of RAM, 20Mb hard disk, and the controller board installed. Local network control software is also available separately on diskettes.

Units are available with a communications and statistical facility. Some work only as an analyzer, and others can function as node or stand-alone personal computer when not being used for network analysis. Most analyzers provide similar types of tests and levels of information. Operators can name the channels or individual terminals to be tested and the types of errors to be sensed and collected. You also can specify your own specific bit-pattern triggers. Figures 8-4 and 8-5 show two types of handheld LAN analyzers.

Most products allow data to be simultaneously displayed in hexadecimal or ASCII formats. The displayed information can indicate the source and destination address, length, and the type of errors detected. These units allow the operator to scroll through the entire buffer or go to selected source and destination addresses within the buffer or to the packets on disk.

Traffic loading

The network management capabilities of most testers are restricted to measuring the traffic loading on each channel. Most testers allow users to inject packets into the

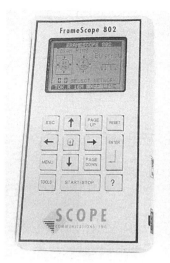

8-4 This pocket-sized LAN analyzer can be used to monitor Ethernet and Token-Ring statistics and noise.

8-5 A low-cost LAN tester for Ethernet and Token-Ring networks.

network data stream to test how well the system reacts to increased traffic. These analyzers allow users to view the traffic-level loading in real time. The screen display might show the following:

The channel loading in the form of a bar graph

The percentage of errors occurring by error type

The number of packets transmitted with and without errors

A count of individual error types occurring on each channel

The number of complete packets received

The source and destination addresses of user-selected channels

The volume of packets set by one address to another

Bar graphs showing the traffic periods measured according to interframe spacing time provide a view of the traffic patterns in real time. The display might show absolute time, acquisition time, the percent of deferred requests, collisions, and percent of aborted attempts.

Most products can measure traffic, provided the volume stays below 40 percent of network capacity. Above that, they tend to lose packets. Packets can be lost in special applications such as setting traps for specific bit patterns. Because setting data traps is used for fault analysis, losing packets can be a problem.

Bar charts that show network loading during specific periods can provide the average packet size gathered over a specific test period. If 95 percent of the packets had 64 bytes, this can be displayed along with the peak traffic rates. Performance statistics can include the number and types of errors occurring during the measurement period.

In addition to analyzing local networks, many products can be used to control measurements at remote locations. Software packages such as Meridian Technology's Carbon Copy can be used to control the remote site.

Although most units provide similar facilities for monitoring and measuring local network performance, some screens incorporate more performance statistics, and some units can be used as a network node for other applications when not being used for analysis. Figure 8-6 represents screens that show some features of a typical protocol analyzer.

Frame number	Time since previous frame	Destination	Source	Highest protocol

Previous frame next frame new capture	Options

8-6 Protocol analyzer screen features.

Scanners

A number of testing tools can be used for troubleshooting networks. Typical of these is the Pair Scanner from Microtest. This scanner is a handheld, battery-powered unit. The scanner works with virtually any cable type. The Pair Scanner solves many of the difficult problems associated with twisted-pair cabling systems. It helps network managers and systems installers work with Ethernet, Arcnet, Token Ring, and all forms of telephone wiring systems used in network communications.

Injectors for the Pair Scanner

Microtest has developed a series of injectors to enhance the testing capability of the Pair Scanner. By injecting a specified frequency into the cable, the scanner can identify errors and certify that the wiring meets the manufacturer's specifications.

Multiline Injector

Use the Multiline Injector with the Pair Scanner or with another Multiline Injector. By pulsing each wire sequentially, it identifies mismatched pairs, short circuits, breaks, and inverted pairs by simple visual inspection of the red/green LEDs on the Pair Scanner display.

Type III Injector

The Type III Injector is used in conjunction with the Pair Scanner to help you certify that your twisted-pair wiring works per the IBM Cabling System Type III specification. By injecting four precisely calibrated frequencies, it will determine dB loss at 256, 512, 776, and 1000 kHz.

The Pair Scanner provides the following troubleshooting functions.

1. Locates breaks, shorts, bad crimps, and, in wiring
2. Isolates faulty Token-Ring MAUs (media access units) and connectors
3. Locates fault in all LAN cabling systems
4. Certifies that wiring lengths are within specification
5. Automatically identifies LAN terminators

Like the other types of scanners (Table 8-3), the Pair Scanner uses TDR (time-domain reflectometry) or cable radar to locate and/or measure cable shorts and breaks, length, resistance and electrical noise (interference). The Pair Scanner includes all of the standard scanner functions, plus it measures signal loss, generates a link bit for hub testing (10BASE-T), supports alarm programming, and includes a built-in relay for rapid switching between transmit and receive pairs. You can use the Pair Scanner to locate and repair problems in your LAN cabling system quickly and accurately. It can even be used to isolate intermittent problems. Network installers can use the Pair Scanner certification capabilities when installing even the most complex systems and print out hard copy reports for clients.

The Pair Scanner Kit comes with the Pair Scanner Unit, the 10BASE-T injector, printer cable, 2RJ45 adapters, Token-Ring adapter cable, and 10BASE-T adapter cable.

The kit comes with an operations manual and a durable hard plastic carrying case able to house an array of additional accessories including injectors, adapter kits, and testers.

Table 8-3. Scanner types

Function/Feature	Pair scanner	Cable scanner	Quick scanner
Prevents network downtime	X	X	X
Locates faults, shorts, or breaks in cabling	X	X	X
10BASE-T hub tests	X		
Isolates intermittent problems	X		
Monitors Ethernet networks	X	X	X
Monitors Token-Ring networks	X		
Maps network wiring	X	X	
Certifies compliance with specifications	X		
Special twisted-pair features	X		X
Hard copy report/printouts	X	X	
Includes wire trace capability	X	X	
SCOPE mode support for TDR displays	X	X	

10BASE-T injector

The 10BASE-T injector certifies that your twisted-pair wiring meets IEEE 10BASE-T specifications. It calculates dB loss by injecting a precisely calibrated 5 and 10 MHz signal into the cable. This injector is included in the Pair Scanner Kit.

Quick Scanner

The Microtest Quick Scanner has the following functions:

1. Pinpoints faults in LAN cabling using Cable Radar.
2. Displays results in plain English.
3. Tests all twisted-pair and coax cables.
4. It is menu driven so it is very easy to use.
5. Monitors Ethernet network activity.

Quick Scanner is the easiest-to-use member of this product family. It tests virtually all coax and twisted-pair cabling for the most common LAN wiring faults instantly. It is designed for network installers and administrators with small to medium-size networks. This handheld, menu-driven scanner will help you install your LAN and keep it up and running properly with minimum time, effort, and training. Because of its small size and low cost, the Quick Scanner is often the best solution for troubleshooting LANs in the field.

The Quick Scanner makes network troubleshooting easier. You turn it on, attach the cable and hit the [Enter] button. It automatically scans the systems and instantly reports any faults in your network cabling. If no problem exists, the scanner indicates this and toggles into network monitor mode to display network traffic statistics (IEEE-802.3 networks only) in any easy-to-understand graphic format. Quick Scanner is the first scanner that is completely menu driven, making it even easier to perform standard diagnostic tests. Press the up arrow or down arrow button and the menu screen changes. When you arrive at the menu option you want, simply hit Enter, and it runs the test, displaying such results as Open at 300 feet, Short at 110 feet, No faults found.

The Quick Scanner Kit comes with the Quick Scanner Unit, a quick-test adapter for twisted-pair cable scanning, and an extensive operations manual. With the proper accessories, the Quick Scanner can troubleshoot all major LAN systems including Token Ring, 10BASE-T, Arcnet, and all twisted-pair and coaxial systems.

Cable scanner

The Microtest cable scanner troubleshooting unit has the following functions:

1. Locates breaks, shorts, and bad crimps
2. Monitors Ethernet network activity
3. Determines when a repeater is needed
4. Finds missing or bad terminators
5. Detects electrical interference

Cable scanner is a handheld network diagnostic tool designed for people who install, service, troubleshoot, or manage LANs. It uses a form of *cable radar* to locate and/or measure cable shorts and breaks, length, resistance, and electrical noise (interference).

The cable scanner supports thin Ethernet, Arcnet, Token Ring, twisted-pair, TV cable, coax, and 10 user-defined cable types. Whatever your network cabling system, Cable Scanner's technology does the work for you by eliminating the problems that often plague network administrators. Eliminating problems reduces network downtime. You can use the Cable Scanner to help produce *as-built diagrams* of LAN cable installation and print system quality reports or determine if existing cabling will support data transmission.

The Cable Scanner can monitor LAN traffic and graphically display or print out a 24-hour daily activity log. Connected to an oscilloscope, the scanner precision, high-speed, pulse-generating circuitry offers you a detailed view of the entire LAN including the transceiver, terminator, and multiple faults at a fraction of the price of a traditional TDR. The Cable Scanner can also be used to determine how many feet of cable are on a spool before installing it in your facility.

The Cable Scanner Kit comes with the Cable Scanner Unit, the Cable Tracer Accessory, an ac adapter/charger, printer cable, three-cable adapter, extensive operations manual, and PC diskette. With the proper accessories, the Quick Scanner can accurately troubleshoot all major LAN systems.

Cable Scanner adapters

Several adapters expand the capabilities of the Cable Scanner. 10BASE-T and Token-Ring testing can be easily performed with the use of these special adapters.

- *Token-Ring adapter.* The Token-Ring adapter allows you to use the scanner to test Token-Ring networks that are using IBM Data Connectors. The adapter has two BNC (bayonet Neill-Concelman) connections to an IBM Data Connector so that the wire pairs are open and data can travel through the connection and into the cable for scanning.

- *10BASE-T adapter kit.* The 10BASE-T adapter kit provides a connection from twisted-pair wiring with various RJ-style connectors to a Microtest Scanner. The

10BASE-T adapter kit includes an RJ-11 to scanner adapter, two RJ-45 to scanner adapters, and an RJ-45 female-to-female coupler.

- *Ring Scanner.* The Ring Scanner is a Token-Ring tester and MAU analyzer with the following functions:
    1. Detects shorts, breaks, and miswires
    2. Automatically switches between 4/16 Mbps
    3. Provides intentional ring fault test
    4. Verifies MAU port and relay
    5. Replaces IBM Token-Ring Cable Tester

Ring Scanner finds cabling problems, isolates defective MAUs, and verifies the proper installation of both 4 and 16 Mbps Token-Ring networks. It was also designed to generate the phantom voltage necessary to test data connectors and MAUs.

The Ring Scanner is a dual-purpose device: as a stand-alone Token-Ring tester it performs the same diagnostic functions as IBM's standard Token-Ring Cable Tester, but it also might be used as an accessory to the Microtest Cable Scanner, Quick Scanner, and/or Pair Scanner for even greater functionality. When interfaced with any of these scanners, the Ring Scanner can provide a graphical display of network traffic that will help pinpoint problems with excess traffic on the LAN. When used with the Cable Scanner or Pair Scanner, it also will allow network activity and test results to be printed out or saved in the scanner memory.

The Ring Scanner is supplied with the necessary cable and connectors along with an extensive operations manual.

Transceiver Monitor

The Transceiver Monitor provides diagnostic capabilities for thick Ethernet and IEEE 802.3 networks. It also enhances the diagnostic capabilities of the Pair Scanner and Cable Scanner when used with these two networks. By using the Cable Scanner or Pair Scanner to monitor network activity, you can monitor activity in real time, save a record of activity over time, and print out activity reports.

With the Transceiver Monitor you can monitor total network activity on the Transceiver Monitor LEDs, verify that a network transceiver (also called a *media access unit* or *MAU*) is receiving power from a network workstation, connect your Cable Scanner or Pair Scanner to the transceiver to monitor and record activity over time plus print reports, Scan the Transmit (TX), Receive (RS), and Collision (COL) wire pairs of your AUI (attachment unit interface) cable for faults. The collision signal pair is often referred to as the Control In (CI) pair.

The Transceiver Monitor Kit includes the Transceiver Monitor Unit, a 3-foot workstation attachment cable, and a scanner connection cable.

Telco adapter

The Telco adapter kit provides local area network installers and administrators, using twisted-pair cable, everything they need to ensure network wiring quality. With the Telco adapter kit, you can check the wiring data transmission efficiency, find faults and monitor network activity. The Telco adapter kit is a combination of Microtest's various twisted-pair adapters in one convenient and cost-effective kit.

The Telco adapter kit includes RJ-45 to alligator clip unterminated cable adapters, an RJ-45 female-to-female coupler, RJ-45 to RJ-11 adapter cables, 100 and 120 W terminating plugs, a shorting plug, 66 punch-down block adapter, a 100 punch-down block adapter, an RJ-45 Y adapter, a connecting cable for punch-down block adapters, and one Smart-T, all packaged in a convenient plastic case.

Coax interface

The Coax Interface Kit provides local area network installers and administrators of coaxial-based LAN systems with the accessories needed to both diagnose problems and maintain network quality. Used with one of the Scanner Units, this coax kit enables the LAN technician to find most all typical coax cable problems, including opens or shorts, exposed shields, and improper connections. It also adds increased functionality to the scanner products. If twisted-pair cabling is being used, the coax to twisted-pair adapter is required to use the SCOPE feature of the Pair Scanner. The Token Ring to BNC adapter allows for scanners to test Token-Ring networks using IBM Data Connectors.

The Coax Interface Kit is a combination of Microtest's various adapters. The coax kit includes an RG-58 male-to-male adapter cable, a BNC male-to-male coupler, an N-Series adapter (#3570-05), a BNC female-to-male adapter, a BNC female-to-female adapter, a coax to twisted-pair adapter, a coaxial T adapter, and a Token Ring to BNC adapter. Figures 8-7 and 8-8 show two other types of handheld cable testers.

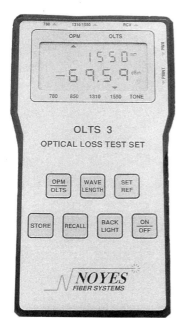

8-7 A fiber optic cable loss tester.

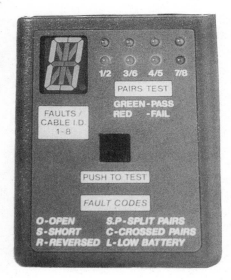

8-8 A 10BASE-T (UTP) cable
fault tester.

Network Probe

Network Communication's Network Probe family consists of four instruments. See
Table 8-4. Each of these network testers can be used at remote field sites to perform
maintenance operations. Their data-line monitoring capabilities are designed for end-to-
end communications networks and can be used for installation, maintenance, and performance measurements.

The Network Probe can perform the following functions: bit error rate tester, digital voltmeter, speaker/monitor, SNA protocol analyzer, up/down line load utility, V.35

Table 8-4. Network Probe specifications

Model	6610	6620A	6630	6640
Internal memory	32K	64K	64K	128K
Baud rate	56 kbps	56 kbps	72 kbps	256 kbps
BERT/BLERT	19.2 kbps	19.2 kbps	64 kbps	128 kbps
Program strings	7	7	16	16
dB meter		X	X	X
Ohmmeter		X	X	X
Vac/Vdc meter		X	X	X
Speaker monitor		X	X	X
Continuity tester		X	X	X
Permanent backup		X	X	X
Async term memory	None	None	4K	8K
Remote control				X
VT100 emulation				X
Graphic lead status				X

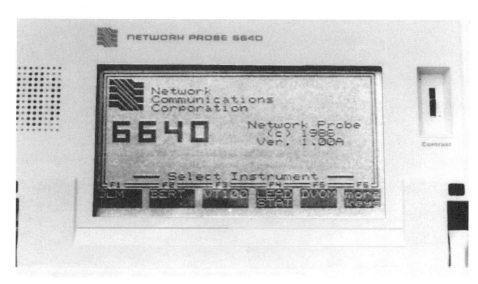

8-9 Network Probe display screen.

protocol monitor, data-line monitor, asynchronous terminal, RS-232 status monitor, X.25 protocol analyzer, Baudot protocol monitor, and DDCMP protocol analyzer.

All models are compact with a simple menu and laptop design. Figure 8-9 shows the display screen. You can program (in English) up to seven transmit strings with the 6610. A mass storage disk drive option is also available.

The 6620A has more nonvolatile internal memory (64K RAM). This instrument also can act as both a speaker/monitor and as a digital multimeter. The speaker/monitor feature allows you to listen to any irregularities that might occur on the transmission line being monitored. The digital multimeter feature provides you with an ac/dc voltmeter, a decibel (or level) meter, an ohmmeter, and a continuity tester.

The 6630 allows 72 Kbps monitoring in SNA and X.25 real-time decode. As a BERT Tester, it allows transmit speeds of 28,000, 38,400, 48,000, 56,000, and 64,000 synchronous. It can perform error-rate calculations that display the percentage of error-free seconds. When it is used as an asynchronous terminal, the unit has a built-in 4K character-capture buffer with a buffer-save feature. The 6630 allows 16 programmable transmit strings (buffers) of 240 characters each.

The 6640 has 128K of nonvolatile RAM and allows monitoring, emulation, and analysis up to 256 Kbps. An auto configuration feature automatically displays line parameters giving you immediate recognition of line configuration or type. The remote-control feature enables the user to control a slave unit from a master control site. The graphic lead status feature provides a visual display of control lead and data activity and can program multiple lead alarms. An optional 3½-inch floppy disk drive can add 800K of real-time mass storage to help track difficult diagnostic problems.

9

Other Input Devices

The words *input device* normally bring to mind the keyboard or mouse, but there are many other devices you can use to input information to the computer. In this chapter, you can learn about some of those input methods such as track ball, pen digitizer, the touch panel, joystick, and modem.

Keyboard technology

You can use many types of input devices, including keyboards. In the common alphanumeric keyboard, each key depression causes a 7-bit code to be stored in a character register in memory. The code can be determined by the program and sent to the monitor or printer in the form of a character. The key might also have a fixed function such as insert or delete or the key function might be determined by the program that is running at that time. Some functions might also require multiple key depressions.

You can accumulate consecutive characters into a buffer until a termination character is typed, thereby producing a character-string input. This process is common in programming applications.

Several technologies detect a key depression, including mechanical contact closures, a change in capacitance, and a change in magnetic coupling. The mechanical contact can take place in a mechanical key switch with a spring or a membrane switch that uses a rubber boot instead of the spring. The membrane switch can be made much smaller since the contacts used are part of the circuit board tracks. This type of switch is often used in handheld units. The entire mechanical movement in either switch is about .14 inch. Use Fig. 9-1 for a troubleshooting keyboard.

There are a number of factors that tend to make one keyboard different from another. These factors include key spacing, slope or shape of the keyboard, shape of the keycaps, and the contact pressure needed to depress a key.

Other differences involve details of the layout such as separating keys—such as Line Delete—from other frequently used keys—such as those for the return function—

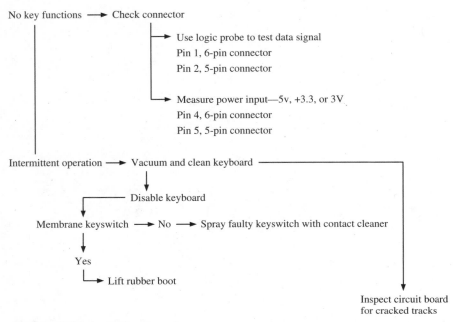

9-1 Troubleshooting keyboards.

and making frequently used correction keys easily reachable without the need to depress the Control or Shift keys simultaneously.

The programmed function keys can be provided as a separate unit. The separate unit is found in some applications, but usually the function keys are integrated with the main PC keyboard. The function keys differ from the other keys in that they are always prelabeled.

The function keys usually have no predefined character meanings. They are generally used for commands or menu options. Dedicated keys have permanent labels. The function keys can be labeled with coded overlays on which the command names are printed. The function keys might also report pressure releases as well as depressions. This operation allows you to start an activity when you press a key and then to terminate the activity when you release the key.

Another type of input device is a *chord keyboard* that has keys shaped like piano keys and is operated by depressing several keys at the same time, like the playing of a chord, and can be used for music or command input. Using 5 keys allows the generation of 31. Learning the chords requires some training, but you can learn to operate these devices rapidly. Chord keyboards are generally not suitable as substitutes for the standard type of alphanumeric keyboard.

Touch panels and pen digitizers

Touch panels allow you to indicate items on them using your finger rather than by moving a screen cursor to the item. The touch panel is mounted across the face of the

CRT (cathode-ray tube) and when your finger touches the panel, this position is detected using one of several different technologies including surface wave, infrared, and pressure sensing. (See Fig. 9-2).

One type of high-resolution touch panel uses two layers of transparent material; one is coated with a thin conductor and the other is resistive. Finger pressure causes a voltage drop across the resistive substrate; the voltage drop is measured to calculate the coordinates of the pressure point.

Similar techniques are used in digiter technology. Graphic pad digitizers use a flat tablet and a stylus pencil. The tablet provides a flat surface over which you move the stylus pencil. The position of the stylus is monitored by the computer. The stylus usu-

Resistive touch screen

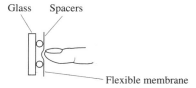

Surface wave touch screen

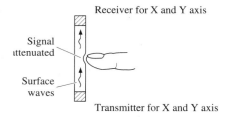

Infrared touch screen

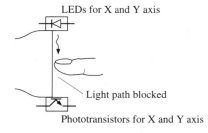

Pressure-sensing touch screen

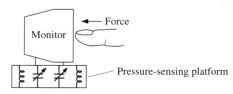

9-2 Touchscreen technologies.

ally may incorporate a pressure-sensitive switch that closes when you push down on the stylus. The switch indicates that the stylus is at a position of interest on the screen and that a menu choice is made.

Most tablets use a resistive electrical sensing system to measure the stylus position. Resistive sensing systems may use a single layer of a conductive film over glass. A controller switches the voltage at the ends of the film to measure the X and Y positions of the stylus. Two-layer systems are also used that operate like the touch panel previously discussed. These techniques are used in low-cost pen computers. The resistive material can change with temperature, humidity, and wear causing problems in the digitizer's output. A grid of wires can also be embedded in the tablet surface. The electromagnetic coupling between the electrical signals in the grid and in a wire coil changes as the stylus is moved to induce an electrical signal in the stylus. The strength of the signal indicates the position of the stylus on the tablet.

The digitizer senses the position of a pen, cursor, or some other pointer and electronically relays this information to the computer as an xy coordinate on the pad. A drawing placed on the tablet can be digitized by positioning the stylus over each point or line to be recorded.

Other digitizer technologies are electrostatic 9 capacitive and magnetostrictive. The electrostatic tablets radiate an electric field that is sensed by the pen. The system changes the frequency of the radiated field as a function of where the pen touches the surface. This frequency changes for each tablet position. The digitizer circuits translate the frequency changes into x-y coordinates, which are then sent to the computer. Electrostatic digitizers can sense the pen position through most media with a low dielectric constant such as paper, plastic, or glass.

Electrostatic systems can have problems digitizing accurately if they are near metal objects or partially conductive materials such as pencil lead or some felt-tip inks.

Magnetostrictive tablets use magnetostrictive wires laid beneath the table to keep track of pen position. A magnetic pulse on one end of the wires produces a small strain wave that propagates across the tablet. The wave is detected by a pickup coil in the pen or cursor. The time elapsed from the start of the pulse and the time that the probe senses can be related to the position of the pen.

Magnetostrictive tablets are not sensitive to conductive materials. However, magnetic objects that are near the tablet surface can disturb the magnetic properties and degrade the operation. You must remagnetize these tablets periodically with large magnets. Other problems include drifting and scratching.

In the electromagnetic tablets, either the table or the pen transmits a small ac signal. This signal is detected by receiver circuits that produce the digital signal defining the pen location. Electromagnetic digitizers are not affected by conductive or magnetic materials on their surface and generally require no periodic recalibration. This technique is used in the better pen computer. Figure 9-3 shows troubleshooting techniques for pen digitizers.

Potentiometric-device technology

Potentiometric devices are input devices that use potentiometers. A set of rotary potentiometers (Fig. 9-4) might be mounted in a unit such as a joystick. Slide poten-

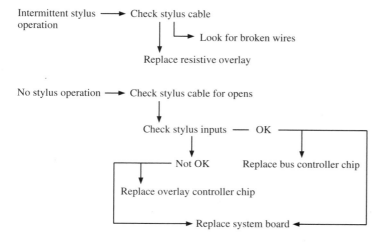

9-3 Troubleshooting pen digitizers.

tiometers, in which a linear movement replaces the rotation, are also used in some designs.

Potentiometers are sampled by devices whose analog values are converted and stored in registers to be read by the microprocessor. The values read from the registers are then converted to equivalent numbers for use by the program.

An analog-to-digital converter and a power supply can be used to determine the potentiometer position by measuring the voltage as shown in Fig. 9-5. The voltage is proportional to the amount of shaft rotation about the axis. When the converter is correctly adjusted, a zero position will correspond to a digital reading of all zeros, and a full-scale position will correspond to all ones.

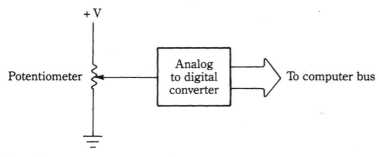

9-4 The potentiometer interface requires a power source for the potentiometer and an analog-to-digital converter to process the signal for connection to the computer bus.

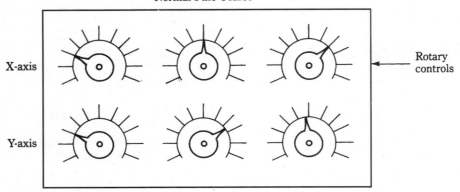

9-5 A set of controls for screen positioning. Two controls are needed for two-axis positioning. The other controls could be used for fine and coarse positioning.

Trackball technology

Trackball controls are large plastic balls mounted with some fraction of the ball surface protruding from the top of the enclosing unit. The ball rotates freely within its mount and is typically moved by drawing the palm of your hand over it. Rotating the ball can be detected by the computer to move the screen cursor.

Trackballs can be used to select commands displayed on the display. The ball positions the cursor to the proper area of a menu. Pushing a keyboard key (usually Return) makes the selection. The computer reads the cursor position at the time when the key is pressed and executes the procedure listed in the menu.

Trackballs (which are sometimes called *crystal balls*) are used as shown in Fig. 9-6. The ball motion turns potentiometers, whose output is converted into digital data for reading by the microprocessor.

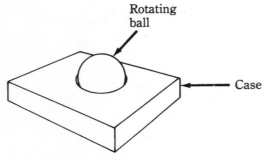

9-6 A trackball control uses a large plastic ball that is moved with the palm of your hand. The ball is connected to potentiometers.

Light-pen technology

You can use light pens as element-indicating devices. The light pen does not emit light to create lines on the screen, but it senses or detects the light from the picture elements on the screen. Some light pens do use a narrow focused light source called a *finder beam* that is directed at the screen to indicate what picture elements are in the field of view of the pen. A handheld light pen consists of a pencil-sized plastic cylinder with a light sensor in one end. One light-pen design is shown in Fig. 9-7. A number of different designs are used. The other end is connected to the computer by a cable. As you position the light-sensitive pen tip to select a point on the screen, the light pen sends a pulse when this screen area is bright. The pulse produced by the light pen is then used to calculate the screen position that the pen was at.

The pen senses the burst of fluorescent light emitted when the electron beam is bombarding the phosphor. The light is emitted during the drawing of the picture element. The pen output is usually connected to the system control logic in such a way that the microprocessor stops executing commands when the pen senses the light. This signal can be correlated with a menu list to detect the particular item being displayed at the time when the light from the pen was detected.

Most light pens also produce a second signal that you generate by pushing a button on the pen to signal the microprocessor of your selection of a point as shown in Fig. 9-8.

When the computer is interrupted by the light-pen signal, its instruction counter will contain the address of the next instruction. This address might be used to give the application program the location of the segment containing the detected element. Using this technique, the light pen acts as a locator for a raster display, stopping the raster scan at the detected pixels. The xy coordinates provide the locations.

Several factors can affect light-pen performance. Many CRT screens use bonded implosion shields over the display tube, leaving a gap between the outer glass surface and phosphor. This gap can cause accuracy problems when positioning the light pen. Unless properly adjusted, a light pen can detect false points such as adjacent characters or fail to detect the desired points.

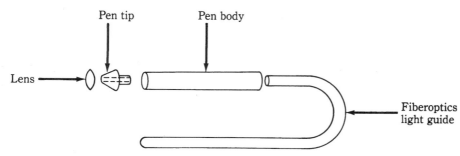

9-7 The basic light-pen design uses a lens with a fiber optics cable.

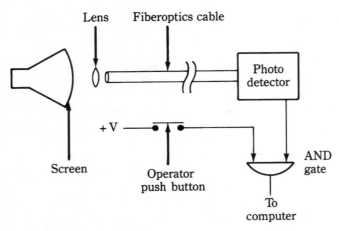

9-8 An operator push button can select a point on the screen.

Joystick technology

A joystick is like an aircraft control stick where you control the motion of a cursor on the screen by pushing it in the direction of the desired motion. The displacement type of joystick actually moves, but with the force-actuated joystick, the stick is fixed and the force from your hand causes the cursor motion.

Force-actuated, or *isometric, joysticks* use strain gauges on the shaft to measure the deflections caused by the force. Joysticks can also be rotated or pushed on the end to control other variables besides the basic position. The joystick can be moved left or right or forward or backward as shown in Fig. 9-9. Potentiometers sense the movements. Springs are sometimes used to return the joystick to its center position. Some joysticks offer a third degree of freedom because the stick can be twisted clockwise and counterclockwise.

In an *absolute joystick,* the travel of the joystick will correspond directly to the screen position. Moving the absolute joystick to its upper position places the cursor at the top of the display. Moving it to its lower-left position places the cursor at the lower-left corner of the display.

In the *rate joystick,* the motion of the joystick imparts a direction of motion to the cursor. If you move the rate joystick to the left, the cursor will move left from its present position. Push it to the lower left, and the cursor will move diagonally in that direction. When you return the joystick to center, then the cursor comes to a halt. In many designs, by varying how far in any direction the rate joystick is moved, you control the speed at which the cursor will move.

The *absolute/rate joystick* is a hybrid design that uses both techniques. A switch on the joystick handle selects the mode. In the absolute mode, a motion to the upper-left corner with the joystick will move the cursor to the upper-left corner of the computer display. Once the general target area is reached, the switch is released, and the cursor positioned using the rate mode. It can be difficult to use a joystick to control the

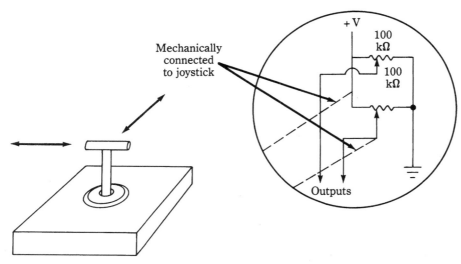

9-9 A displacement joystick acts as a handle to position the cursor. Potentiometers are used to sense the movements.

absolute position of a screen cursor accurately because even a small hand movement is amplified in the position of the cursor. The cursor movements can become erratic because the joystick does not allow fine positioning.

A small dead zone normally allows for drift in the joystick center position. The relationship of cursor velocity to joystick displacement is generally not linear, as shown in Fig. 9-10. A variation of the joystick is the *joy switch*. It can be moved in any direction: up, down, left, right, and in four diagonal directions. A switch allows nine states. In each of the eight on states, the position of the screen cursor can be changed at a constant rate in that direction.

Mouse technology

Mice are handheld units that use rollers or an LED and a ruled metal surface. Movement of the unit causes the rollers to turn internal potentiometers or the LED to sense the ruled lines. These voltage changes are, in turn, used to sense the relative movements of the mouse and track the relative position. The motion is converted to digital values

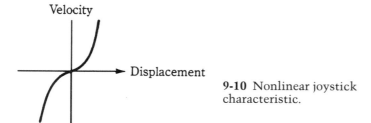

9-10 Nonlinear joystick characteristic.

and used by the microprocessor to calculate the direction and magnitude of the mouse's movement.

The mouse is normally moved on a flat surface called a *mouse pad* (Fig. 9-11). The computer maintains a current mouse position register that is incremented or decremented by the mouse movements. The mouse usually has one or more push buttons that are used to input commands.

Optical, mechanical, optomechanical, optical-mechanical, acoustomechanical, or analog tracking units exist with one to four buttons. The tracking might depend on or be independent of the rotation of the mouse. Resolution ranges from 20 to 2000 counts/inch and serial or parallel interfaces are available with relative or absolute position information in a variety of data formats and at different baud rates.

In general, mice are designed so that the front of the device is low because that is the way your hand naturally falls. Mice are also lightweight because you frequently lift and reposition them. The buttons are often parallel to the surface so the mouse won't be moved accidentally when a button is pressed.

Although there are six different techniques that can be used to perform the tracking function of a mouse, only the optical, mechanical, and opto-mechanical are widely used.

Optical mice

Optical mice track position by counting the number of line (or dot) crossings on a special mouse pad much as a bar-code wand reads bar codes (Fig 9-12). Because there is no contact between the mouse and the surface and there are no moving parts, optical mice are reliable.

Optical mice do not require maintenance, and tracking errors of less than 1 in 100 are typical throughout the life of the mouse. A special mouse pad is needed for optimum performance. Some optical mice track motion relative to the orientation of the mouse pad. The mouse cannot be rotated more than 90 degrees in either direction. Other optical units track motion relative to the orientation of the mouse, which is similar to the tracking characteristics of mechanical mice.

Mechanical mice

Mechanical mice use a metal ball to drive two orthogonal mechanical shaft encoders. This technique is low in cost and lets you track motion on any surface, but

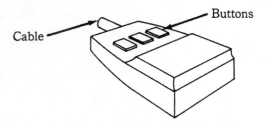

9-11 The mouse is designed so that it will fit your hand. The buttons are arranged so the mouse will not be moved when a button is pressed.

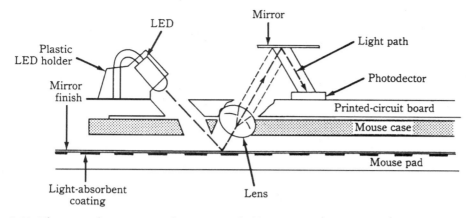

9-12 The optical mouse travels over a grid of lines on the mouse pad. An LED provides a light beam that is either absorbed or reflected.

these units have a limited lifetime (because of the mechanical switching of the encoders) and require periodic cleaning.

Opto-mechanical mice use a ball to drive two orthogonal optical shaft encoders (Fig. 9-13). This technique is low in cost, has a longer life (compared to the mechanical mouse), and lets you track on any surface. Periodic cleaning is required. *Optical-mechanical mice* use an optically sensed spring-loaded plate to determine the direction and optically count the line crossings on a special mouse pad. These units have characteristics that are very similar to optical mice.

Acoustomechanical mice use strain gauges to determine direction and a piezo-electric transducer to determine the magnitude (Fig. 9-14). There are no moving parts, no maintenance, and the mouse can track motion on almost any surface; however, the resolution (counts per inch) depends on the type of surface on which the mouse is used and on the downward pressure placed on the mouse.

Analog mice use either a ball or two orthogonal metal wheels mounted orthogonally that drive the shaft of a potentiometer. This technique is compatible with the interfacing schemes used by personal computers. The disadvantages are that such mice have

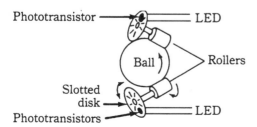

9-13 An optomechanical mouse uses a rotation ball connected to rollers that turn slotted disks. The disks turn between an LED and phototransistor combination.

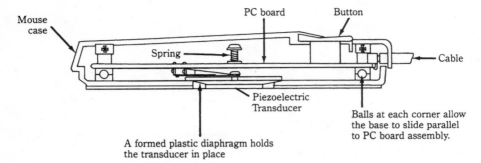

9-14 Acoustomechanical mice determine direction by the pattern of change in resistance in a strain gauge, which is returned to position by a spring action. An A/D converter provides a signal in portion to the *xy* shear. A microprocessor combines this data with velocity information from a piezoelectric transducer to reflect movement by the mouse.

a limited lifetime and a limited amount of travel in any one direction due to the use of the potentiometer.

Generally, you will use some kind of pad with nonoptical mice to reduce slipping, audible noise, and to protect the desktop. This pad is often rigid. Most nonoptical mice do not work well unless they are horizontal.

The major problems that can occur with mouse input devices can be summarized as follows:

1. *Maintenance.*   Optical mice have no moving parts. Because mechanical, opto-mechanical, and analog mice require regular maintenance, some mice have access holes for maintenance.
2. *Slippage.*   Optical mice rarely miss a count, but mechanical mice can slip on the surface.
3. *Audible noise.*   Some mechanical mice that use a metal ball make audible noise on some surfaces. This noise might increase over a period of time. Sometimes you can reduce this noise by running the mouse on a sheet of paper.
4. *Jitter effects.*   When a mouse is positioned between two grid points, a type of jitter called *teasing* might occur. The mouse might jump ahead or back by one count, which also might increase over time. Many devices use hysteresis to eliminate this problem.

Interfacing techniques

Two basic types of interfaces exist for mice: parallel and serial. Parallel mice generally use quadrature encoding for motion and encode switch depressions as a TTL low voltage. Different 9-pin standards are used by the manufacturers.

Serial mice are interfaced to RS-232 ports. A wide variety of protocols can be used but the electrical and mechanical interface is standard. Generally, these protocols send the change in the mouse state (buttons or position) whenever the mouse changes state.

The Mouse Systems serial protocol is typical. It is a 1200 baud relative-position protocol that provides 48 updates/second with a maximum velocity of 50 inches/second.

Information is transmitted only when there is a change of mouse state. Instead of polling the mouse, the microprocessor uses interrupts to service the device.

Serial mouse operation

The settings that a typical mouse uses to communicate through the RS-232C port are as follows:

Baud rate	1200
Data bits	8
Start bits	1
Stop bits	1
Parity	None

Data blocks are sent when there is a change of mouse state. The start of a data block is indicated by a sync byte. The next bits are the debounced state of the switches and the next bytes contain updates of the mouse movement counters, for the horizontal distance moved since the last transmission and the corresponding vertical distance. The coordinate systems are different; some screen coordinate systems that have vertical coordinates getting larger as you move down the screen and some are the opposite. The tracking software scans for a sync byte after receiving the bytes.

Each data byte is read using interrupts. The byte is read in the interrupt service routine, processed, and used to set a counter to indicate which byte has been read. This process minimizes the time you are running with interrupts disabled. Other parts of the program or operating system that run for extended periods with interrupts disabled might cause you to lose mouse bytes.

Sensitivity

Some programs adjust the sensitivity of the mouse by filtering the mouse input. The sensitivity is changed by multiplying or dividing the delta values by a constant before moving the cursor on the screen. Multiplying causes the cursor to move further relative to mouse motion. Dividing provides fine control of the cursor. The sensitivity can also be nonlinear. For example, a fast mouse motion could move the cursor further than slow mouse motion.

Maintenance and troubleshooting

A mouse requires a little maintenance. Some rotating-ball types tend to collect dust and might clog up if the dust and dirt are allowed to accumulate. Most of these have a removable ball that should be checked. Clean the ball with soap and water and allow it to dry before replacing. Remove any dust or dirt from the rollers.

Keep the mouse pad clean and protected from scratches and dents. Clean the pad occasionally with a damp cloth. If the mouse pad gets wet, let it dry thoroughly before using.

A mouse is designed to track accurately and function properly at all times. If you think your mouse is mistracking or is exhibiting undesirable behavior, it could be due to the following problems.

Common problems

The most common problems with a mouse are due to improper orientation of the pad and bad connections. Inadequate grounding of the computer and using an older version of the mouse software with a program that requires a later version are also typical problem causes.

The mouse software also might conflict with older keyboard enhancement software. The system also might conflict with improperly configured COM ports.

Hardware or software might make the mouse appear to stop working. If the mouse suddenly stops working, there are several things you can try. First, reboot and restart the mouse with a program. Run the TEST program.

Power cycle the mouse and turn your computer off (for 15 seconds) and on again and then restart the mouse with a program. If none of the above correct the problem, then look for the following:

LED on mouse does not turn on. Recheck the steps in the mouse setup. Try moving the connectors or pressing the connectors firmly into their receptacles. Make sure the wall outlet is working.

Cursor does not move and computer will not respond to keyboard. Some programs that use the serial ports can, in combination with the mouse, cause the computer system to lock up. The solution is to reboot your computer after using that program before using the mouse.

Strange marks on screen. If you are using some WordStar versions, strange marks will appear if you are moving the mouse too fast. If you wait a moment, the marks will disappear.

Test program works, but mouse button does nothing. Make sure that the mouse driver has been loaded. If you have a two-button mouse, make sure that the test middle button indicator always indicates that the button is up. If it indicates that the button is down, your mouse is defective. If you have an older compatible, it might have an old BIOS PROM. You will need to replace it.

Mouse button works with some programs, but not all. Some older programs do not use the keyboard type-ahead buffer. The button will not work with a program that does not use the type-ahead buffer. Word Vision and Leading Edge Word Processor are two examples of programs that will not work.

Cursor stops moving. If the cursor stops moving while in a program, check to be sure the cable is securely installed and then power-cycle the mouse, unplug the mouse, and plug it back in five seconds later. If there is still no motion, try moving the cables. Try the TEST program and if the problem persists, your mouse is defective.

Some programs, such as basic, will disable the mouse tracking upon exiting. Some VisiCorp's products, such as VisiWord, also might disable the mouse upon exit or while switching applications, going from VisiSpell to VisiWord. This situation is normal and tracking should resume when the mouse is restarted with a program. Rebooting the system also will disable mouse tracking.

Computer beeps when you press a button. Computer beeping is usually a video-mode problem and will occur if the screen is in graphics mode and you do not have a graphics video driver loaded. In some older versions of programs such as SuperCalc, if your computer has both a color and a monochrome monitor connected, then the pop-up menus think that the screen is in graphics mode. This problem has been fixed in later versions. If you are running an older version you can make the color monitor active before you start the program by typing

MODE CO80

You also can cure this problem by using your setup menu for the video mode.

Cursor does not move, even in the test program.   Check that the mouse is getting the proper signals and that all cables are secure. If the cursor does not move but the software has been installed and properly started, verify that the mouse connector is securely plugged into the port on your computer.

Remove any extra components from the RS-232C line, if you are using one, such as break-out boxes and extension cables. Run the test program to see if the mouse will work on one of the three COM: port options. The test program should reset your COM ports to their initial power-on state, this action might correct your problem. If none of these techniques works, your asynchronous communication port might be improperly configured or installed.

Cursor moves erratically.   Be sure that your computer is properly grounded and that the mouse is isolated from strong radio frequency interference. If the cursor moves erratically in the test program, be sure that the mouse pad is properly oriented. Some programs that use the serial ports, such as communications programs, might cause erratic cursor motion. If you use CROSSTALK, and then try to use the mouse, the cursor might move erratically. Reboot your computer to restore normal cursor motion. Some programs, such as WordStar, will let you position the cursor only over the text portion of a document. Therefore, sometimes motion past the beginning or end of a line will cause the cursor to jump on the screen. This behavior is normal and is not caused by the mouse or the software.

Cursor moves only horizontally or only vertically.   If the cursor moves in only one direction, rotate the pad 90 degrees, and/or power-cycle the mouse. If the problem persists, your mouse is defective.

One of the buttons does not function.   If one of the mouse buttons does not work in the test program, then your mouse is defective.

Moving the mouse quickly produces very little motion.   Some programs, such as SuperCalc, empty the keyboard buffer after many repeated arrow keys so that the cursor will stop moving immediately when the cursor key is no longer pressed. There is no way to avoid this behavior.

Your mouse will not work if your system has an incorrect communications port configuration. Typical errors include

1. Two communications boards configured for the same port address and/or IRQ. For example, you might have two ports both configured as COM1:.

2. A communications board or a Bus Plus card with a mismatched port address and IRQ. For example, a board with a COM2: interrupt address and a COM1: I/O address.
3. Port address or IRQ conflicts with another card, such as an internal modem.

Some multifunction cards provide a nonstandard configuration for COM2:. These cards have a design limitation in that they use the same interrupt address for both COM1: and COM2:. The mouse software might work with these boards, but you might be unable to fully use your COM1: port while the mouse driver is active. For example, you might not be able to use a modem or serial printer on COM1: while using the mouse on a nonstandard COM2:.

If you are unable to get your mouse to work with the test program, you should verify that your communications cards are correctly configured. Refer to the documentation that came with your mouse, communications card, modem card, or multifunction card. It should give you the type of configuration information as follows:

	COM1:	*COM2:*	*Nonstandard COM2:*
8259 input	IRQ4	IRQ3	IRQ4
I/O address	3F8	2F8	2F8
Interrupt number	0C	0B	0C
Interrupt address	30	2C	30

Modems

The word *modem* is a contraction of modulator/demodulator. Some devices function like modems but have advantages over true modems in certain applications. Modems are functionally defined as devices that allow communication between data devices over media that would not normally allow data transmission. Based on this definition, a modem might or might not transmit data through modulation and demodulation. Short-haul modems can use techniques as current drive and return to zero. True modems use modulation/demodulation techniques.

Modulation and demodulation

Modulation is a process in which a device generates an analog carrier signal and varies a characteristic of that signal, such as the amplitude, in relation to a digital data signal. *Demodulation* is the reverse process by which the original data signal is recovered.

At the most basic level, a modem can use only two variations of a characteristic. A frequency-modulating modem can use one frequency or tone to represent spaces (0) and another frequency for marks (1).

Modulation techniques

The most common modem modulation techniques are AM (amplitude modulation), PM (phase modulation), and FM (frequency modulation). Some modems can use these techniques in various combinations. Most modems use PM and FM because they are better suited to the requirements of data communications than AM.

Amplitude modulation

AM modems, as the name suggests, vary the amplitude of the carrier signal in relation to the data signal. The number of amplitude levels used determines the amount of information that each level transmits. With two levels, for example, each level transmits either 0 or 1; with four levels, each level transmits either 00, 01, 10, or 11. These levels mean that modems that use four levels transmit twice as much information within the same time span as modems that use two levels.

Some modems can use AM in conjunction with another technique to increase the speed of data transmission over a given bandwidth. For example, a carrier signal modulated with two phases can transmit a maximum of one data bit per cycle (0 or 1). If that carrier signal were also modulated with two amplitudes, as in QAM (quadrature amplitude modulation), the possible number of data bits per cycle would be two (00, 01, 10, or 11).

Although AM is inexpensive to implement in modems, it is not especially popular because of several problems. One problem is a wide bandwidth requirement, which makes it usable only for very low-speed data transmissions. There are also problems from low noise tolerance, which can cause data errors in data transmissions. Phase modulation has good noise immunity but also uses a lot of bandwidth.

Phase modulation

A simple example of phase modulation is a shift between two phases, with each phase shift representing a single data bit (0 or 1). This technique is commonly called *PSK* (*phase-shift keying*). In more complex phase modulation, four or more phase shifts can be used to transmit data, and each phase shift transmits two or more data bits. This operation reduces the required bandwidth and allows higher data rates. Shifts of 90, 180, 270, and 360 degrees, for example, could be used to transmit 00, 01, 10, or 11.

The receiving modems in PM will detect each phase shift by reference to a fixed phase or, more typically, the last phase. The modems must detect each shift as it occurs in order to achieve high data rates.

The modems also must be synchronized with each other to allow rapid shift detection and signal decoding. This requirement makes these modems better suited for synchronous data transmissions, which is their primary use. The complexity of the detection and decoding circuitry is relatively high. Most modems today use specialized chip sets to reduce costs. Figure 9-15 shows the functional blocks of a typical two-chip FAX modem.

Frequency modulation

FM modems do not need to be synchronized and are a simpler design for operation above the voice band. FM modems typically use a technique called *FSK* (*frequency-shift keying*), which means the carrier only shifts between two frequencies (tones).

FSK modems are usually phase coherent, which means each new frequency follows the phase of the previous frequency. There is no forced phase shift and the frequency components that would result from such shift are missing. The receiving modem only needs to be concerned with the two data-carrying frequencies. This feature allows higher data rates because phase-coherent modems can detect these frequencies within a very short period, even within half a cycle.

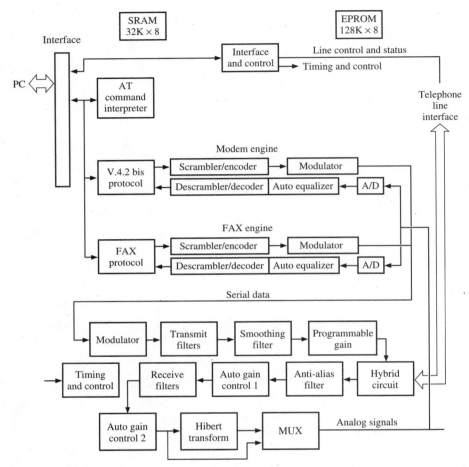

9-15 FAX modem block diagram, the protocol generators can be implemented with an 89C 126 FX chip (68 pins) and the functions below this can be implemented with an 89127 chip (28 pins).

Some modems use the on-off technique to transmit data. In this case, the modems simply turn the carrier signal on or off to transmit 0 and 1. This operation can be viewed as either FM or AM modulation.

Types of modems

Modems and modemlike devices can be grouped into seven basic types: long-haul modems, short-haul modems, medium-distance modems, data-over-voice modems, acoustic couplers, modem eliminators, and line drivers.

Long-haul modems

Long-haul modems allow the transmission of data over large distances. With a long-haul modem, you can access a computer located across the country or ocean.

These modems can be either half-duplex or full-duplex, and some long-haul units have both capabilities.

Normally, long-haul modems modulate a voice frequency carrier signal with the digital data pattern. They are designed to compensate for the variations that occur in the line parameters such as amplitude and phase delay. In theory, the range of long-haul modems is limited only by the quality of the media over which they are transmitted.

These modems can be divided into two subtypes, depending on the type of lines they use. Most long-hauls are designed for operation on the public switched (DDD) network. Others are designed for use on dedicated leased telephone lines (Bell System Type 3002 voice channels). DDD modems are the most common type. DDD modems are typically Bell-compatible and will operate with either Bell System modems or other Bell-compatible models.

All DDD modems require FCC certification (United States) or DOC registration (Canada) for direct connection to the public switched network. Modems that operate on dedicated leased lines do not, but they might require line conditioning (C1, C2, C4, D1, or D2) to eliminate problems on dedicated leased lines. Conditioning controls the frequency response and other channel characteristics to lower the error rate at high speeds.

Microprocessors are used in most long-haul modems for reliability and flexibility. Most long hauls for PCs provide complete menu-driven control with autodialing to store multiple numbers and log-in sequences.

Other features include error detection and control autoanswer, autodial, multiport operation, alternate voice/data transmission, and dial backup.

Short-haul modems

Short-haul modems typically operate at distances of up to 10 miles. Short hauls are widely used for data transmission within metropolitan areas, in campus environments, and within building complexes. Short-haul modems are used because they are less expensive and provide higher data rates, allowing more efficient use of existing leased lines.

The most common data rate for short-haul modems is 9600 bps, but some short hauls operate at much higher rates (256 kbps). Most short hauls, which are also known as *local data sets,* operate on privately owned metallic circuits or leased lines. The distances at which they operate are limited by the transmission speed and the diameter of the wires over which they transmit.

Generally, short-haul modems do not require dc continuity. In addition, the communication line for a short-haul is isolated from the modem through a transformer, which helps to protect the modem from damage and disturbance by transient signals (lightning, for example) on the line. Short hauls also provide high reliability and lower bit-error rates.

Many short-haul modems are not true modems in the sense of having a carrier signal that they modulate. These modems are actually line drivers that send the digital signal directly over the channel by acting as a signal conditioner. Because the integrity of the digital signal depends on the speed and distance involved, these short hauls have a very limited range. The smaller short hauls measure less than four inches in length, weigh only a few ounces, and plug directly into an RS-232 connector.

Medium-distance modems

These devices fall between short hauls and long hauls. They can operate at separation distances of up to 200 miles. These devices are true modems because they generate a carrier signal and modulate it. They do not require all of the complicated long-distance circuitry of long hauls. Medium-distance modems include synchronous and asynchronous models.

Data-over-voice modems

DOVs (data-over-voice modems) are sometimes known as *LADTs* (local area data transports). They allow simultaneous voice and high-speed, full-duplex data communications on a single pair of the existing telephone wires over distances of up to several miles.

DOVs are true modems. They generate carrier frequencies and modulate them with the digital data pattern. Frequency allocation and a sophisticated filtering system prevent the voice and data channels from interfering with each other. Available models are PCC-certified but are not designed for use on the public switched network or leased lines. Some models work as two-wire modems on private telephone lines or other metallic circuits.

Other modems

In addition to long-haul, short-haul, medium-distance, and data-over-voice modems, several other types of modems and modemlike devices are used. These units are used in specialized applications, where conventional modems are not practical or cost-effective.

Acoustic couplers, for example, are found in portable applications. These devices acoustically provide a data path to the switched network directly through a telephone handset. In general, acoustic couplers do not operate at speeds greater than 600 bps. They are low priced and do not need FCC certification. Modem eliminators are another example. They are used when the distance is very short (200 feet) or when a clock source is needed to permit communication over a very short distance. These units extend the possible separation distance between two data devices. Each modem eliminator serves as a substitute for two modems by regenerating the data and control signals and by providing the necessary crossover and clock source.

Line drivers, such as modem eliminators, are alternatives to conventional modems in very local applications. Line drivers, which usually require dc continuity, run on customer-owned (private) twisted-wire pairs or coaxial cable.

The line is not isolated from the equipment, which make line drivers susceptible to damage and interference from transient signals. Line drivers are usually not Bell-approved for use on telco (telephone company) lines. As discussed earlier, some so-called short-haul modems or local data sets are actually line drivers. Because of the limitations of line drivers, they cannot be used as a replacement device for an application requiring the capabilities of a short-haul modem.

Multiplexers

Depending on the number of dedicated communication lines involved, the cost of using multiple modems can quickly become unreasonable. This situation calls for multiplexers.

Multiplexers combine several low-speed inputs into one high-speed output. As a result, they allow two or more data devices to transmit data simultaneously over a single media. Multiplexers concentrate data, which would otherwise be routed over many separate point-to-point lines, into a composite stream transmitted over one link. Some multiplexers have built-in modems.

Two basic techniques of multiplexing exist: frequency division and time division. In *frequency division,* the communications channel is split into different frequencies and the data from the different sources is transmitted together. In *time division,* data from each source is put on a schedule, and only one data signal at a time is transmitted. Time-division multiplexing can allocate time on either a fixed or statistical basis.

Modem and MUX testers

Modem and MUX (multiplexer) test sets are generally microprocessor-based instruments. They can be used to test and monitor a data communications system at the modem-terminal interface. A breakout panel provides access to the conductors of the interface between the terminal and the modem. Synchronous and asynchronous protocols can be used for a variety of tests. Master and remote polling tests can be performed on two- or four-wire systems. An echo test drives received data (RD) back out as transmitted data (TD) to verify message transmission.

Bit-error rate testers

A BERT (bit-error rate test) counts bit errors in different patterns. Transitions can be detected in a steady mark or space pattern. User-constructed messages can be entered and tested. BERTs are handheld, microprocessor-based testers that can perform several tests. A typical BERT tester might be capable of testing synchronous data links to 72 Kbps and asynchronous data links to 38 Kbps. These testers can perform bit-error testing, percent error-free seconds testing, and count-positive and negative transitions on any interface lead. They can also generate Fox messages in ASCII, BAUDOT, and IPARS.

BERT/breakout testers

Some units function as both a basic BERT tester and a battery-powered break-out box. They are capable of analyzing both the bit-error rate of digital data communication channels as well as breaking out and monitoring both sides of the RS-232 interface. They usually have separate transmitter and receiver sections that allow full-duplex tests to be performed in either end-to-end or loop-back configurations.

In some units, the transmitter can generate up to four switch selectable dot patterns including 2047-bit repeating pseudorandom sequences and an alternating mark-space pattern. The receiver section will generate a replica of the selected transmitted data pattern and compares this error-free replica with the received data pattern. The break-out box is line powered and capable of monitoring both sides of the RS-232 interface.

Modem settings

The settings are one of the most frequent problems. The baud rate, parity, data, and stop bits must match those of the remote system to make a successful connection. The sum of the parity, data bits, and stop bits must be equal to or greater than nine. The baud rate is the speed at which the modem sends and receives data. Typical choices are 300, 600, 1200, 2400, 4800, 9600, 19,200 and 38,400. The usual parity settings are None, Even, Odd, Mark, or Space. Normally, the default setting is None, because most online services ignore parity. The possible values for the data bits are 7 and 8. They represent the number of data bits used. The usual choices for stop bits are 1 and 2. A *stop bit* is the last bit of a byte of data.

The echo can be set to on or off. The default setting is off. If set to off, you must depend on the host computer to send back (echo) each character you type. If set to on, the characters you type will be displayed (or echoed) to the screen and sent to the host computer. These options are also called *full duplex* (on) and *half duplex* (off).

If after you are connected, you see two characters for each one you type (such as *ttyyppee*), change this setting to off. If you cannot see the characters you type, set the echo to on.

The mode can be set to call, answer, or direct. When set to call, the communications software will try to establish a connection, using the dial prefix (either standard or MNP) and the phone number. If set to answer, the software will send an answer string to the modem. The answer string tells the modem to stand by for an incoming call. If you select direct, the communications software assumes it has a direct connection with the host computer and sends nothing.

The flow control can be set to None, XON/OFF, or RTS/CTS. Flow control determines the type of handshaking used between the software and the modem. XON/XOFF is usually the default setting. If you use software with MNP 4 or 5, set this field to None. When using an MNP-equipped modem, set this to RTS/CTS.

Terminal settings for online services

Make sure you set up your communications software properly for online services, especially for downloading or uploading files. Dedicated software for online services, such as WinCIM for CompuServe, handle this for you. If you are using a program such as Windows' Terminal or Procomm Plus, you have to do it yourself (Table 9-1).

Table 9-1. Modem settings

Service name	CompuServe	GEnie	TymNet*	SprintNet	BBS
Terminal type	VT100	VT100	VT100	VT100	VT100
Data bits	7	8	8	8	7 or 8
Stop bits	1	1	1	1	1
Parity	Even	None	None	None	Even or None
Duplex CompuServe	Full	½ or Local Echo	Full	Full	Full

*TymNet usually works with VT100, 8N1, but if there is a problem and you receive unreadable text, wait three seconds, then type capital A, set modem to 7E1.

Error-correcting modes

Some modems with hardware error-correction protocols such as MNP5 and V.42 use different modes of operation. These modes are as follows.

Normal mode

The normal mode is used to communicate with nonerror correcting modems. This mode is the default if an autoreliable link negotiation with the remote modem fails. Data buffering takes place in the normal mode but error correction is not active.

Direct mode

The direct mode is the simplest form of operation. There is no error correction, data compression, or data buffering in this mode. The serial port and the modem port must be set for the same data rate.

Direct mode is the mode of operation of a non-error-correcting modem. The data is not buffered; therefore, the port speeds must be the same, and no hardware error correction takes place.

Reliable mode

In the reliable mode, your modem will connect with another modem capable of establishing an MNP reliable (error-correcting) link. When the connection is made, it attempts to establish a reliable link. If this attempt fails, the modem disconnects and the following problems might exist:

1. The remote modem does not support an MNP reliable link.
2. The remote modem is an MNP mode, but it is not in the proper mode.
3. The telephone connection is poor and noisy enough that even an MNP reliable link connection is unable to assure dependable communications.

The reliable mode requires that the remote system have MNP error correction.

Other protocols

If you use some software error-correcting protocols with the reliable link, the redundant error checking will reduce the file-transfer efficiency of the link. File-transfer protocols exist that are designed to be used with hardware error-correcting modems. Two of the best of these file transfer protocols are IMODEM and YMODEM-G. ZMODEM is usually within a few percentage points of these protocols.

If you use reliable mode, you need to know the capabilities and status of the remote system. If you call a non-MNP or V.42 modem while in reliable mode, the connection will fail. If you are unable to obtain the needed information about the remote system, you will probably want to use autoreliable mode.

Autoreliable mode

Because you do not always know the type and status of the remote modem, some modems support an autoreliable mode. In this mode, after the initial connection is made, the local modem looks at the data stream from the remote modem for incoming MNP characters. If the appropriate characters are detected, the local modem establishes an MNP reliable link. If it cannot make this connection, it will fall back to a normal mode connection and use flow control if it is enabled. If flow control is not enabled, the modem will fall back to a direct mode.

If the modem is set to auto-answer incoming calls in autoreliable mode, the handshake period can be reduced using the autoreliable fallback character. When the local modem detects the autoreliable fallback character it stops checking for the identification characters and falls back to a normal connection.

V.42-only reliable mode

In this mode, the local modem will only connect with another modem capable of establishing a V.42-reliable (error-correcting) link. The mode is very similar to the reliable mode except it first looks for the LAPM (link-access protocol) character during the handshake. If an error-correcting connection is not established the modem will disconnect. The following problems might cause the attempt to secure a reliable link to fail:

1. The remote modem does not support the V.42 protocol.
2. The remote modem is a V.42 modem, but it is not in the proper mode.
3. The telephone connection is poor and noisy enough that even a V.42-reliable link connection is unable to assure dependable communications.

Because of the increased complexities during the handshaking procedures, use this mode only with other V.42 modems when you do not want to make an MNP connection. In most cases, you should use the V.42/MNP autoreliable mode. The V.42-only reliable mode requires that the remote system have V.42 error correction.

V.42-only autoreliable mode

The V.42-only autoreliable mode is similar to the V.42-only reliable mode. The difference is that if the V.42 connection is not made, the local modem will establish a normal or direct mode connection. An MNP-reliable (error-correcting) link will not be attempted after the attempted V.42 reliable link fails. A normal or direct mode connection will be established.

V.42/MNP reliable mode

The V.42/MNP reliable error-correction mode is similar to the reliable mode except it first looks for the LAPM character during the handshake. Because the V.42 protocol also includes the MNP protocols, if the LAPM connection attempt fails, the V.42/MNP reliable mode will attempt an MNP-reliable connection. If an error-correcting connection is not established, the modem will disconnect. Due to the increased complexities during the handshaking procedure, the V.42/MNP reliable mode should be used only with other V.42 modems when the data integrity is critical. In most cases, it is better to use the V.42/MNP autoreliable mode.

V.42/MNP autoreliable mode

The V.42/MNP autoreliable mode is among the most sophisticated error-correction operating modes available. The mode is similar to the autoreliable mode except that it first attempts to connect with another modem using the LAPM error-correction protocol. If the LAPM connection is not available, the modem will attempt an MNP autoreliable mode connection. If the error correction is not enabled, the modem will establish a normal or direct mode connection.

Testing

An easy way to test your modem is from the DOS prompt. Type the command

```
Echo ATDT >COM#
```

where # is the number of the comm port you want to use. If there is a modem at that port and it is working, you should hear a dial tone or other indication that the modem has accepted the command. To reset the modem to the original factory settings, replace ATDT with AT&F.

Troubleshooting

Modem communication depends upon several things working together correctly: the computer, modem, software, and the telephone line. These individual pieces must be working correctly on the other side of the connection as well.

Although correcting problems is usually quite simple, the difficulty is in knowing where to look. This section should help you in determining the cause of problems that might occur so you can correct them. Figure 9-16 shows how to troubleshoot some of the more common problems.

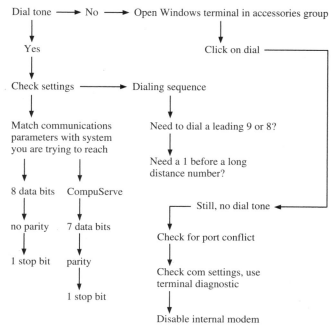

9-16 Modem troubleshooting.

When an internal modem is not working and you think you have it installed correctly, the problem could be a port conflict. You may have to disable a COM port through the BIOS setup program to correct the problem. This conflict can happen when the internal modem wants to use a hard-coded set of interrupts that the BIOS has redirected for use on the system board. After these COM ports are disabled for the system board, the internal modem can use them.

If your fax and communications programs try to use the same modem at the same time, you will get a

Port in Use

error. To fix this, make one application give up control of the port or close down one application and try again. If this occurs often, the solution is to use a communications port-sharing application, such as KingCom from OTC or the shareware program Voodoo Assassin.

Panel lights

When you are troubleshooting your communication program, you can use modem panel lights to check the status of the connection. If you have an external modem, you have the lights. If you have an internal or PCMCIA modem, you can get onscreen lights with one of the shareware programs available for downloading from online services. The most common modem lights are shown in Fig. 9-17.

The send and receive lights will alternately flash when you are sending or receiving a file. On some modems, SD is replaced by TX, which stands for transmit.

CD—Carrier detect, this light indicates whether the modem on the other end answered.

AA—Automatic answer, this lets you know whether the modem has been configured to answer incoming calls automatically.

OH—On hook

SD—Send

RD—Receive

9-17 Modem panel lights.

Call waiting

Call waiting can cause problems if someone calls while you are using your modem. You can lose characters or data, or even be taken off the connection. To avoid this, set up your communications program to dial

    *70

which disables call waiting, before each phone number. Include a comma after the *70 to allow your telephone system time to process the command. If you are using a rotary phone, the code is 1170. Then, if someone calls while you are online, that person will get a busy signal and your communications session will go on uninterrupted.

Screen savers

Turn off your screen saver during downloads, especially if you are downloading large files. If the screen saver switches in, it could cause transmission errors.

Character loss

You may need to change the COMBoostTime value in the [386Enh] section of SYS-TEM.INI in Windows if the characters you type in from the keyboard do not appear on the screen during a communications session. You can use a text editor, such as Notepad. Open SYSTEM.INI and change the COMBoostTime to 20.

Some DOS communications programs may fail to detect and enable the UART buffer because Windows is doing its own buffering of the communications port for the applications. You can fix this by adding the statement

    COM#Buffer=0

where # stands for your comm port number, to the [386Enh] section of your SYSTEM.INI file.

You may also need to increase the size of the communications port buffer. Change the size of the number of bytes to make the buffer, in the line above, to at least 1024 or greater. The default value is 128 bytes, which may not be enough to keep up with faster modems. Increasing the value may slow down communications slightly, but it should give you more reliability.

If your high-speed modem is not giving you the throughput you expect, your communications program may be the problem. High-speed modems normally negotiate with each other when making a connection so that they use the highest speed and best error control and compression for a given line condition.

Modems always use the same commands for setting up the fallback options when the initial negotiation fails, and not all Hayes-compatible modems are fully compatible. You may need to reconfigure your communication program's modem initialization string and change the codes specifying the action the modem takes when the intital error-control negotiation fails. Check the S36=value in the initialization string and compare it with the setting in your modem manual, or check with your modem manufacturer. The default for most communication programs is S36=7. This tells a Hayes-compatible modem to try the V.42 Alternate Protocol and if that doesn't work to try a standard asynchronous connection with automatic speed buffering.

For high-speed modem communications, set the serial port to use hardware handshaking (CTS/RTS). Use the Control Panel Ports icon and click on the port you are using. From the Flow Control list box, select Hardware and then click on OK.

Sometimes a modem will lose characters at high speed even if your computer has a 1655A or other high-speed port installed. Use the procedure of Fig. 9-18(A) to prevent this, add the line

COM#Protocol=XOFF

to the [386Enh] section in SYSTEM.INI in Windows. Replace # with the comm port you are using. This line sets the port to use the Xon/Xoff protocol, which forces the port to wait for an OK before trying to process a buffer full of data.

You can also make this change from the Windows Control Panel. Select Ports, double-click on your COM port, and select Xon/Xoff under Flow Control (Fig. 9-18(B)).

Not all drivers are the same. The COMM.DRV serial port drive that comes with Windows is good, but high-speed modems can use more. TurboCom is a good replacement, as is the shareware CHCOMB.EXE, which lets DOS programs under Windows use the 16550A chip.

If you regularly use your communications software to connect to the same online services or bulletin boards, you can script the communications software to learn your log-on sequences so it will run automatically when you dial the number. This will prevent log-on problems due to mistyping. Most communications programs allow you to create a script and then assign it to a phone book entry.

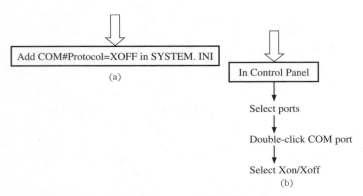

9-18 (A and B) Setting a port to Xon/Xoff protocol.

Fax modem problems

If your communications program has problems resetting a fax modem from fax to data mode, you will have trouble establishing a data connection with another fax modem. Find the modem initalization string in the modem setup of your communications program, and add AT&F to the beginning of this line. This will reset the modem each time you run the program, providing more reliable connections.

Changing your UART

If you have a modem running at 14.4 Kbps or higher, and the serial port on your machine uses a 8250 or 16450 UART, you may be communicating much more slowly than your modem will allow and you may be losing data, too.

The UART (Universal Asynchronous Received/Transmitter) controls the exchange of data between your computer and modem, determining the speed and reliability of communications. If your machine uses one of these chips, replace it with a 16550A UART. You can find out which chip is used by running the Microsoft diagnostic utility, MSD.EXE.

Unlike the 8250 and the 16450, which buffer only one character as they send or receive data, the 16550A UART stores 16 characters for both transmission and reception. As data comes in, the computer must service the UART and translate the incoming data between a serial data stream and a parallel data stream.

The computer's processor must read the UART and copy the data that it contains. Depending upon what else the computer is doing at the time, the UART might not be serviced as quickly as it should be.

In the older chips, this means that data can be lost when the character in the 1-byte buffer is overwritten with incoming data. In the newer 16550A UARTs, 16 bytes of data can be stored before the buffer needs to be read. This allows more time for the computer's processor to read the chip and less chance that data will be lost. With the 16-byte buffers, the 16550A UART running at 9600 bps requires the same service time as an 8250 UART running at 600 bps.

Many newer PCs do not have a separate UART, they use an application-specific integrated circuit (ASIC) with the UART built in. If your PC has a separate UART, you may be able to replace it, but the UART may be soldered to the motherboard or communications card.

Replacing the 8250 is not hard, especially if it is socketed. The 16550A and the 8250 are both 40-pin chips, and only two of the pins (24 and 29) differ between the chips. This makes it possible to plug the 16550A into an existing 8250 socket. If you have a socketed chip, you can get a $10 to $15 UART from an electronics supplier.

The two pins that differ are typically unused for PC-compatible serial ports. They are sometimes used to connect a ground wire. If this is the case, you can clip off that pin or bend it back so that it does not go into the socket.

Another option is to add a new serial board. Adding such a board requires a free slot and at least one free IRQ; dual-port boards will need two IRQs.

Serial ports

Determine what serial ports are installed in your computer. You might have assumed that you only have COM1 in your computer, when you actually have both COM1 and COM2. You might also have other combinations of COM ports.

Most computers with a Serial I/O facility have COM ports 1 and 2 enabled, which allows you to connect an external modem or a mouse to each serial connector. Even if you do not have anything connected to the RS-232 connector, it is still using a COM port. A COM port can only be used by one device. Most communications software includes a modem testing program. This program will check your computer system to determine what COM ports are installed on your computer. It will also suggest a COM port to configure the modem to. The test will inform you if a port is occupied by acknowledging that the port exists.

Many problems are caused by configuring the modem COM port to a port already installed in your computer system. A common problem the modem will experience is the inability to dial.

Common problems

The most common problems that are encountered are as follows:

1. The computer, or communications software, does not recognize the modem.
2. The modem will not dial (and/or answer).
3. You can connect with another computer, but the text (or graphics) that you see is not correct.

Modem recognition

If your modem is not being recognized by your computer (or communications software), the problem often involves COM ports. First, check your communications software. Make sure that the COM port selected on the software is the same as the one you have selected on your modem.

If you have determined that there is not a COM port conflict, then the problem might involve IRQ (interrupt request level) conflicts. Check to see if you have another device (such as a mouse) that shares an IRQ level with the modem. COM1 and COM3 share IRQ4 and COM2 and COM4 share IRQ3. A mouse, even a bus mouse, although it is not serial, has an IRQ level. If you have a mouse installed on your computer, it is usually installed in COM port 1 or 2. A mouse requires a DRIVER, which is a memory resident program to control the mouse. If the modem is using the same IRQ level as your mouse when the modem requests an interrupt from the computer, the mouse drive intercepts the request as if it were coming from the mouse.

If you have this problem, either change the IRQ level used by the mouse, by changing the IRQ level used for the COM port that the mouse is connected to, to an IRQ level that is not used by your system. Many systems give you a choice of IRQ levels for the COM ports. The common choices are IRQ2, IRQ3, IRQ4, and IRQ5. You can also reconfigure the modem to a COM port that uses a different IRQ level or connect the mouse to a port that uses a different IRQ level.

Some communications software uses memory resident programs. This can cause some problems. For example, if you have configured the modem to use COM2 (IRQ3), and you program your FAX to send a FAX at a certain time, but at the same time you attempt to communicate with another modem configured to use COM4 (IRQ3), the other modem will request an interrupt from the computer and the FAX program will intercept the request as if it were coming from your modem. You will need to avoid these time conflicts.

No connection

The communication software dials the host computer. The host answers, and the dial tone changes to a high-pitched tone, indicating the modem is ready, but the CONNECT message does not appear, and the connect clock does not start. Check that you are using the correct baud rate, parity, stop bits, and data bits. These parameters have to match those of the host.

Another common cause of this problem is that another serial device is using the same COM port address as your modem. For example, your mouse and modem are both set to COM1. To correct this problem, you need to either disable the other serial port or change the COM port address of your modem or the other serial device. Most internal modems have switches to change the COM port address to COM1, COM2, COM3, or COM4.

This problem also can occur when the modem is set to echo commands in numeric rather than English words. Check the modem and see which kinds of commands it uses and if it can be switched to use English words. If you cannot switch your modem to use English words, you might be able to use an "o is zero" dialing prefix in the communication configuration menu.

Also, the host computer might have reset the modem.

Connection problems

If the modem will not dial and/or answer, and you have already determined it is not a COM port conflict, check the telephone lines. Make sure that the telephone cord from the wall is firmly connected to the jack in the modem labeled Line. If it is, unplug the cord from the modem and connect it to a telephone, use the same telephone cord that you used to connect to the modem. If you cannot hear a dial tone when you pick up the phone, the telephone line or outlet is the source of the problem.

Try using another telephone cord to ensure it is not defective. If you still cannot hear a dial tone when you pick up the phone, the telephone outlet is defective or the phone line might be out of service. If you do hear a dial tone on the telephone set, but you do not hear the dial tone when the phone is connected to the phone jack on the modem, it might be a problem with the modem.

Line noise

If you can connect to another number, but the screen display is garbled with wrong characters or misplaced characters, the cause is usually one of two problems. Check that your communications program is configured correctly for the modem you are connecting to. Check the baud rate, parity, data bits, and stop bits. These settings should match that of the other computer. Also, check to determine if you need to emulate a terminal when connecting.

If all of the settings in the software are correct, you might have a noisy telephone line. You can contact your local telephone company to have them check the line. Tell them that you are using the line for a modem. If the telephone company technician verifies a good phone line, the problem is probably in the modem.

Communications software will not start

Check that your computer has enough RAM to run the software. Use CHKDSK at the DOS prompt to find out how much RAM memory is available. Check the directory or disk that contains the software for the correct EXE file. Compare this file with the original file on your program disk.

Double characters as you type

Double echo can occur after you have made a connection with the echo on. Set echo to off in the communications parameters menu.

Strange characters on screen

If you get strange characters after you have made a connection, set the input filter on in the communications parameters menu to filter out the high-order bits.

Cursor jumps to start of line

The cursor might jump after connecting to a host computer. Every time you press [Enter] to type a new line, the cursor moves to the beginning of the same line. You need to change the Auto LF field in the communications parameters menu to on. The cursor will then advance a line when you press [Enter].

Double-spaced

If after connecting to a host, everything you type is doubled-spaced, change the Auto LF field in the Communications Parameters Menu to off.

Need to dial 9 for an outside line

If you first have to dial a 9 and then wait for a dial tone before getting an outside line, you might need to add 9,, (the number 9 followed by two commas) to the Phone Number field in your Communications Selection Menu. The two commas stand for a two-second pause.

Redial without waiting for a connection

The redial field in the communication parameters menu is too short. Set this to at least 40, this allows the modem enough time (40 seconds) to wait for a connection before redialing.

COM 1 not functional or NO DSR Signal on COM 1 error message

The not-functional or no-signal message usually indicates a faulty connection, check that all the cables are securely connected and that the modem's DRS light is on. Other error messages can occur when you change your dialing prefix or when you dial a long number. If you change your dialing, make sure you have the proper Hayes commands and that these commands are supported by your modem. Also, the letters should all be uppercase. If you are using a long phone number, your modem might not be able to handle all the digits.

Result codes

Some modems send responses to the computer after a command is issued. Unless they are modified by commands or your communication software, these responses will be shown on the screen. These responses from the modem are known as Result Codes. The modem sends these result codes in a verbal (text) format or a numeric format. Typical responses are listed as follows:

Numeric	Verbal	Meaning
0	OK	The command line has been executed without errors.
1	CONNECT	The modem has connected.
2	RING	A ring signal has been detected by the modem due to an incoming call.
3	NO CARRIER	The modem connection has been lost or was never established after dialing.
4	ERROR	An error was detected in the command line; this might be an invalid character or too many digits in the command line.
5	NO DIAL TONE	A dial tone was not detected when one was expected by the modem.
6	BUSY	A busy signal was detected by the modem.
7	NO ANSWER	No ringback or quiet answer was detected by the modem.

Scanners

Scanners evolved from the large, expensive self-contained units to smaller, printer-sized units and even low-cost handheld units. These smaller units are often grouped together as desktop scanners. The following types are generally referred to, although there is some overlap in classification.

Camera-based scanners use photographic technology to produce very high resolution scans of two- or three-dimensional objects. The scanner head might resemble a 35 mm camera and can be mounted on a moving tower above a flat platform.

Feeder scanners resemble a single-sheet printer. They are usually designed to scan letter-size documents, although larger and smaller sizes can be supported. The document is placed in an input tray or manually fed through the unit.

Flat-bed scanners are used to scan flat, two-dimensional objects such as documents and photographs. Some flat-bed models offer a multiple-page feeder attachment for automatic multiple-page scanning.

Slide scanners are typically used for high-resolution color scans of 35 millimeter slides. Most of these scanners support 256 gray-scale level output for gray-scale conversion of color or black-and-white slides.

Overhead scanners use a scanning platform with the scanning head fixed above the platform. The platform allows the scanning of small three-dimensional objects.

Another type of scanner uses a device that replaces the drawing head of a plotter. This device is called a *plotter add-on* type of scanner and is used for drafting applications because it can scan large-sized drawings.

A similar add-on type of scanner replaces the print head in a dot matrix printer. Software included with this printer add-on scanner controls the movement of the scanner head and the document feed through the printer, allowing a line-by-line scan of documents and photos.

Monochrome handheld scanners are small, low cost, manually operated scanning units. Most handheld models have a scanning width of about four inches and use imaging software for scanning larger documents.

Color handheld scanners can provide full color or 256 gray-scale level scans. The color output is usually produced by combining information from separate red, green, and blue scan passes.

Desktop scanners

The category known as desktop scanners are a popular add-on for personal computers. These products have evolved over the years. In the mid-1980s, desktop publishing pushed the development of desktop scanners for personal computers. Some of the first products included those from Microtek, Datacopy, and DEST. These early desktop scanners used a simple binary technology where the scanned images (line art or photographs) were broken down into cells that are either black or white. In 1987, gray-scale techniques appeared. In gray-scale scanning, each cell in the scanned image can be recorded as a shade of gray, which provides you with more control over the quality of the scanned image before and during the editing process. The first machines to use this technology had 16 shades of gray, but shortly scanners with 256 gray tones appeared (8-bits-per-pixel) that became the gray-scale standard.

As desktop scanners evolved as an important peripheral for personal computers, their design and capabilities were targeted for areas such as desktop publishing, which can be broadly defined as electronic publishing or computer-aided publishing. This area is the main application of desktop scanners. The available products have advanced rapidly from black-and-white to color scanning. Differences exist between the capabilities of both the hardware as well as the software that controls the scanner. Some scanners are designed for color only, but others can handle color and gray scale and some are designed as scanners for transparencies.

There are also larger-size scanners that are capable of scanning documents up to 36 inches wide. Although these will never be as popular as the smaller, lower-cost scanners, they represent some of the most advanced scanners.

Charge-coupled devices

CCDs (charge-coupled devices) are an important component in today's scanners. They have evolved over the years to their present level of capabilities. CCDs have improved along with large-scale integrated circuits and the reduction in size of memory chips. CCD images are being used to bring back photos from distant planets. In the 1970s, they were used in products such as electronic still-video cameras and camcorders.

The actual scanning is performed with an array of CCD elements. Each element is a pixel, or picture element, with the light from the object image on it. In the CCD, a photoconductive material is used similar to that in the vidicon tubes used in video cameras. In the vidicon tube, a single layer is used where the scanning beam defines the picture element. The solid-state CCD sensor has individual picture elements that are accessed by separate leads. This construction makes the solid-state sensor more expensive to manufacture.

In the vidicon tube, changes in the scan velocity and other problems affect performance. Solid-state sensors provide better positional accuracy. Color is created by using a repetitive pattern of color filters. Using this CFA (color-filter array), each pixel is covered with a color filter that allows only that color to pass (Fig. 9-19).

The CCD uses charge coupling as shown in Fig. 9-20. Small amounts of electrical charge are created in the silicon semiconductor material. These areas are created by an electric field between a pair of gate electrodes, which are located close to the surface of the silicon.

The CCD elements are placed next to each other and as the voltages on adjacent gate electrodes change, the individual charge packets beneath them are passed from

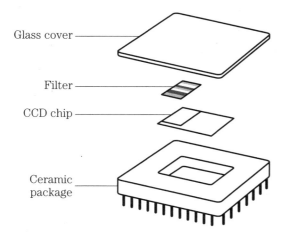

9-19 Components of a charge-coupled device (CCD).

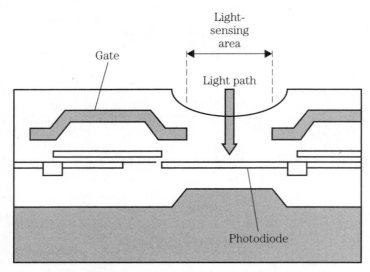

9-20 Cross section of CCD image sensor. The light path to the light-sensitive photodiode acts as a gate electrode.

one element to the next. The CCDs act as shift registers because they transfer their charge to the next element while the amount of charge in each packet stays the same, even as it is passed from one element to another.

When the silicon absorbs the light striking its surface, free electrons are generated. The number of free electrons generated is proportional to the light striking the surface. This light image is a reproduction of the original scene and it generates a proportional electrical charge. The charge packets are transferred by charge coupling, and the value of each charge packet corresponds to a picture element or pixel. The actual CCD sensors are made of a series of horizontal and vertical rows, creating an xy array of elements.

CCD sensors

Monochrome sensors have higher speeds because it is not necessary to have the three alternating systems of red, green, and blue, all of the pixels are available for the collection of photons. The newer sensors transfer energy closer to the surface so more energy can be collected and produce a higher-speed sensor.

CCDs are more reliable compared to vacuum picture tubes. They are a low-power device, but they can accept large amounts of light without damage or change to the photosensitive surfaces. CCDs generate electrical noise but this noise is low enough to give good performance.

Noise in an image appears as granular spots. Most noise in these systems does not come from the CCDs. It comes from adjacent circuits and connections in the system.

The scanners use multielement CCD arrays and some units can be used with large format E-size drawings that are 34 × 44 inches. Some of the larger units have a fixed scan head and a drum on which the paper moves. Others use a flatbed for the document and move the sensor array (Fig. 9-21).

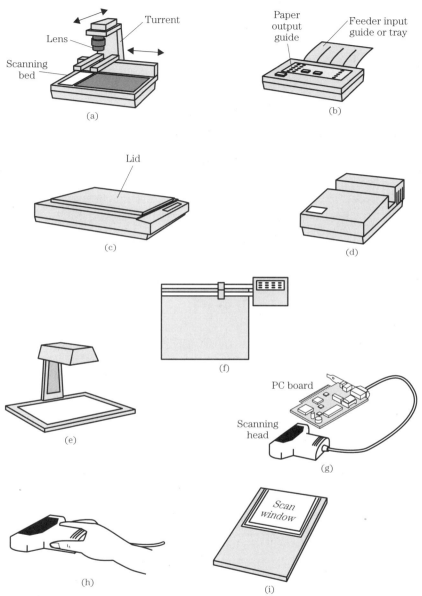

9-21 Types of scanners. Camera type, also called a flat-bed scanner (A). Feeder type, used for letter-sized documents, manually fed using guide or tray (B). True flat-bed scanner; document is placed under lid. Multiple page feeders can be used (C). Slide scanner, used for 35 mm color or black-and-white slides (D). Overhead type, used like a fixed-camera scanner (E). Plotter attachment type; replaces the drawing head of the plotter. Used to scan large drawings (F). Printer attachment type; uses a PC board and a scanning head that replaces the print head (G). Handheld scanner, usually about 4 inches wide, used with imaging software for larger documents (H). Color handheld type used for color photos; needs separate red, green, and blue scans (I).

Gray scale refers to the number of shades of gray the scanner is able to represent per dot or pixel. A scanner that is able to represent only black and white is said to have two levels of gray. The more shades of gray a scanner is able to detect and record, the more closely the scanned reproduction matches the original. Conventional halftone techniques for printing photographs use dots of different sizes to represent the shades. In many digital scanning devices, the dots are the same size. Shading is done by grouping dots into small units called *grains*. A grain can be made up of 4, 9, 16, 25, 36, or 64 dots in a square array. The smaller grain sizes provide more details.

Gray scales are produced by partially filling the grain. A 2×2 grain has 4 possible fill slots, and it provides a five-step gray scale. An 8×8 grain can provide 33 gray levels that means more shades but less detail. Grains are not used for line art.

The *resolution* of a scanner refers to the scanner's sensitivity. A scanner's resolution is measured in dots (or pixels) per square inch. The maximum image size depends on the scanner's physical scanning range. Scanning speed refers to how quickly the scanner operates.

In a color scanner, the color information the scanner detects and records is done for each of the three basic colors: red, green, and blue. Red, green, and blue are mixed to produce other colors. Figure 9-22 shows two filtering techniques that are used. Table 9-2 lists several color scanners. The IEEE-488 interface comes on an expansion board.

Microtek

This manufacturer was one of the first to offer scanners. Its ScanMaker 600Z/ZS is a desktop scanner that can be used to scan 16.8 million colors and 256 shades of gray and black and white. It can capture images at up to 600 dots per inch. Its ScanMaker 1850 can be used to capture 24-bit color and 8-bit gray scale from 35 mm color or black-and-white slide images at resolutions to 1850 dots per inch. The images can be scanned in both portrait and landscape orientations.

The Microtek MS-300A scanner, like most others, uses a CCD sensor array. It can be used to scan photographs, line art, and graphics and text for OCR applications. This desktop scanner uses a roller feed to move the original by the image sensors. A standard page takes less than 10 seconds to pass by the image-sensing array.

During imaging, a bitmap of the original image is produced. As the document is scanned, logic circuits in the scanner determine how the image is to be interpreted. If the copy is black and white, a black area is given a logic 1 and results in an area of dots; a white area is given a logic 0 and results in an area with no dots. If a photograph is scanned, the various shades of gray are interpreted as a pattern of dots.

The MS-II scanner is designed for multiple pages. It has a 50-page automatic document feeder along with 300 dots per inch resolution and a sheet-feed design. It can be used for black-and-white graphics including line art and half-tone scanning.

Setup

The actual scanning operation is automatic after you set up the scanner. Like a manually adjusted camera, the scanner must be adjusted for the document. In the MS-II, adjustment is done with the Scanner Settings screen. Brightness and contrast adjust-

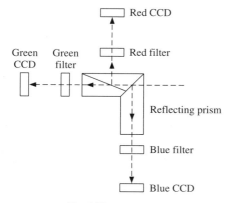

Fixed filter system

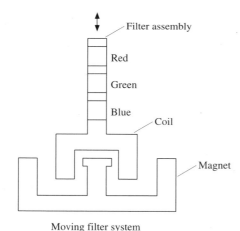

Moving filter system

9-22 Color scanning techniques.

ments must be used to set a threshold value for the scanning process. These adjustments restrict the amount of light that reach the scanner sensor.

When the amount of light is below the threshold value, the data bit is represented as a black dot. When the amount of light is above the threshold value, a white dot is produced. Settings can be saved and used again. Settings that are used often can be installed to automatically load each time the program is run.

Truvel flatbed scanner

The Truvel TZ-3BWC is a reflective flatbed scanner with resolution from 75 to 900 dpi (dots per inch) (Fig. 9-23). This type of scanner uses a moving tower to scan the copy that is placed on the bed. You can scan three-dimensional objects as well as flat documents and open books.

Table 9-2. Color scanners

Manufacturer's part number	Maximum resolution	Maximum gray-scale level	Color resolution	Scanning speed	Maximum image size	Interface
35 mm slide Barneyscan	1,000	256	8 × 3 bits/ pixel	3–4 min	35 mm slide	IBM PC Card
PC/AT Eikonix 1435	2,800	4,096	12 × 3 bits/ pixel	3 min × 24 mm	36 mm	IEEE-488
Flat-bed Sharp JX-300	300	256	8 × 3 bits/ pixel	45 ms/line max	8.5 × 11	IEEE-488
Sharp JX-450	300	256	8 × 3 bits/ pixel	30 ms/line max	11 × 17	IEEE-488
Overhead Truvel TZ-3BWC	300	256	8 × 3 bits/ pixel	0.1 in/s mono; 0.8/s color	14.5 × 24	SCSI

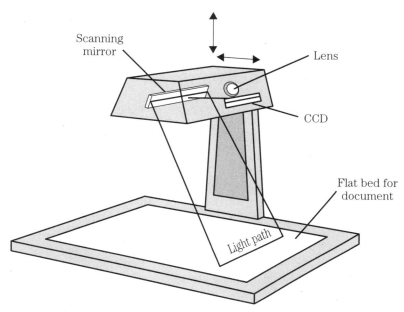

9-23 Flat-bed scanner showing lens, light sensor, and scanning mirror.

The TZ-3BWC scanner requires a tuning procedure before use. The tuning sets the aspect ratio so scans are not distorted or out of proportion. The tuning for black and white is easier than that required for color. The black-and-white tuning consists of a 15-minute warm-up followed by a calibration check. Color tuning requires the tower to make several dozen passes over the target card and takes about 45 minutes. The tuning information can be saved in a file and reused.

Making a scan

You begin the scanning process by selecting black and white or color. The scanner is then calibrated, the resolution is selected, and the scan area defined. Then the scan is performed and the file is saved.

A 15-minute timer is used to warm up the lights so that the scanning illumination is stable. The screen displays a timer showing the elapsed and remaining times. The type of scan (black-white or color) and the line art or gray-scale level are set from a menu.

The scanner is calibrated before scanning by placing a target card on the scan bed. The calibration procedure is similar to tuning. If the focus is out, then the tower needs adjusting. The scan bed is 12×17 inches, which is the maximum size of a scan. You must define the part of the scan bed area that will be active. A prescan can be used to confirm that the scanning area is correct.

Hand scanners

Hand scanners can quickly capture existing text and graphics. Low-cost, handheld scanners are popular for many tasks. An example of a typical hand scanner is ScanMan.

ScanMan

The ScanMan scanner has a 4-inch window, a control unit, and software. The scanning unit is just a little bigger than a mouse. The scanner operates like a desktop accessory so it is accessible from any application. Setup is done from a menu. One of the settings is an adjustable time out. The time out can be set from 1 to 30 seconds. The time out begins when the scanner is not moved after a scan has been started. The scanner width is 4.2 inches wide, and the maximum length depends on the available memory.

Scanning resolutions of 100, 200, 300, and 400 dpi are available. A mode switch allows you to scan either line art or photographs. The line-art setting is used for copy that contains no shades of gray and is made up of black lines on a white background. The photo mode provides shades of gray using groups of dots.

Different size dots are used to create the shades in this scanner. Other scanners might change the concentration of dots to create shades. In either case, the process is called *dithering*. After you set the scanner, you turn it on by selecting Scan from a menu. Place the scanner over the copy, press the Start button, and move the unit in a straight line over the image.

A scanned image can be modified by selecting the complete image or a portion of the image. This area can be moved, deleted, rotated, flipped, mirrored, or resized.

Complete Half-Page Scanner/400

The 400 is another low-cost hand scanner. The unit is about 5 inches long and about 5 inches wide. It can scan a 4-inch wide image up to 14 inches long at a resolution of 200 dpi. The scans can be pieced together to make full pages. The Complete Half-Page Scanner/400 comes with a special card that installs in an available expansion slot.

The scanning resolution can be set to 200, 300, or 400 dpi. The working or display resolution can be 75, 100, 150, 200, 300, or 400 dpi. Position the scanner over the start of the copy, press the scanner button, and move the scanner slowly down the surface of the copy. An image of the scan will appear on the display screen. If the scan is acceptable, it can be edited and saved. If not acceptable, it can be rejected, and the process can be repeated.

When you turn on the scanner, the screen is cleared and the CCD sensors come on. They will sense the light levels reflected from the paper as the scanner is moved over the image. Controls on the side of the scanner are used to adjust the gray scale and brightness. As the scanner is moved, the image begins to appear on the screen.

Troubleshooting hand scanners

If the scanner software does not work properly, the graphics adapter might be specified incorrectly. Check the documentation on your graphics adapter, then correct the configuration in the software installation. An incorrect configuration can also cause the screen to remain black when you start a scan.

If the light in the scanner does not go on when you try to scan, check the cable connection to the scanner interface card in the system unit and be sure the interface card is properly seated in the connector.

The scanner hardware interrupt might be conflicting with another device in the system, or the I/O address you chose in hardware configuration might not match the switch settings on the scanner card. In an IBM XT, some scanner cards will conflict if they are plugged into slot 8, and in a Compaq Deskpro, the same problem can occur with slot 1.

You will need to change either the scanner card switches or the software I/O address range so the settings match. You might also have to move the card into another slot.

If you press the scanner button and the system locks up and you get no response to keyboard inputs, the I/O address setting for the interface card probably conflicts with the setting for another card in the system. The DMA channel you are using might also conflict with another device in the system.

You will need to change the I/O address or DMA channel setting to another option in the configuration part of the software installation.

If the scanner light goes on, but the scanned image does not appear on the display. The following problems might exist:

1. You might not have rebooted your system after installation and saved the settings.
2. The I/O address you have selected might conflict with another interface card in the system.
3. You might have selected the wrong graphics adapter type.
4. The hardware interrupt you selected conflicts with another interface card in the system.
5. The interrupt you selected in the hardware configuration might conflict with the setting on the scanner interface card.

You can reboot the system with the key sequence:

<Ctrl><Alt><Del>

then try the scanner again. Change the I/O address setting on the scanner card switches or software to a different value. Specify the correct graphics adapter in the configuration section of software installation or change the hardware interrupt setting on the interface card switches or software to a different value. Change the software setting or the hardware setting so they match.

The scanner light might turn on but only the first inch of the scanned image appears at the bottom of the screen; then the display freezes. You might have selected the wrong DMA channel and will need to change to the other DMA channel.

If you press the scanner button and the system locks up with no response to a keyboard input, it could be the I/O address setting for the scanner conflicting with the setting for another interface card, or because the DMA channel you are using conflicts with another device in the system.

You might need to change the switch settings on the scanner interface card and change the software setting or reconfigure the other card. You might need to change the DMA setting in the configuration part of the software installation.

Imaging problems

If a black strip runs vertically through the scanned image on the screen, the card might not be completely plugged into the connector, the fingers on the interface card might be dirty, or the scanning window might be dirty. Press the card firmly into the connector by applying pressure to the middle and outer end of the card, not the metal connecting bracket. Remove the scanner card and use alcohol or a pink pencil eraser to clean off the fingers of the card. Use a soft cloth to wipe off the scan window on the bottom of the scanner.

When the scanned image is so large that only one side of it appears on the monitor, this is normal in some scanners at a resolution of 300 or 400 dpi. This situation is not an error. The image will be printed at the same size as the original, but when it is displayed, the dot-to-pixel ratio causes the higher resolution image to appear much larger on the screen.

If the display image seems distorted, it is usually because the monitor does not have equal resolution in the horizontal and vertical dimensions. This problem is due to the monitor characteristics. Print a copy of the image to see how it will look. If the image is displayed in reverse or upside down, you scanned the image in the wrong direction (right to left, or bottom to top) or you pushed it away from you instead of pulling it toward you.

The scanned image will look wavy on the screen if the scanner wobbled as you moved it across the image. You need to scan with a smooth, straight stroke, at a steady rate of about one inch per second. Try using a thick ruler or book as a guide. The scanned image will have sections that are distorted or missing if you scan the image too rapidly because data will be lost. Scan the image more slowly with a rate of about one inch per second. If the scanned image has dark or light blotches, the following problems might exist.

1. The dithering setting is wrong.
2. The original is not flat.
3. The surface of the original is reflective and too much light is bouncing back to the scanner sensors.

You can copy the original to produce a version with a surface that is not shiny; then scan the photocopy.

If the printed copy of the image is too large, you probably specified a different scanning resolution in the software then the resolution switch is set for. Change either the hardware or software setting for the scanning resolution and rescan. If the printed copy of the scanned image is too small, you probably scaled the image down before saving it. Scan the image again and save it at full size, or scale it down less.

The printed copy of the scanned image might be fuzzy for the following reasons.

1. The gray-scale switch is set for a dithering pattern that is not optimal.
2. The nature or quality of the original image makes it unsuitable for scanning.
3. The printer has lower resolution than the scanner and must eliminate dots in the process of printing.

You will need to position the switch to another setting or use an original with higher contrast, such as a line drawing instead of a halftone. You might also need to use a printer with higher resolution.

If lines that are straight in the original image look jagged in the printed copy of the scanned image, the scanner might have jiggled or did not move on a path that was parallel to these lines. The lines look jagged because of the limits of the scanner's resolution. The solution is to run the scanner along a book or thick ruler. You can also tape the original image on lined or graph paper to provide a reference for guidance. Use the pixel edit capability to touch up the scanned image.

The printed copy of the scanned image will be reversed if you scan the image in the wrong direction (right to left, or bottom to top). You can rotate the image (if it is not text) or scan again in the proper direction.

Areas that are red in the original image will appear white in the printed copy of the scanned image if the scanner uses red light to detect the image. You can photocopy the original to produce a monochrome version and then scan this image.

10

CHAPTER

Testing Techniques

An important part of testing is finding out what to do when the computer does not work. The goal is to know what went wrong and why. This testing or troubleshooting process requires some knowledge of the computer hardware; in addition, there are a number of available techniques for identifying and correcting problems. Problems related to component failure and methods for identifying them are discussed in this chapter.

The general troubleshooting tools available to identify and locate these problems will also be described, including voltmeters, continuity testers, logic probes, signature analyzers, oscilloscopes, and digital analyzers.

Common problems

Typical problems that can occur in a computer system include

1. Connection faults; open or short circuits
2. Component failure; wrong value or type of component installed
3. Software or disk media errors
4. Noise or interference errors

Figure 10-1 shows the distribution of failures in desktop PCs.

Connection failures

Connection faults can be detected by a resistance check from point to point in the system. Each wire or circuit track must provide a complete connection. Connection faults can be a troublesome problem, but they are easily solved although they take time (Fig. 10-2). Circuit paths can be buzz tested using a simple continuity checker that emits a tone for a connection and is quiet for an open (Fig. 10-3). Such a tester leaves both hands and eyes free to track the wiring.

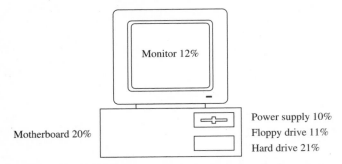

10-1 The components most likely to fail in desktop PCs. Component failure rates reported in response to an October 1993 and February 1994 *PC World* Reliability and Service Monitor survey.

Component failures

Components such as resistors, capacitors, inductors, transformers, transistors, diodes, integrated circuits, and connectors can all experience failures. Resistors can open, and capacitors can become leaky.

Each component can be assigned a figure of merit, known as its *MTBF* (meantime-between-failure). This prediction is a statistical one that estimates, in hours of use, how long an average part will last under typical operating conditions. Table 10-1 lists some typical values of failure rates for good-quality parts and connections. These numbers are often used to estimate those parts that are most likely to fail after a certain period of

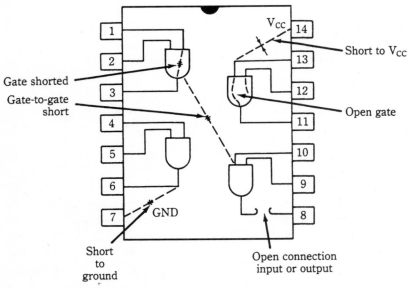

10-2 Typical failures in a small four-gate integrated circuit.

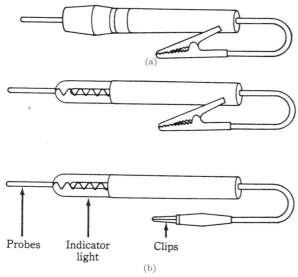

Probes   Indicator   Clips
light

10-3 Audible continuity testers operate with 1.5-Vdc AAA batteries and emit a 70-db audible signal for a connection of less than 150 Ω between the probe and clip ends (A). Continuity testers will test for the presence of voltage from 2 to 500 Vac or Vdc (B).

time. The failure rates are determined from test data and field return data on a large number of parts.

Some parts will last longer, on the average, than others. The values assume that all parts are properly installed and equipment is operated properly.

Because failure rates are defined as 1/MTBF (meantime-between-failures), knowing the failure rate of each component in the computer will provide the failure rate for the complete system. If the failure rates of all the components in the computer are summed, the result is the computer failure rate. The inverse of this number is the system meantime-between-failures.

Electronic components exhibit a bathtub type of lifetime characteristic, which means that many failures occur when the parts are new, most of the other failures occur when the parts are old, and fewer failures occur in between.

Initial burn-in tests are often used to root out most of the initial failures, which means the computer is left running for a specific period of time, often for several days. Most of the initial failures will occur during this time.

Software problems

Software can be the cause of problems. For example, there might be a routine in a program for restoring data to an internal register during a power interruption. Suppose a mistake was made when copying this program that restores conditions when power

Table 10-1. Average failure rates for typical computer parts and connections

Component or connection	Percent per 1000 hours failure rate
1. Capacitor	0.02
2. Connector contact	0.005
3. Diode	0.013
4. Integrated circuit	0.015
5. Quartz clock crystal	0.05
6. Resistor	0.002
7. Soldered joint	0.0002
8. Transformer	0.5
9. Transistor	0.04
10. Variable resistor	0.01

returns. If this routine does not work when the power fails, the unit might go into a foreign state.

Another potential problem could be an arithmetic calculation that causes an overflow and halt condition when an input value exceeds the capability of a register. The system might work well until this condition is exceeded. Then the system might stop mysteriously.

These types of software problems, or bugs, can be difficult to identify. You will usually have to contact the software vendor or developer and report this type of problem. They might have a patch or fix worked out already, or they might have advice on how to back away from the problem and how to avoid it in the future.

Noise problems

Noise can be a problem in circuits with low-level signals. Noise is generally kept under control by the circuit design but drift in components or a break in a shield or ground connection can cause a noise problem to surface.

When there is current in a wire, there is an electromagnetic field, which can be from power transformers, motors, and electrical wiring. When these fields become large enough to generate signals in wires or components, they become a problem. Even a small length of wire can act as an antenna for noise.

When integrated circuits switch, they can cause current changes in their power requirements. When many circuits switch at once and the system logic changes are not balanced, the power supply voltage changes might affect other parts of the circuit. Bypass capacitors are often installed near each integrated circuit to prevent this type of noise.

A noise spike can occur from turning on a piece of equipment on the same power line. In a system without noise filters, if that spike occurs at a critical time, data can be lost.

If two wires are close together, a pulse traveling along one induces a pulse in the other, due to transformer action between the two wires. This type of induced pulse might cause reflections in the wiring and toggle a logic circuit or cause read-write data errors. To prevent errors, twisted and shielded lines are often used (Fig. 10-4).

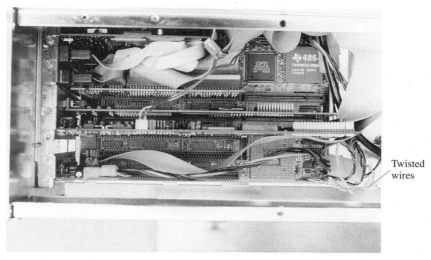

Twisted wires

10-4 Interior of 486 tower system showing twisted wires used to reduce noise problems.

The power supply is always filtered (Fig. 10-5) but there is always a small amount of 60-Hz ripple at the output of the filter. If this becomes large enough, it can affect the contents of memory and cause an improper read or write. The power supply will also have a small droop in voltage under heavy load before actual regulation occurs.

Troubleshooting tools

There are a number of tools you can use to find problems. When you have a problem with your computer, the first step is analyzing the symptoms of the problem. Analysis requires that you be able to indicate the circuits that are likely to contain the defect. To do this you need some tools that will tell you the condition of the circuit.

Typical hardware tools include a low-voltage continuity tester, a logic probe, and a VOM (volt-ohm-milliammeter). You can use the continuity tester to find shorts and opens. This type of tester is used when the computer is disconnected from power. The logic probe can be used to check high- and low-logic levels and pulses on the pins of the digital circuits. The logic probe is used when the computer is powered on. The VOM is an all-around instrument that can be used to measure voltages as well as resistance and continuity.

A common technique is to make some measurements with the test equipment and/or run some diagnostic tests. Based on the results of these hardware or software tests, you can make a replacement of the suspect part. For example, if the microprocessor is suspected from the results of software tests, you can unplug it and try a replacement.

However, not all chips are socketed, like the microprocessor, and a desoldering and resoldering operation is required. This operation can be time-consuming and unless you

Filter choke   Filter
capacitors

10-5 XT power supply. The filter components are located at the rear.

have experience working with small components, other procedures such as diagnostic software, are best used to determine the trouble. If you do suspect a socketed chip though, and have or can borrow a replacement, it can be worth a try. Many memory chips as well as arithmetic processors are socketed in addition to the microprocessor.

Continuity, logic, and voltage tests are usually simple but are time-consuming and might not be able to indicate some problems. Additional test equipment includes the following. A signal injection device called a *logic pulser* can be used, and another unit is the *current tracer.* Various types of oscilloscopes as well as frequency counters are available.

Diagnostic software is another important tool for testing. There are the simple programs on the ROMs in the computer or on a disk. There are specialized diagnostic programs for most parts of the computer. These programs usually exercise various circuits in the computer and if a circuit will not perform properly, a special trouble number or code will appear on the screen indicating the suspected part or circuit.

Following is a list of test equipment that can be used for troubleshooting.

Power on	*Power off*
Voltmeters	Ohmmeters and continuity testers
Oscilloscopes	
Frequency counters	
Logic probes and analyzers	

Digital signature analyzers

Signal and function generators

Automatic testers

Most of the troubleshooting tools that are available are designed for certain kinds of problems. You should know the limitations of these tools.

Open conductors and incorrect voltages are among the most common problems. They are also the easiest to detect. An ohmmeter can be used to check for opens and shorts and a DVM (digital voltmeter) or VOM can be used to check voltages and currents. If you have the proper schematics and the time, it is possible to make sure every component draws the right currents and receives the proper voltages. Figures 10-6 and 10-7 show several types of digital meters.

To measure a voltage, place a VOM in parallel with the circuit element. Consider the measurement of a power supply output voltage. The VOM can be used to measure such voltages, but it will not detect excessive ripple or noise riding on the power supply outputs. You must use an oscilloscope to measure this output. To measure a current, place the meter in series with the component, which means you must break the circuit. It is always possible that some connections can be made without cutting wires or traces. In the power supply example previously discussed, the meter can measure the voltage across the load and then by disconnecting the load and reconnecting it in series through the meter, the current can be measured. These measurements should be within the required tolerances. Incorrect values might indicate later problems.

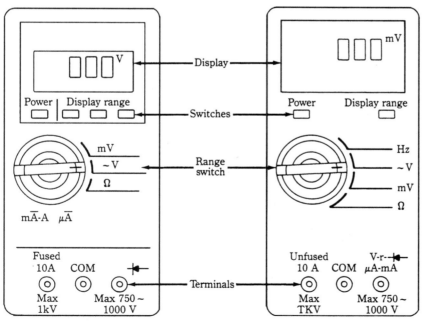

10-6 Two examples of handheld digital VOMs.

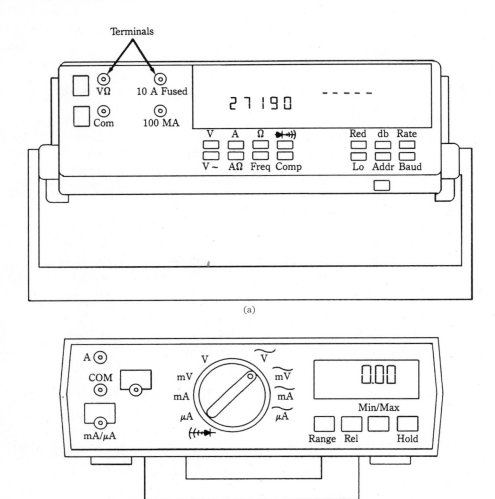

10-7 Bench-type digital multimeters. This model measures frequency to 1 MHz. The dc current accuracy is 0.05 percent, and a dual display allows two measurements from the same signal (A). This model will measure voltages from 100 to 1000 Vac or Vdc, currents from 0.1 to 10 A ac or dc, resistance from 0.1 to 10 Ω ac or dc, or resistance from 0.1 Ω to 10,000 MΩ with a relative mode that calculates the difference between the present reading and following readings (B).

Component substitution

Resistors, capacitors, diodes, and transistors can all be checked against known good devices. They can be measured with the DVM or VOM to determine if they are basically functional. For example, a good diode will have a low resistance in the forward direction, usually less than a few ohms. The resistance in the reverse direction should be much greater by a factor of 100 or 1000. A bipolar transistor can be quickly checked in much the same way, because it is made up of two diodes connected back to back.

Special test equipment is needed for diodes and transistors to measure the actual device characteristics (Fig. 10-8). Integrated circuits can be difficult to test without expensive equipment; instead consider having several of each device available to replace a device with a possible malfunction. Intermittent problems are often due to connector or solder-joint failures. You can check these connections first, before going on to other components.

Intermittent problems will generally require an oscilloscope (preferably with some storage capabilities) or a logic analyzer that stores logic states can be used. Static problems are easier to solve.

Voltmeters

The *voltmeter* is a versatile and convenient piece of equipment for checking computer circuits. But, be careful using the ohmmeter in the VOM to check resistance in the computer. The ohmmeter section uses batteries, and these batteries can apply a dangerous voltage to the component under test.

One cell might be used to provide 1.5 V for the low ranges, but the higher ranges could have several cells added in series to furnish 6 V. A small transistor junction could be destroyed by the higher voltage. The small transistors used in the more complex integrated circuits are even sensitive to the lower voltages, although most have some form of protection on the input. To avoid unneeded problems, use a low-voltage ohmmeter scale. The voltmeter function of the VOM does not furnish any voltage to components.

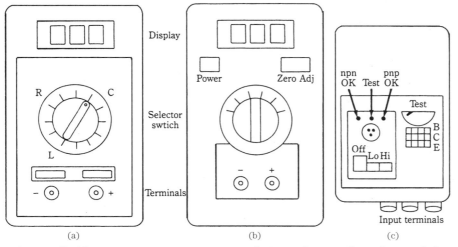

10-8 Handheld instruments. LCR meter with 3½-inch LCD (liquid crystal display) display. It measures capacitance from 200 pF (picofarads) to 2 mF (microfarads), resistance from 20 Ω to 20 MΩ (megohms), and inductance from 2 mH (millihenrys) to 200 H (henrys) (A). Digital capacitance meter with nine ranges from 200 pF to 20 mF, fuse protection to prevent damage from a charged capacitor and +0.5 percent accuracy (B). Transistor tester. A GO/NO-GO tester with LEDs to indicate NPN-OK or PNP-OK. It can be used to test FETs (field-effect transistors) and SCRs (silicon-controlled rectifiers) in or out of the circuit (C).

When the VOM is used to check the logic states, the negative lead is attached to ground volts and the logic states can be checked on a pin by pin basis. TTL (transistor-transistor logic) voltage levels are typical of those you will find. If you measure the voltage levels on TTL devices, a high can range from +2.5 to +5 V, and a low will range from 0 to +0.8 V.

A voltage between +0.8 and +2.5 V indicates a *tristate condition.* The test point is in a high-impedance state and a logic-probe LED would not be triggered by this voltage. In a CMOS (complementary metal-oxide semiconductor) chip, the voltage levels are similar but not the same as TTL. A high level is above +4.2 V. The low state is below +1.8 V. The range +1.8 to +4.2 V represents the tristate condition.

In both TTL and CMOS chips, the tristate condition could indicate a failure. Or the chip could be in a normal condition. If you find a tristate condition, check the part number and function of the chip to see if it represents a failure.

Continuity testing

A *resistance continuity tester* will light up or buzz if there is a complete circuit present. Many continuity testers use 1.5-V batteries that can damage a sensitive junction.

A low-voltage tester can be purchased or built using the circuit shown in Fig. 10-9. The circuit as well as the rest of the tester can be built from available parts or the circuit can be built or installed to modify an existing continuity tester.

If you are modifying an existing tester, the circuit can use the same batteries and bulb. The additional parts needed are the npn transistor and a CMOS comparator such as the CA3130. A few resistors are needed for biasing the circuit. The transistor switches the bulb on and off and the comparator is used to turn the transistor on and off.

The completed circuit delivers about 0.2 V to the component under test. This voltage is low enough to protect most sensitive junctions and is below the voltage necessary to turn most components on. If a device is switched on during testing, it could cause the computer circuits to change state and indicate a malfunction.

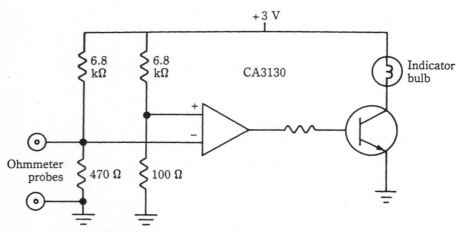

10-9 Voltage limiter for ohmmeter.

Logic pulsers

The *logic pulser* is a type of signal injection device. It has two connections that are made to +5 V and ground. The pulser is touched to a test point, and it has a button that can be used to send a pulse to the test point. The pulse voltage is usually high and pressing the button will cause it to go low and then high again. These pulses can be used to test digital circuits. A test point that is low can be switched to a high state.

Current tracers

The *current tracer* is a current probe device that you can use to detect an ac current. It has a small magnetic pickup coil in its tip, and when this coil is close to the magnetic field produced by an ac current, an indicator light glows. The tracer can be used to trace the path of or detect a continuous pulse train. The sensitivity is adjustable and the detectable current range is typically a few hundred microamps (a very dim indication) to a few milliamps that lights the bulb to full brightness. The current path must be in line with the pickup coil, if the current flow is at an angle of 90 degrees there will not be enough coupling for the pickup to work.

The current tracer is useful when a circuit has several parallel branches and a problem, such as a short, could be in any one of the branches (see Fig. 10-10). To isolate the branch with the short, you would need to disconnect each branch and test each separately. This procedure would require cutting or desoldering each branch to separate them and then resoldering to connect them.

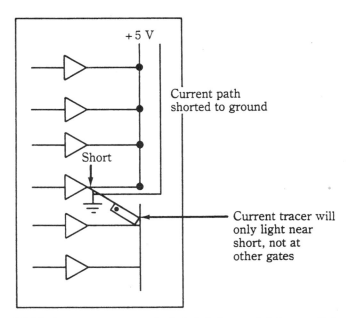

10-10 A current tracer is helpful for multiple parallel paths. You can use it to find the shorted point.

The current tracer allows you to test the current in each branch. A TTL high output would normally have a current of about 40 mA (microamps). A TTL low output will normally have a current of about 1.6 mA. If there is a short circuit, the high current would be about 55 mA (milliamps). The normal high current of 40 mA will not light the lamp of the current tracer, but a current of 55 mA would cause a very noticeable bright light. The current tracer can be quickly touched to the suspected circuits and the bright light will point to the faulty track or circuit.

Logic probes

The *logic probe* is designed to test digital circuits for the proper logic states. No actual measurement of voltage is made, the probe will indicate a high, low, or pulse condition. Switches usually are available to select CMOS or TTL levels and multiple or single pulses. Two leads are connected to power the probe. One connection goes to ground and the other goes to +5 V to provide the power for the indicator lights. The logic probe connection is made by touching the test probe to the IC under test.

The probe usually has at least three LEDs (light-emitting diodes) to indicate, high, low, and pulse conditions (Fig. 10-11). When only the high LED lights up, this indicates that there is a high at the test point. When only the low LED is lit, there is a low on the test point. In either case, there is no pulsing activity taking place, and the duration of the signal is constant at the test point.

If both the high and pulse LEDs are lit, this indicates that there is a series of positive pulses. When both the low and pulse LEDs are lit, it means there is a series of negative pulses. You also get an indication of the frequency. Usually, if the frequency of a square wave is less than 100 kHz, all three LEDs will light up. The square wave has a 50 percent duty cycle for both the high and low durations, so both LEDs light up. When one state (high or low) has a larger duration, then the light for that state will light up. When the frequency is above a 100-kHz square wave, only the pulse LED will light.

Logic probes are a useful tool for checking logic levels on integrated circuits and they are helpful in isolating static or steady conditions. A quick indication is possible and it will show that a signal is a 0, 1, or undetermined. The undetermined state usually indicates a problem unless it is a tristate floating output as discussed. Figure 10-12 shows several types of logic probes as well as a logic pulser and a clip-on logic monitor. The VOM and logic probe do not indicate time, so they are of limited use for dynamic problems. What is needed are devices that can indicate that the timing is correct.

The oscilloscope

To obtain timing information, an *oscilloscope* can be used. By using one or more traces, critical events can be measured as a function of time. A general-purpose oscilloscope has a horizontal frequency range of about 100 kHz. With this range, the oscilloscope can be used to view and measure frequencies up to this range. The minimum clock frequency of an IBM PC is 4.77 MHz, so one cycle of the clock cannot be viewed. You would see 47.7 complete cycles if the maximum frequency of the oscilloscope is 100 kHz. This image would appear as an envelope (Fig. 10-13) and you would not be able to recognize individual cycles, but you would know that the clock is running.

LED states			Signal sensed	Explanation
high	low	pulse		
○	○	○	No signal	Open circuit three-state
✸	○	○	5 V ⌐ ¯ ⌐ ¯ 1 0 V	High level
○	✸	○	5 V ⌐ ¯ 0 0 V ⌐ ¯	Low level
✸	○	✸	⌐‖‖‖‖ 1	Negative pulses from high level
○	✸	✸	‖‖‖‖ 0	Positive pulses from low level
○	○	✸	⊓⊔⊓⊔⊓⊔	Square wave greater than 100 kHz
✸	✸	✸	⊓⊔⊓⊔⊓	Square wave less than 100 kHz

10-11 Typical logic probe signal sensing states.

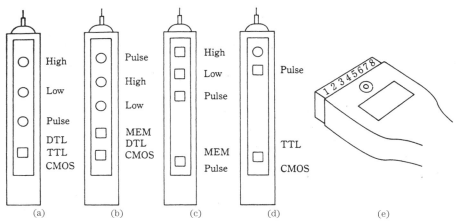

10-12 Logic probes and pulsers. 50 ns to 10 MHz (A). 50 ns to 35 MHz (B). ECL (emitter-collector logic) 3 ns to 100 MHz (C). Logic pulser 100-Hz train; 100 mA, 1 μs for TTL, 10 μs for CMOS (D). Clip-on logic monitor; 16 channels for 8-, 14-, or 16-pin ICs, 16 LED light for high logic levels (E).

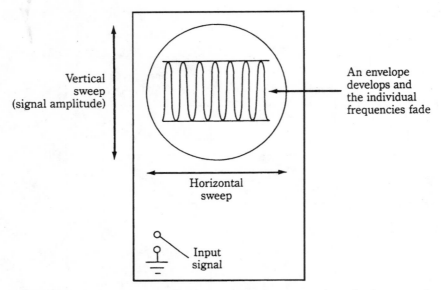

10-13 If the vertical input frequency is much greater than the horizontal sweep, the individual frequencies will be lost with only the outside envelope left.

In addition to the clock circuit, other signals can be tested with a general-purpose oscilloscope, such as the video signals in the video circuits. Figure 10-14 shows how oscilloscopes are used to measure the signals of these and other circuits. Figure 10-15 shows a handheld unit that functions as an oscilloscope, multimeter, and frequency counter.

The multitrace oscilloscope can be used to check the timing between critical chips such as the microprocessor and the memory, using a timing diagram such as the one shown in Fig. 10-16.

In microcomputer systems, you might need to observe events as short as 10 ns. A 10-ns square wave will be filtered and will look like a sine wave on a 10-MHz oscilloscope. A unit with a 50- or 100-MHz bandwidth is needed to see these faster events clearly.

Transitions from one logic level to the other would generally occur in less than 1 ms to avoid noise problems. An oscilloscope can be used to indicate if a logic level error is present.

Such a measurement, along with the knowledge of the correct logic timing, will indicate to the troubleshooter that a line is at fault. By observing chip-select, control, and bus lines with an oscilloscope, loading, timing, and noise problems can be found. The logic levels should fall between accepted limits; voltage levels that fall between states indicate problems.

Frequency counters

You can use a *frequency counter* to measure the actual frequency of the clock or the frequency of circuits driven by the clock. This measurement is possible with a magnetic pickup loop or a direct physical connection. The advantage of using a magnetic

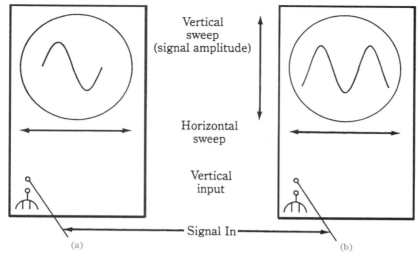

Vertical
sweep
(signal amplitude)

Horizontal
sweep

Vertical
input

Signal In

(a) (b)

10-14 Using a scope to check signal amplitude and frequency. Horizontal same as vertical (A). Horizontal one-half vertical (B).

loop is that loading effects on the circuits are minimized or eliminated. Capacitive coupling can also be used to reduce loading effects.

You can move the loop close to the clock-generating crystal quickly and measure the crystal frequency. A defective crystal or frequency-determining circuit can be found in this way.

10-15 A combination oscilloscope, multimeter, and frequency counter in a handheld unit.

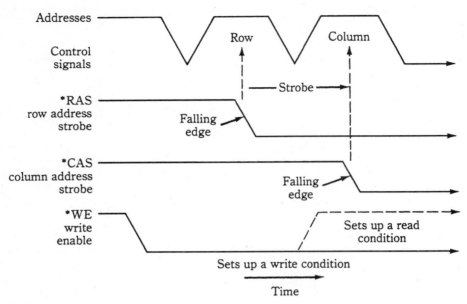

10-16 Timing diagram for 4164 control signals. The falling edges of the CAS signals are timed to strobe the row and column addresses. The *WE signal will set up either a read or a write condition as shown.

Logic-state measurement

Individual system timing and system logic levels might appear to be correct when observing a single bit or line or pair of lines, but in some cases a number of lines might need to be observed at the same instant in time. Logic analyzers that are sometimes called *digital-domain analyzers* are used for this test. These instruments allow the observation of up to 32 lines simultaneously. They can generally display these bits in binary, octal, hexadecimal, or in the form of conventional oscilloscope traces. The display can be triggered when a given combination of bits occurs.

State analyzers can store a number of clock cycles, and they are able to display several sets of signals before and after the trigger set. Each set of signals in time is known as a *state*.

The available analyzers are designed to provide two types of information—those that provide mostly timing information and those that provide mostly logic state information. The timing information analyzers are configured like multichannel oscilloscopes. These devices are most useful where logic spikes, noise, or logic-level problems are to be investigated.

Signature analyzers

Signature analyzers are based on storing repetitive sequences of signal values in a recirculating shift register. The values are clocked into a display each time around. The sequence of values will generally have a unique signature unless similar points or lines are being measured.

Each node in a system will have its own signature when it is working properly. It will also have a special signature for each possible problem. By using fault-tree methods, developed by using the signature analyzer, you can debug faulty equipment quickly, down to the faulty component. It will not find software problems or the cause of intermittent failures in a system. A typical unit is the HP 5004A Signature Analyzer.

Testing problems

An example of improper testing is passing too much current through a sensitive IC, which can cause damage such as an open. Applying too much voltage to a device can cause arcing and eventual breakdown. Every device has its limits.

Another problem is the loading effect on a single output line on an IC. A parameter drift can cause the system to read or write improper data values on an intermittent basis, which might depend on temperature.

Other subtle errors include timing problems of a particular part. Suppose the address for a particular memory part must be stable for 30 ns. If the address gated to this memory part must be stable for 30 ns before the data and write pulses arrive and this is not true any longer, the system timing will be incorrect.

Some problems require specialized equipment for quickly completing the troubleshooting effort, but a VOM and oscilloscope can be used for most problems if time is not as critical.

Intermittent problems require that the suspect components or operations be exercised. The system can be operated at different temperatures to localize sensitive components. You can sometimes use a can of freeze spray and a heat lamp to locate temperature sensitive problems. Locate the problems by heating and cooling the suspected parts.

Comparison tests

In this method, a device or board under test is compared to a known good device or good board. They share the same common input, and outputs are compared. This method is a hardware method, and the required tools have been discussed. The underlying principle of this testing technique is to compare an existing board, component, or system to a properly functioning unit.

The problem is to know how a proper unit functions and how to implement a reasonable procedure for performing the comparison in a systematic manner. Other problems include making the measurements themselves and recording a time history of these measurements for the comparison. The basic test instruments and techniques needed for performing such comparisons have already been described.

Components, software, and noise can sometimes cause problems to occur. Figure 10-17 describes some basic methods of approaching typical related problems. The equipment needed for troubleshooting has been discussed and several examples have been given.

Future hardware tools will be oriented toward the more specialized types of testers or analyzers. A large number of logic-state, trace, and test capabilities, as well as the

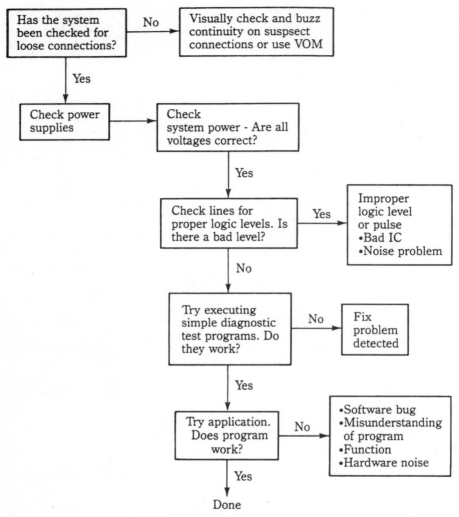

10-17 Troubleshooting flowchart.

ability to display all of the various states of computer operations, will be features of the newer test units. Figures 10-18 to 10-21 show examples of specialized testers.

Printed circuit board repair

Today's printed circuit boards are manufactured in a highly automated factory. The printed circuit board starts as a laminated fiberglass or plastic fiber board with a copper foil layer on both sides. A circuit connection pattern is designed for the particular part layout.

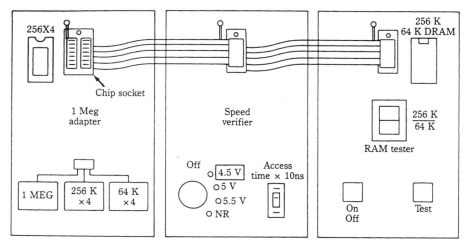

10-18 A portable DRAM chip tester. It has an 8088 microprocessor that writes, reads, and refreshes each memory cell at least four times. It has current limiters that protect the chip and prevent damage if the chip is inserted backward. The speed verifier measures the chip's access time and can be used to find a slow chip that could be causing a problem. An autoloop test can be used for finding intermittent problems.

This pattern is used to control an etching solution that removes the copper that is not needed for the desired connections. Components such as the common dual inline packages will require holes through the board so the pins can be soldered to the copper foil tracks. Surface-mount devices use solder pads so the SMD legs can be soldered to the pads. Factory robotics can produce completed printed circuit boards with very small pin-to-pin spacings. The specialized equipment used can solder small pins quickly. If a chip fails, then you must desolder the package and resolder a new one in place. Unless you have experience with close tolerance ICs, the replacement of an IC can seem to be a difficult job. However, it is not so important that your replacement have the physical appearance of the original manufactured connections. Complete all the connections properly without disturbing nearby connections and components.

Chip packages

The printed circuit board will hold the IC chips that make up the bulk components. However, there are usually other support components such as capacitors, switches, and jumpers. The larger of these are relatively easy to desolder, replace, and resolder. This ease is especially true of those components with only a few connections such as capacitors. IC chips are more difficult to replace unless they are socketed. These chips usually have many pins, and the pins are close together.

DIPs

Most older PCs used ICs with a dual inline package. The pins on the DIP package are placed in holes in the circuit board. Then the pins are soldered to the circuit tracks on the board.

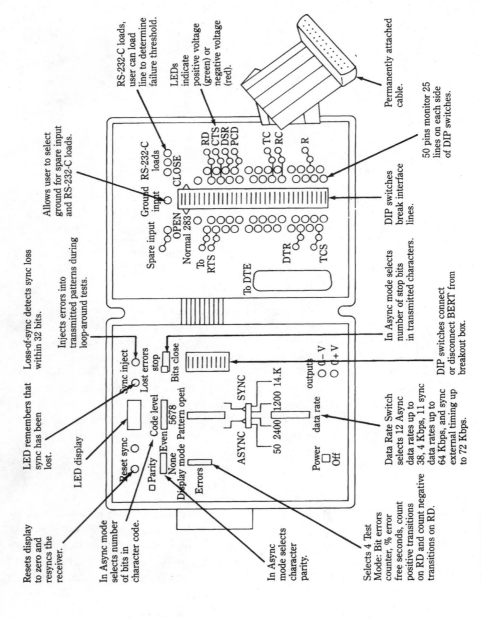

Resets display to zero and resyncs the receiver.

LED remembers that sync has been lost.

Loss-of-sync detects sync loss within 32 bits.

Injects errors into transmitted patterns during loop-around tests.

In Async mode selects number of bits in character code.

LED display

Allows user to select ground for spare input and RS-232-C loads.

RS-232-C loads, user can load line to determine failure threshold.

LEDs indicate positive voltage (green) or negative voltage (red).

Permanently attached cable.

50 pins monitor 25 lines on each side of DIP switches.

DIP switches break interface lines.

In Async mode selects number of stop bits in transmitted characters.

DIP switches connect or disconnect BERT from breakout box.

In Async mode selects character parity.

Data Rate Switch selects 12 Async data rates up to 38, 4 Kbps, 11 sync data rates up to 64 Kbps, and sync external timing up to 72 Kbps.

Selects 4 Test Mode: Bit errors counter, % error free seconds, count positive transitions on RD and count negative transitions on RD.

10-19 RS-232 tester.

430

10-20 32-bit memory tester with 30/72-pin test head.

The pins are numbered counterclockwise, from the top, as shown in Fig. 10-22. The marks might be a half circle or dot indentation or a painted dot. Plastic DIPs are usually found in PCs. The pins are 0.1 inch apart. The plastic DIP usually has tin-plated pins and 60/40 solder works well.

SMDs

Surface-mount devices use solder pads. Chips can be mounted on both sides of the board. The SMD package is smaller because four sides can have pins. The SMD can be made 40 to 60 percent smaller in surface area than a DIP containing the same chip. One type of SMD is called the CCP (chip-carrier package). These devices use pins that are bent over and resemble feet. These feet are designed to be soldered to pads.

When the boards are manufactured, the feet are positioned over the pads and the board is heated, the solder melts and the feet become attached to the pads. The connection provides both a physical and electrical bond. The surface-mount technology is both cheaper and faster to manufacture than using DIPs. Two of the SMD foot styles used include the gull-wing and J-shape shown in Figs. 10-23 and 10-24. An SMD board will cost about ½ that of a DIP board, but it is harder to repair. The distance between pins are tighter and the solder pads are harder to get to. However, you can test and replace SMDs with the proper tools and techniques.

Another type of SMD is the COB (chip on board). These assemblies are not replaceable except with factory equipment. The COB chip is wired and bonded directly to the board using a type of foil for connections. The chips and leads are all part of the board assembly. A plastic sealant is molded over the chips and leads for protection. Once the assembly is complete, you can remove the chip without damaging it.

Chip replacement

Integrated circuit chips (Fig. 10-25) are harder to troubleshoot and repair than the discrete components on the print board. The larger components such as vacuum transistors, diodes, capacitors and resistors are larger and easier to test and replace. When

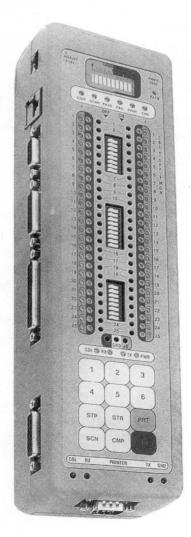

10-21 Cable breakout box and monitor for fiber-optic and Ethernet testing.

these components are shrunk to microscopic size and put on a silicon chip, they can have the same types of electrical shorts, opens, and leaks. When one of these chip components fail, the complete chip must be replaced.

If the package is socketed (Fig. 10-26), the replacement is simple. You must pull the bad chip out of its socket and install a new one. Even a DIP with a low pin count that is soldered through holes in the printed circuit board is not too difficult. You can test this type of chip on a pin-by-pin basis with a logic probe, VOM, or oscilloscope.

Soldering

To replace a small DIP, use a low-wattage soldering iron with a solder sucker as shown in Fig. 10-27. The solder sucker has a small rubber bulb that is used to take up

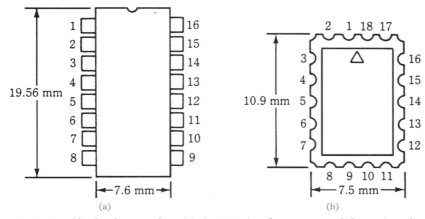

10-22 DIP (dual inline package) (A). SMD (surface-mounted device) package (B).

melted solder. This type of iron is designed for desoldering chips; for resoldering you will need a regular low-wattage iron.

When desoldering the DIP, heat the iron and squeeze the bulb while you hold the tip of the hot iron on the bottom of the board under the first plated through pin. It helps to have a bright light on the bottom of the board. Hold the bulb closed while the solder melts. When the solder is liquid, then release the bulb. The solder at the heat pin is sucked into the bulb. Remove solder from the bulb by squeezing it. Repeat the process until all the pins are free and the chip can be removed. If there is still some solder in the holes, clear it using a toothpick to open the holes.

You can install chips backward, so be sure you install the new chip with the marker in the correct orientation. Use a regular iron of 30 W or less for resoldering. Use a small-diameter solder because only a spot of solder is needed for each pin. The solder must not drip because it could form shorts across circuit tracks.

Changing low–pin count DIPs does not take too long but the higher–pin count chips can become tedious. Desoldering equipment with vacuum pumps and hollow tip irons are also available. These devices prevent damage because some pins require repeated heating and sucking efforts to free the pin. Sometimes you must pick at the solder to remove it. Picking might create additional problems from damage to the printed circuit board. A vacuum desoldering system will usually prevent these problems.

Surface-mount device replacement

Replacing an SMD is more difficult than replacing DIPs because SMDs are soldered to only one side of the circuit board. The pads on the circuit board are slightly larger than the foot for the SMD pin. These pads are sometimes called *footprints*. During the manufacturing process, each pad has a layer of solder paste applied, using a stencil or screen. You can use a hand syringe to apply solder paste during a chip replacement. The paste aids in the soldering process by allowing a smooth flow of solder as it holds the chip in place.

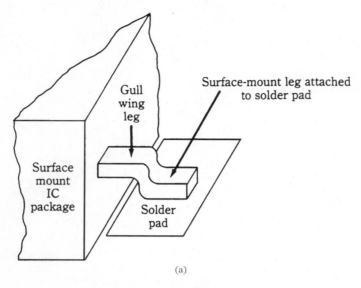

(a)

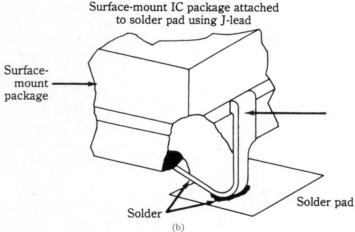

(b)

10-23 Gull-wing legs on surface-mounted packages are representative of the different foot sizes and shapes. This type is called the gull-wing leg style because of its shape (A). Another leg shape for an SMD is the J-lead. The solder tends to accumulate in the hook of the leg. This provides a stronger solder joint (B).

During manufacture, the heating is done in an oven. If chips need to be replaced, special soldering irons are used that heat all the pins on a chip at the same time. These irons also have grippers to hold the chip. A cleaning solvent is needed to remove solder flux residues.

You can desolder SMDs using pieces of solder braid or wick with a fine-tipped low-wattage iron. Dip the solder braid in rosin and place it across the pins on one of the four

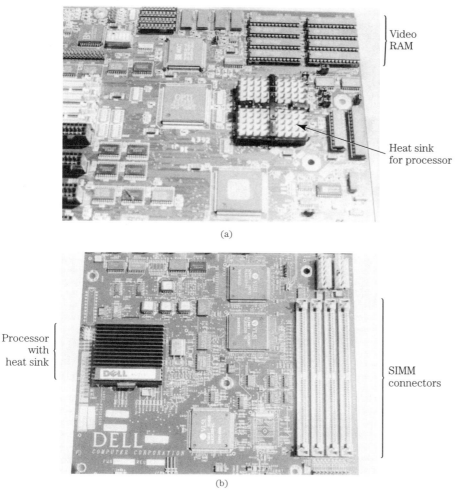

Video RAM

Heat sink for processor

(a)

Processor with heat sink

SIMM connectors

(b)

10-24 Sections of 486 boards showing SMDs, processor video memory, and SIMM connectors. A 486 board showing SMDs, processor, video RAM, and heat sink for 486 (A). A 486 board showing SMDs, processor, and SIMM connectors (B).

sides of the chip. When the braid is heated, it will tend to melt the solder holding the pins. The melted solder will be attracted to the braid by capillary action. Rubbing the braid over the pins also helps. When the braid has filled with solder, cut the end off and use a new section of braid.

When most of the solder has been removed, the pins can be heated with the iron and separated from the pads using a pick—one pin at a time until you can lift the chip from the board.

To install a replacement SMD, you can apply the solder paste with a hand syringe on the pads. Then place the new chip on the pads and solder the corner pins first. The corner pins will hold the chip while you solder the other pins.

10-25 A printed circuit board. The integrated circuit chips are labeled with U, and the capacitors next to them are labeled C and used for filtering.

Static electricity

ESD (electrostatic discharge) is a concern whenever chips are handled. The problem is the small size of the MOS transistors used in many ICs. The insulator that protects these is very thin because of the method of constructing these devices. Static discharge can break down these insulators and cause damage to the small devices. In most high-density chips such as RAMs, the insulator protects very small current paths on the silicon chip. There are thousands of these paths on the silicon chip, and damage to any one of them means a functional failure. Precautions are necessary to protect these chips from static electricity.

When the RAM chips had only a few thousand transistors, the spacing between the leads of the transistors was about five times as wide as it is today. The lead spacing has

10-26 The 8088 microprocessor is socketed, and replacement chips are available for quick substitution.

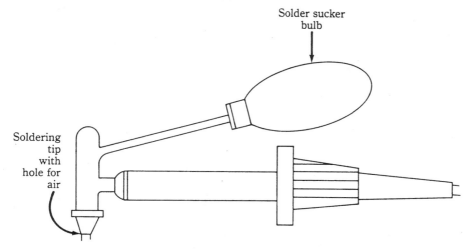

10-27 A rubber bulb is available with a special hollow soldering tip for desoldering DIP packages. When the bulb is released, some of the melted solder will be vacuumed into the hole in the iron.

been reduced and the leads themselves are much smaller. This metallization is vulnerable to static electric currents.

Because these chips are sensitive to ESD, take care when replacing chips. Handling techniques have been developed over time. The human body is capable of providing several hundred volts of static electricity. When the air is humid, this potential is lower and might only be about 100 V because of leakage. When the air is drier, there is less leakage and the potential will build up as you move around. You can build up a static charge of almost 1000 volts under the right conditions. If this charge is passed on to a high-density MOS device, some damage is possible if the energy is large enough. Most devices have some type of protection on their input leads, but the protection can be lost if the energy of the static charge is greater than the burnout energy of the protection devices. The energy that is left over will then burn out functional devices inside the chip.

When the chip is connected to other circuits on the printed circuit board, its pins are connected to ground paths and other low-impedance paths. The major danger exists when it is disconnected and being handled.

Grounding techniques

Before you handle a chip, take precautions to lower any static charge on your body. You must connect your body to an earth ground such as a grounded computer chassis. The work table should also be connected to ground.

A number of products are available for static protection. The wrist strap goes around your wrist and carries away the electrostatic charge before it builds up (Fig. 10-28). These lightweight wrist straps have a coiled cord that acts as the grounding cable and connects to earth ground.

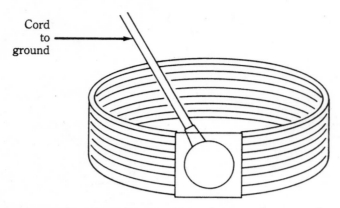

10-28 Static control wrist straps fit around your wrist and have a grounding cord. Some units use a 1-MΩ resistor to prevent the current from exceeding 0.5 mA for voltages to 220 Vac.

Always use the grounding bracelet on the same hand that you use to hold the probe or soldering iron. The closer the strap is to the hand that works on the chips, the safer the chips will be.

Because you are now grounded to earth, you have to be especially careful not to touch any electrical lines. If that should happen, you would provide a short circuit path to ground!

Two things are done to reduce this danger. The outside of the wrist strap is insulated and a 1-MW resistor is connected in series with the ground line at the wrist-strap connection. This resistor prevents the current through the ground line from exceeding 0.5 mA for voltages up to 220 V.

Table and floor mats (Fig. 10-29) are available in a semiconductive vinyl. The semiconductive material provides discharging for static effects but prevents shorting of circuit board pins. The floor mat works best for leather-soled shoes. Other types of soles will be insulated from the mat.

Observe the following guidelines when you work on printed circuit boards.

1. Never insert or remove a device unless all power to the circuits is removed. Remove the power plug so there can be no question of electrical power removal.
2. Keep chips in conductive foam pads. The pads will keep the pins shorted together.
3. Handle the chip only with the hand that has the ground strap.
4. Ground tools that are used to touch the chip just before they make contact. This precaution applies to chip pullers and inserters, pliers, and solder picks.
5. The soldering iron should have its tip grounded. Remove the power plug when solder is touched to the iron and when the iron touches the pins of the chip. Removing the plug prevents any possibility of damage to the chip from line power.

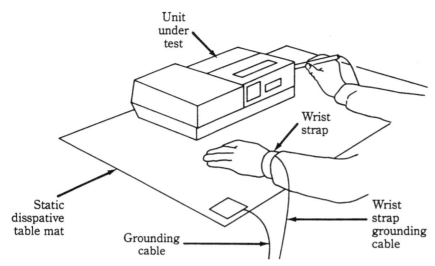

10-29 Static electricity can be shorted to ground using a static mat and a wrist strap to drain the static charges to ground.

Never handle an IC unless you are properly grounded, especially when the ambient humidity is low. A static charge, such as the one generated by walking on carpeting on a dry day, can destroy many MOS chips.

Do not install a board in the computer unless power is off and you have waited at least 15 seconds for all charges to be dissipated.

Finally, do not trust specified voltages and currents; always measure them.

Service facilities

The testing of printed circuit boards and replacing defective components can be a difficult job that requires special equipment. Technical service firms are available that specialize in the repair of the various computer parts. These facilities usually have an inventory of good circuit boards that they will swap with you or will repair if they do not have the right board in stock.

Service facilities are equipped with the required service tools in addition to the stock of good printed circuit boards for the computers they service. The boards can range from printer boards with a few chips to system or motherboards with hundreds of chips.

The specialized equipment and training allows these facilities to quickly troubleshoot and repair printed circuit boards. They are able to desolder and then resolder large pin count chips in DIP and SMD packages.

Another type of service that is available is field service. When a computer system breaks down, a field technician is dispatched to the computer site to analyze the trouble. The technician is usually able to isolate the problem to a single printed circuit board. Once the suspect printed circuit board is identified, the technician removes the suspect board and replaces it with a good board. If the trouble was in the suspected board, the computer is repaired and the technician goes on to the next service call.

Later, a technician will check out the board using the required servicing equipment. The bad component is found and replaced. The system is then tested and given a final okay.

If you can determine that board or section of the computer is faulty, you are essentially doing the work of a field technician. You could remove the board or disk drive and take or send it to a service facility. They might be able to do the repair while you wait or perhaps service it in the next day or two. Some will give you an allowance for your defective unit and furnish a rebuilt unit. This procedure is often followed for disk drives.

Following is a list of many service firms and their specialities.

ACI
550 E. Thornton Parkway, Suite 100
Denver, CO 80229
1-800-231-0743
Floppy drives, monitors, print heads

AEG Olympia, Inc.
1255 Viceroy Dr.
Dallas, TX 75247
(214) 630-4608
Monitors

BL Memories
17070 Royal View Rd.
Hacienda Heights, CA 91745
(818) 913-1851
Disk drives

CAP Industries, Inc.
600 Ansin Blvd.
Hallandale, FL 33009
Boards, printers

Capital Computer Solutions, Inc.
50210 W. Pontiac Trail
Wixom, MI 48393
(313) 624-3260
Keyboards, printers

CTS Services, Inc.
31 Hayward St.
Franklin, MA 02038
(508) 528-7720
Monitors

Decision Data
One Progress Ave.
Horsham, PA 19044
(800) 633-2863
Printers

Depot II
2968 W. Ina Rd., #167
Tucson, AZ 85741
1-800-345-9331
Monitors

Independent Computer Support Services
400 Devon Park Dr.
Wayne, PA 19087
(215) 687-0900
Monitors, printers, tape drives

Intron Corporation
7420 Fullerton Rd., Suite 114
Springfield, VA 22153
(703) 569-1500
Monitors

Maxdata Technologies, Inc.
8100 Remmet Ave., #9
Canoga Park, CA 91304
(818) 702-8836
Floppy drives, tape drives

MicroLogic Systems, Inc.
5111 Troup Hwy, #105
Tyler, TX 75707
(903) 561-0007
Printers

Midwest Computer Support
1946 N. 13th St.
Toledo, Ohio 43624
(419) 259-2600
Hard drives, monitors, printers

OMNI CEO, Inc.
70 Industrial Ave., E.
Lowell, MA 01852-9923
(508) 937-5004
Keyboards

PTS Electronics Corporation
5233 S. Hwy. 37
Bloomington, IN 47401
1-800-333-7871
Monitors

Quality High-Tech Services, Inc.
11865 Forestgate Dr.
Dallas, TX 75243
(214) 231-6696
Monitors, printers

Reset
49 Strathearn Pl.
Simi Valley, CA 93065
(805) 584-4900
Disk drives, printers

Stingray
607 Swan Dr.
P.O. Box 558
Smyma, TN 37167
1-800-467-0242
Printers

Technical Equipment Services
83 Harwood Ave.
Littleton, MA 01460
(508) 486-0600
Keyboards

Texas Computer Brokers
1305 Summit Station 10
Plano, TX 75014
(214) 881-0777
Monitors, printers

Tech Zam
7745 Alabama Ave., Unit #8
Canoga Park, CA 91304
(818) 887-3046
Hard drives

URS Information Systems, Inc.
44 Concord St.
Wingmington, MA 01887
(508) 657-6100
Monitors, printers

Zenith Data Systems
611 Development Blvd.
Amery, WI 54001
(715) 268-8106
Monitors, printers

Most service outlets try to have a quick turnaround time so you can get your system back running quickly. With a little knowledge and some basic tools, you can usually get the faulty components out and back in without much trouble.

In-circuit component testers

In-circuit component testers are general-purpose troubleshooting test instruments. These testers are designed to evaluate and visually compare digital, analog, and hybrid semiconductor devices and reactive components in or out of the circuit with the power off. They can be used to detect leakage problems and bonding problems, shorts, opens, and other failure modes. In many cases, these problems can be the cause of intermittent failures.

The operating principles used are similar to those used in a semiconductor curve tracer. A current-limited sine wave voltage is injected across the two points of the device under test. The resulting signature is displayed as a current and voltage trace on the built-in CRT display (Fig. 10-30). The display indicates the dynamic conditions of the semiconductor junction.

A well-defined junction appears as a straight line that indicates a normal semiconductor. Poorly defined junctions show up as curved lines and indicate excessive leakage. These displays represent the condition of the semiconductor and can be used to find defective devices as well as marginal components.

A comparison mode can be used that alternately displays CRT signatures of both a unit under test and a known good board or component, allowing you to identify defective boards and troubleshoot to the component level. When you have identified a defective component, use the tester to verify if the replacement component is good.

You can test the following components:

- *Diodes.* General-purpose, zener, tunnel, varactor, and high-voltage
- *Transistors.* npn and pnp bipolar, Darlington, JFET (junction field-effect transistor), MOSFET, (metal-oxide semiconductor field-effect transistor), and unijunction
- *Thyristors.* SCR, SGS, GCS, triac, and diac

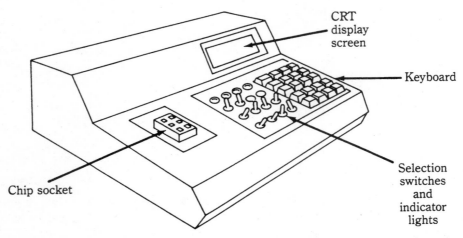

10-30 An in-circuit tester can be programmed with a device interface such as the one shown. It has component and chip sockets, a keyboard, and control panel.

- *Optoelectronic devices.* LEDs, LED displays, photo transistors, and optocouplers
- *Integrated circuits.* Digital, CMOS, NMOS, PMOS, and TTL
- *Analog operational amplifiers, voltage regulators, and timers*

Component switching

An interface unit is also available for switching circuit boards and components. A set of IC clips are used to route the signals from both the board being tested and a known good board through an automatic switch. The rate at which the signals are compared on the display are controlled by the interface unit.

You can also use the switching unit with general-purpose test equipment for power-on troubleshooting. This tester can be used to make voltage, signal level, resistance, or other measurements of powered circuits and components.

IC sockets on the unit allow A/B comparisons of 40-pin DIP packages, allowing pin-for-pin comparisons for replacing ICs.

Power supply testers

Power supply testers monitor the voltage of a suspect dc power supply. It can aid the troubleshooting process by isolating a problem to either the power supply or the system under power. It can be used to detect and store out of range conditions and provides a test vehicle to see whether or not a power supply has stayed within specifications over a period of time. This information can then be checked against any intermittent failures that might have occurred in the system under power, replacing the need for chart recorders or digital storage scopes.

Power problems

PC downtime can be caused by a number of factors. The reliability of hardware and the quality of software are certainly key to keeping a PC functioning and available. But another important, yet often neglected, factor is the quality and reliability of the computer's electrical power supply.

Although the quality of the hardware and software are controlled to a large extent by the manufacturing process and correct usage of the products, the quality of the electrical supply depends on many factors that are often beyond your control.

Although high-quality electric power might be generated by the utility, it can be corrupted by special circumstances such as lightning or grid switching by the utility during high-demand peak periods. These factors interrupt the continuous flow of power, which means the power that reaches a computer might not always meet the electrical requirements of the system.

Additional power contamination might be created by influences internal to the building. When other equipment is turned on, the starting inrush power requirements can temporarily cause transient voltages and surges resulting in data errors and equipment damage.

Most studies show that power disturbances occur on the average of two times a week for a typical commercial facility and most disturbances are generated within the building.

Power-line disturbances

The following types of disturbances have been found to cause problems by both IBM and Bell Labs.

1. *Sags.* Sags are cycle-to-cycle decreases in the power-line voltage below 80 percent of the nominal value usually lasting less than several seconds. Sags occur frequently at the wall-socket level and account for the majority of total power-line disturbances. These disturbances are a major cause of data loss.
2. *Surges.* Surges are cycle-to-cycle increases in the power-line voltage above 110 percent of the nominal value lasting less than several seconds. Surges cause most of the hardware damage in computers.
3. *Outages.* An outage results in a zero-voltage condition. Outages account for about 15 percent of the total number of power-line disturbances that occur at the wall-socket level.
4. *Oscillations.* Oscillations are fluctuations also known as *noise.* Oscillations usually decay within a cycle of line voltage and have a frequency range from 400 Hz to 5 kHz.
5. *Spikes.* Spikes are also known as impulses and show up as overvoltages superimposed on the line voltage. They can last between 0.05 and 100 μs.

Power transients can force too much power into the computer or deprive the computer of the necessary power. The first type of transients includes surges and spikes, and the second type includes sags, brownouts, and blackouts. Because spikes are rapid excursions of voltage with a large amplitude, they can propagate through the system and cause sensitive components to break down. See Fig. 10-31 for typical power-line problems.

Power sags

All disturbances can cause malfunctions in computers. Power disturbances can affect a system differently depending on their duration and which part of the system was being used when the disturbance occurred. Sags can result in two types of problems in computers, depending on their duration.

If the sag lasts longer than one or two cycles, it can cause the computer power supply to detect a low voltage on its output, resulting in computer shutdown. The computer must then be rebooted.

If the sag lasts for a cycle and its duration is approximately equal to the holdup time of the power supply in the computer, the problem can be more critical. The power-supply voltage of the computer will decrease near the end of sag and then increase. This transient condition can cause the reversal of 1s and 0s in memory. These changes will be transferred to disk storage as bugs or data errors. They can result in program hang-ups. Power blackouts can create the same types of problems as sags.

Power surges

A *surge* is an overvoltage or increase in the ac line voltage. A *spike* is more of an instantaneous or short-term overvoltage. It lasts from 0.05 to 100 μs and acts like a large but faster surge. Insurance company data shows that 40 percent of transient problems are surge-related. Surges stress computer components, particularly in the power supply, and can cause premature component failure.

A transient dip in the voltage is usually called a *sag,* but it is an undervoltage condition. A long sag becomes a *brownout.* Undervoltage problems cause more damage than surges, but the surge that follows a sag can cause serious damage. When the power goes out completely, as long as it goes out quickly enough, there will be no damage to the computer. When the power returns to normal, it does it in a series of surges, producing

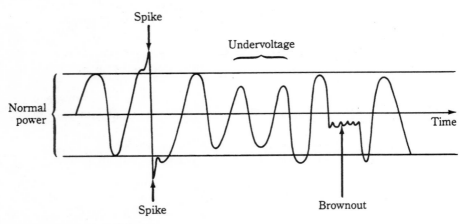

10-31 Power-line problems.

an effect called *hammering*. Hammering can cause the hard disk head to fall down onto the surface of the disk and then lift up and drop down again with each surge.

Noise and oscillations

Electrical noise can enter the computer through the power cable. The noise can be interference from fluorescent lights and other equipment. Noise can cause fluctuations in the voltage and cause lost or corrupted data.

If the amplitude of oscillations is less than 50 percent of the nominal voltage over a period of time, the power supply can break down. If it does not break down, then the oscillations will appear on the output of the power supply and have the same effects as sags on the power-supply lines to integrated circuits.

Causes

Power is affected by a number of devices between the service entrance and the workstation. Air conditioners can cause surges on power lines. Fluorescent lights generate noise that, if it gets through to the machine, can cause erratic performance. Other devices that can cause problems include copiers and printers.

All computers have some type of filtering capacitor that acts to reduce transients. The computer internal logic circuits require a clean, continuous source of power; these filter capacitors along with the power-supply shutdown are designed to deliver it. But any capacitor has a finite storage capacity (the *capacitance*). The transient on the ac power line might swamp the capacitor if it has enough energy.

Surge suppressors

You can protect devices using a variety of methods. The methods range from surge suppressors (Fig. 10-32) to IPS (intelligent power systems). Surge suppressors are probably the most common and least effective of the power protection devices. They reduce the voltage of a surge, using a device such as a varistor to limit the maximum voltage, which means that voltages of less than 200 to 300 V might get into the computer. Varistors have a long response time that can allow short spikes to pass through. Varistors are used in about 90 percent of the surge suppressors sold.

Surge suppressors also use gas tubes or inductive chokes in series with the line. Gas tubes can handle large amounts of energy and can provide some protection for lightning effects. Series-choking devices allow the normal ac line power through but limit the effects of surges.

Standby power systems

The problem with surge suppressors is that they have no power reserve to apply in the event of an undervoltage. This type of power problem requires a standby or uninterruptible power system. An *SPS* (standby power system) is also called an *offline system*. It contains a battery that will support the computer in the event of a power sag, brownout, or blackout.

The SPS is plugged into the wall outlet, and the machine is plugged into the SPS. When the power drops below a certain level, the SPS switches from ac power to battery backup power.

(a)

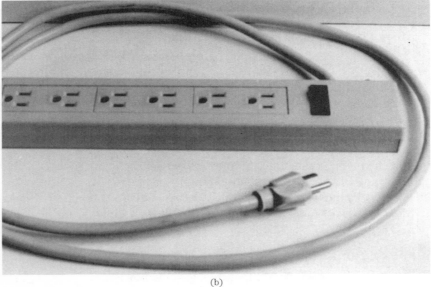

(b)

10-32 Two types of surge suppressors. Single-outlet surge or spike suppressor (A). Multiple outlet surge suppressor with switch (B).

An important part of SPS performance is the *switching time,* which is the time it takes the system to switch from line to battery power. If the time is too long, even though the hardware might not notice it, the data generally will notice it. This problem is especially true on a network where information is traveling over some distance. The maximum allowable switching time is about 1 ms. Most SPSs have switching times from 1 to 4 ms.

Uninterruptible power systems

A *UPS* (uninterruptible power system) is known as an *online system.* Although an SPS lets the normal line power through until it senses an irregularity, a UPS provides the power from its own battery, which is continuously charged from utility power. There is no switching time, and line conditioning is built into the system. When a blackout occurs, the UPS provides backup long enough to allow a systematic shutdown of the computer.

A disadvantage of a UPS is that it can generate heat that reduces the lifetime of internal components. The battery also needs to be replaced periodically. The usual approach to the heating problem is to oversize the components so they generate less heat.

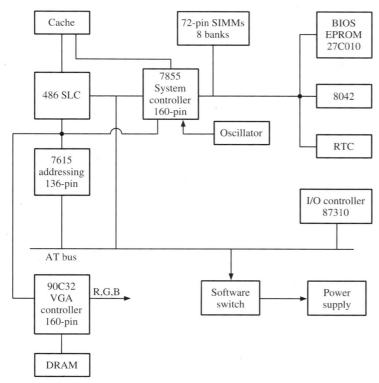

10-33 Green power-managed system.

Intelligent power systems

The IPS is like a UPS, but it has software that sends a warning message the computer is going down in a certain time. It then goes into an orderly shutdown of the system, saving and closing files without any loss of data. When the power comes back on, the software brings up the system and reopens the files to where the system was when the power went down. This shutdown and startup is done with no loss of data.

A major advantage of an IPS is that a system or network that is protected by an IPS can be left unattended. A UPS can provide an orderly shutdown, but there must be someone available to perform the shutdown before the battery runs out. An IPS will shut down the network automatically.

Green PCs

A related development is the use of green or energy-saving system boards as shown in Fig. 10-33. These use a software switch to power-down the processor during idle periods (between keystrokes). Although this feature is primarily designed to reduce power requirements, it can also improve surge protection to some degree.

Index

A

Above Disk, 110
absolute joystick, 374
access methods, local area
    network (LAN), 342
Acer Computers:
    AcerFramer 300MP, 29–30
    AcerPower 486 SX, 25
    Pentium Systems, 25
    486 SX XP 486 computers
    clone, 24–25
acoustic couplers, 386
acoustomechanical mice,
    377–378
active matrix, 101
active matrix addressing, 98
adapter cards, 16–17, 271
add-in boards, 92–93
ADD PC, cover removal, 47
addressing, 103–105
address parity check, 78
ADP, 146
advanced data path, 146
air spaces, 80
alignment tester/exerciser,
    floppy drives, 235–236
ALR computers:
    Pentium systems, 25–26
    PowerFlex SX 386 clone 19
ALU, 68
AM, 382
American Standard Code for
    Information Interchange
    (ASCII), 127
analog-to-digital converter,
    371

antiglare coating, 263
Appletalk, 349
application-specific integrated
    circuits, 21
Arcnet, 351–352
    cards, 351
arithmetic logic unit (ALU), 68,
    112
ASCI Code, 106
AST Premium II, 19
asymmetrical multiprocessing,
    38
audio CDS, 245
AUTOEXEC.NCF, 349
auto LF field, 398

B

backbone, 343
bad RAM chip, 170
bank switching, 109
baseband networks, 341
baseband transceivers, 341
basic input-output system, 12
beep codes, 180
BERT, 387
BIOS, 12
bit error rate test, 387
bit error rate tester, 364
bit rate, 64
bit stuck, 172
black strip, 409
Blue Lightning, 33
board repair, 430
booting, 111
boot-up diagnostics, 204

branch prediction, 31
bridges, 349
broadband networks, 339
brouter, 349
brownout, 448
bus, 78
bus master interface controller,
    66
BUSY condition, 327
butterfly read, 333
byte, 1

C

cable scanner, 361
cache memories, 134
cachable BIOS, 25
cache controller, 65
cache hit, 64, 134
cache memory, 64, 82
cache miss, 64, 134
caddy, 240
call waiting, 393
Carbon Copy, 350
CCDs, 401
CD audio, 236
CD burner, 238
CD drive, 238
CD Miracle Mender, 247
CD-ROMs, 236
    drive problems, 242–246
    drives, 239–240
Centronics printer interface,
    324
CGA, 87–256
    monitor, 252

ABOUT THE AUTHOR

Michael F. Hordeski is an experienced computer systems consultant and licensed professional engineer. He has written or co-written more than two dozen books on microcomputing hardware and networking, including the *Illustrated Dictionary of PCs, 4th Edition* and *Personal Computer Interfaces*, and he has been involved in computer system design, repair, and analysis for such corporations as Rockwell International, General Motors, and Bell Atlantic.